THE
CLARE
WAR DEAD

THE
CLARE
WAR DEAD

A HISTORY OF THE CASUALTIES OF THE GREAT WAR

TOM BURNELL

The
History
Press
Ireland

First published 2011

The History Press Ireland
119 Lower Baggot Street
Dublin 2, Ireland
www.thehistorypress.ie

British Library Cataloguing in Publication Data.
A catalogue record for this book is available from the British Library.

ISBN 978 1 84588 703 2
Typesetting and origination by The History Press
Printed in Great Britain

Contents

Acknowledgements

Special thanks Peter Beirne, Ennis Local Studies, Ennis Library, Co. Clare and Jimmy Taylor, Wexford town. Many thanks to Philip Lecane, author of *Torpedoed! The R.M.S. Leinster Disaster*, for the extra information on all the RMS *Leinster* casualties.

Introduction

This is record of the 653 Co. Clare men and women who died in the military and associated services during the First World War and just after. This list also includes First World War service personnel from other locations who died during this and period who are buried in the Co. They died in the service of the British Army, the Australian Army, the New Zealand Army, the American Army, the Indian Army, the Canadian Army, the South African Army, the Royal Navy and the British Mercantile Marine, Territorial Force Nursing Service, Queen Alexandra's Imperial Military Nursing Service and Queen Mary's Army Auxiliary Corps.

Glossary of Place Names

Clare place names and their various spellings found in the records:

Athy

Ballinagim
Ballmaclure
Ballybhon
Ballymaclure
Ballymagh
Ballyorughia
Ballyvaughan
Balycoyney
Barefield
Belturbet
Bindon Street Ennis
Birdhill
Bridgetown
Bunratty
Burane
Burrane
Burrin

Carnaghclogan
Carrigaholt
Castlebank
Clare
Clare Abbey
Clarecastle
Clonana
Clonawhite
Clonlara
Clonloun
Cooraclare

Corofin
Corrovorin
Corrovorin
Corrovorrin
Cratloe
Cregluce
Cross Carrigahold
Cross Carrigaholt
Crusheen

Deerpark
Derrymeelick
Derrynavegh
Donbeg
Doolin
Doonbeg
Dromcliffe
Drumbiggle
Drumcliffe
Drumecliffe
Drumeliffe
Druncliffe
Dysart

Enagh
Enmis
Ennis
Ennistymon
Ennistynan
Erinagh
Erinah

Farkel
Feakle
Fothera
Foynes
Fulla

Garteen

Inagh
Inch

Kedington
Kelmaley
Kilaloe
Kilbaher
Kildysart
Kilfenora
Kilfinane
Kilkee
Kilkeling
Kilkerrin
Kilkisheen
Kilkishen
Killaloe
Killanon
Killarboy
Killimer
Killuran
Kilmacduane
Kilmaley
Kilmihill

Kilmilgil
Kilmurray
Kilmurry McMahon
Kilmurrybricam
Kilmurrysbricken
Kilnaboy
Kilrush
Kilush
Kimale
Kimurray
Knock
Kuilty
Kyldsart

Labasheeda
Lahinch
Layalmeh
Leitreim
Lifford
Lisannon
Liscannon
Liscannor
Lisconner
Liscullane
Lisdoonvarna
Lisdornvarna
Lisgreen
Lissycasey

Malbay
Maynore

Meelick
Miltown Malbay
Mont Shannon
Moyasta
Moylesky
Mullagh
Mullough

Newmarket
Newmarket-on-Fergus

O'Brien's Bridge
O'Callaghans Mills
O'Gonnelloe
Ogomelloc

Parteen

Quin
Quinn

Scarrif
Scarrip
Sixmile Bridge
Sixmilebridge
Skibbereen
Starrell

Teakle
Tiermaclane
Tomgraney

Trough
Tubber
Tulla
Tullabrack
Tullagh
Twoclay

Whitegate

Glossary of Terms

CWGC: Commonwealth War Graves Commission.

ODGW: Officers Died in the Great War.

SDGW: Soldiers Died in the Great War.

IMR: Ireland's Memorial Records.

Killed in action: The soldier was killed during engagement with the enemy.

Died of wounds: The soldier was not killed outright and may have made it back to the Regiments Aid Post or Casualty Clearing Station before he eventually died of his wounds.

Died at home: Death by drowning, suicide, accident or illness in the UK. Home in these cases means back in England and not necessarily where he lived. Many times I have come across this and it turned out to be that the soldier died in a UK hospital.

Died of wounds at home: The soldier was not killed outright and may have made it back to the Regiments Aid post or Casualty Clearing Station before he eventually died of his wounds back in the UK or Ireland.

Died: Death by drowning, suicide, accident or illness.

ADAMS, HERBERT GEORGE:
Rank: Aircraftman, 2nd Class. Regiment or service: Royal Air Force. Date of death: 26 October 1919. Age at death: 18. Service No.: 161234.

Supplementary information: Son of Joseph and Catherine Adams, of No. 94 Church Road, Horfield, Bristol. Late of Ennis, Co. Clare. Left the Bristol Aeroplane Company to enlist.

Grave or memorial reference: Haidar Pasha Memorial in Istanbul, Turkey.

ALLINGHAM, EDWARD: Rank: Private. Regiment or service: Irish Guards. Unit: 1st Battalion. Date of death: 27 August 1918. Age at death: 20. Service No.: 11433. Born in Killarboy Co. Clare. Enlisted in Dublin. Killed in action.

Supplementary information: Son of Sarah Allingham and the John Allingham, of No. 57 Lower Mount, Pleasant Avenue, Dublin.

From the *Limerick Leader*, January 1916:

On Monday night the Constabulary at William Street Police Barracks entertained Constable Robert C. Allingham, who volunteered for the front, and who proceeded last evening en route to Catherham, where he will undero training in the Irish Guards, the regiment which he has selected for service. A very pleasant evening was spent, and a handsome presentation, including a silver cigarette case from

District-Inspector Craig, was made to Constable Allingham, who is a native of the County of Clare.

Robert C. Allingham is a brother of Edward, and their parents wre John and Sarah Allingham from Miltown Malby, County Clare. Robert survived the war.

Grave or memorial reference: Panel 3. Memorial: Vis-en-Artois Memorial in France.

ARMSTRONG, CHARLES MARTIN: Rank: Lieutenant. Regiment or service: Royal Dublin Fusiliers. Unit: 10th Battalion. Date of death: 8 February 1917. Age at death: 23. Killed in action.

Supplementary information: Student of Trinity College, Dublin. Son of the Revd Chancellor S.C. and Eliza Armstrong (*née* Martin), of The Rectory, Finglas, Co. Dublin.

From the *Clare Journal*, September 1915:

Armstrong, Charles Martin, 2nd Lieutenant, Royal Dublin Fusiliers. 8th son of Chancellor Armstrong of the Rectory, Kilrush Co. Clare. Educated Privately and at Trinity College, Dublin, where he was studying with a view to entering the Ministry of the Church of Ireland. Enlisted in the 7th Battalion, Royal Dublin Fusiliers after the outbreak of war. Served with the Mediterranean Expeditionary Force in Gallipoli. Took part in the landing of the 10th Division at Suvla Bay, was invalided to Malta, and subsequently to England. Was gazetted 2nd Lieutenant. Joined his battalion in France just after Christmas, 1916 and was killed in action, 8th February 1917. His Captain wrote: "About 7 o'clock in the morning he had gone down our line to relieve a brother officer. In passing an exposed part of the line and enemy sniper caught him. He was killed instantaneously. He was buried in a military cemetery behind the lines … We all admired him for his willingness to undertake any hard work. His unselfishness, and particularly his courage … I may also tell you that all the men in the company feel the loss of your son very much … I cannot tell you too often how much I feel the loss," and another officer; "I had seen a good deal of him since he joined the 10th Division, and I can assure you that he was much liked by his fellow officers and respected by his men. His manly keenness was infectious, and no matter what the circumstances, and I can assure you that they have of late been very trying, he was always cheery and optimistic. His loss mourned by every one of my fellow officers."

Letters from the front
The following extracts are from a letter which Canon S. C. Armstrong of Kilrush, has received from one of his sons, a Private. in the 7th Battalion Royal Dublin Fusiliers:

"We took a hill just before dark. The Turks did not wait for the bayonet, but cleared when we got near their trenches, leaving their slippers, etc., behind. We had a very stiff time of it for about nine days, getting practically no sleep, as the Turks used to threaten us with attacks every night, sometimes coming very near the trenches. We had to clear out a lot of unexploded shrapnel shells, which the Turks had stored up in a dug-out-running along with them while snipers were landing bullets rather too near to us to be comfortable. However, we captured all the shells, without any casualties. We had to get our water supply under fire, and the only way to escape the bullets was to keep on the move. I have trotted a couple of miles, over and over again, with water bottles, while the snipers were potting for all they were worth, often getting half-a-dozen bullets, running, within a few feet of me. Then they would sometimes turn shrapnel on the wells, and cause a good many casualties. However, thank God, I have not had a bullet in me yet, although I have had some very narrow shaves. I am here (Valetta Hospital Malta), recovering from dysentery. We are very well cared for – nice porridge for breakfast, with an egg, bread and butter and ripping tea. Chicken, nicely boiled, for dinner, then tea and supper. The hospital seems like a palace after Gallipoli. "

From the *Clare Journal*, April 1917:

Clare Clergyman's Son Killed
We see in recent casualties, the name of second Lieutenant Charles M.

Armstrong, R. D. F., killed in the late fighting. He was son of Canon S. C. Armstrong, Kilrush, and was only 23 years old. There is general sympathy with Rev Mr Armstrong in his loss.

From the *Court Journal*, 16 March 1917:

The Late Lieutenant Armstrong
Second Lieutenant Charles Martin Armstrong, who was killed on the 18th February, 1917, was the eighth so of Canon and Mrs Armstrong, the Rectory, Kilrush, and was nearly 24 years of age. He was educated at home, was an undergraduate of Trinity College, Dublin, and purposed entering the Ministry of the Church of Ireland. Shortly after the beginning of the war he joined D Company, 7th Battalion, Royal Dublin Fusiliers, commonly known as "The Pals" and made up mostly of members of the Rugby football clubs, Dublin, graduates and under-graduates of Trinity College. He was at the landing of the 10th Division at Suvla Bay, and went through a large part of the fighting there until invalided to Malta, and subsequently home. He got a commission and joined the Royal Dublin Fusiliers at the front just after Christmas, 1916.

The Captain of his company writes—"About seven o'clock in the morning he had gone down our line to relieve a brother officer. In passing an exposed part of the line an enemy sniper caught him. He was killed instantaneously and was buried in a military cemetery behind the lines. We all admired him for his willingness to undertake any hard work, his unselfishness, and particularly his courage … I may also tell you that all the men of the company feel the loss of your son very much … I cannot tell you too often how much I feel the loss."

Another officer writes—"I had seen a good deal of him since he joined the 10th Division, and I can assure you that he was much liked by his fellow officers ad respected by his men. His manly keenness was infectious, and no matter what the circumstances, and I can assure you they have of late been very trying, he was always cheery and optimistic. His loss is regretted by every one of my fellow officers."

Grave or memorial reference: VII. C.28. Cemetery: Ancre British Cemetery, Beaumont-Hamel in France.

B

BAIRD, ROBERT: Rank: Private. Regiment or service: Royal Irish Regiment. Unit: 2nd Battalion. Date of death: 1 June 1918. Age at death: 25. Service No.: 8040. Born in Killaloe, Co. Clare. . Enlisted in Roscrea, Co. Tipperary. Killed in action.

Supplementary information: Son of Robert and Elizabeth Baird, of No. 13 Normanston Road, Oxton, Birkenhead. Born at Clarisford, Killaloe, Co. Clare.

Grave or memorial reference: A.3. Cemetery: Fienvillers British Cemetery in France.

BAKER, THOMAS: Rank: Lieutenant (Acting Captain). Regiment or service: Royal Garrison Artillery. Unit: 203rd Siege Battery. Date of death: 28 July 1917. Age at death: 39. Born in Co. Clare. Killed in action.

Supplementary information: Husband of Maude Mary Baker, of No. 2 Lodge Sreet, Lancaster.

Grave or memorial reference: II. B.2. Cemetery: Coxyde Military Cemetery in Belgium.

BARLOW, THOMAS: *see* **HEAVY, THOMAS.**

BARRON, PATRICK: Rank: Private. Regiment or service: Royal Irish Regiment. Unit: 1st Garrison Battalion. Date of death: 1 January 1917. Age at death: 39. Service No.: 11322. Formerly he was with the Royal Munster Fusiliers where his number was 6413.

Supplementary information: Husband of Mary Barron (*née* Sheehan), of Kilmoon, Lisdoonvarna, Co. Clare. Born in Drumcliffe, Co. Clare. Enlisted in Tralee, Co. Kerry while living in Lisdoonvarna, Co. Clare. Died at Sea.

Grave or memorial reference: Mikra Memorial in Greece.

BARRY, MICHAEL: Rank: Private. Regiment or service: Leinster Regiment. Unit: 2nd Battalion. Date of death: 12 April 1917. Service No.: 5241.

Supplementary information: Date of last will and testament: 12 April 1916. Property and effects received: Mrs Maggie O'Connor, of No. 2 Upper Market Street, Ennis, Co. Clare, Ireland. Born in Kilmaley, Co. Clare. Enlisted in Nenagh, Co. Tipperary while living in Ennis.

Grave or memorial reference: Bay 9. Memorial: Arras Memorial in France.

BARRY, PATRICK: Rank: Private. Regiment or service: Australian Infantry, AIF. Unit: 55th Battalion. Date of death: 22 October 1916. Service No.: 5339. Killed in action. Born in Ennis, Co. Clare.

Supplementary information: Occupation on enlistment: Labourer. Went to Australia when he was 44. Born, Kilnamona, Ennis, Co. Clare. Occupation on enlistment: Labourer. Age on enlistment: 43 years 3 months. Next of kin details: Dave Barry (brother), of No. 130 Burren Street, Victoria. Place and date of enlistment:

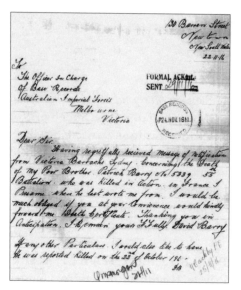

A letter from Private Patrick Barry's brother David.

The Town Hall, Liverpool, N.S.W.; 10 January 1916, while living at Tarana, N.S.W. Weight: 14st 2lbs. Height: 5ft 10in. Complexion: Fresh. Eyes: Blue. Hair: Brown. His mother, Margaret Barry of 'Waratah' Clarfendon Road, Strathfield was awarded a pension of £2 per fortnight from 13 January 1917. His father died in March 1914, and his mother died in November 1917. His sister was Mrs Bridget Smark, of 'Bruntwood', Australia Street, Camperdown, N.S.W. when a letter was sent to her from the military authorities she was known at that address. His eldest brother, Johnny Barry, lived with his sister, Bridget.

Grave or memorial reference: He has no known grave but is listed on the Villers-Bretonneux Memorial in France.

BAXTER, ARTHUR EDWARD:

Rank: Private. Regiment or service: Australian Infantry, AIF. Unit: 20th Battalion. Date of death: 12 November 1916. Age at death: 23. Service No.: 4371. Killed in action; however, he was listed in the casualty lists as 'died of illness'.

Supplementary information: Next of kin: Mrs M. Baxter (mother), of No. 131 Grove Road, Edinburgh, Scotland, later changed to Mrs Margaret Baxter, Public Library, Prestonpans, Haddingtonshire, Scotland. Born in Sixmilebridge, Co.Clare. Occupation on enlistment: Labourer. Age on enlistment: 22 years 7 months. Place and date of enlistment: Casula, N.S.W., 18 November 1915 while living at Peoples Palace, Pitt Street, Sydney. Weight: 14st 3lbs. Height: 5ft 7½in. Complexion: Fresh. Eyes: Hazel. Hair: Brown. His sister was Dorothy Baxter, Public Library, Prestonpans,

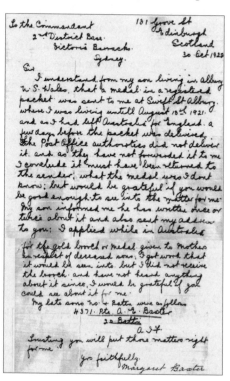

A letter from Margaet Baxter, mother of Private A. Baxter.

Haddingtonshire, Scotland. A pension of £2 per fortnight was awarded to his mother from 29 January 1917.

Grave or memorial reference: He has no known grave but is listed on the Villers-Bretonneux Memorial in France.

BAXTER, JOHN: Rank: Gunner. Regiment or service: Royal Garrison Artillery. Unit: 206th Siege Battery. Date of death: 24 April 1917. Age at death: 45. Service No.: 3575. Born in Killaloe, Co. Clare. Enlisted in Limerick. Killed in action.

Supplementary information: Son of Michael and Mrs M. Baxter, of Killaloe; husband of E. Baxter, of Killaloe, Co. Clare.

Grave or memorial reference: L. 23. Cemetery: Ste. Catherine British Cemetery, Pas-De-Calais, France.

BAYLISS, HUBERT GERALD: Rank: Driver. Regiment or service: Royal Horse Artillery. Unit: 7th Brigade; Ammunition Column. Date of death: 12 March 1919. Age at death: 25. Service No.: 68238.

Supplementary information: Son of Thomas Alfred and Sarah Ann Bayliss. Born in Co. Clare.

Grave or memorial reference: 1846. Cemetery: Newport (Christchurch) Cemetery, Monmouthshire, UK.

BEAKEY, MARTIN: Rank: Private. Regiment or service: Royal Irish Regiment. Unit: 2nd Battalion. Date of death: 22 October 1920. Age at death: 21. Service No.: 7109830.

Supplementary information: Son of Patrick and Bridget Beakey, of Cahersherkin, Ennistymon, Co. Clare.

Grave or memorial reference: R.C. 939. Cemetery: Netley Military Cemetery, Hampshire, UK.

BEHAN, JOHN: Rank: Stoker 1st Class. Regiment or service: Royal Navy. Unit: H. M.S. *Monmouth*. Date of death: 1 November 1914. Age at death: 23. Service No.: SS/112719.

On 1 November 1914, the HMS *Monmouth* received an 8.2in shell from the SMS *Gneisenau* which almost blew her to pieces. She limped away and later that day was sent to the bottom by SS *Nurnberg*. There were no survivors.

Supplementary information: Son of Austin and Annie Behan, of Kilkee; husband of Mary Kate Behan, of Miltown Road., Kilkee, Co. Clare.

Grave or memorial Reference: 3. Plymouth Naval Memorial, UK.

BENNETT, PATRICK: Rank: Private. Regiment or service: Royal Dublin Fusiliers. Unit: 2nd Battalion Date of death: 13 October 1916. Age at death: 30. Service No.: 43152. Born in Scariff, Co. Clare. Enlisted in Nenagh while living in Killaloe. Killed in action. Formerly he was with the Royal Irish Regiment where his number was 8747.

Supplementary information: Son of Patrick and Mary Bennett, of Killaloe, Co. Clare.

Grave or memorial reference: Pier and Face 16 C. Memorial: Thiepval Memorial in France.

BENTLEY, WILLIAM: Rank: Private. Regiment or service: Royal Munster Fusiliers. Unit: 1st Battalion. Date of death: 22 November 1918. Age at death: 27. Service No.: 8521.

Supplementary information: Son of Mrs Margaret Bentley, of Brick Hill, Cratloe, Co. Clare.

Grave or memorial reference: I.B. 7. Cemetery: Lille Southern Cemetery, Nord in France.

BERGIN, DENIS: Rank: Private. Regiment or service: Royal Irish Fusiliers. Unit: 1st Battalion. Date of death: 12 October 1916. Service No.: 11101. Born in Drumcliffe, Co. Clare. Enlisted in Dublin while living in Cheriton, Kent. Killed in action.

Grave or memorial reference: Pier and Face 16 C. Memorial: Thiepval Memorial in France.

BLAKE, FRANCIS: Rank: Private. Regiment or service: Royal Dublin Fusiliers. Unit: 2nd Battalion. Date of death: 20 July 1916. Service No.: 23497. Enlisted in Naas while living in Ennis. Died of wounds.

Supplementary information: Son of James and Elizabeth Blake, of Corbally, Quin, Co. Clare.

From the *Saturday Journal*, July 1916:

Missing

Pte Blake was son of Mr James Blake, Corbally, and much sympathy is felt with him in his bereavement. He died at Bellahouston Hospital, Glasgow.

Grave or memorial reference: H. 1324A. Cemetery: Glasgow Western Necropolis, Scotland. (We have a bit of a mystery here as Private Blake and Private John Quinlan from Lismore, Co. Waterford are both listed as occupants of this grave – Author.)

BLAKE, MARTIN: Rank: Private. Regiment or service: The King's (Liverpool Regiment). Unit: 1st/7th Battalion. Date of death: 22 September 1917. Age at death: 35. Service No.: 267371. Born in Scariff, Co. Clare. Enlisted in Bootle, Liverpool while living in Killaloe, Co. Clare. Died of wounds.

Supplementary information: Son of Martin and Mary Blake, of Long Gardens, Killaloe, Co. Clare.

Grave or memorial reference: I. C. 9. Cemetery: Nine Elms British Cemetery, Popeninghe, West-Vlaanderen in Belgium.

BLOOD, BINDON: Rank: Captain. Regiment or service: 4th (Queen's Own) Hussars and the Royal Flying Corps. Date of death: 29 September 1915. Age at death: 33. Killed in action.

Supplementary information: Son of Bagot Blood and Florence Blood.

From the article *Our Heroes*, 1916:

Captain Bagot Blood, 4th Hussars and Royal Flying Corps, was killed at Hounslow whilst flying. He was the eldest son of the late Captain Bagot Blood, of Rockforest and Gleninagh, Co. Clare. He had seen extensive service during the South African War and later at Burma, and was for some time at the Curragh. He went to Belgium with the 4th Hussars in August, 1914, and served with them continuously until last summer, when he joined the Royal Flying Corps.

From the *Clare Journal*, September 1915:

Clare Officer's Terrible Experience
Fying in Flames.
Whilst flying at Hounslow Heath on Friday afternoon an aeroplane took fire. The pilot, Captain Blood, of the Royal Flying Corps, managed to descend safely, and escaped from the machine with his clothing in flames. He received immediate assistance, and was taken to hospital. Although badly burned, hopes were entertained on Friday that he would recover. It has since been reported that he has succumbed, but we have not heard it definitely.

Captain Blood is eldest son of the late Mr Bagot Blood, J. P., of Templemaley, and grandson of Major C. W. Studdert, J. P., of Cragmoher. He had been on service in India, but came home just before the outbreak of war. He had been at the front, but joined the Flying Corps lately.

The Late Captain Bindon Blood
On Monday we reported the shocking accident, while flying, to our gallant countryman, Captain Bindon Blood, who has since succumbed to his terrible burns. At the Hounslow Coroner's Court on Tuesday, a verdict of "accidental death" was returned.

Captain Blood was a member of the well-known family, the Bloods, of Cranagher, Co. Clare. He was elder son of the late Mr Bagot Blood, J. P., Rock Forest, and Templemaley, and was a cousin of General Sir Bindon Blood. He served through the South African War, first in the ranks of the South African Constabulary and then as officer in the East Yorkshire Regiment. Afterwards he was transferred to the Indian Army and then in the Essex regiment. In 1913 he joined the 4th Hussars. He served with the regiment from the beginning of the present war, and was mentioned in despatches. Last February he was attached to the Royal Flying Corps, and had recently been gazetted Flight Commander.

He was flying at Hounslow on Friday when his machine took fire, and though he was able to descend, his clothing had taken fire, and he had sustained shocking burns. He died on the following day, yet another Clare victim to this terrible war, though not in the firing line.

From the *County Offaly Chronicle*, September 1915:

Sept, 24, as a result of an accident, while flying at Hounslow, Capt, Bindon Blood, IV, Queen's Own Hussars and Royal Flying Corps, elder son of the late Bagot Blood, of Rock Forest, Co, Clare, aged 33.

From the *County Offaly Chronicle*, October 1915:

Intrepid Irishman killed
At the Hounslow Coroner's Court a verdict of 'Accidental death', was returned in the case of Captain Bindon Blood, aged 34, attached to the Flying Corps, who died from burns received in an accident with an aeroplane. He was a member of

the Bloods of Cranagher, Co. Clare, and a cousin of General Sir Bindon Blood. He served through the South African War, afterwards in the South African Army, and then in the Essex Regiment. He served with the 4th Hussars from the beginning of the war, and was mentioned in despatches. Last February he was attached to the Royal Flying Corps, and had recently been gazetted flight commander. Mentioned in Despatches.

Served in the Boer War as a Captain with the Indian Army (8th Cavalry). Began the war with the 8th Hussars. During practice with an aeroplane he met with an accident and died of his injuries.

Grave or memorial reference: 360. Cemetery: Woking (St John's) Crematorium.

BLOOD, PATRICK: Rank: Private. Regiment or service: Royal Munster Fusiliers. Unit: 8th Battalion. Date of death: 4 September 1916. Service No.: 5844. Born in Ennistymon, Co. Clare. Enlisted in Limerick while living in Ennistymon, Co. Clare. Died of wounds.

Grave or memorial reference: XXI. F. 3. Cemetery: Delville Wood Cemetery, Longueval in France.

BOTHWELL, GEORGE ALFRED: Rank: Private, 2nd Class. Regiment or service: Royal Air Force. Unit: Wireless School (Winter). Date of death: 4 October 1918. Age at death: 20. Service No.: 294023.

Supplementary information: Son of James and Margaret Bothwell, of No.

48, New Road, Chippenham, Wiltshire. Born at Kilkee. Co. Clare.

Grave or memorial reference: 1985. Cemetery: Winter (West Hill) Old Cemetery, Hampshire, UK.

BRADY, GEORGE: Rank: Corporal. Regiment or service: Leinster Regiment. Unit: 1st Battalion. Date of death: 5 July 1917. Service No.: 7616. Killed in action in Salonika.

Supplementary information: Date of informal will: 21 May 1917. Property and effects received: Mrs Katherine Flynn (aunt), Butter Market, Ennis, Co. Clare. Born in Ennis, Co. Clare. Enlisted in Ennis.

Grave or memorial reference: III. E. 1. Cemetery: Lahana Military Cemetery in Greece.

BRAZIL, JAMES: Rank: Private. Regiment or service: Canadian Infantry (Eastern Ontario Regiment). Unit: 2nd Battalion. Date of death: 4 May 1915. Age at death: 29 Service No.: 22939.

Supplementary information: Son of James and Bridget Brazil, of Hector Street, Kilrush, Co. Clare. Also com-memorated as 'Jas. Brassil' in the 'List of Kilrush Men engaged in the First World War from August 1914'. This pamphlet lists the Kilrush men who were involved in the First World War until 11 November 1918. Included in this pamphlet is a Corporal Michael Brassil who served in the Dardanelles and was invalided out of the army with a pension. Also Private Patrick Brassil, RAMC, 'Captured and prisoner in Germany'. They may all be related. James is also commemorated in the

'List of Employees of Messrs. M. Glynn and Sons. Flour and Meal Millers and Steamship Owners. Kilrush, Co. Clare, who took part in the First World War, 1914 to 1918.' Dated 11 November 1918'.

Grave or memorial reference: IV. A. 9. Cemetery:

BREEN, JOHN: Rank: Private. Regiment or service: Connaught Rangers. Unit: 1st Battalion. Date of death: 15 April 1917. Service No.: 5623. Killed in action in Mesopotamia.

Supplementary information: Born in Stratford, England. Enlisted in Kilrush while living in Kilrush, Co. Clare.

Grave or memorial reference: He has no known grave but is listed on the Chatby Memorial in Egypt.

BREEN, MICHAEL: Rank: Private. Regiment or service: Royal Munster Fusiliers. Unit: 2nd Battalion. Date of death: 25 September 1915. Age at death: 27. Service No.: 4155. Killed in action.

Supplementary information: Son of John and Margaret Breen, of Burton Street, Kilrush, Co. Clare. Born in Kilrush, Co. Clare. Enlisted in Kilrush, Co. Clare while living there. Also commemorated in the 'List of Kilrush Men Engaged in the War from August 1914'. This pamphlet lists the Kilrush men who were involved in the First World War until 11 November 1918.

Grave or memorial reference: Panel 127. Memorial: Loos Memorial in France.

BREEN, MICHAEL JOSEPH: Rank: Private. Regiment or service: Australian Infantry, AIF. Unit: 25th

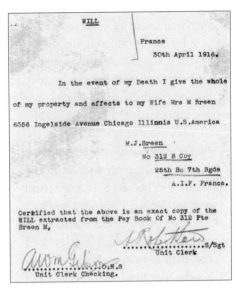

The will of Private M.J. Breen.

Battalion. Date of death: 14 September 1916. Age at death, 41. Service No.: 12. Died of gunshot wounds to the back (received in action in France) in London General Hospital.

Supplementary information: Born, Cooraclare, Kilmihil, Co. Clare. Occupation on enlistment: Labourer. Age on enlistment: 34 years 6 months. Next of kin details: Mr P.J. Breen (brother), of Kilrush, Ireland, his address is also given as Royal Munster Fusiliers. This was later changed to his wife as he married after enlisting. Place and date of enlistment: Queensland, 2 September 1914. Previous military experience: 12 years with the 88th Infantry (Galway). Weight: 9st 13lbs. Height: 5ft 6½in. Complexion: Dark. Eyes: Hazel. Hair: Brown. Promoted to Sergeant in November 1915 and reverted to Private by his own request Sentenced to penal servitude for life in June 1916. Mentioned in Despatches for gallant conduct. Divisional Orders:

'Complimented as rendering good service by staunchly remaining at his post with a supply of bombs ready for use when required by the patrol in charge of Lieutenant H, Page on the 29th, October 1915.' Charged with:

Discharging his rifle near his billet and striking his superior Officer in the execution of his office. Awarded penal servitude for life, suspended by G. O. C. Reserve Army. Breen was mortally wounded during the Brigades third time in the trenches at Pozieres where his behaviour from a fighting point of view was an example to all. Further for his good work at Armentieres and Messines, Breen was recommended for the Military Medal. For the above reasons it is recommended that the sentence be remitted. Sentence was remitted by G. O. C.

Grave or memorial reference: Aust 7. Cemetery: Wandsworth (Earlsfield) Cemetery, London, UK.

BREEN, MICHAEL: Rank: Private. Regiment or service: Royal Munster Fusiliers. Unit: 2nd Battalion. Date of death: 9 May 1915. Age at death: 30. Service No.: 6217. Killed in action.
Supplementary information: Son of Thomas and Bridget Breen, of Lower Burrane, Knock, Ennis, Co. Clare. Born in Kilrush, Co. Clare. Enlisted in Limerick while living in Burrane, Knock, Co. Clare. Also commemorated in the 'List of Kilrush Men engaged in the War from August 1914'. This pamphlet lists the Kilrush men who were involved in the First World War until 11 November 1918.

Grave or memorial reference: Panel 43 and 44. Memorial: Le Touret Memorial in France.

BREEN/BREENE, PATRICK: Rank: Private. Regiment or service: Royal Irish Regiment. Unit: 2nd Battalion. Date of death: 3 September 1916. Age at death: 36. Service No.: 18009. Killed in action.
Supplementary information: Born in Kilrush, Co. Clare. Enlisted in Ennis while living in Kilrush, Co. Clare. Also commemorated in the 'List of Kilrush Men engaged in the War from August 1914'. This pamphlet lists the Kilrush men who were involved in the First World War until 11 November 1918.

Grave or memorial reference: XVII. A. 3. Cemetery: Serre Road Cemetery No. 2 in France.

BRENNAN, JAMES: Rank: Private. Regiment or service: Royal Munster Fusiliers. Unit: 1st Battalion. Date of death: 27 July 1916. Service No.: 4352. Killed in action.
Supplementary information: Born in Bunratty, Co. Clare. Enlisted in Limerick while living in Limerick. Husband of M.K. Brennan, of No. 5 Creagh Lane, Limerick.

Grave or memorial reference: I. J. 25. Cemetery: Philosophe British Cemetery, Mazingarbe in France.

BRENNAN, JOSEPH: Rank: Private. Regiment or service: Royal Munster Fusiliers. Unit: 1st Battalion. Date of death: 21 August 1915. Age at death: 44. Service No.: 6228. Killed in action in Gallipoli.

Supplementary information: Born in Kilrush, Co. Clare. Enlisted in Ennis, Co. Clare while living in Kilrush, Co. Clare. Husband of Bridget Brennan, of Grace Street, Kilrush, Co. Clare. Also commemorated in the 'List of Kilrush Men engaged in the War from August 1914', Burton Street. This pamphlet lists the Kilrush men who were involved in the First World War until 11 November 1918.

Grave or memorial reference: Panel 185 to 190. Memorial: Helles Memorial in Turkey.

BRESLIN, THOMAS: Rank: Private. Regiment or service: Australian Infantry, AIF. Unit: 59th Battalion. Date of death: 19 July 1916. Service No.: 1914. Died on the Somme.

Supplementary information: From the CWGC; Son of Thomas and Mary Breslin; husband of Mary Breslin, of North Clermiston Farm, Davidson's Mains, Edinburgh, Scotland. Native of Co. Clare, Ireland. His records, however, state he was born in Carlow.

Grave or memorial reference: VI. D. 46. Cemetery: Ration Farm Military Cemetery, La Chapelle-Darmentieres, Nord in France. .

BROGAN, JOHN: Rank: Private. Regiment or service: Royal Munster Fusiliers. Unit: 6th Battalion. Date of death: 21 March 1918. Service No.: 1891. Killed in action in Palestine.

Supplementary information: Born in Drumcliffe, Ennis, Co. Clare. Enlisted in Wigan while living in Wigan, Lancashire.

Grave or memorial reference: U. 60. Cemetery: Ramleh War Cemetery in Israel.

BROGAN, THOMAS: Rank: Sergeant. Regiment or service: Lancashire Fusiliers. Unit: 1st Battalion. Date of death: 25 October 1916. Service No.: 561. Killed in action

Supplementary information: Born in Clarecastle, Co. Clare. Enlisted in Wigan, Lancashire while living in Sydney, Australia.

Grave or memorial reference: I. C. 13. Cemetery: Bulls Road Cemetery, Flers, France.

BROWN, J.: Rank: Private. Regiment or service: Highland Light Infantry. Unit: 9th (Glasgow Highlanders) Battalion. Date of death: 14 July 1920. Service No.: 71979. One of four British soldiers drowned at Carrigaholt on that day.

Grave or memorial reference: In South-East corner. Cemetery: Kilrush (Shanakyle) Cemetery, Co. Clare.

BROWNE, HENRY GEORGE: Rank: Private. Regiment or service: Bedfordshire Regiment. Unit: 7th Battalion. Date of death: 1 July 1916. Age at death: 29. Service No.: 20097. Killed in action.

Supplementary information: Born in Enmis (*sic*), Co. Clare. Enlisted in Bedford while living in Stevenage, Hampshire. Son of Henry George and Jane Brown; husband of Catherine Ann Brown, of No. 7 Albert Street, Stevenage, Hertfordshire.

Grave or memorial reference: Pier and Face 2 C. Memorial: Thiepval Memorial in France.

BROWNE, JOHN: Rank: Private. Regiment or service: Household

Cavalry and Cavalry of the line including the Yeomanry and Imperial Camel Corps. Unit: South Irish Horse. Date of death: 29 March 1917. Age at death: 27. Service No.: 1942.

Supplementary information: Born in Ballenacally. Enlisted in Limerick while living in Ballenacally. Son of John and Mary Browne, of Ballenacally, Co. Clare.

Grave or memorial reference: VI. F. 3. Cemetery; Warlincourt Halte British Cemetery, Saulty in France.

BROWNE, MICHAEL: Rank: Private. Regiment or service: Irish Guards. Unit: 1st Battalion. Date of death: 1 November 1914. Service No.: 1655. Killed in action.

Supplementary information: Born in Kilmacduane, Co. Clare. Enlisted in Manchester, Lancashire while living in Clonana, Co. Clare.

Grave or memorial reference: Panel 11. Memorial: Ypres (Menin Gate) Memorial in Belgium.

BROWNE, THOMAS: Rank: Private. Regiment or service: Royal Munster Fusiliers. Unit: 8th Battalion. Date of death: 22 June 1916. Service No.: 5670 and 8/5670. Killed in action.

Supplementary information: Born in Clare Abbey, Co. Clare. Enlisted in Ennis while living in Clarecastle, Co. Clare.

From the *Saturday Journal*, July 1916:

A credit to the Co. Clare and T
to the Munsters
Another of our brave young Claremen, Private Thomas Browne, who responded to the call of his country, and has it creditably recorded of him that he was a credit to his country and to the Munsters, to which regiment he belonged. The sad news of his having fallen on the field of battle, was conveyed to his sister. Mrs McMahon, of Ballygreene, Newmarket-on-Fergus, by Lieutenant Hugh M. V. O'Brien, who wrote as follows:

"I am extremely sorry to have to tell you of the death of your brother, Pte Thomas Browne, C Company, 8th R. M. F. he was killed by a German shell on the 21st of this month in the front trench, and has been buried in a soldier's graveyard He was a very good boy, and we shall all kiss him. Sergeant O'Connor, of Newcastle West, who was his platoon Sergeant, tells me he would sooner have lost a brother. He was killed instantly, and so suffered no pain. He was a credit to the Co. Clare, and the Munsters."

Mrs McMahon's husband also received a similar communication apprising him of the death of his brother, Private Jim McMahon, of the Munsters, who belonged to Clarecastle. In his will, his personal effects and property were received by: Miss L. McMahon, Ballygreen, Newmarket on Fergus, Co. Clare, Ireland

Grave or memorial reference: I. D. 5. Cemetery: St Patrick's Cemetery, Loos in France.

BUCKLEY, JAMES: Rank: Private. Regiment or service: Royal Munster

Fusiliers. Unit: 2nd Battalion. Date of death: 9 May 1915. Service No.: 5613. Killed in action.

Supplementary information: Born in Kilrush, Co. Clare. Enlisted in Kilkee while living in Kilkee, Co. Clare.

Grave or memorial reference: Panel 43 and 44. Memorial: Le Touret Memorial in France.

BURDETT, THOMAS: *see* **DICKS, THOMAS.**

BURKE, JOHN: Rank: Private. Regiment or service: Leinster Regiment. Unit: 2nd Battalion. Date of death: 14 October 1918. Age at death: 18. Service No.: 4737. Killed in action.

Supplementary information: Born in Kilrush, Co. Clare. Enlisted in Ennis, Co. Clare while living in Kilrush, Co. Clare. Son of James and Mary Burke, of Glen Street, Kilrush.

Grave or memorial reference: Panel 143. Memorial: Tyne Cot Memorial in Belgium.

BURKE, JOHN: Rank: Private (Lance Corporal). Regiment or service: Royal Irish Regiment. Unit: 6th Battalion. Date of death: 7 June 1917. Service No.: 8503. Killed in action.

Supplementary information: He won the Military Medal and is listed in the *London Gazette*. Born in Foynes, Co. Clare. Enlisted in Ennis while living in Limerick. Grave or memorial reference: X. 75. Cemetery: Kemmel Chateau Military Cemetery in Belgium.

BURKE, MICHAEL: Rank: Corporal. Regiment or service: Royal Munster Fusiliers. Unit: 1st Battalion.

Date of death: 12 January 1917. Service No.: 8202. Killed in action.

Supplementary information: Born in Drumcliffe, Co. Clare. Enlisted in Ennis while living in Clarecastle, Co. Clare.

Grave or memorial reference: H. 10. Cemetery: Pond Farm Cemetery in Belgium.

BURKE, PATRICK JOSEPH: Rank: Private. Regiment or service: Australian Infantry, AIF. Unit: 4th Battalion. Date of death: 15 April 1917. Age at death: 21 (his records state he was 25 when he died). Service No.: 1325.

Supplementary information: Son of Patrick and Elizabeth Burke, of Rock Cottage, Clonlara, Co. Clare, Ireland. Born in Rock Cottage, Clonlara, Co. Clare. Occupation on enlistment: Shop assistant, draper and tram conductor. He went to Australia when he was 19. He won several silver and gold medals

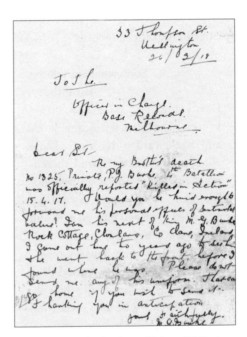

A letter from the brother of Private P.J. Burke.

at athletic sports, for running events in Ireland, and for weight throwing.

From the official records:

Name listed as Jospeph Pat Burke.
Born, Conty Clare, near Limerick.
Age on enlistment; 23 years 4 months.
Apprenticiship?; J. H. Ellis, Draper, 3 years.
Next of kin details: P. Bourke (father), of Clonlara, Co. Clare.
Place and date of enlistment, Liverpool, N. S. W. 03-November-1914.
Weight, 176 lbs. Height, 5 feet, 8 ½ in. Complexion, medium. Eyes, Blue. Hair, Dark Brown. Hospitalised from May, 1915 to August, 1915 with the 'effects of shell shock'rigin of disability, Gallipoli. Parents were each awarded a pension of 15/6d from May 1918.
Killed in action.

A letter in his official records:

> Somewhere in France.
> Jan 17th, 17.
>
> Dear Lettie.
> I received your very welcome letter and Xmas card today. You ask me about going over to Ireland, there is no chance yet Lettie as we have not too many men to spare, but if I get wounded I will certainly go over, and I hope it will be in the summer time.
> It is very cold now here, it is snowing a treat, and it rains a good deal. I have just come out of the trenches and am having a bit of a spell. I did four weeks in the trenches and will be going back next week.
> I only wish the war was over. I would like it to be so. Did you get the receipt for the ten pounds I paid into the Commonwealth Bank of Australia, and in case I do get killed you can have it. Will you tell May to be sure and get all my money in Sydney if I get killed. I will conclude with best wishes to you and all at home, hoping this will find you and all quite well.
> Your fond brother.
> (sgd) Pat.

He has no known grave but is listed on the Villers-Bretonneux Memorial in France.

BURKE, WILLIAM: Rank: Lance Corporal. Regiment or service: Royal Munster Fusiliers. Unit: 2nd Battalion. Date of death: 27 April 1916. Service No.: 10206. Killed in action.

Supplementary information: Born in St Johns in Limerick and enlisted in Limerick while living in Ennis Co. Clare. Husband of Louisa Tierney (née Burke), of John Street, Nenagh, Co. Tipperary.

Grave or memorial reference: A. 82. Cemetery: Bully-Grenay Communal Cemetery, French Extension in France.

BURLEY, MICHAEL: Rank: Private. Regiment or service: Royal Munster Fusiliers. Unit: 1st Battalion. Date of death: 24 May 1915. Age at death: 22. Service No.: 5936 (SDGW), 9536 (CWGC).

Supplementary information: Born in Drumcliffe (SDGW) Kilmore (Records), Co. Clare. Enlisted in Ennis while living in Ennis, Co. Clare. Killed in action in Gallipoli. Son of Peter and Mary Burley, of Cornmarket, Ennis, Co. Clare. Michael died on his first day on the battlefields.

From the *Clare Journal*, June 1915:

Ennis Men Killed in action
News has reached Ennis of the death in action of Private. Michael Burley, in France, of the Munster Fusiliers.

The poor lad came of a fighting family, for his father, also a Munster, has been 14 years in the army. An uncle, who was in the Royal Garrison Artillery, was killed in the Boer War, and another who was in the Munsters fell on the Indian North-Western frontier.

Private. James Murphy, of the Munsters, a native of Ennis, has also been killed.

Also see article attached to **REGAN, JOHN**.

In his will, his personal effects and property were received by: Mrs Mary Burley (mother), Corn Market Street, Ennis Co. Clare, Ireland.

Grave or memorial reference: Panel 185 to 190. Memorial: Helles Memorial in Turkey.

BURNS, JAMES: Rank: Able Seaman. Regiment or service: Royal Navy. Unit: H. M. S. *Indefatigable*. Date of death: 31 May 1916. Age at death: 30. Service No.: 226313.

Supplementary information: Born in CGS, Liscannor, Co. Clare. Son of Michael and Mary Burns, of Rose Cottage, Ballybunion, Co. Kerry.

During the Battle of Jutland the German Battlecruiser *Von Der Tann* fired 11in shells at the *Indefatigable*. The first two entered 'X' magazine area and blew out the bottom of the ship and she began sinking by the stern.

More 11in shells from the *Von Der Tann* destroyed 'A' turret and also blew up the forward magazine and she then sank. There were only two survivors of her crew of 1,017 men. The *Von Der Tann* was scuttled in Scapa Flow in June 1919.

Grave or memorial reference: 11. He has no known grave but is listed on the Plymouth Naval Memorial, UK.

BUTLER, MICHAEL: Rank: Private. This man is in *Soldiers died in the Great War* twice as Burley and Butler (*see* **BURLEY, MICHAEL**) with just the names and numbers slightly different. He is not in the Commonwealth War Graves Commission under Butler at all.

BYRNE, JOHN FRANCIS: Rank: Corporal. Regiment or service: Australian Infantry, AIF. Unit: 58th Battalion. Date of death: 5 January 1918. Age at death: 29 (his records state he was 36 when he died in the Military Hospital in Colchester). Service No.: 2182. Died of illness (Pleurisy).

Supplementary information: Son of Patrick and Alicia Byrne, of Bally Valley, Killaloe, Co. Clare, Ireland. Born in Bally Valley, Killaloe, Co. Clare. Occupation on enlistment: Grocer's assistant. He went to Australia when he was 26. His records state he was born in Dublin.

Grave or memorial reference: T. 5. 62. Cemetery: Colchester Cemetery, Essex, UK.

The Australian Roll of Honour.

BYRNE, WILLIAM: Rank: Private. Regiment or service: Australian Infantry, AIF. Unit: 12th Battalion. Date of death: 20 May 1915. Age at death: 23. Service No.: 1015. Killed in action at Gaba Tepe.

Supplementary information: Killed in action in Gallipoli. Born, Ennis, Co. Clare. He went to Australia when he was 20. Occupation on enlistment: Farmer. Age on enlistment: 21 years 2 months. Next of kin details: Mrs Mary A Byrne (mother), Ardelough, Straffan, Co. Kildare. Place and date of enlistment: Blackboy Hill, Western Australia, 16 September 1914. Weight: 14st 3lbs. Height: 5ft 5½in. Complexion: Dark. Eyes: Brown. Hair: Dark brown. Reported missing in action in the Dardanelles, later pronounced killed in action. Buried in a temporary grave (60 yards from Brigade headquarters by Revd F.R. Richards) and later re-interred in Shell Green Cemetery. His mother received a pension of £2 per fortnight from 21 May 1915.

Grave or memorial reference: Artillery Road Plot. 22. Cemetery: Shell Green Cemetery in Turkey.

C

CAHILL, THOMAS: Rank: Sapper. Regiment or service: Corps of Royal Engineers. Unit: 55th Field Company. Date of death: 29 September 1915. Service No.: 25506. Died of wounds.

Supplementary information: Born in Ennis, Co. Clare. Enlisted in Ennis while living in Lifford, Co. Clare.

From the *Clare Journal* and *Ennis Advertiser*, October 1915:

Ennis Victims of the War
In a letter from an hospital "Somewhere in France," an Ennis man, who took part in the recent heavy fighting, which was successful for the British army, describing how Lance-Corporal John Tuttle of the Munster Fusiliers, son of Mr Edward Tuttle … says he was the first of the Munsters to fall, shot through the head, death being instantaneous. The deceased man was reputable for his quiet and amiable disposition and was very popular amongst friends before leaving Ennis.

Other Ennis men, Private. J. Savage and Private. Cahill, have, we hear, also died. The latter died of wound's.

Grave or memorial reference: Panel 4 and 5. Memorial: Loos Memorial in France.

CAHILL, WILLIAM FRANCIS: Rank: First Lieutenant. Regiment or service: US Army. Unit: 307th Infantry, 77th Division. Date of death: 29 August 1918. Age at death: 25.

Supplementary information: Enlisted in New York, USA.

From the *Saturday Record*, November 1918.

Clareman's Death from Wounds
U. S. Officer
Lieutenant William Francis Cahill, who died of wounds, was a member of the law firm of Byrne and McCutcheon, of New York. Lieutenant Cahill was a graduate of Fordham University and of the Harvard Law School. He received his preliminary military training at Plattsburg, and went to France in Company M, 307th Infantry, Upton Div. Lieutenant Cahill was 25 years old. He was a son of Mrs Cahill, Deerpark, Doora.

From the *Saturday Record*, November 1918:

Death of Lieutenant william Cahill
In a recent issue, we mentioned, with deep regret, the death of a gallant young American officer, from wounds, Lieutenant W. Cahill, one of the most brilliant young men of the day in New York. He was son of Mr Michael Cahill, New York, and grandson of Mrs Cahill, Deerpark, Doora. The deceased had just finished his career as a Law Student at the university of Harvard, where he distanced all competitors, win-

ning the Gold Medal at the end of his term, and his friends had good reason to anticipate for him a distinguished career in his profession. Just then America entered the war, and Mr Cahill was among the first to offer his services, receiving a Lieutenant's Commission.

An Irishman to the core, he would go where the danger was greatest and the battle fiercest We desire to convey to Mrs Cahill and her family the assurance of our sincere sympathy in their bereavement.

On Tuesday High Mass was celebrated for the repose of the soul of deceased, at Doora Church. The celebrant was Rev. J. Scanlan, P. P., deacon; Rev. M. McGrath, C. C., Clarecastle; and sub deacon, Rev M. Crowe, C. C., Doora.

The choir was conducted by Very Rev. Canon Bourke, and Very rev. Father Chrysostom, O. F. M., Ennis.

Grave or memorial reference: Plot A, Row 15, Grave 12. Cemetery: Oise-Aisne American Cemetery, Fere-en-Tardenois, France.

CANTY, MICHAEL: Rank: Lance Corporal. Regiment or service: Rifle Brigade. Unit: 8th Battalion, also listed as the London Regiment, (Post Office Rifles). Date of death: 3 November 1918. Service No.: 52032. Killed in action.

Supplementary information: Born in Sheringham, Norfolk. Enlisted in Norwich while living in Co. Clare, Ireland.

Grave or memorial reference: IX. C. 15. Cemetery: Terlincthun British Cemetery, Wimille, France.

CAREY, DANIEL: Rank: Private. Regiment or service: Irish Guards. Unit: 1st Battalion. Date of death: 15 September 1916. Service No.: 9440. Killed in action.

Supplementary information: Born in Kilmacduane, Co. Clare. Enlisted in Dublin while living in Ballinagim, Co. Clare.

From the *Clare Journal*, October 1916:

Irish Guardsmen's Deaths Intelligence has been received that Constables Dan Carey and Edward Luby were Killed in action while fighting at the front on the Somme—Carey on the 15th and Luby on the 25th September. At the commencement of the war both gallant, fine strapping young fellows manfully volunteered in the Irish Guards, and met a soldier's death. The greatest sympathy is felt by their comrades. Carey was a native of Kilrush and Luby, Tipperary. [Luby is listed in his records under Looby.] His Nuncupative [or missing] will was witnessed by;- Michael Carey, Ballynagun ?, Honora Carey, Ballynagnn, Bridget Tubridy, Dromelihy? After his death, his personal effects and property were received by: (Sister) Mary Carey, Ballynagun ?, Doonbeg, Co. Clare, Ireland.

Grave or memorial reference: Pier and Face 7 D. Memorial: Thiepval Memorial in France.

CARMODY, DANIEL: Rank: Private. Regiment or service: Leinster Regiment. Unit: 1st Battalion. Date of death: 9 May 1915. Age at death: 39. Service No.: 4381. Died of wounds.

Supplementary information: Born in Ennis, Co. Clare. Enlisted in Ennis. Son of Patrick and Mary Carmody (*née* Corloran), of Ennis, Co. Clare.

Grave or memorial reference: Enclosure No 4. XIII. C. 12. Cemetery: Bedford House Cemetery in Belgium

CARMODY, EDWARD: Rank: Private. Regiment or service: Connaught Rangers. Unit: D Company, 5th battalion. Date of death: 25 March 1917. Age at death: 22. Service No.: 5113. Killed in action in Salonika.

Supplementary information: Born in Craughwell, Co. Galway. Enlisted in Galway while living in Craughwell, Co. Galway. Son of Michael and Delia Carmody, of No. 5 Montpelier Terrace, Galway.

Private Edward Carmody.

From De Ruvigny's Roll of Honour:

Carmody, Eddie. Corporal, No 5112, 5th (Service) Battalion, Connaught Rangers. 2nd son of Michael Carmody, Sergeant, Royal Irish Constabulary, Monivea, Co. Galway, by his wife, Delia, daughter of the late Michael Nestor, Kilshanny, Co. Clare. Born Craughwell, 14-June-1895. Educated, Sligo Municipal School, was employed on commercial work, and was Corporal of the Local National Volunteers at Craughwell. Enlisted 10-december-1914. Served with the Mediterranean Expeditionary Force at Gallipoli; from thence proceeded to Salonika. Took part in the retreat from Serbia, 1915, was slightly wounded, and was killed in action at Lake Worino, Greece, 25-March-1917, by a sniper while on outpost duty. Buried at Kumli. His Commanding Officer wrote; "He died nobly, and was one of the best N. C. O.'s in his battalion. He was an exceedingly good boy, and was deeply regretted by his officers and comrades," and a comrade; "Whilst we regret his death, he died manfully as he lived. He was a favourite with all, and many a tear was shed at his grave."

Grave or memorial reference: He has no known grave but is listed on the Doiran Memorial in Greece.

CARPENTER, PATRICK: Rank: Private. Regiment or service: Royal Munster Fusiliers. Unit: 1st Battalion.

Date of death: 26 April 1915. Service No.: 8015. Killed in action in Gallipoli.

Supplementary information: Born in Dromcliffe, Ennis, Co. Clare. Enlisted in Nenagh, Co. Tipperary while living in Ennis. Date of last will and testament: 21 April 1915. Property and Effects received by: Bridget Carpenter, No. 4A Clare Road Cottages, Ennis Co. Clare, Ireland.

Grave or memorial reference: Special Memorial, A. 114. Cemetery: Redoubt Cemetery, Helles in Turkey.

CARROLL, CORNEY: Rank: Private. Regiment or service: Royal Horse Artillery and Royal Field Artillery. Unit: 76th Battery. Date of death: 2 February 1917. Service No.: 52389. Died in Turkey.

Supplementary information: Born in Clare, Ireland. Enlisted in Ennis, Ireland.

Grave or memorial reference: Angora Memorial, 39. Cemetery: Baghdad (North Gate) War Cemetery in Iraq.

CARROLL, WILLIAM: Rank: Lance Corporal. Regiment or service: Household Cavalry and Cavalry of the Line including the Yeomanry and Imperial Camel Corps. Unit: Corps of Lancers, 5th Lancers (Royal Irish). Date of death: 2 May 1915. Age at death: 24. Service No.: 3961. Killed in action.

Supplementary information: Son of John and Augusta Carroll, of Eden Vale, Ennis, Co. Clare. Born in Killaloe, Co. Clare. Enlisted in Ennis.

From the *Clare Journal*, 1915:

Claremen lost at the Front
Lance Corporal Carroll

In a late issue we reported the death from German poison gas, of Lance Corporal Carroll, Fifth Lancers, son of Mr John Carroll, Edenvale. From a letter received this week by his afflicted mother, from a comrade of the deceased, it should appear that death was due to a shell fragment, not the gas. The writer, Lance Corporal Musgrave, says—"It was on Sunday, may 2nd, and we were preparing to be relieved from our trenches where we were reserved. At about 5.30 in the evening, the enemy made an attack with poisonous gases (which, no doubt, you have heard about). Our infantry were overcome by the fumes, and we were ordered to advance to take their places. As we were advancing the shells fell very thick and our squadron happened to catch brunt of the fire. Will was knocked over by one shell, and was trying to rise when another came and killed him on the spot. A married Private with him was also killed, another died later, and several were badly wounded. It was impossible to get a message from him as he was dead when we found him, but I know he had your photo with him. It is impossible to tell the name of the place, but I can tell you it is where all the fighting has been going on for several months, and where thousands of out brave men have fallen. You have the knowledge that he did not suffer much, if at all. Our losses that day were 4 killed, and about twenty wounded."

From the *Limeric Leader*, May 1915:

One of the victims in the recent desperate fighting at the western war front was Private William Carroll, Fifth Royal Irish Lancers, who was killed by the murderous poisn gas of the Huns. He was son to Mr John Carroll, Edenvale, Ennis, County Clare, and had been home on furlough three months ago.

Grave or memorial reference: He has no known grave but is listed on Panel 5 on the Ypres (Menin Gate) Memorial in Belgium.

CASEY, PETER: Rank: Sergeant. Regiment or service: Royal Munster Fusiliers. Unit: 9th Battalion. Date of death: 28 May 1916. Service No.: 3347. Died of wounds.

Supplementary information: Born in Miltown Malbay, Co. Clare. Enlisted in Ennis while living in Kilkee, Co. Clare.

From the *Saturday Journal*, June 1916:

Kilkee Fatality at the Front

Events at the front in France have been painfully brought for the past few weeks to several families in Kilkee. Private. P. Nevin of the Munsters was killed in the trenches. Sergeant P. Casey, of the same gallant corps, had both his legs blown off, and died at the base hospital at Boulogne, last week.

Grave or memorial reference: Plot D, Row 2, Grave 17. Cemetery: Calais Southern Cemetery in France.

CASEY, THOMAS: Rank: Private. Regiment or service: Australian Infantry, AIF. Unit: 16th Battalion. Date

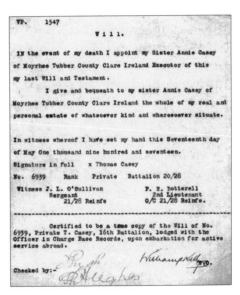

The will of Thomas Casey.

of death: 8 August 1918. Age at death: 41 Service No.: 6939.

Supplementary information: Son of Michael and Honora Casey (*née* Howard), of Moyrhee, Tublier, Co. Clare, Ireland. Born in Moyrhee, Tubber, Co. Clare. Went to Australia when he was 35. Occupation on enlistment: Farm Manager. Location of death, near Merricourt in France.

From the official records:

Born, Clare, Ireland.
Age on enlistment; 35 years.
Address on enlistment, 495 Hay Street, Perth, W.A.
Occupation on enlistment, Labourer, Yardman.
Apprenticiship?;
Next of kin details; (father) Michael Casey, Moyrhee, Tubber, Co. Clare.
Place and date of enlistment, Bboy(Blackboy) Hill, 28-March-1917.
Weight, 126lbs. Height, 5 feet, 7½ in.
Complexion, dark. Eyes, blue. Hair, dark.

'Private. Clancy was part of a Lewis Gun team that went forward in a tank on the 8th of August The tank to which Pte Casey was attached was hit by a shell and the crew and Lewis Gun team evacuated the tank. They went forward about 50 X when a shell exploded in the middle of the Lewis Gun team and they were all either killed or wounded as far as I can ascertain Pte Casey was not killed outright. This took place on the outskirts of the village of Mericourt.'

He was buried in a temporary grave and later exhumed and reburied in Heath Cemetery.

Grave or memorial reference: I. H. 20. Cemetery: Heath Cemetery, Harbonnieres in France.

CASSERLEY/CASSERLEY, THOMAS: Rank: Lance Corporal. Regiment or service: Corps of Royal Engineers. Unit: 74th Field Company. Date of death: 1 April 1918. Age at death: 21. Service No.: 34426. Killed in action.

Supplementary information: Born in St Andrews, Co. Dublin. Enlisted in Dublin while living in Ennis. Son of James and Margaret Casserly, of Dublin.

Grave or memorial reference: I. D. 17. Cemetery: Wanquetin Communal Cemetery Extension, Pas-De-Calais, France.

CHAMBERS, JAMES FRANCIS: Rank: Private. Regiment or service: Wellington Regiment, NZEF. Unit: 2nd Battalion. Date of death: 15 September 1916. Service No.: 11828. Killed in action.

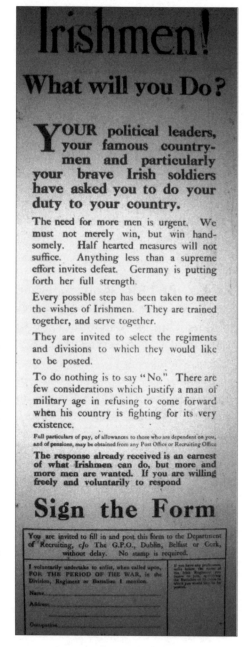

Newspaper recruitment appeal.

Supplementary information: Son of John Chambers, of Clonfineen, Cooraclare, Co. Clare, Ireland. Occupation on enlistment: Bushman. Next of kin details: John Chambers (brother), of No. 2 Murphy Street, Wellington, New Zealand.

Embarked with the 12th Reinforcements Wellington Infantry Battalion, B Company, New Zealand Expeditionary Force on 1 May 1916 from Wellington, New Zealand aboard the *Ulimaroa* bound for Suez, Egypt.

Grave or memorial reference: Caterpillar Valley (New Zealand) Memorial, Longueval France.

CHARLESWORTH, JOHN: Rank:
Private. Regiment or service: Sherwood Foresters (Notts and Derby Regiment). Unit: 2nd/8th Battalion. Date of death: 16 May 1916. Service No.: 2863. Died at sea.

Supplementary information: Born in Mansfield, Nottinghamshire. Enlisted in Mansfield. Son of E. Charlesworth, of No. 5 Broomhill Lane, Mansfield.

From the *Saturday Record*, May 1916:

Soldier Drowned at Killaloe
On Tuesday morning three soldiers out of a large number which arrived that morning in Killaloe, went boating from the Lakeside shore. The men, who had no local knowledge of the very fast and dangerous current which prevailed at the time, especially as a heavy flood was running down and the sluice gates wide open, were quickly in difficulties, and the boat was swept along at a dangerous rate until it struck one of the gates. One man succeeded in gripping a support of the structure, and was quickly rescued. The other two disappeared, but a second was rescued by some fishermen several hundred yards down the stream. He was unconscious at the time, but artificial respiration set him right, little the worse for his immersion.

The body of the other man has not yet been recovered.

From the *Tipperary Star*:

Soldier Drowned
One of the soldiers who arrived in Killaloe on Tuesday afternoon has been drowned as the result of an accident. From information to hand it appears that about an hour after their arrival in the town on Tuesday three soldiers took out a boat for a row in the Shannon. Not knowing the river and not presumably being skilled oarsmen they got into a strong current which took the boat from their control and dashed it against the weir gates which unfortunately were closed at the time, breaking it to pieces. Two of the solders were recovered in an unconscious condition, but as the resolute of artificial respiration they slowly recovered consciousness. The body of the third soldier has not yet been recovered, and it is presumed that the poor fellow lost his life. All belonged to the Notts and Derby Regiment.

From the *Tipperary Star*, June:

Found Drowned
"Found Drowned." Was the verdict of the Coroner's jury at the inquest, at Killaloe, on Tuesday, on Private John Charlesworth, who was drowned at Killaloe as a result of a boating accident on may 16th. Charlesworth belonged to a detachment of Sherwood Foresters, which visited Killaloe. The body

was discovered on Monday in the Shannon about two miles outside Killaloe. The jury commended two of Charlesworth's companions were poorly equipped for the high river and swift current. They also commended the action of Constable Jeremiah Mahoney who gave instructions as to the positions of the drowning soldiers from the battlement of the bridge. As two Rosary Beads were found in Charlesworth's pocket, and as the Chaplain of the Battalion, before his departure from Killaloe informed Canon Archdale that the deceased belonged to the Church of England, and asked him in the event of the body being found near Killaloe to carry out the burial according to the rites of his Church, some doubt existed as to the deceased's religion. This was cleared up by Mr McClelland, D. I., who while the inquest was proceeding received a wire from deceased's relatives stating that he belonged to the Church of England, and another from the military to the same effect. The internment took place on Tuesday evening at Killaloe.

Grave or memorial reference: Between the Cathedral and the Oratory. Cemetery: Killaloe (St Flannan) Cathedral Graveyard, Co. Clare.

CLAHANE, WILLIAM: Rank: Gunner. Listed as CLAHANE (SDWG) and CULHANE (CWGC), Culhane seems to be the correct name. Regiment or service: Royal Garrison Artillery. Unit: 37th Trench Mortar Battery. Date of death: 29 June 1916. Age at death: 30. Service No.: 3673.

Supplementary information: Born in Drumcliffe, Co. Clare. Enlisted in Limerick while living in Tipperary. Killed in action. Son of John and Johanna Culhane. Listed as Gr W. Clahane, Kildysart, R.G.A in the *Clare Journal*, August 1916.

Grave or memorial reference: K. 8. Cemetery: Berles-Au-Bois Churchyard, Pas-De-Calais, France.

CLANCY/CLANEY, THOMAS: Rank: Private. Regiment or service: Machine Gun Guards, Guards Machine Gun regiment. Unit: 4th Battalion. Date of death: 9 October 1917. Age at death: 23. Service No.: 1051. Formerly he was with the Irish Guards where his number was 9847. Killed in action.

Supplementary information: Son of Pat and Mary Clancy, of Ballynacragga, Kildysart, Ennis, Co. Clare.

Grave or memorial reference: Panel 11. Memorial: Tyne Cot Memorial in Belgium.

CLANCY, WILLIAM JOSEPH: Rank: Second Lieutenant. Regiment or service: Army Service Corps Date of death: 16 October 1918. Age at death: 38. Died as 'result of after operation'.

Supplementary information: Son of John and Winifred Clancy, of Moore Street, Kilrush, Co. Clare. Also commemorated in the 'List of Kilrush Men engaged in the War from August 1914'. This pamphlet lists the Kilrush men who were involved in the First World War until 11 November 1918.

From the *Saturday Record,* November 1918:

Roll of Honour
Private. W. J. Clancy, Liverpool
Scottish

We take the following from the Central Argentine Railway Magazine of Buenos Aires;--

We regret to record that a cable received from the London Office announced the death in hospital on the 16th October, from meningitis, of the above Central Argentine Volunteer, formerly connected with the Chief Engineer's Department. Mr Clancy, who was born in Kilrush, Co. Clare, Ireland, on 16th-January-1879, entered the service of this Company, in August-1906, having previously held positions in the British South African Police, Rhodesia. He volunteered for active service in October 1914, and at the time of his departure he filled the position of Chief Clerk in the Sectional Engineer's Office, La Banda. On arrival in England he immediately joined King Edward's Horse, subsequently transferring to the Liverpool Scottish, and at the time of his death he spent nearly three and a half years on active service. A big, smiling, jovial Irishman, with a heart as large as his frame, his genial presence ad kindly disposition will be greatly missed by a wide circle of friends both in business and social life.

This man is only in the Commonwealth War Graves database. Grave or memorial reference: 3 "C". Z. 26. Cemetery: Greenwich Cemetery, UK.

CLARK, CHRISTOPHER: Rank: Third Mate. Regiment or service: Mercantile Marine. Unit: SS *Eupion* (London). Date of death: 3 October 1918. Age at death: 29.

Supplementary information: Son of Christopher Granger Clark and Hannah Hodgson Clark, of 'Hazelwood' Langholm Road, East Boldon, Sunderland. Born at Robin Hood's Bay, Yorkshire.

The 3,575 ton SS *Eupio* was built in Alloa, Clackmannanshire in 1914 for the Eupion Steamship Company. She was torpedoed and sunk west of Loop Head, Co. Clare by German submarine U-123, the same submarine that sank the *Leinster* a week later.

Grave or memorial reference: In north-east corner. Cemetery: Kilrush Church of Ireland Churchyard, Co. Clare. Two other Eupion casualties are buried in this cemetery.

CLARKE, JAMES: *see* **MURPHY, JAMES.**

CLEARY, DANIEL: Rank: Fireman. Regiment or service: Mercantile Marine. Unit: SS *Coningbeg* (Glasgow). Date of death: 18 December 1917. Age at death; 45.

Supplementary information: Son of Timothy and Johanna Cleary; husband of Ellen Cleary (*née* Plasteon), of No. 13 Henrietta Street, Waterford Born in Co. Clare. Torpedoed by German Submarine U-62. There were no survivors. U-62 surrendered in November 1918.

Grave or memorial reference: He has no known grave but is listed on the Tower Hill Memorial in the UK. He is also listed on the Formby-Coningbeg Memorial, Adelphi Quay in Waterford City.

CLEARY, JOHN JOSEPH: Rank: Private. Regiment or service: Australian Infantry, AIF. Unit: 9th Battalion. Date of death: 2 July 1916. Service No.: 4160. Died of wounds received in action (gunshot wound to the head, compound fracture of the skull) at 1st Australian Casualty Clearing Station.

Supplementary information: Born, Killaloe, Co. Clare. Age on enlistment: 40 years 6 months. Occupation on enlistment: Miner. Next of Kin: Abbe/Abby Cleary (mother), of Millchester Road, Charters Road, Queenstown. She died in 1922 and it changed to Mrs Ellen Roberts (sister) of Boundary Street, Clarkes Towers. Date and location of enlistment: 16 August 1915. Charters Towers, Queensland. Height 5ft, 6in. Weight: 8st 7lbs. Complexion: Fresh. Eyes: Blue. Hair: Light brown.

Grave or memorial reference: II. T. 9. Cemetery: Estaires Communal Cemetery and Extension in France.

CLEARY, STEPHEN: Rank: Private. Regiment or service: Royal Munster Fusiliers. Unit: 1st Battalion. Date of death: 2 September 1918. Service No.: 4599. Killed in action.

Supplementary information: Born in Drumcliffe, Co. Clare. Enlisted in Limerick while living in Limerick. In his will, his effects and property were received by: Mrs B. Cummins (sister), 2 Custom House Place, Limerick City, Ireland.

Grave or memorial reference: I. E. 23. Cemetery: Dominion Cemetery, Hendecourt-les-Cagnicourt, Pas-De-Calais, France

CLOHESSY, JOHN: Rank: Private. Regiment or service: Royal Munster Fusiliers. Unit: 1st Battalion. Date of death: 21 August 1915. Age at death: 28. Service No.: 3856.

Supplementary information: Born in Ennistymon, Co. Clare. Enlisted in Limerick while living in Ennistymon, Co. Clare. Killed in action in Gallipoli. Son of Mrs Anne Foran, of Deerpark, Ennistymon, Co. Clare.

Grave or memorial reference: Panel 185 to 190. Memorial: Helles Memorial in Turkey.

CLOHESSY, MATHEW: Rank: Private. Regiment or service: Royal

A letter from the sister of J. Cleary.

Irish Regiment. Unit: 2nd Battalion. Date of death: 21 March 1918. Service No.: 18013. Formerly he was with the Royal Munster Fusiliers where his number was 6063. Killed in action.

Supplementary information: Born in Corofin, Co. Clare. Enlisted in Ennistymon, Co. Clare.

Grave or memorial reference: Panel 30 and 31. Memorial: Pozieres Memorial in France.

COALPOISE, FRANK: Rank: Private. Regiment or service: Irish Guards. Unit: 1st Battalion. Date of death: 17 November 1917. Service No.: 4586. Died of wounds.

Supplementary information: Born in Ennistymon, Co. Clare. Enlisted in Cork while living in Ennistymon, Co. Clare.

Grave or memorial reference: I. M. 13. Cemetery: Poperinghe Old Military Cemetery in Belgium.

COFFEE, FRANCIS WARREN: Rank: Second Lieutenant. Regiment or service: Royal Irish Rifles. Unit: 5th Battalion attached to the 14th Battalion. Date of death: 16 August 1917. Age at death, 28. Killed in action.

Supplementary information: Son of Francis Richard Coffee, of 8 Fairfield Park, Rathgar, Dublin, and Evelyn Coffee (*née* Warren). Born 20 November 1888 at Whitechurch, Kilkenny. Entered Trinity College in 1906.

From *Irish Life*, October 1917:

… was killed in an advanced position whilst gallantly leading his men forward during an attack on the enemy's lines on August 16th, 1917,

was the eldest and only surviving son of Mr F. R. Coffee, Inspector, Board of Works, of 8 Fairfield Park, Rathgar. He was educated at Bishop Foy's School, Waterford; Fermoy College, and Trinity College. He was gazetted to the Royal Irish Rifles in October 1915, proceeded to France in June 1916 and went through the Somme campaign of that year. He again arrived in France in January last and was on active service there until his death.

Grave or memorial reference: He has no known grave but is listed on Panel 138 to 140 and 162 to 162A and 163A on the Tyne Cot Memorial in Belgium. Also Listed on the Bishop Foy School Memorial located in Christ Church Cathedral (Church of Ireland), Henrietta Street, Waterford

COFFEY, JOHN: Rank: Private. Regiment or service: Irish Guards. Unit: 1st Battalion. Date of death: 9 May 1918. Service No.: 4583. Killed in action.

Supplementary information: Born in Kilkishen, Co. Clare. Enlisted in Ennis, Co. Clare.

Grave or memorial reference: B. 7. Cemetery: Ayette British Cemetery in France.

COGHLAN/COUGHLAN, THOMAS: Rank: Private. Regiment or service: Leinster Regiment. Unit: 2nd Battalion. Date of death: 5 April 1916. Service No.: 6516. Died at home.

Supplementary information: Son of Mrs E. O'Leary, of Chapel Street, Ennis, Co. Clare. Born in Tubber, Co. Clare. Enlisted in Gort, Co. Galway (*see* **NEYLON, SINON**) Private Coughlan was one of the escort detailed to bring Private Neylon to the Curragh.

Grave or memorial reference: RC. 470. Cemetery: Grangegorman Military Cemetery in Dublin.

COLE, RICHARD: Rank: Fireman. Regiment or service: Mercantile Marine. Unit: S. S. *Keepe*r (Limerick) Date of death: 10 June 1917. Age at death: 23.

Supplementary information: Husband of Delia Cole, of Mill Road, Ennis, Co. Clare. SS *Keeper* was built in 1906 and owned by J. Bannatyne & Sons Ltd, Limerick. She was torpedoed and sunk possibly by German submarine UC-66 during a voyage from Belfast to Limerick. Twelve seamen were lost including four Clare men; **CONSIDINE, ARTHUR**; **COLE, RICHARD**; **McCREADY, WILLIAM** and **McMAHON J**.

Grave or memorial reference: Tower Hill Memorial, UK.

COLEMAN, MICHAEL: Rank: Private. Regiment or service: Connaught Rangers. Unit: 6th Battalion. Date of death: 1 August 1916. Age at death: 23. Service No.: 5818. Died of wounds.

Supplementary information: Born in Sixmilebridge, Co. Clare. Enlisted in Limerick while living in Sixmilebridge, Co. Clare. Son of John and Elizabeth Coleman, of Mill Street, Sixmilebridge, Co. Clare.

Grave or memorial reference: V. G. 74. Cemetery: Bethune Town Cemetery in France.

COLEMAN, MICHAEL: Rank: Driver. Regiment or service: Royal Horse Artillery and Royal Field Artillery. Unit: 82nd Battery. Date of death: 30 November 1916. Service No.: 53840. Died in Turkey.

Supplementary information: Born in Kilrush, Co. Clare. Enlisted in Kilrush.

From the *Limerick Leader*, August 1916:

Intelligence has been received by his relatives in Sixmilebridge that Private Michael Coleman, Connaught Rangers (Maxim One Section), has died of wounds received in action during the recent British advance in France. The deceased was most popular in his native district and the news of his death has cuased much regret. He was the first of a number of Sixmilebridge volunteers to fall in the fighting.

Grave or memorial reference: XXI. P. 24. Cemetery: Baghdad (North Gate) War Cemetery in Iraq.

COLFER, JAMES RICHARD: Rank: Lieutenant. Regiment or service: Royal Munster Fusiliers. Unit: 9th Battalion. Date of death: 26 February 1917. Age at death: 25.

Supplementary information: Son of John Redmond Colfer and Martha Colfer of New Ross, Co. Wexford

From an article in the *Enniscorthy Guardian*:

Mr John R Colfer, solocitor, New Ross, has received the following letter concerning the death of his son, Lieut, James R Colfer, R. M. F., from Major L, Roche, R. M. F.:

Lieutenant James Colfer.

"Dear Mr Colfer, I have learned with the greatest possible regret of the death of your dear son in action. I knew him well, and stood side by side with him in the trenches in France for nine months in the Loos and Helloch sectors and at the Somme in September, 1916, and a more gallant fellow I never met.

We of the old 9th Munsters shall sorely miss his genial presence. His bravery at the taking of Guillemont and Ginchy will never be forgotton by his old comrades, Sincerely Yours, L Roche, Major 8th, R. M. F."

Mr Colfer also received the following wire from Buckingham Palace "The King and Queen deeply regret the loss you and the army have sustained by the death of your son in the service of his country. Their majesties truly sympathise with you in your sorrow-

Keeper of the Privvy Purse! Vow of Condolence.

At the New Ross Harbour Board on Wednesday, on the proposition of Mr John O'Sullivan, J. P. chairman seconded by Mr James Power, a vote of condolence was passed with Mr Colfer, solicitor to the board, on the death of his son Lieut James R Colfer, in France, and adjourned the meeting as a mark of respect.

From an article in a Wexford newspaper:

Lieut James. R. Colfer, youngest son of Mr John. R. Colfer, New Ross, Lieut, Colfer volunteered his services last summer and was gazetted 2nd Lieut in the 9th Royal Munster Fusiliers. At present he is serving in Flanders as machine gun officer to the battalion. Lieut Colfer was a popular figure in New Ross and was highly esteemed by all.

From the *Clare Journal*, March 1917:

We also regret to see the death recorded of Lieutenant Colfer, of the machine gun section. Before entering the Army, he was a very popular member of the staff of the Munster and Leinster Bank, Ennis.

Grave or memorial reference: III. F. 1. Cemetery: Wimereux Communal Cemetery in France.

COLGAN, EDMOND: Rank: Drumer. Regiment or service: Royal Munster Fusiliers. Unit: 1st Battalion. Date of death: 30 June 1915. Service No.: 8414. Died of wounds in Gallipoli.

Supplementary information: Born in Tralee, Co. Kerry. Enlisted in Limerick while living in Ennis. His personal effects and property were sent to his mother, Mrs M.E. Colgan, Clonroad Cottage, Ennis, Co. Clare, Ireland and 10s was sent to Miss Blacke, Caswell, of No. 7 Ivanhoe Road, Lichfield, England.

Grave or memorial reference: Special Memorial B. 12. Cemetery: Twelve Tree Copse Cemetery, Gallipoli.

COLLINS, EDWARD: Rank: Private. Regiment or service: Royal Dublin Fusiliers. Unit: 2nd Battalion. Date of death: 24 May 1915. Service No.: 7836. Killed in action.

Supplementary information: Born in Glenamaddy, Co. Galway. Enlisted in Tullamore while living in Clare.

Grave or memorial reference: Panel 44 and 46. Memorial: Ypres (Menin Gate) Memorial in Belgium.

COLLINS, THOMAS: Rank: Private. Regiment or service: Royal Munster Fusiliers. Unit: 1st Battalion. Date of death: 31 March 1916. Service No.: 5673.

Supplementary information: Born in Sixmilebridge, Co. Clare. Enlisted in Limerick while living in Parteen, Co. Clare.

Grave or memorial reference: In the north-west corner. Cemetery: Maison-Roland Churchyard, France.

COMBER, EDWARD: Rank: Private. Regiment or service: Royal Irish Regiment. Unit: 2nd Battalion. Date of death: 7 September 1914. Age at death: 28. Service No.: 7726.

Supplementary information: Born in Ennistymon, Co. Clare. Enlisted in Liverpool while living in Ennistymon, Co. Clare. Son of Thomas J. Comber, of Lahinch. Co. Clare. Born at Ennistymon. Co. Clare.

From the *Clare Journal*, 1914:

Young Lahinch Victim of the War Our obituary column last week had an announcement of the death from wounds at the front, of Mr Eddie Comber, a well-known and popular young Lanhich man, and member of one of the oldest families in the district. He had been in Melbourne for about five years, and came home last year. When the war opened he joined the 18th Royal Irish, with whom he fought in some of the hottest days of the earlier stages of the campaign, being so badly wounded that he died in hospital.

Mr Comber was son of Mr T. J. Comber; formerly auctioneer, of Ennistymon, and brother of Mr Harry Comber, Lahinch. He was nephew of the late Surgeon General Comerford, of Galway. There is general sympathy with his relatives.

Grave or memorial reference: IX. E. 10. Cemetery: Mons (Bergen) Communal Cemetery in Belgium.

CONNELL, PATRICK: Listed in the CWGC under **O'CONNELL, PATRICK**. Rank: Private. Regiment or service: Royal Inniskilling Fusiliers. Unit: 7th Battalion. Date of death: 27 April 1916. Age at death: 41. Service No.: 27702. Formerly he was with the Royal

Irish Regiment where his number was 9656. Killed in action.

Supplementary information: Born in Kilrush, Co. Clare. Enlisted in Clonmel. Son of Peter and Annie O'Connell, of No. 5 Cecil Street, Limerick.

Grave or memorial reference: Panel 60. Memorial: Loos Memorial in France.

CONNELLY, J.: Rank: Private. Regiment or service: Royal Scots. Unit: 2nd Battalion. Date of death: 4 August 1920. Service No.: 65529.

From the *Saturday Record*, August 1920.

Soldiers Fatal Accident

Private. Connolly, of the Royal Scots Regiment, quartered at Kilmihill, had a revolver on his side on duty on Wednesday morning, and which went off accidentally through contact with his arm or some othere unaccountable way, and the contents lodged in his body inflicting such wounds from which he died soon after.

Grave or memorial reference: In south-east corner. Cemetery: Kilrush (Shanakyle) Cemetery, Co. Clare.

CONNOLLY, THOMAS: Rank: Private. Regiment or service: Household Cavalry and Cavalry of the line including the Yeomanry and Imperial Camel Corps. Unit: (Old) 7th Reserve Cavalry Regiment (9th and 21st Lancers). Date of death: 3 October 1914. Service No.: 8500. Died at home.

Supplementary information: Born in Ennis, Co. Clare. Enlisted in Walham Green while living in Dundalk. Records also have him as being born in Dundalk.

Co. Louth. This is a case where two databases conflict with the place of birth.

Grave or memorial reference: A. 24. Cemetery: Tidworth Military Cemetery, UK.

CONROY, JOHN: Rank: Private. Regiment or service: Leinster Regiment. Unit: 2nd Battalion. Date of death: 21 July 1916. Service No.: 3892. Killed in action.

Supplementary information: Born in Tulla, Co. Clare. Enlisted in Tuam, Co. Galway.

Grave or memorial reference: C. 23. Cemetery: Knightsbridge Cemetery, Mesnil-Martinsart, France.

CONSIDINE, ARTHUR: Rank: Seaman. Regiment or service: Mercantile Marine. Unit: SS *Keeper* (Limerick). Date of death: 10 June 1917.

Supplementary information: SS *Keeper* was built in 1906 and owned by J. Bannatyne & Sons Ltd, Limerick. She was torpedoed and sunk, possibly by German submarine UC-66, during a voyage from Belfast to Limerick. Twelve seamen were lost including four Clare men; **CONSIDINE, ARTHUR**; **COLE, RICHARD**; **McCREADY, WILLIAM** and **McMAHON J.**

Grave or memorial reference: He has no known grave but is listed on the Tower Hill Memorial in the UK.

CONSIDENE, PATRICK: *see* **KELLY, PATRICK.**

CONSIDINE, PETER: Rank: Private. Regiment or service:

Canterbury Regiment, NZEF. Date of death: 6 May 1918. Age at death: 44. Service No.: 29149. Died of disease.

Supplementary information: Son of Patrick and Maria Considine (*née* Cain), of Co. Clare, Ireland. Occupation on enlistment: Labourer. Next of kin details: John Considine (brother), of East Trentham, Victoria, Australia. Embarked with the 18th Reinforcements Canterbury Infantry Battalion, C Company, New Zealand Expeditionary Force on 11 October 1916 in Wellington, New Zealand aboard the *Tofua* bound for Plymouth, England. Born in Australia.

Grave or memorial reference: C. 307. Cemetery: Tidworth Military Cemetery, UK.

CONSIDINE, WILLIAM: True name is O'CONNOR, THOMAS. Rank: Private. Regiment or service: Australian Infantry, AIF. Unit: 13th Battalion. Date of death: 1 May 1919. Age at death: 29. Service No.: 302.

Supplementary information: Son of Patrick and Margaret Considine, of Danganelly, Cooraclare, Co. Clare, Ireland. Born in Danganelly, Cooraclare, Co. Clare. Occupation on enlistment: Agriculturist Location of death, in the Red Sea at Bullecourt, France.

From the official records:

Born, Miltown, Tralee, Co. Kerry. [Another copy of his documents states he was born in Cooraclare, Kilrush.] Occupation on enlistment, Labourer. Age on enlistment; 33 years 10 months.

Next of kin details; Mr M P Considine (changed from his father Mr Patrick O'Connor) Danganelly, Cooraclare, Co. Clare.

Previous military experience, 8 years as a driver in the Royal Engineers.

Place and date of enlistment, Rosehill, N. S. W. 29-September-1914.

Weight 12st 10. Height, 5 feet, 8 ½ in. Complexion, fair. Eyes, brown. Hair, black Wounded in the right shoulder and forearm 2 May 1915. Reported missing in April 1917 and later found to be a prisoner of war in Germany after he was captured in Raincourt. Interned at Limburg. Repatricated and arrived

```
Officer i/c Records,
   A.I.F.Headquarters,
      130 Horseferry Road,
         Westminster,
            LONDON.      S.W. 1
      --------------------

      re the late No. 302 Private Thomas O'CONNOR,  13th Battalion.
      --------------------------------------------

         Advice is to hand from O.C. Troops, H.T."Medic", that the
   above mentioned soldier made a statement a few days prior to his
   death, to the effect that his correct name was CONSIDINE William,
   and that next-of-kin was Mrs.Patrick Considine (mother), Danganelly,
   Coora Clare, Co.Clare, Ireland.

         The records have been amended in accordance with King's
   Regulations, para 1901.
```

Record document showing true name and alias.

in England in December, 1918. Died of Syncope at Sea and buried in Cape Town.

Grave or memorial reference: Sec. 4. 97708C. Cemetery: Cape Town (Maitland) Cemetery in South Africa.

CONWAY, JOHN: Rank: Private/ Lance Corporal. Regiment or service: Canadian Infantry (Saskatchewan Regiment). Unit: 28th Battalion. Date of death: 17 October 1915. Age at death: 38 years and 3 months. Service No.: 73535.

From De Ruvigny's Roll of Honour:

... eldest son of Patrick Conway, of Ivy Cottage, Ennistymon. co. Clare. ex-Sergt Royal Irish Constabulary, by his wife, Hanna, daughter. of William O'Sullivan. Bonane, Kenmare, Co. Kerry; Born in Iries, Castletownhere, Co. Cork, 13 July. 1874; educ. Bantry and Castletownhere; enlisted in the Grenadier Guards about 1894. and served with the Sudan Expedition, including the Battle of Omdurman and the capture of Khartoum; and through the South African war. 1899-1902 (receiving three medals). He then went to Canada about 1906 and settled in Ottawa, and was working on the railroad, but on the outbreak of the European war joined the Canadian Expeditionary Force, came over with the second contingent and was Killed in action in Belgium 17 Oct. 1915. He was in charge of a machine gun, when a shell fell within 15 yards of his post, killing him and three more instantly. His commanding officer. . Major C. R. Mill, wrote: "He was a splendid soldier, and on the 16th had been promoted L. -Corpl. He died at his post, and no man could do more."

Next of kin listed as Patrick Conway (father), Ennistymon, Co. Clare, Ireland. Place of birth: Ennistymon, Co. Clare, Ireland. Date of birth, 17 July 1877. Occupation on enlistment: Labourer. Previous military experience: 7 years with the British Regulars. Place and date of enlistment: 27 October 1914, Saskatoon. Address on enlistmen: Height, 5ft 10in. Complexion: Dark. Eyes: Grey. Hair: Black.

Grave or memorial reference: I. E. 30. Cemetery: Wulverghem-Lindenhoek Road Military Cemetery in Belgium.

CONWAY, MARTIN: Rank: Private. Regiment or service: Irish Guards. Unit: No. 5 Coy. 2nd Battalion. Date of

Private John Conway.

death: 30 September 1915. Age at death: 28. Service No.: 541.

Supplementary information: Born in Drumcliffe, Co. Clare. Enlisted in Ennis, Co. Clare. Killed in action. Son of Peter and Mary Conway, of Old Mill Street, Ennis, Co. Clare.

Grave or memorial reference: Panel 9 and 10. Memorial: Loos Memorial in France.

CONWAY, PATRICK: Rank: Private. Regiment or service: Royal Munster Fusiliers. Unit: 8th Battalion. Date of death: 20 July 1916. Service No.: 6771. Died of wounds.

Supplementary information: Born in Drumcliffe, Co. Clare. Enlisted in Ennis while living in Ennis.

From the *Clare Journal*, August 1916:

Another Brave Young Ennis Man Lieutenant's Letter
The creditable circumstances under which another brave young Ennis man has had his name attached to the roll of honour are recalled in a letter to his mother, Mrs Maria Conway, Mill Street, written by Lieutenant Hugh M.V. O'Brien, R. M. F., who writes---

"Dear Mrs Conway—You must have been told before this of the death of your son, Pte Conway, 8th R. M. F. He was mortally wounded on the night of the 18th, July, at the same time as Lieutenant Becker [sic] who was his officer, and nearly at the same place, close up to the German trench, which they were attacking. I believe they both died the next evening in hospital. He received the rites of the

Church, and has been buried in a soldier's cemetery, with a cross with his name on it, marking his grave. He was a bomber, which is one of the most dangerous jobs, but also one of the most honourable. He was a good and fearless soldier, and did his work well in helping to beat the Germans, and we are all sorry to have lost him. I am told this is your second son killed. All the Ennis and Clare soldiers I have met have done well, and are a great credit to their Co."

Grave or memorial reference: I. C. 8. Cemetery: Mazingarbe Communal Cemetery Extension in France.

CONWAY, PATRICK: Rank: Leading Seaman. Regiment or service: Royal Navy. Unit: HMS *Monmouth*. Date of death: 1 November 1914. Age at death: 32. Service No.: 215609.

Supplementary information: On this day HMS *Monmouth* received an 8.2in shell from the SMS *Gneisenau* which almost blew her to pieces. She limped away and later that day was sent to the bottom by SS *Nurnberg*. There were no survivors.

Son of Michael and Bridget Conway, of Pound Street, Kilrush, Co. Clare. Also commemorated in the 'Kilrush Men belonging to or who joined the Naval Service since commencement of the War.' This pamphlet lists the Kilrush men who were involved in the First World War until 11 November 1918.

Grave or memorial reference: 1. Memorial: Plymouth Naval Memorial, UK.

COONAN, THOMAS: Rank: Private. Regiment or service: Guards

Machine Gun Regiment. Unit: 4th Battalion. Date of death: 7 May 1918. Age at death: 23 Service No.: 76. Killed in action. Formerly he was with the Grenardier Guards where his number was 18123.

Supplementary information: Born in Ogemelloc, Co. Clare. Enlisted in Llanelly, Glamorganshire. He won the Military Medal and is listed in the *London Gazette*.

Son of william and Margaret Coonan, of O'Gonnelloe, Killaloe, Co. Clare. His personal effects and property were sent to his mother Mrs Coonan, Killaloe, Co. Clare.

Grave or memorial reference: II. E. 15. Cemetery: Gommecourt Wood New Cemetery, Foncqueviller, Pas-De-Calais, France.

COONEY, MICHAEL: Rank: Private. Regiment or service: Australian Machine Gun Corps. Unit: 1st Company. Date of death: 24 September 1917. Age at death: 23. Service No.: 459.

The grave of Private Michael Cooney.

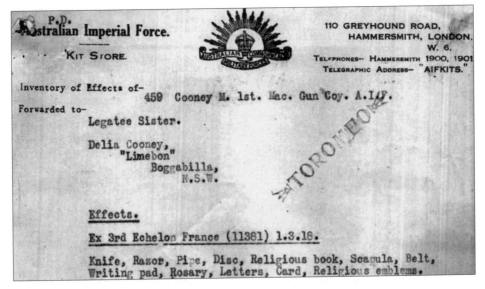

The Inventory of Effects of Private Michael Cooney.

Supplementary information: Son of Patrick and Katie Cooney, of Killuran, Broadford, Co. Clare, Ireland. Died of wounds at the Battle of Polygon Wood. From the official records:

Born, Broadford, Co. Clare. Occupation on enlistment, Labourer. Age on enlistment; 21 years 9 months. Next of kin details; (father) Patsey Cooney, Killuran More, Broadford Co. Clare.
Place and date of enlistment, 01-June-1916, location unreadable. Weight, 154lbs. Height, feet, in. Complexion, reddish. Eyes, grey. Hair, brown. Wounded in action in Belgium in September, 1917, gunshot wound to the right shoulder penetrating his chest. Died of wounds at 2nd Canadian Casualty Clearing Station. His will left all his estate to his sister, Delia Cooney, of 'Limebon' Boggsbills, N.S.W.

Grave or memorial reference: XIX. C. 13. Cemetery: Lijssenthoek Military Cemetery in Belgium.

COONEY, PATRICK: Rank: Private. Regiment or service: Royal Irish Fusiliers. Unit: 1st Garrison Battalion. Date of death: 26 June 1916. Service No.: G/494. Formerly he was with the Royal Munster Fusiliers where his number was 6007. Died in India.
Supplementary information: Born in Kilrush, Co. Clare. Enlisted in Kilrush, Co. Clare. Son of Thomas and Bridget Downes Cooney, of Kilrush; husband of Kate Cooney, of Chapel Street, Kilrush, Co. Clare.

Grave or memorial reference: Face E. Memorial: Kirkee 1914-1918 Memorial in India.

COPELAND, JOHN: Rank: Guardsman. Regiment or service: Irish Guards. Unit: 2nd Battalion. Date of death: 26 October 1914. Service No.: 5116. Killed in action.
Supplementary information: Born in Toyness, Co. Limerick. Enlisted in London while living in Toyness. In the 1911 Census he is listed as boarding with the Kenny family at No. 54 Old Mill Street, Ennis. His occupation on enlistment: Stone cutter. Age on enlistment: 30.
From the *Clare Journal*, 1914:

Clare Victims of the War
News has reached Ennis that Pte John Copeland, Scots Guards; Pte Michael Scully (Ballyea), Irish Guards; and Pte Murphy, Clarecastle, Irish Guards, have been Killed in action.
Grave or memorial reference: XXI. H. 5. Cemetery: Hooge Crater Cemetery Zillebeke, Belgium.

COPLEY, JOSEPH: Rank: Private. Regiment or service: Royal Munster Fusiliers. Unit: 2nd Battalion. Date of death: 22 March 1918. Age at death: 19. Killed in action. Service No.: 18207. Formerly he was with the Royal Dublin Fusiliers where his number was 26583.
Supplementary information: Enlisted in Ennis, Co. Clare while living in Kilrush, Co. Clare. Son of William and Mary Copley, of Chapel Street, Kilrush, Co. Clare.

Also commemorated in the 'List of Kilrush Men engaged in the War from August 1914'. This pamphlet lists the Kilrush men who were involved in the First World War until 11 November 1918 and states that he was 'missing since 21 March last Presumed killed'.

Grave or memorial reference: Panel 78 and 79. Memorial: Pozieres Memorial in France.

CORBETT, JOHN PATRICK: Rank: Sergeant. Regiment or service: East Lancashire Regiment. Unit: 1st Battalion. Date of death: 2 November 1914. Age at death: 24. Service No.: 9479. Killed in action.

Supplementary information: Born in Fulla, Ennis, Co. Clare. Enlisted in Dublin while living in Tulla. Son of James and Ellen Corbett, of Main Street, Tulla, Co. Clare.

Grave or memorial reference: I. A. 2. Cemetery: Lancashire Cottage Cemetery in Belgium.

CORBETT, MICHAEL: Rank: Private. Regiment or service: Royal Munster Fusiliers. Unit: 8th Battalion. Date of death: 20 July 1916. Service No.: 3431. Killed in action.

Supplementary information: Born in Kilrush, Co. Clare. Enlisted in Ennis while living in Kilrush, Co. Clare. Also commemorated in the 'List of Kilrush Men engaged in the War from August 1914', Grace Street. This pamphlet lists the Kilrush men who were involved in the First World War until 11 November 1918.

Grave or memorial reference: Panel 127. Memorial: Loos Memorial in France.

CORRY, JOSEPH: Rank: Private. Regiment or service: Royal Dublin Fusiliers. Unit: 1st Battalion. Date of death: 5 October 1917. Age at death: 19. Service No.: 40916. Formerly he was with the Royal Munster Fusiliers where his number was 6600. Killed in action.

Supplementary information: Born in Miltown Malbay, Co. Clare. Enlisted in Limerick while living in Miltown Malbay, Co. Clare. Son of Bridget Corry, of Braffa, Milltown Malbay, Co. Clare. Joseph also appears in the list of wounded in the *Clare Journal*, July 1916.

Grave or memorial reference: Panel 144 to 145. Memorial: Tyne Cot Memorial in Belgium.

CORRY, RICHARD: Rank: Private. Regiment or service: Loyal North Lancashire Regiment. Unit: 10th Battalion. Date of death: 1 July 1916. Service No.: 17124. Killed in action.

Supplementary information: Born in Cregluce, Co. Clare. Enlisted in Bolton while living in Cregluce.

Grave or memorial reference: III D. 2. Cemetery: Bienvillers Military Cemetery in France.

CORRY, THOMAS: Rank: Private. Regiment or service: Canadian Infantry (Central Ontario Regiment). Unit: 75th Battalion. Date of death: 30 September 1918. Age at death: 22. Service No.: 850463.

Supplementary information: Son of Bridget Corry, of Breffa, Miltown Malbay, Co. Clare. Next of kin listed as Mrs Bridget Corry (mother), Miltown

Malbay, Co. Clare. Place of birth: Miltown Malbay, Co. Clare. Date of birth: 1 January 1895. Occupation on enlistment: Labourer. Place and date of enlistment: Bridgeburg; 11 April 1916. Address on enlistment: No. 84 King Street, New York City. Height: 5ft 9½ in. Complexion: Medium. Eyes: Blue. Hair: Light.

Grave or memorial reference: F. 32. Cemetery: Cantimpre Canadian Cemetery, Sailly, Nord in France.

COSGROVE, JOHN: Rank: Private. Regiment or service: Royal Munster Fusiliers. Unit: 2nd Battalion. Date of death: 17 August 1916. Service No.: 9681. Killed in action.

Supplementary information: Born in Trough, Castlebank, Co. Clare. Enlisted in Limerick while living in Castlebank.

Grave or memorial reference: I. M. 12. Cemetery: Albert Communal Cemetery Extension in France.

COSTELLO, CORNELIUS: Rank: Private. Regiment or service: Royal Munster Fusiliers. Unit: 2nd Battalion. Date of death: 13 May 1915. Service No.: 6016. Died of wounds.

Supplementary information: Born in Kilkee, Co. Clare. Enlisted in Kilrush while living in Kilkee, Co. Clare.

Grave or memorial reference: III. A. 37. Cemetery: Lillers Communal Cemetery in France.

COSTELLO, JAMES: Rank: Private. Regiment or service: Royal Munster Fusiliers. Unit: 7th Battalion. Date of death: 3 November 1915. Service No.: 6012. Died of wounds in Greek Macedonia.

Supplementary information: Born in Mullagh, Co. Clare. Enlisted in Ennis, Co. Clare while living in Kilrush, Co. Clare. Son of Mrs Norah McGrath, of Ennis Road, Kilrush, Co. Clare.

Grave or memorial reference: 1597. Cemetery: Salonika (Lembet Road) Military Cemetery in Greece.

COSTELLO, JOHN: Rank: Corporal. Regiment or service: Royal Munster Fusiliers. Unit: C Company, 1st Battalion. Date of death: 30 September 1918. Age at death: 24. Service No.: 5565. Killed in action.

Supplementary information: Born in Kilkee, Co. Clare. Enlisted in Limerick while living in Kilkee, Co. Clare. John also appears in the list of badly wounded in the *Clare Journal*, June 1916.

Son of Mrs B. Costello, of Gratton Street, Kilkee, Co. Clare.

Grave or memorial reference: Panel 10. Memorial: Vis-en-Artois Memorial in France.

COSTELLO, JOHN: Rank: Private. Regiment or service: Connaught Rangers. Unit: 6th Battalion. Date of death: 5 February 1916. Service No.: 4600. Killed in action.

Supplementary information: Born in Drumcliffe, Co. Clare. Enlisted in Sligo while living in Grange, Co. Sligo.

Grave or memorial reference: Panel 124. Memorial: Loos Memorial in France.

COUGHLAN/COGHLAN JOHN: Rank: Private. Regiment or service: Royal Munster Fusiliers. Unit: 1st Battalion. Date of death: 9 September 1916. Age at death: 26. Service No.: 6359. Killed in action.

Supplementary information: Born in Drumcliffe, Co. Clare. Enlisted in Ennis, Co. Clare while living in Ennis, Co. Clare. Son of Michael and Mary Coughlan, of 'The Cottage', Circular Road, Ennis, Co. Clare.

Grave or memorial reference: I. G. 2. Cemetery: Delville Wood Cemetery, Longueval in France.

COUGHLAN, MICHAEL JOSEPH: Rank: Private. Regiment or service: Royal Munster Fusiliers. Unit: 8th Battalion. Date of death: 14 May 1916. Age at death: 24. Service No.: 4379. Died of wounds.

Supplementary information: Born in Kilrush, Co. Clare. Enlisted in Limerick while living in Kilrush, Co. Clare. Son of Mrs M. Coughlan, of Burton Street, Kilrush, Co. Clare. Also commemorated in the 'List of Kilrush Men engaged in the War from August 1914'. This pamphlet lists the Kilrush men who were involved in the First World War until 11 November 1918.

Grave or memorial reference: V. C. 55. Cemetery: Bethune Town Cemetery in France.

COUGLAN/COGHLAN, THOMAS: Rank: Private. Regiment or service: Leinster Regiment. Unit: 2nd Battalion. Date of death: 5 April 1916. Service No.: 6516. Died at Home.

Supplementary information: Son of Mrs E. O'Leary, of Chapel Street, Ennis, Co. Clare. Born in Tubber, Co. Clare. Enlisted in Gort, Co. Galway.

Grave or memorial reference: R. C. 470. Cemetery: Grangegorman Military Cemetery in Dublin.

COURTNEY, PATRICK: Rank: Private. Regiment or service: Irish Guards. Unit: 2nd Battalion. Date of death: 12 April 1918. Age at death: 19. Service No.: 11902. Killed in action.

Supplementary information: Born in Corofin, Co. Clare. Enlisted in Limerick, Co. Limerick. Son of Nicholas and Mary Courtney, of No. 29 Upper Clare Street, Limerick.

Grave or memorial reference: Panel 1. Memorial: Ploegsteert Memorial in Belgium.

COURTNEY, PAUL JAMES: Rank: Private. Regiment or service: Royal Army Service Corps. Date of death: 26 July 1920. Service No.: DM2/155419.

Supplementary information: Husband of Mrs Courtney, of Ballina, Killaloe, Co. Clare. This man is only in the Commonwealth War Graves database.

Grave or memorial reference: Near south-east corner. Cemetery: Ballina (Templehollow) Graveyard in Tipperary.

COYNE, JOHN: Rank: Private. Regiment or service: Labour Corps. Date of death: 10 October 1918. Age at death: 40. Service No.: 638667. Formerly he was with the Royal Munster Fusiliers where his number was 7139. Died at Sea.

Supplementary information: Born in Carran Co. Galway. Enlisted in Ennis, Co. Clare while living in Tuamgraney, Co. Clare. Private Coyne was a passenger on the ill-fated RMS *Leinster*. Husband of Bridget O'Farrell (*née* Coyne), of Raheen Road, Tuamgraney, Co. Clare.

Grave or memorial reference: Hollybrook Memorial, Southampton UK.

CRAWFORD, WILLIAM ROBERT: Rank: Sapper. Regiment or service: Royal Engineers. Unit: Inland Water Transport. Date of death: 4 May 1917. Age at death: 36 Service No.: 156938. Died at sea.

Supplementary information: Born in Dublin and enlisted in Blackrock, Co. Dublin Son of William Robert and Elizabeth J.L. Crawford, of Miltown Malbay, Co. Clare.

Grave or memorial reference: III. A. 24. Cemetery: Mazargues War Cemetery, Marseilles in France.

CREAGH, O'MOORE CHARLES: Rank: Lieutenant. Regiment or service: Royal Field Artillery. Unit: C Battery. 108th Army Brigade. Date of death: 23 March 1918. Age at death: 21. Killed in action.

Supplementary information: Son of Charles Vandeleur Creagh, CMG, and Blanche Frances Creagh, of Cahirbane, Co. Clare.

From the *Saturday Record* and *Clare Journal*, May 1918:

Lieutenant O'M. C. Creagh Lieutenant O'Moore Charles Creagh, R. F. A., was Killed in action on March 23rd, near Mont St Quentin. He was the younger son of the late Mr Charles Vandeleur Creagh, C. M. G., of Cahirbane, Co. Clare, and of Mrs Creagh, Charlton Road, Blackheath, and a nephew of General Sir O'Moore Creagh, V. C., late Commander-in-Chief in India. He entered the Roayl Military Academy, Woolwich, and obtained his commission in February, 1915,

and on going to France in the following April, was appointed to the R. F. A. he volunteered for trench mortars, was wounded, and on recovering was appointed to a R. H. A., Battery. He afterwards returned to his old Battery at the request of the major. Writing of him his Major says—"I can honestly say I know of no-one whose loss I should feel more, and the battery as a whole feel the same, officers and men."

From De Ruvigny's Roll of Honour:

Creagh, O'Moore Charles, Lieutenant, R.F.A. Youngest son of the late Charles Valdeleur Creagh, C.M.G., of Cahirbane, Co. Clare (Governor of British North Borneo and Governor and Commander-in-Chief of Labaun, retired 1895), and Mrs Creagh, of 32, Charlton Road, Blackheath, S.E., and grandson of the late Captain F. A. Edwardes, 30th Foot, of Rhyd-y-gors, Co. Carmarthen, and nephew of General Sir O'Moore Creagh, V.C.G.C.S.I., late Commander-in-Chief in India. Born at Southsea, Co. Hants, 7 December 1896. Educated at Eastman's, Southsea, and Cheltenham College (Boyne House), from where he passed into the Royal Military Academy, Woolwich, and obtained his commission 10 February 1915. Served with the Expeditionary Force in France and Flanders from 17 April following, being appointed to the 117th Battery, R. F. A. He subsequently volunteered for the Trench

Mortars, and when in command of the 67th Trench Mortar Battery was wounded in the head, and invalided into hospital in England from November to the end of December. On his recovery he returned to the Western front July-1916, and joined the 96th Brigade, C Battery. Was later transferred to the 108th Army Brigade, R.F.A. In March, 1917, he was appointed to the R.H.A., G Battery, and took part in the celebrated cavalry charge at Monchy on Easter Monday. The Major of his old battery applied for his return, which was effected. At the Battle of Messines he was taking signals from the infantry to his headquarters for fifteen hours, and on 1 September was on liaison for the third attack, when he was reported Killed in action at Fevillacourt, near Mont Street Quentin, 23 March 1918. He took part in the actions at Richebourg 17 May 1915, and those at the Hohenzollern Redoubt, Loos, Vermelles, Ypres, on the Somme, at Messines and asschendale, etc, and when he was killed was within a few days of obtaining his Captaincy. His Major, writing of him, said; "I can honestly say I know of no-one whose loss I should feel more, and the battery as a whole feel the same, both officers and men. He was one of the best officers I have ever met."

He was mentioned in Despatches (*London Gazette*, 21 May 1918) by F.M. Sir Douglas Haig, 'for gallant and distinguished service in the field'. On his mother's side he was related as nearly as his generation would allow to General Sir Thomas Picton, of Peninsular and Waterloo fame.

Grave or memorial reference: Bay 1. Memorial: Arras Memorial in France.

CRIMMINS, PATRICK: Rank: Private. Regiment or service: Royal Irish Fusiliers. Unit: 1st Battalion. Date of death: 24 August 1918. Age at death: 24. Service No.: 18385. Killed in action.

Supplementary information: He won the Military Medal and is listed in the *London Gazette*. Born in Ennis, Co. Clare. Enlisted in Tipperary while living in Dublin. Husband of Teresa Crimmins, of No. 31 Chancery Lane, Dublin. Native of Co. Limerick.

Grave or memorial reference: III. G. 85. Cemetery: Bailleul Communal Cemetery (Nord) in France.

CROFTON, EDWARD VIVIAN MORGAN: Rank: Lieutenant. Regiment or service: Royal Engineers. Unit: 61st Field Company. Date of death: 14 July 1917. Age at death: 28. Killed in action.

Supplementary information: Son of Everard Hugh Robert Crofton and Wilhelmina Frances Westropp Harrison Moreland. Birthday: 24 June 1889, Dublin, Ireland.

From De Ruvigny's Roll of Honour:

... Son of Edward Hugh Robert Crofton, of Marlton House, Wicklow, by his wife, Wilhelmina Francis Westropp Harrison, dau, of William John Harrison Moreland, of Raheen manor, Co. Clare; and a great-garndson of Sir Hugh

Lieutenant Edward Crofton.

Crofton, of Mohill Castle, Co. Leitrim, Bart.; b, Dublin; underwent training at Chatham; afterwards served with a Field Coy, at Gibraltar; returned home in July, 1914; was stationed at Chatham; he assisted in training 62nd Field Coy; served with the Expeditionary Force in France and Flanders from May, 1915; took part in the operations in the Ypres salient; was invalided home suffering from shell concussion; rejoined his regiment at Chatham on his recovery in March, 1916, and again went to France, Aug, 1916; was Killed in action, 14 July, 1917, near Vlerstraat. Buried there. His Commanding Officer wrote; "He was a very gallant officer and a loyal friend, hard working and conscientious, always ready to carry through any work, even in difficult circumstances.

The following incident is typical; Before the attack of 9 April, 1917,

your son was responsible for laying out certain assembly trenches in no mans land, and a covering party had been arranged for, but had failed to get into position; nevertheless, your son, at great personal risk, went out and correctly laid out and finally dug the trenches; he did this with great fearlessness and efficiency, and one of his N. C. O's received the Military Medal for this very work. His loss will be much felt and his place hard to fill," and a brother officer; "Your son had been one of the brave men who have sacrificed everything for the sake of his principles; he was always admired and popular among us and we all feel his loss, both as a fine soldier and a fine man." Another also wrote; "Your son's sense of duty led him to get away from the job he had at the Base and come to the front. Many men would have preferred to have stayed at the Base at the expense of their better feelings," and another; "Your son was one of the most fearless officers I have met."

Grave or memorial reference: II. D. 10. Cemetery; Klein-Vierstraat British Cemetery in Belgium.

CROWE, MARTIN: Rank: Private. Regiment or service: Canadian Infantry (Central Ontario Regiment). Unit: 8th (Reserve) Battalion. Date of death: 29 March 1918. Service No.: 3031023 and 3031823.

Supplementary information: Son of Patrick Crowe, of Querin. Next of kin listed as, Margaret Crowe (wife), of

No. 52 S. Huntington Ave, Roxbury, Mass, USA. Place of birth: Co. Clare. Date of birth: 29 February 1889. Occupation on enlistment: Chauffeur. Place and date of enlistment: Toronto, Canada, 9 November 1917. Address on enlistment: 52 S. Huntington Ave, Roxbury, Mass, USA. Height: 5ft 8in. Complexion: Medium. Eyes: Hazel. Hair: Dark brown.

Grave or memorial reference: Northwest part. Cemetery: Querrin (Temple Made) Cemetery, Co. Clare.

CROWE, THOMAS HEPPEL: Rank: Private. Regiment or service: Canadian Infantry (Manitoba Regiment). Unit: 16th Battalion. Date of death: 9 October 1916. Age at death: 24. Service No.: 420031.

Supplementary information: Born in Newcastle-on-Tyne, England. Occupation on enlistment: Accountant. Previous military experience: 79th C.H. of C. Age on enlistment: 22 years 8 months. Date of birth; 27 July 1892. Next of kin: Michael Joseph (father), Crowe, Ennis, Co. Clare. Place and date of enlistment: Winnipeg, 4 January 1915. Height: 5ft 9in. Complexion: Fresh. Eyes, Brown. Hair: Dark Brown.

From the *Clare Journal*, December 1916:

Gallant Young Soldier Killed
There is very general sympathy with Mr M. J. Crowe, the esteemed Surveyor of Excise and Customs, Ennis, on the loss of his gallant son. Corporal Thomas. H. Crowe, news of whose death in action in France came this week. Corporal

Crowe, who was a fine, athletic young man, of only 25 years, was in Canada when the war broke out, and promptly joined the 16th Battalion of the Canadian Scottish, and was attached to the Grenade Company. He quickly won promotion. He had several narrow escapes, and was wounded by shell fragments in the ear. His death is understood to have taken place on the 8th or 9th October. The deceased was in Ennis for a long time during the summer, and was very popular here.

Grave or memorial reference: He has no known grave but is listed on the Vimy Memorial in France.

CULHANE, WILLIAM: *see* **WILLIAM, CLAHANE.**

CULLEN, MYLES: Rank: Private. Regiment or service: Royal Irish Regiment. Unit: 6th Battalion. Date of death: 22 July 1916. Age at death: 25. Service No.: 8112. Died of wounds

Supplementary information: Born in St Mary's, Enniscorthy, Co. Wexford Irelands Memorial Records state he was born in St Marty's, Ennis, Co. Clare. Enlisted in Enniscorthy. Son of Robert and Mary Cullen of 20; Irish St, Enniscorthy, Co. Wexford

From an article in the *Enniscorthy Guardian*:

Third Son Killed. His bereaved parents have received the sad news that Private Myles Cullen, Irish Street, Enniscorthy, has died of wounds received in action.

He was the son of Mr and Mrs Robert Cullen of the above address, and is the third of six sons in the army to fall in this deadful war. Another son is at present at home recovering from wounds also received at the front. Much sympathy is felt with Mr and Mrs Cullen in their great bereavement.

From and article in the *Enniscorthy Guardian* in 1916:

Mr and Mrs Cullen, Irish Street, Enniscorthy, have received the sad news that their youngest son, Christopher Cullen, a Private in the Royal Irish Fusiliers, has been severely wounded.

He lost his arm in the recent fighting, also receiving a shrapnel wound to the back. He is at present in a military hospital, and is doing as well as can be expected. Private Christy Cullen is the fourth of six sons in the army to fall a victim of the Germans. Three of the brothers are already killed; only two weeks ago an account of the death of Private Myles Cullen, with photo, was published in this column. Another son is at present home discharged from the army, part of one hand being blown away. Much sympathy is felt with Mr and Mrs Cullen in their many troubles.

Grave or memorial reference: V. G. 20. Cemetery: Bethune Town Cemetery in France.

CULLINAN, CHARLES: (Listed in Soldiers Died in the Great War as

The grave of Private Charles Cullinan.

CUNNIENE, CHARLES). Rank: Private. Regiment or service: Leinster Regiment. Unit: 1st Battalion. Date of death: 7 May 1915. Age at death: 41 Service No.: 3716. Died of wounds.

Supplementary information: Born in Ennis, Co. Clare. Enlisted in Coatbridge, Lanarkshire. Son of Patrick and Ann Cullinan, of Ennis, Co. Clare.

Grave or memorial reference: A. 16. Cemetery: Divisional Cemetery in Belgium.

CULLINAN, EDWARD PATRICK: Rank: Sergeant. Regiment or service: Lord Strathcona's Horse (Royal Canadians). Date of death: 30 March 1918. Age at death: 30. Service No.: 6168.

Supplementary information: Born in Ennis, Co. Clare. Enlisted in Sewell,

Manitoba on 23 June 1915. Date of birth: 15 March 1885. Next of kin listed as Thomas Cullinan, of Fountain House, Ennis, Co. Clare on his enlistment documents, this indicates that he got married after enlistment as there is a line struck through that entry. Occupation on enlistment: Rancher. Previous military experience: 7 years in the 6th Dragoon Guards. Son of Thomas and Angela P. Cullinan, of No. 16 Victoria Avenue, Cork, Ireland; husband of Alice Anastasia Cullinan, of Cumberland Terrace, Birr, King's County, Ireland.

From the *King's County Chronicle*, April 1918:

Captain Robert Cullinan.

Roll of Honour
March, 30, 1918, Killed in action, Squadron Sergt-Major, E. P. J. Cullinan, of Lord Strathcona's Candian Horse, youngest son of Mr Cullinan, Ennis, aged 30.

Grave or memorial reference: He has no known grave but is listed on the Vimy Memorial in France.

CULLINAN, JOHN: Rank: Private. Regiment or service: Royal Munster Fusiliers. Unit: 2nd Battalion. Date of death: 18 May 1915. Age at death: 35. Service No.: 2/6476 and 6476. Died of wounds.

Supplementary information: Born in Drumcliffe, Co. Clare. Enlisted in Ennis, Co. Clare while living in Ennis, Co. Clare. Son of Patrick and Annie Cullinan, of Ennis, Co. Clare.

From the *Clare Journal*, 1915:

Private Cullinan
His father, Mr Patrick Cullinan, we

hear also received news of the death of his son, John, who was in the Munsters, in the late fighting. He had been home on leave wounded, about three months ago.

Grave or memorial reference: I. H. 6A. Cemetery: Wimereux Communal Cemetery, Pas-De-Calais, France.

CULLINAN, ROBERT HORNIDGE: Rank: Captain. Regiment or service: Royal Munster Fusiliers. Unit: 7th Battalion. Date of death: 8 August 1915. Age at death: 34. Killed in action.

Supplementary information: Son of John and Martha Cullinan, of No. 6 Bendon Street, Ennis, Co. Clare. He was a member of the Munster Bar.

From De Ruvigny's Roll of Honour:

Cullinan, Robert Hornidge, B.A., Barrister-at-Law, Captain, 7th Battalion, Royal Munster Fusiliers.

2nd Surviving son of John Cullinan, of 6, Bindon Street, Ennis, Solicitor, by his wife, Martha. Daughter of the Rev Francis Faris, Rector of Dovena, Co. Wicklow. Born Ennis, Co. Clare 09-August-1881. Educated in Tipperary Grammer School and having obtained Senior Erasmus Smith Exhibition, entered Trinity College, Dublin in October 1899. Here he gained numerous honours and prizes in History and Political Science and Logic and obtained on leaving a Senior Moderatorship with gold medal for History and Political Science. He was called to the Irish Bar in Trinity Term, 1904, and was a member of the Munster Circuit.

On the outbreak of war he offered his services and secured a commission in September, being gazetted Lieutenant, (afterwards confirmed) Captain, 27-February. He was Killed in action after the landing at Suvla Bay, 8th August-1915. Major Drage, commanding C Company, wrote; "Captain Cullinan, C Company, with D on its left, and the 6th Munsters on the right of it, had to advance early on Saturday afternoon along, below and parallel to a high ridge, on which were many skilful Turkish snipers. Your son, on the 7th, commanded the first line of C Company, and went on leading his men under heavy fire most determinedly and gallantly, till he got to an open patch, where he was struck down, mortally wounded. 2nd Lieutenant Bennett bravely went to his side, to find Captain Cullinan riddled with five or six bullets and

dead." And Major Hendricks; "I was in the firing line with him not half an hour before he was shot. We were in a thunder storm together and were wet to the skin. Suddenly I received an order to reinforce our other battalion, on a flank, and sent Major Drage's company, to which your son belonged, to carry out the duty. Your son died, as he had lived, a noble hero, never thinking for one moment of himself, telling the men to go on and leave him. He was then shot through the head. His death was practically instantaneous. After the 12 months I have known your son, I must say I looked on him as a dear pal, and one of the best officers in the regiment. He had endeared himself to one and all." At Dublin University he was a member of the rugby football club, and played for the first fifteen for three years, obtaining his colours in the year 1900-1, and was also record secretary of the University Historical Debating Society.

From the *Clare Journal*, August 1915:

Young Ennis Officer Killed in the
Gallipoli Peninsula
Captain R H Cullinan
The sad news reached here on Wednesday afternoon of the death in action during the new landing on the Gallipoli Peninsula on Sunday last, of Captain Robert H Cullinan, of the 7th Munster Fusiliers, the second surviving son of Mr John Cullinan, Sol. Bindon, Street Ennis, and brother of Mr F F Cullinan, C. S., and of Mr G. C. Cullinan, B. L.

Captain Cullinan, who was only 34, was enjoying a very successful position at the Munster Bar, when soon after the war began he answered the call of his country, and joined the Munsters. He was speedily given a commission, and his earnest-ness and devotion to his new sphere of action augured further success. Of fine physique, a few years the gallant young officer was one of the most dashing Rugby Players of Trinity. The sad news has caused very general sorrow amongst his immediate friends and acquaintances in his native country.

From the *Clare Journal*, 2 September 1915:

The Late Captain Robin H. Cullinan.
How he Died.
'A Hero of the War'

Mr John Cullinan, Bindon Street, has had a number of letters of sympathy on the death of his gallant son, Captain Robin H. Cullinan, who was, as our readers already know, one of the victims in the terrific struggle in the Dardanelles. Major Drage, commanding "C" Company, Seventh Battalion, of the Munsters, writes—"I have the sad duty to tell you (though you may already have seen it in the officers casualty lists, if they are telegraphed) of the death of your gallant son, Captain Cullinan, "C" Company, with "D" on its left, and the 6th Munsters on the right of it, had to advance early on Saturday afternoon, along, below, and parallel to a high ridge, on which were many skilful Turkish snipers. Your son, on the 7th, commanded the first line of "C" Company, and went on leading his men under heavy fire most determinedly and gallantly, till he got to an open patch, where he was struck down mortally wounded. Second Lieutenant Bennett bravely went to his side, to find Captain Cullinan riddled with five or six bullets and dead. Bennett himself was shot through the chest and only lived a short time after he was brought in by the men round them to a little to the right rear, where Lieutenant Harper had collected the men round us. Harper examined your son's body, but could not find his disc, or any small article of value. Lieutenant Harper was himself killed on the 9th, in another attack "C" Company made over nearly the same ground. I cannot say how grieved I am to lose the cool, determined, wise support of your son, who was my second in command. He was esteemed by all the officers of the Regiment, and I and the men of "C" Company had the greatest confidence in him, and would follow him anywhere. My wife and I used to see your son in St Anne's Church, Dublin, and I knew he was a friend of the Rector, and a good sound Christian himself.

Major Henricks of the Munsters, writing form the Netley Hospital says—"I have been intending to write to you for some time about your son, but unfortunately am in hospital with a broken right arm, and a bullet through my right lung

… I cannot say what a terrible blow the loss of your son was to us all. I was in the firing line with him, not half an hour before he was shot. We were in a thunderstorm together, and were wet to the skin. Suddenly I received an order to reinforce our other Battalion on a flank, and sent Major Drage's Company, to which your son belonged, to carry out the duty. Your son died as he had lived, a noble hero, never thinking for one moment of himself, telling the men to go on and leave him. He was then shot through the head. His death was practically instantaneous. After the twelve months I have known your son, I must say I looked on him as a dear pal, and one of the best officers in the Regiment. He had endeared himself to one and all. He was one of the real heroes of the war, who gave up everything at his country's call, and it seems a bitter thing that we shall never see his cheery, determined, honest face again. "

We take the following from another letter—"I expect you will by now have heard from several sources how bravely your son died ….Young Fitzmaurice, now in hospital in the Isle of Wight, wrote me about him—'Poor old Cull'. I am not ashamed to say that I nearly wept in the middle of a tremendous fight when I heard he was knocked over. He was one of the first officers of our lot hit, and he was knocked over quite close to the Turkish position. He would not let anyone near him bandage him up for fear the snipers who got him might get

anyone else who tried to help him. He was still cheering his men on when he was shot through the head. It was the fourth bullet that had hit him. The man who told me this was a Private in my platoon, who had strayed and was wounded trying to get Cull. Under cover, and the poor fellow was almost in tears.' What a splendid man he was! If he was given but little opportunity to show what a brave soldier and fighter he was, at least he proved how bravely he could die. As my brother said on writing home on first hearing of his death—'I feel sure he died, as he lived, a man!' … I again quote Fitzmaurice's letter-"We were under fire the whole time, of course, and out in the open all Saturday and Sunday, because we could not dig trenches more than three feet deep on the account of the rocky ground. On Monday (the 8th) we pushed on. The men were marvellous. A perfect hail of bullets from Turks hidden in the hills all round! Nothing to fire at, because there was not an enemy to be seen. It was simply a case of pushing on with fixed bayonets and never getting a chance of getting our own back. Men were being hit on all sides, but the others pushed on, and never wavered. In the end we had to fall back on our old line about two or three miles from the beach. However, two or three miles was a good gain. This was the new landing at Suvla Bay, or rather our share of it. "

Another officer writes—"We landed on the 7th, and nothing of any great importance came about on the actual landing. There were a few shells going, and when on shore a few land mines. We were fortunate in missing these; however, some of our 6th Battalion were not so fortunate. On Monday we advanced under heavy fire, and when coming on an open patch, Captain Cullinan was mortally wounded. Your son gallantly went to his side and was shot through the chest The advance stopped, as "C" Company was in advance of all others, and the men and we could only lie down until dark came, when Lieutenant Harper, who was near me, with some men, carried your son in close behind us."

From *Our Heroes*:

Killed in action at the Dardanelles on August 8th. He was the second son of Mr John Cullinan, Ennis, and was called to the Bar in 1904. He was one of a number of young barristers who at the outbreak of the war offered their services to their country. He obtained a commission in the 7th Royal Munsters, and in February last was promoted Captain.

From the *Saturday Record*, May:

The Late Captain R. H. Cullinan A handsome tablet has been placed in Ennis Parish Church in memory of the late Captain Cullinan, son of Mr John Cullinan, Bindon Street, Ennis. The inscription is as follows— "In memory of Captain Robert Hornidge Cullinan, Barrister-at-Law, 7th Battalion, Royal Munster

Fusiliers, who gave his life for King and country at the Dardanelles on the 7th Aug., 1915; aged 34 years. 'Greater love hath no man than this, that a man lay down his life for his friends.' St John XV. 13.

"This tablet was erected by parishioners of Drumcliffe and Clare Abbey as a token of their esteem and regret."

Grave or memorial reference: Panel 185 to 190. Memorial: Helles Memorial in Turkey.

CUNNEEN, JOHN: Rank: Private. Regiment or service: Royal Munster Fusiliers. Unit: 2nd Battalion. Date of death: 27 August 1914. Age at death: 26. Service No.: 7614. Killed in action

Supplementary information: Born in Newmarket-on-Fergus, Co. Clare. Enlisted in Ennis, Co. Clare while living in Newmarket-on-Fergus, Co. Clare. Son of Patrick and Johanna Cunneen, of Latoon, Newmarket-on-Fergus, Co. Clare.

Grave or memorial reference: I. 28. Cemetery: Etreux British Cemetery, Aisne, France.

CUNNIENE, CHARLES: *see* **CULLINAN, CHARLES.**

CUNNINGHAM, JOHN: Rank: Lance Sergeant. Regiment or service: Royal Munster Fusiliers. Unit: 2nd Battalion. Date of death: 9 May 1915. Age at death: 25. Service No.: 5509. Killed in action.

Supplementary information: Born in Drumeliffe (*sic*), Co. Clare. Enlisted in Ennis, Co. Clare while living in Ennis,

Co. Clare. Son of John and Margaret Cunningham, of Turnpike, Ennis, Co. Clare.

From the *Saturday Record*, May:

Ennis Fusiliers Killed and Wounded Prayers have been asked at the Cathedral for the repose of the soul of Private J. Cunningham, of the Munster Fusiliers, Killed in action. He belonged to The Turnpike, Ennis.

Grave or memorial reference: Panel 43 and 44. Memorial: Le Touret Memorial in France.

CUNNINGHAM, THOMAS: Rank: Private. Regiment or service: Manchester Regiment. Unit: 18th Battalion. Date of death: 22 March 1917. Service No.: 47847. Killed in action.

Supplementary information: Born in Ennis, Co. Clare. Enlisted in Manchester.

Grave or memorial reference: Bay 7. Memorial: Arras Memorial in France.

CUNNINGHAM, WILLIAM: Rank: Private. Regiment or service: Leinster Regiment. Unit: 2nd Battalion. Date of death: 20 October 1914. Age at death: 29. Service No.: 7346. Killed in action.

Supplementary information: Born in Kilrush, Co. Clare. Enlisted in Limerick. Son of John and Margaret Cunningham, of Turnpike, Ennis, Co. Clare; husband of Bessey Cunningham.

Grave or memorial reference: Panel 10. Memorial: Ploegsteert Memorial in Belgium.

CURRY, MICHAEL: Rank: Private. Regiment or service: Irish Guards. Unit: 1st Battalion. Date of death: 6 November 1914. Service No.: 2508. Killed in action.

Supplementary information: Born in Cratloe, Co. Clare. Enlisted in Ennis, Co. Clare while living in Clydebank, Lanarkshire.

Grave or memorial reference: I. C. 9. Cemetery: Zantvoorde British Cemetery in Belgium.

CURTIN, LAWRENCE: Rank: Private. Regiment or service: Royal Munster Fusiliers. Unit: 1st Battalion. Date of death: 12 May 1915. Age at death: 17. Service No.: 9787. Died of Wounds in Gallipoli.

Supplementary information: Born in Kilbaher, Carrigaholt, Co. Clare. Enlisted in Tralee, Co. Kerry, while living in Kilrush, Co. Clare. Son of Mrs Mary Curtin, of Grace Street, Kilrush, Co. Clare. Also commemorated in the 'List of Kilrush Men engaged in the War from August 1914'. This pamphlet lists the Kilrush men who were involved in the First World War until 11 November 1918.

Grave or memorial reference: H. 84. Cemetery: Alexandria (Chatby) Military and War Memorial Cemetery in Egypt.

CUSACK, JAMES: Rank: Private. Regiment or service: South African Infantry. Unit: 1st Regiment. Date of death: 18 July 1916. Age at death: 39 Service No.: 1125.

Supplementary information: Son of James and Catherine Cusack, of Oil Mill Road, Sixmilebridge, Co. Clare, Ireland.

Grave or memorial reference: Pier and Face 4 C. Memorial: Thiepval Memorial in France.

CUSACK, OLIVER: Rank: Sapper. Regiment or service: Corps of Royal Engineers. 11th Field Company, Royal Engineers. Date of death: 28 June 1915. Age at death: 20. Service No.: 26169. Died of wounds at home.

Supplementary information: Born in Thurles. Enlisted in Ennis Co. Clare. Son of Thomas and Margaret Cusack of Clarecastle, Co. Clare. His personal effects and property were sent to Margaret Cusack (mother), Clarecastle, Co. Clare, Ireland.

From the *Clare Journal,* July 1915:

Another Clarecastle Victim
Sapper Oliver Cusack, R.E.
Our obituary columns to-day contain the announcement of the death of Sapper O Cusack, R. E., which took place in a London Hospital on Monday last as the result of wounds received whilst fighting "somewhere in France".

Deceased, who was only in his twentieth year, was, after leaving school, appointed as junior in the office of the Ordnance Survey Department in Ennis, and some time ago when changes were about to take place in that Department, young Cusack, with a number of his colleagues, joined the Corps of the R. E. Since the beginning of the war he has been practically at the front, and his letters home to his people were always most cheery, the last one received being from Edmonton Hospital in London, where he had just arrived, and in which he described the wounds he had received from the shrapnel of the 'Huns'. This letter was followed next day by an official intimation of the death of the poor fellow.

Kindly and generous, beloved by all his comrades, the news of his death was received with sincere sorrow in the district where he was so well known, and was tender to his sorrowing father and mother, and the other members of the poor young soldier's family, our sincere sympathy in their sad loss.

Grave or memorial reference: Gen 7377 (Screen Wall). Cemetery: Tottenham Cemetery, UK.

CUSACK, THOMAS: Rank: Private. Regiment or service: Royal Munster Fusiliers. Unit: 2nd Battalion. Date of death: 24 October 1916. Age at death: 38. Service No.: 6173. Died of Wounds.

Supplementary information: Born in Kilrush, Co. Clare. Enlisted in Limerick while living in Kilrush, Co. Clare. Son of Tom and Mary Cusack, of Glynn Street, Kilrush; husband of Anne Cusack, of Pound Street, Kilrush, Co. Clare. His personal effects and property were sent to Mrs Annie Cusack, Pound Street, Kilrush, Co. Clare, Ireland. He was also commemorated in the 'List of Kilrush Men engaged in the War from August 1914'. This pamphlet lists the Kilrush men who were involved in the First World War until 11 November 1918.

Grave or memorial reference: At the far east of the end of the main path. Cemetery: Feuquières-en-Vimeu Communal Cemetery in France.

D

DALY, MICHAEL FRANCIS:
Rank: Trimmer. Regiment or service: Royal Naval Reserve. Unit: HM Trawler *Romilly*. Date of death: 10 February 1918. Age at death: 22. Service No.: 7185/TS. Blown up by a mine.

Supplementary information: Son of Michael and Bridget Daly, of John Street, Kilrush, Co. Clare. Also commemorated in the 'Kilrush Men belonging to or who joined the Naval Service since commencement of the War'. This pamphlet lists the Kilrush men who were involved in the First World War until 11 November 1918.

Grave or memorial reference: S. D. 556. Cemetery: Ardrossan Cemetery, Ayrshire, UK.

DANAHER, PATRICK: Rank: Sergeant. Regiment or service: Royal Irish Regiment. Unit: 2nd Battalion. Date of death: 5 August 1916. Age at death: 35. Service No.: 3258. Killed in action.

Supplementary information: Born in Nenagh, Co. Tipperary. Enlisted in Tipperary while living in Killaloe, Co. Clare. Son of Dan and Catherine Danaher; husband of Bridget Danaher, of New Street, Killaloe, Co. Clare.

He has no known grave but is listed on Pier and Face 3A of the Thiepval memorial in France.

DAVIS, FRANCIS: Rank: Private. Regiment or service: Royal Irish Fusiliers. Unit: Depot Secondary Regiment: Royal Munster Fusiliers Secondary. Unit: Formerly (5990) 5th Battalion. Date of death: 8 December 1918. Age at death: 29. Service No.: G/534.

Supplementary information: Son of Bridget Davis of Church Hill, Ennistymon, Co. Clare. This man is only in the Commonwealth War Graves database.

Grave or memorial reference: West part, South of ruin. Cemetery: Ennistymon Cemetery, Co. Clare.

DAVIS, THOMAS: Rank: Private. Regiment or service: Royal Munster Fusiliers. Unit: 1st Battalion. Date of death: 2 July 1915. Age at death: 21. Service No.: 1/9804.

Supplementary information: Executed on Gully Beach, Gallipoli at sunrise for 'quitting his post'. For more information see *Shot at Dawn* (Pen & Sword Books Ltd, 1998) by Julian Putkowski and Julian Sykes. Also see article in the *Clare Champion*, 18 August 2006, p. 1.

Son of Mrs Margaret Davis, of Turnpike Road, Ennis, Co. Clare. This man is only in the Commonwealth War Graves database

Grave or memorial reference: Addenda Panel. Memorial: Helles Memorial in Turkey.

DAVOREN/ DAVERON, DELIA:
Rank: Nursing Sister at the General Infirmary, St Giles, Northamptonshire. Regiment or service: Unknown. Date of death: 10 October 1918. Age at death: 37.

The National Health Insurance Certificate of Davoren.

Supplementary information: Residence; Claureen House, South of the Lahinch Road, Ennis. Drowned when the Packet SS RMS. *Leinster* was torpedoed and sunk by German Submarine U-123 on 10 October 1918. Delia was, or had been, a member of the Territorial Force Nursing Service, and has a file at The National Archives (WO399/10811) in the name Delia Davoreen.

Both Delia and her sister Norah (*see* below) nursed in England for ten years. Delia spent three months as part of the Territorial Force Nursing Service at the 3rd General Southern Hospital, Oxford from 1 August 1914 to 1 December 1914.

She was discharged due to impending marriage. It has been pointed out by the nursing archivist who supplied Delia's documents that using the excuse 'marriage' on an application for discharge would make that process easier and the applicant may not actually intend to marry. I have not found anything in her

records or newspaper articles that's portrays her as a married woman. As Nurse Davoren did not complete six months service she was required to repay £4 for her uniforms, and she unsuccessfully applied for this not to be deducted.

From the *Clare Champion*:

Clare Victims

The first intimation the family received was a wire from Northampton, from the Matron of the hospital there, to which place the ladies were going, expressing anxiety as to their safety. Mr Jerry Davoren proceeded to town at once, and was shocked on discovering that the boat on which his sisters were travelling had gone down, and that the name of one of them, Norah, was amongst the victims. The ladies left Ennis by the one p. m. train on Wednesday, having spent two months at home, and an unfortunate and tragic feature in the whole sad affair was that they were due to leave on the previous day, and only kissed the train by a few minutes. Mr Davoren proceeded to Dublin on Friday night, and on Saturday at St Michael's hospital, Kingstown, had the awful experience of identifying the remains of his sisters amongst 50 others bodies laid out in the morgue. He was able to ascertain that his sisters were amongst the first to be picked up after the disaster. To add to his grief, it was only with difficulty he could obtain coffins, as the employees of the undertakers in Dublin and Kingstown were on strike. It was only on Saturday afternoon that the coffins were procured at Bray. The remains were removed to Ennis on Saturday night and were laid in the mortuary at the Cathedral over night whither they were conveyed by a large concourse of people. On Sunday there was Solemn Requiem High Mass for the repose of their souls, of which the Rev. W. Grace was celebrant. The other priests were Very Rev. Canon O'Dea, Rev. P. J. Hogan, Adm.; Rev. Fr. Molony, Rev. F. Roche, and Rev. P. Gavan, P.P., Tubber. The funeral subsequently to Drumcliffe was one of the most remarkable demonstrations ever witnessed in Ennis. The deceased ladies who were just cut short in the prime of life, were well known in Ennis and district. Their kindly, genial and affable manner made them hosts of friends. In the nursing profession of which they were members, they held a leading and respected place, and this was more than borne out by the messages of sympathy received from the hospital.

At the Cathedral, Ennis, on Sunday last Rev. W. Molony, C.C., said that the awful occurrence was one of the most cruel things which had been done since the beginning of the war. Rev. P. J. Hogan, Adm, spoke similarly.

The chief mourners were; Andrew and Jerry Davoren (brothers); Marian and Mrs Neylon (sisters); Michael Davoren, Ballymurphy (uncle), Mrs Kelly, Drumcliffe (aunt); Martin Neylon, Tubber (brother-in-law).

DAVOREN/DAVERON, NORA/ NORAH/HONORA: Rank: Nursing Sister at the General Infirmary, St Giles, Northamptonshire. Regiment or service: No military or naval connection. Date of death: 10 October 1918.

Supplementary information: Residence: Claureen House, South of the Lahinch Road, Ennis. Date of birth: 30 March 1876. Drowned when the packet SS RMS *Leinster* was torpedoed and sunk by German Submarine U-123 on 10 October 1918. Parents, Michael and Margaret Daveron (aged 70 and 66 in 1901 census respectively). Unmarried, Norah had a daughter and named her Elizabeth but this was later changed to Norah, she had been born in September 1912 in Bristol. Both Nora and Delia had nursed in England for ten years. Norah and Delia Davoren, were meant to return to Nottingham, England on Tuesday, 8 October but missed the train, the consequence of which was to be disastrous. The following day they caught the midday train from Ennis en route for Kingstown, where they boarded the doomed ship. Their bodies were recovered and later identified by their brother. Many thanks to PhilipLecane – author of *Torpedoed! The R.M.S. Leinster Disaster* (Periscope Publishing Ltd, 2005) – for the extra information on all the RMS *Leinster* casualties. He also gives the Davoren sisters ages as 37 (Delia) and 35 (Norah) respectively.

From the *Saturday Record*, December 1918:

Ennis Victims of the Leinster Outrage
On Sunday the funeral of the two Ennis victims of the infamous

Leinster outrage, took place, and was an eloquent expression of public indignation and horror, and sympathy with the friends ad relatives of those who had lost their lives. These were the Misses Norah and Delia Davoren, sisters of Messrs Andrew and Jeremiah Davoren, --and daughters of the late Mr Michael Davoren, Claureen House, Ennis. They had adopted the nursing profession, and had been resident in England for about ten years. They had been home on holidays and were returning to Northampton when they met their doom. A remarkable story is told of their last journey. They were to have left Ennis on the Tuesday, and only missed the train by a few minutes. They left by the midday train next day, with the result now so widely known. The bodies were identified by their brothers at St Michael's Hospital, Kingstown, on Saturday, and after some difficulty in procuring coffins from Bray, were brought to Ennis on Saturday evening. Late as the hour was an immense crowd awaited the remains at the Ennis station, and accompanied them to the Cathedral, where they were received by the parochial clergy. Very Rev Canon O'Dea was also present.

At the Cathedral the following morning, references were made to the appalling outrage. Very Rev P. J. Hogan, Adm., made a touching allusion to it, when asking for prayers for the souls of the deceased, at early Mass. At 10 o'clock Rev J. H. Molony, C.C., also asked for prayers for the souls of the victims, many of the large congregation being visibly affected. He said he was sure their hearts were all filled with thoughts of the awful outrage of the previous Thursday. It was the most cruel thing that had occurred since the beginning of the war.

The funeral from the Cathedral to the family burial place was one of the largest seen here for a long time, and was representative of all sections in the community, and the spectacle of the silent cortege in the falling rain, with two hearses at its head, each containing a coffin, was sad and solemn in the extreme.

The chief mourners were— Jerry amd Andrew, brothers; Marion and Mrs Neylon, sisters; Michael Davoren, Ballymurphy, uncle; Martin Neylon, brother-in-law; Mrs Kelly, Drumcliffe, aunt; Mrs McBamara, Kilmaley; Mrs J Davoren, Kilmaley; Mrs O'Keeffe, Drumcliffe; The Misses Kenny, Corofin; John and Miko Davoren, Kilmaley; Patrick Kelly, V. C., D. C., Clonina, Cree; Tommie Kelly, do; Thomas Neylon, Boston; Joe Neylon, Kilfenora; John Markham, Corofin; Michael Markham, Tubber; Miss E Culliney, Kilfenora, Paddy Moran, do; Frank McNamara, Kilmaley; iko Moran, Kilfenora; Mrs and James Cahill, Corofin; Thos Kenny, do; James Neylon, Tubber, cousins.

There were many other relatives in the procession and the clergy present were Rev P. J. Hogan, Adm.; Revs W. Grace, C. C., J. H. Molony, C. C. Ennis; and J. Roche, C. C,

Kilmaley; Rev J. Gavin, P. P., Tubber; and Very Rev. Canon O'Dea, President, Street Flannan's College, Ennis; and these assisted at the final prayers at the graveside.

Ennis Lives Lost

Amongst those who lost their lives were the Misees Nora and Delia Davoren, Claureen House, Ennis, who were returning after holidays at home, to a Nursing Home at Northampton; Head Constable Ward, Ennis, who was going on official business to Birmingham, it is stated; the Misses Margaret and B. O'Grady, daughters of Mr Frank O'Grady, Manser, Newmarket-on-Fergus, nurses in England, who were home on holidays; Miss Nellie Hogan, daughter of Mr Hogan, Ralshile, and niece of Mr P Power, Clarecastle, also a nurse, who was returning to Brighton; and a Mr Hynes and his daughter, from Tulla who were returning to their residence in England. The bodies of the Misses Davoren were found, with lifebelts attached, quite close together, and the body of Miss Margaret O'Grady has also been recovered, but we have not yet heard if the other bodies have yet been found. It was feared that a girl named Chapman, from the town, had also been lost, but it transpired that she had travelled the previous day, and so escaped a terrible fate.

Davoren (Ennis)-Lost in the Leinster, Delia (Dillie), third daughter of the late Michael Davoren, Claureen House, Ennis.

Davoren (Ennis)-Lost in the Leinster, Nora, youngest daughter of the late Michael Davoren, Claureen House, Ennis. Both attached to a Nursing Home at 30 Hazelwood Road, Northampton.

There is a Private Michael Davoren, No 5805, 2nd Battalion Royal Munster Fusiliers listed in the absent voters list of 1918 for Ennistymon under Old Churchill Street. He may be related.

Both sisters are buried in Drumcliff cemetery, Graves No. 522 & 523, Ennis.

DEENIHAN, THOMAS: Rank: Private. Regiment or service: Royal Munster Fusiliers. Unit: 6th Battalion. Date of death: 11 August 1915. Service No.: 333. Died of wounds in Gallipoli.

Supplementary information: Born in Kilrush, Co. Clare. Enlisted in Kilrush while living in Kilrush, Co. Clare. Also commemorated as Thos Dinihan in the 'List of Kilrush Men engaged in the War from August 1914', Burton Street. This pamphlet lists the Kilrush men who were involved in the First World War until 11 November 1918.

Grave or memorial reference: Panel 185 to 190. Memorial: Helles Memorial in Turkey.

DELMEGE, JAMES O'GRADY: Rank: Second Lieutenant. Regiment or service: Household Cavalry and Cavalry of the Line including the Yeomanry and Imperial Camel Corps. Unit: 4th (Royal Irish) Dragoon Guards. Date of death: 27 May 1915. Age at death: 24. Killed in action at Ypres.

Supplementary information: Date of birth: 18 March 1891. Son of James

Second Lieutenant James Delmege.

O'Grady Delmege and Mrs Delmege, of Castle Park, Limerick.

From *Our Heroes*, 1916:

Lieutenant J. O'Grady Delmege, 4th Royal Irish Dragoons, who was only in his 21st year, died on the 27th May last, from the effects of gas poisoning. He was educated at Clifton, Bath College and Trinity College. He was a very promising young officer, a fine horseman, and devoted to cricket and football. Much sympathy is felt with his father, Mr J. O'Grady Delmege, Castle Park, Limerick.

From the *Clare Journal*, July 1915:

The Late Lieutenant Delmege
At Doonass petty sessions, the presiding magistrate being Mr P.J. Kelly, R. M., a letter was received from Mr J. O'Grady Delmege, conveying sincere thanks for the resolution of sympathy passed by the magistrates on the death at the front of Mr Delmege's son, Lieutenant O'Grady Delmege.

From De Ruvigny's Roll of Honour:

Delmege, James O'Grady, Lieutenant, 4th (Royal Irish) Dragoon Guards. Second son of Captain James O'Grady Delmege, of Castle Park, Co. Limerick, J.P., D.L., late South of Ireland Imperial Yeomanry and South Irish Horse, by his wife, Caroline, daughter and co-heir of Marmaduke Coghill Cramer, of Rathmore, Kinsale, D.L. Born in Limerick, 18 March 1891. Educated at Clifton Bath College (where he took, when 14 years of age, 6ol and 4ol Scholarships, open to all schools), and Trinity College, Dublin; and was gazetted 2nd Lieutenant to the 4th Dragoon Guards, 23 January 1914, and promoted Lieutenant, 15 November following. After the outbreak of war he went to France with the Expeditionary Force and was appointed Assistant Adjutant, and put of the Headquarters Staff. On 24 May 1915, the 4th Dragoon Guards, after a long spell in the trenches, were relieved y the 18th Hussars, but Lieutenant Delmege was left behind to instruct the 18th in the plan of the trenches. During the night and early morning they were heavily gassed by the enemy, and he succumbed to gas poison, on 27 May 1815. He was buried at Bailleul.

Numerous letters received from all ranks testify to the estimation he was held in. Major C. Hunter wrote; "I personally had a high opinion of his prospects as a cavalry officer"; and Lieutenant E. G. Warlock, 4th Dragoon Guards; "He has left behind him a splendid name, being so popular with all who knew him, not only officers, but N. C. O.'s, and men. He was an officer of great promise, and had it not been for his untimely death 'In Action' would have had an illustrious future." Sergeant W. Jones, 4th Dragoon Guards, also wrote; "Lieutenant Delmege was picked up unconscious. I was very sorry to hear of his death, as he was a brave young officer, so cheerful and patient with all ranks, and I know he will be missed by all, especially our Rugby team, as he was a fine sportsman, and took a great interest in his troop, and we were very sorry when he was transferred from his troop to Head Quarters."

Lieutenant C. Jackson, York and Lancaster Regiment, "The last time I saw him, he was going on in front with a patrol to find out where their place in trenches was, in order to lead the Regiment up after dark, he was in such good spirits, and I am sure enjoyed every minute of the war,"; and Captain R. D. Brownson, R.A M.C.; "Being in hospital with some of the Regiment, I thought you would like to hear what a very high opinion they all seem to have of him. He was so popular and such a good officer, in fact he was kept specially to go up into any special trench or take any special message, because he could always be trusted to get there 'Somehow.'"

Grave or memorial reference: I. F. 39. Cemetery: Bailleul Communal Cemetery Extension, (Nord) in France.

DELOHERY/ DOLOHERY, MICHAEL: Rank: Private. Regiment or service: Royal Irish Regiment. Unit: 3rd Battalion. Date of death: 30 December 1916. Age at death: 38. Service No.: 1987. Died at home of illness contracted during service.

Supplementary information: Born in Kilrush, Co. Clare. Enlisted in Limerick. Husband of Ellen Delohery. Also commemorated in the 'List of Kilrush Men engaged in the War from August 1914'. This pamphlet lists the Kilrush men who were involved in the First World War until 11 November 1918.

Grave or memorial reference: Southwest end of the Church. Cemetery: Kilrush Church of Ireland Churchyard, Co. Clare.

DEVINS, OWEN: Rank: Private. Regiment or service: Irish Guards. Unit: 1st Battalion. Date of death: 15 September 1916. Service No.: 2981. Killed in action.

Supplementary information: Born in Drumcliffe, Co. Clare. Enlisted in Dublin while living in Castlegal, Co. Sligo.

Grave or memorial reference: Pier and Face 7D. Memorial: Thiepval Memorial in France.

DICKS, THOMAS: Served as **BURDETT, THOMAS**. Rank: Bombardier. Regiment or service: Royal Garrison Artillery. Unit: 121st Heavy Battery. Date of death: 24 April 1917. Age at death: 26. Service No.: 35270. Killed in action.

Supplementary information: Born in Naas, Co. Kildare. Enlisted in Leicester while living in Liscullane, Co. Clare. Son of George Dicks, of Leicester; husband of Agnes B. Dicks, of Liscullane, O'Callaghan's Mills, Co. Clare. In his will, dated 21 August 1916, his personal effects and property were received by Agnes Dicks (wife), Liscullane, O Callaghn's Mills, Co. Clare, Ireland.

Grave or memorial reference: V. G. 23. Cemetery: Ecoivres Military Cemetery Mont-St Eloi in France.

DILLON, PATRICK: Rank: Private. Regiment or service: Royal Munster Fusiliers. Unit: 8th Battalion. Date of death: 28 June 1916. Age at death: 22. Service No.: 5762. Killed in action.

Supplementary information: Born in Corofin, Co. Clare. Enlisted in Limerick while living in Corofin, Co. Clare. Son of Timothy and Bridget Callinan Dillon, of Dromoher, Kilnaboy, Co. Clare.

Grave or memorial reference: I.D. 14. Cemetery: Street Patrick's Cemetery, Loos in France.

DOHERTY, CORNELIUS: Rank: Private. Regiment or service: Royal Munster Fusiliers. Unit: 9th Battalion. Date of death: 4 April 1916. Service No.: 3435. Killed in action.

Supplementary information: Born in Miltown Malbay, Co. Clare. Enlisted in Ennis while living in Miltown Malbay, Co. Clare. Brother of John Doherty, of Ennistymon Road, Milltown Malbay, Co. Cork.

Grave or memorial reference: Panel 127. Memorial: Loos Memorial in France.

DOHERTY, EDWARD PATRICK: Rank: Sergeant. Regiment or service: East Lancashire Regiment. Unit: 3rd Battalion. Date of death: 21 March 1916. Service No.: 9305. Died at home.

Supplementary information: Born in Knock, Ballyhaunis, Co. Mayo. Enlisted in Moate, Co. Westmeath while living in Clare.

Grave or memorial reference: R. C. C. 3444. Efford Cemetery, Devon, UK.

DOHERTY, GEORGE: Rank: Sergeant. Regiment or service: Royal Irish Rifles. Unit: 2nd Battalion. Date of death: 7 July 1916. Service No.: 8687. Killed in action

Supplementary information: Born in Liscomer, Co. Clare. Enlisted in Belfast. He has no known grave but is listed on Pier and Face 15A and 15B of the Thiepval Memorial in France.

DOHERTY, MICHAEL: Rank: Private. Regiment or service: Leinster Regiment. Unit: 2nd Battalion. Date of death: 12 April 1917. Age at death: 24. Service No.: 4216. Killed in action.

Supplementary information: Born in Drumeliffe, Co. Clare. Enlisted in Ennis while living in Ennis. Son of Mr and Mrs William Doherty.

Grave or memorial reference: Bay 9. Memorial: Arras Memorial in France.

DOHERTY, PATRICK: Rank: Second Lieutenant. Regiment or service: Royal Irish Rifles. Unit: 1st Battalion. Age at death: 26. Date of death: 1 August 1917. Died of Wounds.

Supplementary information: Son of John and Lizzie Doherty, of Caherkinalla, Kilshanny, Co. Clare.

Grave or memorial reference: XIV. A.18. Cemetery: Lijssenthoek Military Cemetery in Belgium.

DOLAGHTY, WILLIAM L. Rank: Gunner. Regiment or service: Royal Garrison Artillery. Date of death: 12 March 1921. Age at death: 45 Service No.: 21267.

Supplementary information: Son of Michael and Anne Dolaghty, of Ballyhannon, Quin, Co. Clare.

This man is only in the Commonwealth War Graves database Cemetery: Sandown (Christ Church) Churchyard, Isle of Wight, UK.

DOLOHERY, MICHAEL: *see* **DELOHERY, MICHAEL.**

DONELAN, MARTIN: Rank: Sapper. Regiment or service: Corps of Royal Engineers. Unit: 171st Tunnelling Company. Date of death: 13 June 1917. Service No.: 112512. Killed in action.

Supplementary information: Born in Ennis, Co. Clare. Enlisted in London while living in Swansea.

Grave or memorial reference: V. F. 14 Cemetery: Wulverghem-Lindenhoek Road Military Cemetery in Belgium.

DONNELLAN, JAMES: Rank: Sapper. Regiment or service: Corps of Royal Engineers. Unit: 12th Field Company. Date of death: 9 August 1915. Service No.: 15726. Killed in action.

Supplementary information: Born in Ennis, Co. Clare. Enlisted in Inch, Co. Clare. In his will, dated 22 February

1915, his personal effects and property were received by, John Donnellan, Pragnagour, Ennis, Co. Clare, Ireland.

Grave or memorial reference: He has no known grave but is listed on Panel 9 on the Ypres (Menin Gate) Memorial in Belgium.

DONNELLAN, THOMAS: Rank: Private. Regiment or service: Australian Infantry, AIF. Unit: 13th Battalion. Date of death: 4 May 1915. Service No.: 844. Killed in action in the Gallipoli Peninsula.

Supplementary information: Born, Drumcliffe, Ennis, Co. Clare. Age on enlistment: 32, in another document in his files it says he was 28 when he enlisted. Occupation on enlistment: Labourer. Next of kin: Mick Donnellan (mother), G.P.O. Sydney.

Previous military experience: Garrison Artillery – 3 years. Date and location of enlistment: 19 September 1914; Rocky Park Camp, New South Wales. Height: 5ft 8 in. Weight: 10st 11 lbs. Complexion: Dark. Eyes: Blue. Hair: Black. After the First World War his next of kin could not be traced and his personal effects were disposed of. No medals were issued.

Grave or memorial reference: 37. He has no known grave but is listed on the Lone Pine Memorial in Turkey.

DONNELLY, JOHN: Rank: Private. Regiment or service: Royal Munster Fusiliers. Unit: 6th Battalion. Age at death: 39. Date of death: 19 October 1915. Service No.: 6/2809 and 2809. Died of wounds at home.

Supplementary information: Enlisted in Pontypridd, Glamorganshire, while living in Pontypridd, Glamorganshire. Son of James and Susan Donnelly, of Lisdeen, Co. Clare.

Grave or memorial reference: Screen Wall. II. R. C. 89B. Cemetery: Liverpool (Kirkdale) Cemetery, UK.

DONOGHUE, THOMAS: Rank: Private. Regiment or service: Royal Munster Fusiliers. Date of death: 11 February 1920. Age at death: 24. Service No.: 4617.

Grave or memorial reference: Near West boundary. Cemetery: Kilrush Church of Ireland Churchyard, Co. Clare.

DONOHOE/DONOHUE, HENRY: Rank: Private. Regiment or service: Leinster Regiment. Unit: 1st Battalion. Date of death: 6 December 1917. Service No.: 10186. Died in Egypt.

Supplementary information: Born in Ennis, Co. Clare. Son of John and Mary Donohoe, of No. 46 Harold's Cross Cottage, Harold's Cross, Dublin. Enlisted in Dublin.

Grave or memorial reference: XXI. U. 27. Cemetery: Baghdad (North Gate) War Cemetery in Iraq.

DONOHOE, JOHN: Rank: Private. Regiment or service: Machine Gun Corps. Unit: 8th Battalion, Infantry. Date of death: 24 April 1918. Service No.: 105359. Formerly he was with the South Irish Horse (T.F.) where his number was 2459. Killed in action.

Supplementary information: Born in Ballyvaughan, Co. Clare. Enlisted in Athy while living in Ballyvaughan, Co. Clare.

Grave or memorial reference: He has no known grave but is listed on Panels 90 to 93 on the Pozieres Memorial in France.

DOOLEY, JOHN: Rank: Lance Corporal. Regiment or service: Irish Guards. Unit: 2nd Battalion. Date of death: 31 July 1917. Service No.: 2331. Killed in action.

Supplementary information: Born in Starrell, Co. Clare. Enlisted in Dublin, Co. Dublin.

Grave or memorial reference: Panel 11. Memorial: Ypres (Menin Gate) Memorial in Belgium.

DOWLING, J.: Rank: Captain. Regiment or service: South African Medical Corps. Date of death: 19 October 1918.

Supplementary information: Husband of A. Dowling, of Ballymacally, Co. Clare, Ireland.

Grave or memorial reference: 3. R.C. 18. Cemetery: Roodiam Military Cemetery, South Africa.

DOYLE, JOSEPH: Rank: Gunner. Regiment or service: Royal Horse Artillery and Royal Field Artillery. Unit: 11th Battery Battalion. Date of death: 30 October 1914. Service No.: 30256. Killed in action.

Supplementary information: Born in Ennis, Co. Clare. Enlisted in Ennis.

Grave or memorial reference: Panel 1. Memorial: Le Touret Memorial in France.

DRONEY, PATRICK: Rank: Private. Regiment or service: Royal Munster Fusiliers. Unit: 2nd Battalion. Date of death: 22 September 1916. Service No.: 6831. Killed in action.

Supplementary information: Born in Ballymagh, Co. Clare. Enlisted in Ennis, Co. Clare while living in Ballymagh.

Grave or memorial reference: He has no known grave but is commemorated on Pier and Face 16C on the Thiepval Memorial in France.

DUFFY, MICHAEL: Rank: Private. Regiment or service: The King's (Liverpool Regiment). Unit: 13th Battalion. Age at death: 36. Date of death: 16 July 1916. Service No.: 18898. Died of wounds.

Supplementary information: Born in Tulla, Co. Clare. Enlisted in Liverpool while living in Liverpool. Son of Michael and Johanna Duffy, of Rathclooney, Carrahan, Quin, Co. Clare; husband of Edith Duffy, of No. 31 Daisy Street, Stanley Road, Liverpool. He volunteered for service in September 1914.

Grave or memorial reference: Plot 1. Row D. Grave 14. Cemetery: Corbie Communal Cemetery Extension in France.

DUGGAN, JOE: Rank: Private. Regiment or service: Cheshire Regiment. Unit: 8th Battalion. Date of death: 9 April 1916. Service No.: 26864. Killed in action in Mesopotamia.

Supplementary information: Born in Teakle, Co. Clare. Enlisted in Birkenhead.

Grave or memorial reference: He has no known grave but is listed on Panel 14 and 64 on the Basra Memorial in Iraq.

DUGGAN, JOHN: Rank: Gunner. Regiment or service: Royal Garrison Artillery. Unit: 141st Heavy Battery. Date of death: 18 August 1917. Service No.: 3633. Formerly he was with the Cork Royal Garrison Artillery 'S.R.' where his number was 6164.

Supplementary information: Born in Drumcliffe, Ennis, Co. Clare. Enlisted in Ennis.

Grave or memorial reference: II. E. 13. Cemetery: Ebblinghem Military Cemetery in France.

DWYER, JOHN: Rank: Private. Regiment or service: Australian Infantry, AIF. Unit: 9th Battalion. Date of death: 4 August 1915. Died of acute alcoholism at the General Hospital in Brisbane.

Supplementary information: Born in Co. Clare. Occupation on enlistment: Labourer. Age on enlistment: 28 years 6 months. Next of kin: Mr J. Dwyer (father) of Co. Clare, Ireland.

Previous military experience: Royal Garrison Artillery – 12 years; tour expired. Place and date of enlistment: Brisbane, Queensland. 1 May 1915. Weight: 12st 3lbs. Height: 5ft 10in. Complexion: Dark. Eyes: Grey. Hair: Dark.

Grave or memorial reference: 15. 12. 2. L1/379. (GRM/4★). Cemetery: Brisbane General Cemetery, Queensland, Australia.

DWYER, JOHN FRANCIS: Rank: Trooper. Regiment or service: Australian Light Horse. Unit: 2nd. Date of death: 7 August 1915. Service No.: 741. Killed in action on the Gallipoli Peninsula.

Supplementary information: Born in Ennistymon, Co. Clare. Age on enlistment: 40 years 10 months. Occupation on enlistment: Labourer. Date and location of enlistment: 2 November 1914. Queensland. Height 5ft 8½in. Weight: 11st 6lbs. Complexion: Dark. Eyes: Hazel. Hair: Black

Previous military experience: Royal Artillery, Fort West, Moreland, finished time. Sent from Egypt for duty with the regiment to Turkey and posted with A Squadron on 6 August 1915.

Grave or memorial reference: Special Memorial, 38. Cemetery: Quinn's Post Cemetery in Turkey.

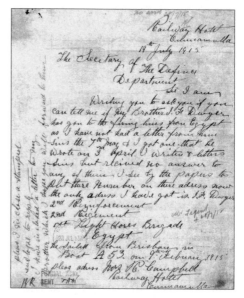

A letter from the sister of Trooper John Dwyer.

E

EARLES/EARLS, MARTIN: Rank: Private. Regiment or service: Royal Munster Fusiliers. Unit: 1st Battalion. Date of death: 25 April 1915. Service No.: 3332. Killed in action in Gallipoli.

Supplementary information: Born in Kilfarboy, Miltown Malbay, Co. Clare. Enlisted in Limerick while living in Miltown Malbay, Co. Clare. In his will, dated 7 April 1915, his personal effects and property were received by; Mrs Bridget Earls (wife), Miltown Malbay, Co. Clare, Ireland.

Grave or memorial reference: He has no known grave but is listed on the Special Memorial, A, 51. Cemetery, V Beach Cemetery in Turkey.

EDWARDS, PATRICK: Rank: Private. Regiment or service: Royal Munster Fusiliers. Unit: 2nd Battalion. Date of death: 21 December 1914. Service No.: 5752. Killed in action.

Supplementary information: Born in Ennistymon, Co. Clare. Enlisted in limerick while living in Ennistymon, Co. Clare.

Grave or memorial reference: Panel 43 and 44. Memorial: Le Touret Memorial in France.

EGAN, FRANCIS M.: Rank: Rifleman. Regiment or service: London Regiment (City of London Rifles). Unit: 2nd/6th Battalion. Age at death: 19. Date of death: 16 April 1918. Service No.: 345071. Killed in action.

Supplementary information: Born in New York, USA. Enlisted in London

while living in Marylebone. Son of T. M. and Catherine Egan, of Main Street, Corofin, Co. Clare.

Grave or memorial reference: Panel 86 and 87. Memorial: Pozieres Memorial in France.

EGAN, MICHAEL: Rank: Private. Regiment or service: Irish Guards. Unit: 1st Battalion. Date of death: 1 November 1914. Service No.: 3829. Killed in action.

Supplementary information: Born in Kilkishen, Co. Clare. Enlisted in Ennis, Co. Clare.

Grave or memorial reference: Panel 11. Memorial: Ypres (Menin Gate) Memorial in Belgium.

EGAN, PIERCE JOHN: Rank: Chaplain 4th Class. Regiment or service: Royal Army Chaplain's Department. Unit: attached to the 1st Battalion, British West Indies Regiment. Date of death: 6 April 1916. Died of dysentery in Alexandria.

Supplementary information: Educated at Trinity College, Dublin, where he graduated in 1888. Held a Curacy at Drumragh, Co. Tyrone until 1893, and then became Curate at St Columb's Cathedral, Derry. Appointed Curate at St Mary's Cathedral, Edinburgh in 1901 and later became Chaplain there (1903) until 1912. Became Chaplain Rector in Saint Peters, Galashiels, Selkirkshire, in 1913.

He was entitled to the British War Medal and the Victory Medal. On the back of Revd Egans Medal Index card is written, Mrs J.H. Egan (Widow), No. 7A Spencer Road, Eastbourne.

He is listed in 'Roll of the Sons and Daughters of the Anglican Church clergy throughout the world and of the naval and military chaplains of the same who gave their lives in the Great War, 1914-1918'. Gazetted, 5 July 1915. He is also listed on the Reading Room Memorial in Trinity College, Dublin, and on the Great War Memorial in St Columb's Cathedral in Derry where his address was in Bennet Street and is also in 'Scottish Episcopal Clergy, 1689-2000.'

From the *Saturday Record*:

Death of Military Chaplain
The Reverend Pierce Egan, M.A., Military Chaplain, died of dysentery at Alexandria, on 6th inst, to the deep grief of many friends and relations, including his only surviving brother, Professor Egan, of Lahinch. The deceased clergyman was a distinguished preacher, of splendid physique, and much beloved by the troops.

Grave or memorial reference: Q. 568. Cemetery: Alexandria (Chatby) Military and War memorial Cemetery in Egypt.

ENSKO, JOHN: Rank: Private. Regiment or service: Royal Munster Fusiliers. Unit: 1st Battalion. Date of death: 21 August 1915. Service No.: 6437. Killed in action in Gallipoli.

Supplementary information: Born in Drumcliffe, Co. Clare. Enlisted in Ennis while living in Ennis, Co. Clare.

From the *Clare Journal*, May 1915:

Ennis Prisoners of War
Mr P. E. Kennealy, Chairman of the Urban Council, has handed us the following letter which he has received from Drummer Hynes, Munster Fusiliers, one of the Ennis prisoners of war at Limberg (Lahn) Germany; Pte, Timmins, Brewery Lane, Ennis, Pte, Flynn, Butter Market, Ennis, Pte, Burke, Lifford, Ennis, Pte, Ensko, Lifford, Ennis, Dr Hynes, Lower Market Street, Ennis, Cpl, Kelly, Upper Turnpike, Ennis.

4 May 1915

Sir—I, Dr Hynes, on behalf of the above-mentioned names, all natives of Ennis, now interned in Germany as prisoners of war, owing to the circumstances we are in, in connection with our parents, who are unable to supply us with money to buy what we want most, beg to request your kindness if you could see you way to send us some cigarettes now and again, and also some tobacco. It is very hard on us, exiled from our far-away home as prisoners of war. There are others belonging to other town lands who are assisted and supplied from funds which have been temporarily formed for that purpose. We would thank you to have this card placed before the eyes of the kind people of our beloved town of Ennis.
I remain, sir, yours faithfully.
Drummer J. Hynes.

(We have personal knowledge that the writer of the foregoing letter has been sent some cigarettes, etc, by a local lady, and that the gift will be continued from time to time, as far as he is concerned– Ed. C. J.)

Grave or memorial reference: Panel 185 to 190. Memorial: Helles Memorial in Turkey.

F

FALVEY, DANIEL: Rank: Private. Regiment or service: Royal Munster Fusiliers. Unit: 1st Battalion. Date of death: 10 August 1917. Age at death: 25. Service No.: 7977. Died of wounds.

Supplementary information: Born in Rathkeale, Co. Limerick. Enlisted in Limerick while living in Ennis, Co. Clare. Son of Daniel and Anne Falvey, of Inchbeg, Ennis, Co. Clare.

Grave or memorial reference: P. II. E. 1B. Cemetery: St Sever Cemetery Extension, Rouen in France.

FANNING, PATRICK: Rank: Private. Listed in the CWGC under FANNING, E.P. Regiment or service: Royal Army Service Corps. Unit: Traction Depot (Aldershot). Date of death: 23 March 1916. Age at death: 19. Service No.: M2/138182. Died at home.

Supplementary information: Enlisted in Nenagh while living in Killaloe, Co. Clare. Son of Francis Fanning, of No. 26 Raphael Street, Knightsbridge, London.

Grave or memorial reference: AF. 1976. Cemetery: Aldershot Military Cemetery, UK.

FARNAN, PATRICK: Rank: Corporal. Regiment or service: Royal Dublin Fusiliers. Unit: 2nd Battalion (SDGW) 4th Battalion (CWGC). Date of death: 21 November 1914. Age at death: 27. Service No.: 5344. Died of wounds.

Supplementary information: Born in Castledermott, Co. Kildare. Enlisted in Naas while living in Kilkee, Co. Clare. Son of John and Mary Farnan, of Ballyvass, Castledermot, Co. Kildare.

Grave or memorial reference: A. 2. Cemetery: Bailleul Communal Cemetery (Nord) in France.

FARRELL, PATRICK: Rank: Private. Regiment or service: Royal Dublin Fusiliers. Unit: 2nd Battalion. Date of death: 24 May 1915. Age at death: 22. Service No.: 11666. Killed in action.

Supplementary information: Born in Kilrush, Co. Wexford. Enlisted in Enniscorthy, Co. Wexford while living in Wexford. Son of Mary Farrell of Clohamon, Ferns, Co. Wexford and Peter Farrell (*see* **FARRELL, PETER.** No.: 3851).

From the *People*, 1915:

> Bunclody soldiers killed
> Bunclody people generally regret to hear of the death of Private. Peter O'Farrell of the Army Service Corps, who subsequently transferred into the R. I. R. some time ago and was killed in France. About the same time came the news of the death of his son, Private. Patrick O'Farrell, R. I. R. who was killed in the trenches in France.

Grave or memorial reference: Panel 44 and 46. Memorial: Ypres (Menin Gate) Memorial in Belgium.

FARRELL, PETER: Rank: Private. Regiment or service: Royal Irish

Regiment. Unit: 2nd Battalion. Age at death: 23. Date of death: 25 May 1915. Service No.: 3851. Died of wounds.

Supplementary information: Born in St Mary's, Co. Wexford. Enlisted in Wexford. Son of Michael and Mary Farrell of King Street, Wexford (This father and son are also in 'The Wexford War Dead').

From an article in the *Enniscorthy Guardian*:

Mr Michael Farrell of King Street, Wexford has been informed by the War Office that his son, Peter Farrell, a Private in the Royal Irish Regiment, has died in a French hospital from the effects of gas poisoning. His first cousin, Private. T. Farrell, who was also gassed has practically recovered, and is expected home in a few days.

From another article in a Wexford newspaper:

Died from Gas Poisoning

Since the Germans have adopted their cowardly tactics of sending noxious fumes to sweep away the brave soldiers who are undaunted by shot, shell or steel, several gallant young Wexford men have fallen victims to the savagery of the Huns. Each succeeding week brings sorrow to many homes, and the hearths of Wexford are not immune from grief for some dear ones who have gone to their last home. The latest victim of the foul fumes is Private. Peter Farrell of the 4th Battalion of the Royal Irish Regiment. On Thursday morning,

his father Mr Michael Farrell, who resides at Stonebridge, Wexford, was officially notified that his son died from gas poisoning on the 25th May. With the letter conveying the sad news was a message of sympathy from the King and Queen and Lord Kitchener.

Another brother of the deceased, Private. Michael Farrell, is serving in the same Regiment, and is fondly hoped that he will be spared to comfort his bereaved parents.

From another article in the *People*, 1915:

Bunclody soldiers killed

Bunclody people generally regret to hear of the death of Private Peter O'Farrell of the Army Service Corps, who subsequently transferred into the R.I.R. some time ago and was killed in France. About the same time came the news of the death of his son, Private Patrick O'Farrell, R. I. R. who was killed in the trenches in France.

Grave or memorial reference: I. F. 73. Cemetery: Bailleul Communal Cemetery Extension (Nord) in France.

FENNELL, JAMES: Rank: Private. Regiment or service: Royal Munster Fusiliers. Unit: 6th Battalion. Date of death: 31 July 1916. Service No.: 548.

Supplementary information: Born in Kilkee, Co. Clare. Enlisted in Ennis while living in Kilkee, Co. Clare. Died in Greek Macedonia. Grave or memorial reference: 289. Cemetery: Salonika

(Lembet Road) Military Cemetery in Greece.

FITZGERALD, PATRICK:

Rank: Private. Regiment or service: Worcestershire Regiment. Unit: 1st/7th Battalion. Date of death: 26 August 1917. Service No.: 41313. Killed in action.

Supplementary information: Born in Tulla, Co. Clare. Enlisted in Woodford, Essex while living in Chigwell, Essex. Son of Charles and Margaret Fitzgerald, of Dromleigh, Co. Clare; husband of Gladys Greaves (*née* Fitzgerald), of No. 1 Brunel Terrace, Brunel Road, Woodford Bridge, Essex.

Grave or memorial reference: Panel 75 to 77. Memorial: Tyne Cot Memorial in Belgium.

FITZGERALD, WILLIAM:

Rank: Sapper. Regiment or service: Corps of Royal Engineers. Unit: 90th Field Company. Date of death: 20 September 1917. Service No.: 121416. Killed in action.

Supplementary information: In his informal will: 28 July 1916, his personal effects and property were received by: Mrs Mary Fitzgerald, Moore Street, Kilrush, Co. Clare. Born in St Michaels, Limerick. Enlisted in Kilrush Co. Clare.

Grave or memorial reference: VI. P.4. Cemetery: Dochy Farm New British Cemetery in Belgium.

FITZGIBBON, MICHAEL:

Rank: Private. Regiment or service: Australian Infantry, AIF. Unit: 3rd Battalion. Date of death: between 7 August 1915 and 12 August 1915. Service No.: 1551. Reported missing in action, later

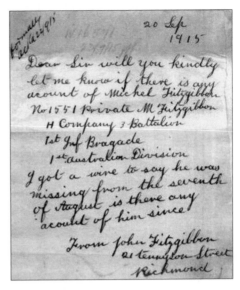

A letter concerning Private Michael Fitzgibbon.

changed to killed in action on the Gallipoli Peninsula.

Supplementary information: Born, Ennis, Co. Clare. Age on enlistment: 21 years. Occupation on enlistment: Labourer. Next of kin: Mr J Fitzgibbon (father), No. 7 Lennox Street, South Richmond. Date and location of enlistment: 7 September 1914. Sydney, N.S.W. Height: 5ft 10½in. Weight: 11st 11lbs. Complexion: Ruddy. Eyes: Brown. Hair: Dark brown.

Witness statements from his records– 7-12 August 1915:

Informant states that in the beginning of August during the Lone Pine charge "some of the chaps saw M. Fitzgibbon lying dead in the open between the trenches not very far from our parapet. He has a set of gold teeth, and that was why they noticed him, as they recognised him by his teeth". Informant was told this some time later in Egypt, but he could not give me no names of the men who told him. Informant went through the Lone Pine charge and states that Gaba tepe was on their right and the New Zealanders at Anzac on their left. They started early in the morning and took and held two or three lines of trenches. Informant states that he saw a number of dead lying between the trenches, when they were relieved. They went for a six weeks rest at Lemnos afterwards.

Reference: Thomas Eaglesham, 1526, 3rd Australians, A Company (III Platoon then) 3rd Southern General Hospital, Oxford:

On 6th August at Lone Pine, Fitzgibbon was alongside Informant as they climbed over the parapet of our trench to take part in the charge. Informant did not see him again, and believes that Fitzgibbon must have fallen at the crest of the attack. A number of men in Fitzgibbon's Company afterwards identified his body owing to two gold teeth which showed prominently in the upper jaw. Informant believes he got these teeth in Egypt. Fitzgibbon was young, about medium height, and build, and Informant believes he came from England.

Reference; McCrae, Private J.C. 3rd Battalion. Details Camp, George's Head, Sydney.

About seven weeks after the charge at "Lone Pine" on the 5th August, 1915, a sapper (I do nor remem-ber his name) told me that a party of sappers, of which he was one, brought in the body of a man for burial; he had five or six gold front teeth, and I think most likely it was Fitzgibbon, as I know he had about the same number of gold teeth in front. Fitzgibbon was about 5' 11", had dark hair.

Reference: Corporal Voss, No 1187, 3rd Australians, A Company, Havre Hospital.

Grave or memorial reference: M. 11. Cemetery: Lone Pine Cemetery, Anzac.

FITZMARTIN, PATRICK: Rank: Sergeant. Regiment or service: Leinster regiment. Unit: 2nd Battalion. Date of death: 11 April 1915. Age at death: 21. Service No.: 3262. Killed in action.

Supplementary information: Son of Bridget Fitzmartin, of George's Street, Durrow, Co. Laois, and John Fitzmartin. Born in Kilmurray, Co. Clare. Enlisted in Maryborough, Co. Laois

Grave or memorial reference: B. 13. Cemetery: Ferme-Buterne Military Cemetery, Houplines in France.

FITZPATRICK, JOHN: Rank: Private. Regiment or service: Royal Munster Fusiliers. Unit: 1st Battalion. Date of death: 21 August 1915. Age at death: 21. Service No.: 6162. Killed in action in Gallipoli.

Supplementary information: Born in Ennistymon, Co. Clare. Enlisted in Ennis, Co. Clare while living in Ennistymon, Co. Clare. Son of John Fitzpatrick, of No. 5 Even Road, Ennistymon, Co. Clare.

Grave or memorial reference: Panel 185 to 190. Memorial: Helles Memorial in Turkey.

FITZPATRICK, PATRICK: Rank: Sergeant. Regiment or service: Leinster Regiment. Unit: B Company, 2nd Battalion. Date of death: 11 April 1915. Age at death: 23. Service No.: 3262. Killed in action.

Supplementary information: Born in Killmurray, Co. Clare. Enlisted in Maryborough, Co. Laois. Son of William and Mary Fitzpatrick, of Crinkle, Birr, Co. Offaly, Ireland. Eight years service, wounded three times and gassed once.

Grave or memorial reference: II. F. 24. Cemetery: La Kreule Military Cemetery, Hazebrouck in France.

FLAHERTY, PATRICK: Rank: Private. Regiment or service: Royal Munster Fusiliers. Unit: 2nd Battalion. Date of death: 30 September 1914. Service No.: 9772. Died of wounds.

Supplementary information: Born in Ennis, Co. Clare. Enlisted in Ennis while living in Ennis.

Grave or memorial reference: I.H. 27. Cemetery: St Souplet British Cemetery in France.

FLANAGAN, JOHN: Rank: Private. Regiment or service: Royal Munster Fusiliers. Unit: B Company, 2nd Battalion. Date of death: 8 March 1916. Age at death: 37. Service No.: 5663. Killed in action.

Supplementary information: Born in Ennistymon, Co. Clare. Enlisted in Ennis while living in Ennistymon, Co. Clare. In his will, his personal effects and property were received by: Mrs P. McCurma? (sister), Riv? Cottage, Ennistymon, Co. Clare, Ireland. Son of John and Katherine Flanagan.

Grave or memorial reference: I. D. 1. Cemetery: Maroc British Cemetery, Grenay in France.

FLYNN, ARTHUR: Rank: Private. Regiment or service: Royal Munster Fusiliers. Unit: 1st Battalion. Date of death: 27 September 1918. Service No.: 1490.

Supplementary information: Born in Adare, Co. Limerick. Enlisted in Limerick while living in Killaloe, Co. Clare.

Grave or memorial reference: I. D. 1. Cemetery: Le Quesnoy Communal Cemetery Extension, Nord, France.

FOGARTY, JOHN: Rank: Private. Regiment or service: Royal Munster Fusiliers. Unit: 1st Battalion. Date of death: 27 December 1918. Age at death: 25 Service No.: 5/6838. Died of wounds at home.

Supplementary information: Born in Crusheen, Co. Clare. Enlisted in Ennis, Co. Clare while living in Quin, Co. Clare. Son of Thomas Fogarty, of Corbally, Quin, Co. Clare.

Grave or memorial reference: Near north-west boundary. Cemetery: Crusheen (Kylwince) Cemetery, Co. Clare.

FOGERTY, JOHN FREDERICK CULLINAN: Rank: Lieutenant. Regiment or service: Royal Engineers. Unit: 227th Field Company. Date of death: 25 September 1917. Age at death: 21. Killed in action.

Supplementary information: Son of William Henry and Emily Georgina Fogerty, of No. 1 Bank Place, Ennis, Co. Clare. Educated at Galway Grammar School and R. M. A. (Woolwich). Born Westbourne, Limerick.

From De Ruvigny's Roll of Honour:

FOGERTY, JOHN FREDERICK CULLINAN, Lieutenant, R.E. Eldest son of William Henry Fogerty of No. 1 Bank Place, Ennis, Co. Clare, Solicitor and Notary by his wife. Emily Georgina, daughter of John Cullinan of Ennis. Born Westbourne, Limerick, 1 June 1896. Educated at Galway Grammar School where he obtained an intermediate Exhibition, a fist place in Ireland in Chemistry (with medal) and fist place (with gold medal) in Ireland in Greek Testament intending to study with the view to taking Holy Orders, but on the outbreak of war entered the Royal Military Academy, Woolwich, being gazetted Lieutenant, R.E., 22-October-1915, a dn promoted Lieutenat, 17-September-1917. Served with the Expeditionary Force in France and Flanders frok July 1-1916 and was Killed in action near Hill 60, Ypres, 25th September 1917, while returning from night duty. Buried in Voormezeele Cemetery, near Ypres.

Grave or memorial reference: I. J. 40. Cemetery: Voormezeele Enclosures No 1 and No 2 in Belgium.

FOGERTY, WILLIAM PERROTT: Rank: Lieutenant. Regiment or service: 57th Wilde's Rifles (Frontier Force) attached to the 58th Vaughan's Rifles (Frontier Force) Secondary. Date of death: 19 October 1919. Age at death: 20.

Supplementary information: Born in Limerick. Last surviving child of W.H. Fogerty (Solicitor) and Mrs E.G. Fogerty, of No. 1 Bank Place, Ennis, Co. Clare. Died while on active service at Ras-el-tin Military Hospital in Alexandria.

Grave or memorial reference: G. 18. Cemetery: Alexandria (Hadra) War Memorial Cemetery in Egypt.

FOKES, HENRY: Rank: Lance Sergeant. Regiment or service: Royal West Surrey Regiment. Unit: 3rd Battalion. Date of death: 15 October 1915. Service No.: G/6241 and 6241. Died at home.

Supplementary information: Born in Ennis, Co. Clare. Enlisted in Leeds, Yorkshire while living in Leeds.

Grave or memorial reference: 1339. Cemetery: Fort Pitt Military Cemetery in Kent, UK.

FOLEY, TIMOTHY: Rank: Lance Sergeant. Regiment or service: Irish Guards. Unit: 2nd Battalion. Date of death: 13 April 1918. Age at death: 23. Service No.: 8218. Killed in action.

Supplementary information: Born in Ennistymon, Co. Clare. Enlisted in Ennistymon, Co. Clare. Son of Michael and Bridget Foley, of Callura, Ennistymon, Co. Clare.

Grave or memorial reference: Panel 1. Memorial: Ploegsteert Memorial in Belgium.

FORAN, MICHAEL: Rank: Private. Regiment or service: Royal Munster Fusiliers. Unit: 1st Battalion. Date of death: 27 December 1916. Service No.: 4663. Killed in action.

Supplementary information: Born in Kilkee, Co. Clare. Enlisted in Kilkee, Co. Clare while living in Kilkee, Co. Clare. In his will, his personal effects and property were received by, Mrs Curtin, Pound Road, Kilkee, Co. Clare, Ireland.

Grave or memorial reference: G. 5. Cemetery: Pond Farm Cemetery in Belgium.

FORAN, WILLIAM: Rank: Private. Regiment or service: Manchester Regiment. Unit: A Company, 1st/8th Battalion. Date of death: 7 August 1915. Age at death: 18. Service No.: 2579. Killed in action in Gallipoli.

Supplementary information: Born in Miltown Malbay, Co. Clare. Enlisted in Manchester while living in Romily, Cheshire. Son of Matthew and Margaret Foran, of No. 74 Ducie Grove, Whitworth Park, Manchester.

Grave or memorial reference: Panel 158 to 170. Memorial: Helles Memorial in Turkey.

FORDE, JOHN: Rank: Rifleman. Regiment or service: London Regiment (Post Office Rifles). Unit: 8th Battalion. Date of death: 15 September 1916. Age at death: 21. Service No.: 4032. Killed in action.

Supplementary information: Enlisted in London while living in Newmarket-on-Fergus, Co. Clare. Son of Patrick and Mary Forde, of Newmarket-on-Fergus, Co. Clare.

Grave or memorial reference: XIV. B. 26. Cemetery: Caterpillar Valley Cemetery, Longueval in France.

FORSTER, ROBERT BURKE: Rank: Private. Regiment or service: Machine Gun Corps. Unit: 11th Company, Infantry. Date of death: 11 May 1917. Service No.: 66624. Killed in action.

Supplementary information: Born in Mohill, Co. Leitrim. Enlisted in London while living in Lisdoonvarna, Co. Clare.

Grave or memorial reference: Bay 10. Memorial: Arras Memorial in France.

FRANCIS, JOHN L.: Rank: Company Sergeant Major. Regiment or service: Royal Scots. Unit: 11th Battalion. Date of death: 21 March 1917. Service No.: 11968. Killed in action.

Supplementary information: Born in Killaloe, Co. Clare. Enlisted in Edinburgh while living in Ohio, USA.

Grave or memorial reference: Bay 1 and 2. Memorial: Arras Memorial in France.

FRAWLEY, PATRICK: Rank: Private. Regiment or service: Royal Munster Fusiliers. Unit: 1st Battalion. Date of death: 25 April 1915. Service No.: 6334. Killed in action in Gallipoli.

Supplementary information: Born in Drumcliffe, Co. Clare. Enlisted in Ennis, Co. Clare while living in Ennis, Co. Clare. Son of Michael Frawley, of Turnpike, Ennis, Co. Clare. One of six brothers who served, two of whom fell (*see* article attached to **REGAN, JOHN**).

Grave or memorial reference: Panel 185 to 190. Memorial: Helles Memorial in Turkey.

FRAWLEY, PETER: Rank: Private. Regiment or service: Leinster Regiment. Unit: D Company, 2nd Battalion. Date of death: 20 October 1914. Age at death: 27. Service No.: 9309. Killed in action.

Supplementary information: Born in Kilmaley, Ennis, Co. Clare. Enlisted in Ennis, Co. Clare. Son of Michael and Bridget Frawley, of Turnpike, Ennis, Co. Clare.

Grave or memorial reference: X. N. 8. Cemetery: Cite Bonjean Military Cemetery, Armentieres in France.

FRAZER, ROBERT MARTIN: Rank: Private. Regiment or service: Royal Irish Fusiliers. Unit: 1st Battalion. Date of death: 4 May 1915. Service No.: 8272. Died of wounds.

Supplementary information: Born in Ennis, Co. Clare. Enlisted in Galway while living in Ennis.

From the *Clare Journal*, May 1915:

Ennis Men Killed at the Front Intelligence has reached town that two young Ennis men have just fallen at the front. One was Corporal Robert Frazer, of the Royal Irish Fusiliers, who, in a recent engagement, was terribly wounded in the legs, and while one was being amputated, succumbed under the operation. The second was Gunner Pat O'Loghlen [*sic*], 46th Battery, Royal Field Artillery, nephew of Mr Martin O'Loghlen,

contractor, Ennis, who was killed with his Major, by the bursting of a shell. This was the third Major this battery had lost since the war began.

Grave or memorial reference: Officers, A. 8. 26. Cemetery: Street Sever Cemetery, Rouen in France.

FRAZER, THOMAS: Rank: Private. Regiment or service: Royal Irish Regiment. Unit: 7th Battalion. Date of death: 15 October 1918. Service No.: 10611. Died of wounds.

Supplementary information: Enlisted in Ennis while living in Killanon, Co. Clare. In his will, dated 16 September 1918, his personal effects and property were received by, Mrs Kate Frazer (wife), of Main Street, Lulla, Co. Clare, Ireland.

Grave or memorial reference: Panel 51 to 52. Memorial: Tyne Cot Memorial in Belgium.

FRIEL, GEORGE: Rank: Private. Regiment or service: Royal Munster Fusiliers. Unit: 2nd Battalion. Date of death: 10 November 1917. Service No.: 6331. Killed in action.

Supplementary information: Born in Liscannon, Ennistymon, Co. Clare. Enlisted in Limerick while living in Lahinch, Co. Clare.

Grave or memorial reference: IX. F. 10. Cemetery: Poelcapelle British Cemetery in Belgium.

G

GALLAGHER, JOHN HENRY:
Rank: Private. Regiment or service: Royal Dublin Fusiliers. Unit: 1st Battalion. Date of death: 4 September 1918. Age at death: 40. Service No.: 43166. Formerly he was with the Royal Irish Dragoon Guards where his number was 14773. Killed in action.

Supplementary information: Born in Clare. Enlisted in Miltown Malbay while living in Oakham, Rutland. Husband of Annie C. Gallaher, of No. 41 King's Road, Oakham, Rutland.

Grave or memorial reference: II. P.14. Cemetery: Trois Arbres Cemetery, Steenwerck in France.

GALLAGHER, JOHN: (Alias, family name is McCann). Rank: Stoker 2nd Class. Regiment or service: Royal Navy. Unit: HMPMS. Erin's Isle (a minesweeper). Date of death: 7 February 1919. Age at death: 23. Service No.: K54407. Killed by a mine explosion in the Thames Estuary.

Supplementary information: Born in Clare/Limerick. Son of James McCann, of 12 Chalmers Street, Greenock, and Mary McCann. Native of Derry.

Grave or memorial reference: 32. He has no known grave but is listed on the Chatham Memorial. UK.

GALLAGHER, THOMAS: Rank: Rifleman. Regiment or service: Royal Irish Rifles. Unit: 1st Battalion. Date of death: 24 April 1917. Age at death: 35. Service No.: 8797. Died of wounds.

Supplementary information: Born in Drumcliffe, Co. Clare. Enlisted in Ennis, Co. Clare. Son of Thomas and Anne Gallagher, of Clonroadmore, Ennis; husband of Susan Gallagher, of No. 32 Street Flannan's Terrace, Ennis, Co. Clare.

Grave or memorial reference: Pier and Face 15A and 15B. Memorial: Thiepval Memorial in France.

GALVIN, MICHAEL: Rank: Civilian. Date of death: 7 May 1915. Age at death: 20. Missing presumed drowned.

From the *Saturday Record*, 1919:

Lusitania Hero
Presumption of Death of Clare
Emigrant
Before Mr Justice Kenny, in the Probate Court, in the matter of the goods of Mr Michael Galvin, deceased.

Mr C Kenny (instructed by Mr M Killeen) applied on behalf of John Galvin for liberty to presume the death of Michael Galvin, formerly of Derryshane, Kilmurry-McMahon, Co. Clare, who has for several years resided in New York. On Sunday, May 9-1915, his brother John, the present applicant, received a letter from him stating that he was embarking on the Lusitania at New York with the intention of coming home to Co. Clare. The Lusitania was sunk off the south coast of Ireland on May 7, and it was presumed that Michael

Galvin was lost with the ship, as he was never since been seen or heard of. The Cunard Co., in reply to a letter from Mrs Killeen, stated that Michael Galvin was, according to the official record, a third class passenger on the Lusitania. The deceased, who was a general labourer, was unmarried, and had made no will. His assets amounted to nearly £500.

My Justice Kenny made an order presuming the death of Galvin, and granted the applicant an order for administration of his estate.

Grave or memorial reference: He has no known grave and is not listed on any known memorial.

GARDINER, THOMAS: Rank: Private. Regiment or service: Irish Guards. Unit: 1st Battalion. Date of death: 12 August 1916. Age at death: 25. Service No.: 3812. Killed in action.

Supplementary information: Born in Ennis, Co. Clare and enlisted in Dublin while living in Cloughjordan Co. Tipperary. Son of Patrick and Anne Gardiner, of Northland, Cloughjordan, Co. Tipperary.

Grave or memorial reference: I. X. 5. Cemetery: La Brique Military Cemetery, No. 2 in Belgium.

GARRAHY, JOHN JOSEPH: Rank: Private. Regiment or service: Royal Irish Regiment. Unit: 2nd Battalion. Date of death: 3 September 1916. Service No.: 18055. Formerly he was with the Leinster Regiment where his number was 5888. Killed in action.

Supplementary information: Born in Lahinch, Co. Clare. Enlisted in Ennis while living in Lahinch, Co. Clare.

Grave or memorial reference: Pier and Face 3 A. Memorial: Thiepval Memorial in France.

GARRY, JOSEPH: Rank: Assistant Surgeon. Regiment or service: Mercantile Marine. Unit: SS *Lusitania* (Liverpool) Date of death: 7 May 1915. Age at death: 25.

Supplementary information: The *Lusitania* was sunk by German submarine U-20. Son of Patrick Garry, and Mary Garry (*née* Murphy), of Shanahea, Ennis, Co. Clare. Born in Co. Clare.

Grave or memorial service: Tower Hill Memorial, UK.

GEORGE, FREDERICK RALPH: Rank: Lieutenant. Regiment or service: Connaught Rangers. Unit: 1st Battalion. Date of death: 5 November 1914. Killed in action.

From the *County Offaly Chronicle*, March 1915:

Lieutenant F.R. George, Connaught Rangers, and formerly of Ballyburley, King's Co., Killed in action, left estate valued at £12, 573. He bequeathed his swords and personal effects to his sister May. £500 each to Judge and Mrs R. Wakely. £333 to each of their three daughters, and all other property to his uncle, J. F. George, for life, with remainder equally between his sisters and brothers.

From De Ruvigny's Roll of Honour:

George, Frederick Ralph, Lieut and Adjutant, 1st Battn. (88th Foot) The Connaught Rangers. Son of the late Barry George. Born Mountshannon House, Co. Clare, 9 Sept, 1883. Educated at Abbey School, Tipperary and Trinity College, Dublin. Was gazetted 2nt Lieut, Connuaght Rangers, 13 Jan, 1906, and promoted Lieut, 2 Jan, 1909 being appointed Adjutant in June, 1914. Served in the European War, and was Killed in action 5 Nov, 1914, during a bayonet attack.

From *Bond of Sacrifice*, Volume 1:

Lieutenant Frederick Ralph George, Adjutant, 1st Battalion, the Connaught Rangers, who was killed on the 5th November, 1914, son of the late Barry George, 13th Foot, was born at Mountshannon House, Co. Clare, the residence of his uncle, on the 9th September, 1883. He was educated at Abbey School, Tipperary, and Trinity College, Dublin, where he was presented with Professor John Wardell's sword. He joined the Connaught Rangers in January, 1906, became Lieutenant in January, 1909, and was appointed Adjutant of his Battalion n June, 1914. he was very fond of all kinds of sport, polo, hunting, shooting, fishing, and football. He played rugby for Trinity. He was also fond of sailing. Lieutenant volunteered to take part in a bayonet attack on the night of the 5th November, and was shot during the charge.

Grave or memorial reference: II. A. 2. Cemetery: Rue-du-Bacquerot No. 1 Military Cemetery, Laventie in France.

GILES, FREDERICK: Rank: Gunner. Regiment or service: Royal Horse Artillery and Royal Field Artillery. Unit: 115th Battery, 25th Brigade. Date of death: 8 September 1918. Age at death: 30. Service No.: L/21921. Died of wounds.

Supplementary information: Born in Ennis, Co. Clare. Enlisted in Camberwell, London, S.E. Son of Florence Jane Giles, of No. 8 Grove Road, Brixton, London.

Grave or memorial reference: IV. A. 64. Cemetery: Aubigny Communal Cemetery Extension in France.

GISSANE, JAMES: Rank: Sapper. Regiment or service: Royal Engineers. Unit: Base Signal Depot ('L' Signal Battalion, Royal Engineers). Date of death: 5 July 1918. Age at death: 40. Service No.: 31390.

Supplementary information: Born in Killaloe, Co. Clare. Enlisted in Limerick. Son of Michael and Annie Gissane, of New Street, Killaloe, Co. Clare. Served in the South African Campaign.

Grave or memorial reference: Div. 62. III. L. 2. Cemetery: St Marie Cemetery, Le Havre in France.

GLEESON, THOMAS: Rank: Private. Regiment or service: Royal Munster Fusiliers. Unit: 2nd Battalion. Date of death: 24 August 1916. Age at death: 20. Service No.: 6776. Killed in action.

Supplementary information: Born in Clare Commons, Clarecastle, Co. Clare on 16 December 1896. Enlisted in Ennis on 22 December 1915 while living in Clarecastle, Co. Clare. Age on enlistment: 19 years. Height: 5ft 6in. Complexion: Fresh. Eyes: Brown. Hair: Light brown. Son of John and Mary Gleeson (née Kitson), of Clare Abbey, Clarecastle, Co. Clare.

Grave or memorial reference: Pier and Face 16C. Memorial: Thiepval Memorial in France.

GLOSTER, FRANCIS BERESFORD: Rank: Lieutenant. Regiment or service: Army Service Corps (21st Div. Train) and Royal Flying Corps. Unit: 20th Squadron. Date of death: 3 December 1917. Age at death: 20. Initially reported missing after his aircraft was shot down by artillery fire this was later changed to killed in action.

Supplementary information: From Parteen. Son of George and Mrs A.J. Gloster, of Parteen House, Limerick. Named in 'Flight' Roll of Honour, December-1917 where he is as listed as a Second Lieutenant and missing.

There is a good article on this man by Patrick McNamara in the *Clare Champion*, 25 April 2003, p. 17.

Grave or memorial reference: Initially buried behind enemy lines he has no known grave and is listed on the Villers-Bretonneux Memorial in France.

GLOSTER, HENRY COLPOYS: Rank: Lieutenant. Regiment or service: Gordon Highlanders. Unit: 6th Battalion. Date of death: 13 March 1915. Age at death: 20. Killed in action.

Supplementary information: Son of Dr J. Gloster and Mrs J. Gloster, of No. 29, Elsham Road, Kensington, London.

Article below from *Our heroes*, 1916. The same article appears in the *Carlow Sentinel*:

Lieutenant Henry Colpoys Gloster, 6th Gordon Highlanders, was the only son of Dr and Mrs Gloster, of Phillimore Place, Kensington, London. His mother is a Co. Clare lady, and Lt Gloster was well known in Kilkee. At the outbreak of the war he left his Co. and was Killed in action at Neuve Chapelle in his twentieth year.

From De Ruvigny's Roll of Honour:

... only son of James Cockburn Gloster, of 15, Upper Phillimore Place, Kensington, B.A., M.B., by his wife, Aphra Jane, only child of Henry Keane. Born 15 Upper Phillimore Place, Kensington, 03 August 1894. Eductaed at St Paul's School, and Gonville and Caius College, Cambridge, where he was a medical undergraduate, and a member of the O.T.C. Volunteered on the outbreak of the war and received a commission in the 6th Gordon Highlanders on 15 August 1914, being promoted Lieutenant, 31 October following. He joined the Regiment at Perth and went from there to Bedford for training, leaving England for the front, 9 November 1914. He was killed in action at Neuve Chapelle, 13 March 1915, and was buried in Esterre Cemetery. He was unmarried. His Colonel spoke highly of him as an officer whose work in the trenches deserved special praise. He suggested improvements and saved several lives of his men when wounded by close attention and skill. He was very popular with his men who respected, admired and loved him for his kindness and intelligent command in times of great danger. He was in command of his platoon in a German trench on the morning of his death. Lieutenant Gloster was a good tennis player, and won the Caius College Fresher's Tournament in 1914.

Grave or memorial reference: Panel 39 to 41. Cemetery: Le Touret Memorial, Pas de Calais, France.

GLYNN, JOHN: Rank: Guardsman. Regiment or service: Grenadier Guards. Unit: 2nd Battalion. Date of death: 13 September 1916. Age at death: 32. Service No.: 14423. Killed in action.
Supplementary information: Born in Ballyorughia, Co. Clare. Enlisted in Manchester.
Grave or memorial reference: Pier and Face 8D. Memorial: Thiepval Memorial in France.

GLYNN, THOMAS: Rank: Private. Regiment or service: Royal Munster Fusiliers. Unit: 2nd Battalion. Date of death: 26 September 1916. Age at death: 30. Service No.: 9511. Died of wounds.
Supplementary information: Born in Ballyvaughan, Co. Clare. Enlisted in Ennis, Co. Clare while living in Ballyvaughan, Co. Clare. Son of James and Bridget Glynn, of Ballyvaughan, Co. Clare.

Grave or memorial reference: I. F. 20. Cemetery: Flatiron Copse Cemetery, Mametz in France.

GORDON, FRANCIS PATRICK: Rank: Corporal. Regiment or service: US Army. Unit: 103rd Field Artillery Regiment, 26th Division. Date of death: 20 April 1918. Died of wounds.
Supplementary information: Enlisted in District of Columbia, Washington, USA.
From the *Saturday Record*, October 1918:

Gordon Died in Heroic Manner.

The following is taken from the *Newhaven Courier*:

COURAGE IS RECOGNISED
AWARDED CROIX DE
GUERRE
BY FRENCH AND OUR
DISTINGUISHED SERVICE
CROSS
It will interest the many friends locally of the late Corporal Frank P. Gordon to know that the Croix de Guerre, the highest prize within the gift of the French Government for heroic service, was posthumously conferred upon him, and also, that the United States Government conferred upon him the highest award for bravery in battle the distinguished service cross. These two awards are unusual honours to be received by one man.
Corporal Gordon voluntarily went to the succour of a wounded comrade and died in the act.

The following is the letter which his brother received from Adjutant-General N. L. McLeod, Captain of the 103rd Field Artillery of the American Expeditionary Force in France, dated June 30, in which the Croix de Guerre was enclosed;--

"Dear Mrs Gordon— There is enclosed the Croix de Guerre awarded by the French Government in recognition of the sacrifice of your son, Frank P. Gordon. The division Commander and the residential commander have directed me to express to you their deepest sympathies. In attempting to rescue a wounded comrade, he made the supreme sacrifice. His action was prompted by true courage and devotion to duty and called forth the admiration of his comrades and his allies —Yours sincerely."
N. L. MacLeod
X Captain 103rd F. A. Adjutant.

Cited by Commander
The General commanding the 32nd Army Corps of France has in a general order also referred to the death of Corporal Gordon as an "example of courage, devotion and sacrifice. He voluntarily went to the aid of a wounded comrade and died in the accomplishment of his action. "

The late Corporal Gordon was youngest son of Mr P. Gordon, late of the Ennis Ordnance Survey, with whom much sympathy is felt on the death of his gallant son.

From the *Saturday Record* and *Clare Journal*, May 1918:

Roll of Honour
Gordon—Killed in action, April, 1918, Francis Patrick (Frank) Gordon, dearly loved son of Mr and Mrs Gordon, 8 Park Grove, York, and late of Clarecastle, Co. Clare, R. I. P.

Grave or memorial reference: Plot B, Row 5, Grave 19. Cemetery: St Mihiel American Cemetery, Thiaucourt, France.

GORMAN, MARTIN: Rank: Private. Regiment or service: Royal Munster Fusiliers. Unit: 2nd Battalion. Date of death: 4 October 1918. Age at death: 24. Service No.: 3621. Killed in action.
Supplementary information: Born in Kilrush, Co. Clare. Enlisted in Limerick while living in Kilrush, Co. Clare. Son of Martin and Ellen Gorman, of Pound Street, Kilrush, Co. Clare. Also commemorated in the 'List of Kilrush Men engaged in the War from August 1914'. This pamphlet lists the Kilrush men who were involved in the First World War until 11 November 1918.

There is a Private Matthew Gorman, Royal Munster Fusiliers, in this pamphlet listed as 'Captured at Mons, Prisoner in Germany' and Private James Gorman RNAS who was awarded the DSM for bravery. They may be related. In his will, dated July 1918, his personal effects and property were received Mr Martin Gorman (father), Pound Street, Kilrush, Co. Clare, Ireland.

Grave or memorial reference: I. J. 6. Cemetery: Templeux-le-Guerard British Cemetery in France.

GREEN, JOHN: Rank: Rifleman. Regiment or service: Rifle Brigade. Unit: 4th Battalion. Date of death: 4 May 1915. Service No.: B/1945. Killed in action.

Supplementary information: Born in Kilkee, Co. Clare. Enlisted in Birmingham while living in Fulham, Middlesex, UK.

Grave or memorial reference: He has no known grave but is listed on Panel 46-48 and 50 on the Ypres (Menin Gate) Memorial in Belgium.

GRIFFEY, MATTHEW: Rank: Private. Regiment or service: Leinster Regiment. Unit: 2nd Battalion. Date of death: 20 October 1914. Age at death: 29. Service No.: 6870. Killed in action.

Supplementary information: Born in Drumcliffe, Co. Clare. Enlisted in Ennis, Co. Clare. Son of Matthew and Mary Anne Griffey, of Jail Street, Ennis, Co. Clare; husband of Maria Griffey.

Grave or memorial reference: Panel 10. Memorial: Ploegsteert Memorial in Belgium.

GRIFFIN, JOHN: Rank: Private. Regiment or service: Royal Munster Fusiliers. Unit: 1st Battalion. Date of death: 25 April 1915. Age at death: 24. Service No.: 9510. Killed in action in Gallipoli.

Supplementary information: Born in Ballyvaughan, Co. Clare. Enlisted in Ennis, Co. Clare while living in Ballyvaughan, Co. Clare. Son of John and Bridget Griffin, of Ballyvaughan, Co. Clare.

Grave or memorial reference: Panel 185 to 190. Memorial: Helles Memorial in Turkey.

GRIFFIN, JOHN: Rank: Able Seaman. Regiment or service: Royal Navy. Unit: HMS. *Bulwark*. Date of death: 26 November 1914. Age at death: 29. Service No.: 215611.

Supplementary information: Son of John and Mary Griffin, of Pound Street, Kilrush, Co. Clare. Commemorated in the 'Kilrush Men belonging to or who joined the Naval Service since commencement of the War.' This pamphlet lists the Kilrush men who were involved in the First World War until 11 November 1918.

From an article in the *Enniscorthy Guardian*, November 1914:

> British Battleship blown up. Terrible loss of life, London, Thursday
> It was announced in the House of Commons this afternoon that the battleship 'Bulwark' was blown up in Sheerness Harbour this morning. Only twelve lives were saved. The 'Bulwark' was a battleship of fifteen thousand tons. She was completed in 1902 and re-commissioned at Chatham in June, 1912. She had a compliment of seven hundred and fifty men, and carried four twelve inch guns. The 'Bulwark' cost £997, 846. It is believed that the cause of the disaster was an internal magazine explosion, which rent the ship asunder. There was no upheaval of water, and when the smoke cleared, the ship had entirely disappeared. An inquiry into the affair will be held tomorrow.

From the *Clare Journal*:

> Clare and Kerry Victims of the Bulwark

The sixteenth inquest on the victims of the Bulwark disaster was held at Chatham on Monday. Two stokers were identified by marks on their clothing, as Daniel Johnson, of Blackfields, Co. Kerry, and Edward Henry Buckingham, of … London, and an able seaman's body proved to be that of John Griffin, Kilrush, West Clare. The jury returned a verdict of accidental death in each case. Twenty-five bodies have now been recovered.

Grave or memorial reference: Naval. R.C. 8. 389. Cemetery: Gillingham (Woodlands) Cemetery, UK.

GRIFFIN, JOSEPH: Rank: Private. Regiment or service: Royal Munster Fusiliers. Unit: T Company. 1st Battalion. Date of death: 22 March 1918. Age at death: 35. Service No.: 5798. Killed in action.

Supplementary information: Born in Miltown Malbay, Co. Clare. Enlisted in Ennis, Co. Clare while living in Miltown Malbay, Co. Clare. Son of Mrs Anne Griffin, of Armagh, Miltown Malbay, Co. Clare. Joseph also appears in the list of wounded in the *Clare Journal*, June 1916.

Grave or memorial reference: Panel 78 and 79. Memorial: Pozieres Memorial in France.

GRIFFIN, MICHAEL: Rank: Private. Regiment or service: Royal Munster Fusiliers. Unit: 2nd Battalion. Date of death: 6 October 1915. Age at death: 30. Service No.: 5890. Died of wounds.

Supplementary information: Born in O'Brien's Bridge, Co. Clare. Enlisted in Limerick while living in O'Brien's Bridge, Co. Clare. Son of Patrick and Ellen Griffin, of O'Brien's Bridge, Co. Limerick.

Grave or memorial reference: I. K. 30. Cemetery: Vermelles British Cemetery in France.

GRIFFIN, PATRICK: Rank: Private. Regiment or service: Royal Irish Regiment. Unit: B Company, 2nd Battalion. Date of death: 24 November 1918. Age at death: 25. Service No.: 16552.

Supplementary information: This man is only in the Commonwealth War Graves database. Son of Patrick and Maria Griffin, of Kilrush, Co. Clare. In his will, dated 2 September 1918, his personal effects and property were received John D. Lorigan (uncle), of Derrycrissane, Kilmihill, Co. Clare, Ireland.

Grave or memorial reference: I. E. 18. Cemetery: Valenciennes (St Roch) Communal Cemetery in France.

GRIFFIN, PATRICK. Rank: Private. Regiment or service: Royal Munster Fusiliers. Unit: 2nd Battalion. Date of death: 27 March 1915. Age at death: 26. Service No.: 4946. Died of wounds.

Supplementary information: Born in Kilkee, Co. Clare. Enlisted in Limerick while living in Kilkee, Co. Clare. Son of Mrs Kate Griffin, of No. 45 O'Connell Street, Kilkee, Co. Clare.

From the *Clare Journal*, April 1915:

Death of a Kilkee Man at the Front
The mother of a young man named Patrick Griffin, of the Munsters, has received official notice of his death, in action at the front. She also received a letter from the Rev.

Father Gleeson, Chaplain, giving a detailed account of the occurrence, from which it would appear Griffin was with a digging party in the trenches when he received his death wound, and as the bleeding could not be stopped, the poor fellow only lived about two hours, but died a splendid death. His poor mother is deaf and dumb, which makes the case more pitiful.

Grave or memorial reference: XXVII. A. 8. Cemetery: Cabaret-Rouge British Cemetery, Souchez in France.

GRIFFIN, STEPHEN: Rank: Second Lieutenant. Regiment or service: Royal Air Force. Unit: 88th Squadron. Date of death: 18 May 1918. Age at death: 28.

Supplementary information: Son of Michael Griffin, of Cahermore, Kilmaley, Ennis, Co. Clare.

Grave or memorial reference: Arras Flying Services Memorial in Faubourg D'Amiens Cemetery, Arras in France.

GRIFFIN, THOMAS: Rank: Private. Regiment or service: Royal Munster Fusiliers. Unit: 2nd Battalion. Date of death: 21 December 1914. Age at death: 20. Service No.: 5298. Killed in action.

Supplementary information: Born in O'Brien's Bridge, Co. Clare. Enlisted in Limerick while living in O'Brien's

Bridge, Co. Clare. Son of the late Patrick and Ellen Griffin.

Grave or memorial reference: Panel 43 and 44. Memorial: Le Touret Memorial in France.

GROGAN, PATRICK: Rank: Gunner. Regiment or service: Royal Field Artillery. Unit: 2nd Reserve Brigade. Date of death: 18 June 1918. Age at death: 33. Service No.: 95034.

Supplementary information: This man is only in the Commonwealth War Graves database. Son of Mr and Mrs Paul Grogan, of Co. Clare, Ireland; husband of Edith Mary Grogan, of Egremont Station, Alberta, Canada.

Grave or memorial reference: Y. W. 47. Cemetery: Luton Church Burial Ground, Bedfordshire, UK.

GUTHERIE/GUTHRIE, MICHAEL: Rank: Guardsman. Regiment or service: Grenadier Guards. Unit: 3rd Battalion. Date of death: between 14 and 17 September 1916. Age at death: 27. Service No.: 20229. Killed in action.

Supplementary information: Born in Ennis, Co. Clare. Enlisted in Wigan. Brother of Miss Margaret Guthrie, of No. 79 Queen Street, Wigan.

Grave or memorial reference: Pier and Face 16 C. Memorial: Thiepval Memorial in France.

H

HALLINAN, MARTIN: Rank: Private. Regiment or service: Leinster Regiment. Unit: 2ⁿᵈ Battalion. Date of death: 20 October 1914. Service No.: 9829. Killed in action.

Supplementary information: Born in Barefield, Co. Clare. Enlisted in Ennis, Co. Clare.

From the *Clare Journal*, 1914:

Ennis men Killed
Intelligence has also been received that the following Ennis men have been killed in the late desperate fighting—

Private. J(sic) Hallinan, 2ⁿᵈ Leinsters. He was son of Mr J Hallinan, Ennis Railway Station.

Grave or memorial reference: Panel 10. Memorial: Ploegsteert Memorial in Belgium.

HALLINAN, MICHAEL: Rank: Private. Regiment or service: Royal Munster Fusiliers. Unit: 7ᵗʰ Battalion. Date of death: 15 August 1915. Service No.: 153. Killed in action in Gallipoli.

Supplementary information: Born in O'Callaghan's Mills, Co. Clare. Enlisted in Limerick while living in O'Callaghan's Mills, Co. Clare. Brother-in-law of Mary Dooley, of Tierovannan, O'Callaghen's Mills, Co. Clare.

Grave or memorial reference: Panel 185 to 190. Memorial: Helles Memorial in Turkey.

HALLORAN, MARTIN: Rank: Private. Regiment or service: Scots Rifles. Unit: 9ᵗʰ Battalion. Date of death: 12 October 1917. Service No.: 266353.

Supplementary information: Born in Kilkee, Co. Clare. Enlisted in Leith. Killed in action.

Grave or memorial reference: XVI. A. 13. Cemetery: Gaza War Cemetery in Israel.

HALLORAN, MICHAEL: Rank: Private. Regiment or service: Connaught Rangers. Unit: 1ˢᵗ Battalion. Date of death: 17 August 1917. Service No.: 5038 (SDGW) 4/5938 (CWGC).

Supplementary information: Born in Tulla, Co. Clare. Enlisted in Galway while living in Ennis, Co. Clare. Died in Mesopotamia. Grave or memorial reference: XI. K. 7. Cemetery: Baghdad (North Gate) War Cemetery in Iraq.

HALLORAN, PATRICK: Rank: Private. Regiment or service: Connaught Rangers. Unit: 1ˢᵗ Battalion. Date of death: 29 April 1915. Service No.: 9143. Died of wounds.

Supplementary information: Born in Ennistymon, Co. Clare. Enlisted in Gort while living in Ennistymon, Co. Clare. In his will, dated 12 February 1915, his personal effects and property were received by Mrs M. Halloran (mother), No. 6 Victoria Terrace, Ennistymon, Co. Clare, Ireland.

Grave or memorial reference: II. H. 13. Cemetery: Hazebrouck Communal Cemetery, Nord, in France.

HANRAHAN, JAMES: Rank: Private. Regiment or service: Royal Munster Fusiliers. Unit: 2nd Battalion. Date of death: 27 August 1914. Age at death: 48. Service No.: 6392. Killed in action.

Supplementary information: Born in Drumcliffe, Co. Clare. Enlisted in Ennis while living in Ennis, Co. Clare. Son of James and Mary Hanrahan; husband of Mary Cullinan Hanrahan, of Ennis, Co. Clare.

Grave or memorial reference: I. 22. Cemetery: Etreux British Cemetery, Aisne in France.

HANRAHAN, JOHN: Rank: Private. Regiment or service: Royal Munster Fusiliers. Unit: 2nd Battalion. Date of death: 9 May 1915. Service No.: 6417. Killed in action.

Supplementary information: Born in Barefield, Co. Clare. Enlisted in Ennis, Co. Clare while living in Barefield, Co. Clare.

Grave or memorial reference: XXVII. E. 16. Cemetery: Cabaret-Rouge British Cemetery, Souchez in France.

HARDING, JAMES GOLDING: Rank: Captain. Regiment or service: Royal Field Artillery. Unit: 21st Trench Mortar Battery. Date of death: 30 October 1917. Age at death: 21. Killed in action.

Supplementary information: Son of Charles Furlouge Harding and Elanor Harding, of Bank House, Ennistymon, Co. Clare. Late of National Bank, Ennistymon.

Grave or memorial reference: VII. E. 17. Cemetery: Hooge Crater Cemetery Zillebeke, Belgium.

HARTIGAN, MARTIN: Rank: Pioneer. Regiment or service: Corps of Royal Engineers. Unit: 12th Labour Battalion. Date of death: 19 September 1916. Service No.: 163432. Died in Salonika.

Supplementary information: Born in Drumcliffe, Co. Clare. Enlisted in Ennis.

Grave or memorial reference: 435. Cemetery: Salonika (Lembet Road) Military Cemetery in Greece.

HARTIGAN, PATRICK J.: Rank: Private. Regiment or service: Sherwood Foresters (Notts. and Derby Regiment). Unit: 2nd Battalion. Date of death: 26 April 1918. Age at death: 26. Service No.: 72743. Formerly he was with the Royal Army Medical Corps where his number was S/4/094904. Killed in action.

Supplementary information: Born in Maynore, Co. Clare. Enlisted in Boyle, Co. Roscommon while living in Ennistynan (*sic*), Co. Clare. Son of James and Jane Hartigan, of Moymore, Ennistymon, Co. Clare.

Grave or memorial reference: I. O. 20. Cemetery: Brandhoek New Military Cemetery No 3 in Belgium.

HARTIGAN, PATRICK: Rank: Private. Regiment or service: Royal Munster Fusiliers. Unit: D Company, 2nd Battalion. Date of death: 21 December 1914. Age at death: 33. Service No.: 4922. Killed in action.

Supplementary information: Born in St John's, Limerick. Enlisted in Limerick while living in Parteen, Co. Clare. Son of Patrick and Mary Hartigan, of No. 20 Donovan's Row, John Street, Limerick.

Grave or memorial reference: Panel 43 and 44. Memorial: Le Touret Memorial in France.

HASTINGS, PATRICK MICHAEL:
Rank: Guardsman. Regiment or service: Scots Guards. Unit: 1st Battalion. Date of death: 14 September 1914. Service No.: 7958. Killed in action.

Supplementary information: Born in Kyldsart, Co. Clare. Enlisted in Edinburgh.

Grave or memorial reference: He has no known grave but is listed on the La Ferte-sous-Jouarre Memorial in France.

HAUGH, FRANCIS: Rank: Private.
Regiment or service: Royal Irish Regiment Secondary Regiment: South Irish Horse Secondary. Date of death: 27 February 1920. Age at death: 22. Service No.: 25355.

Supplementary information: Son of John and Elizabeth Haugh, of No. 43 St Flannans Terrace, Clare Road, Ennis. In his will, dated 23 March 1917, his personal effects and property were received by Mrs Lizzie Hough (mother), of No. 43 St Flannans Terrace, Ennis, Co. Clare, Ireland.

Grave or memorial reference: South-east part of new ground. Cemetery: Ennis (Drumcliff) Cemetery, Co. Clare

HAYES, DENIS ALPHONSUS:
Rank: Private. Regiment or service: Leinster Regiment. Unit: 7th Battalion. Date of death: 9 July 1916. Age at death: 29. Service No.: 3502. Died of wounds.

Supplementary information: Born in Parteen, Co. Clare. Enlisted in Camberley, London while living in Kilmallock, Co. Limerick. Son of Thomas and Mary Hayes, of Bulgaden, Kilmallock, Co. Limerick. Professor in St Kieran's College, Kilkenny.

Grave or memorial reference: II. C. 33. Cemetery: Longuenesse (St Omer) Souvenir Cemetery in France.

HAYES, JAMES: Rank: Private.
Regiment or service: Irish Guards. Unit: 1st Battalion. Date of death: 7 July 1917. Age at death: 27. Service No.: 5332. Died of wounds.

Supplementary information: Born in Ennis, Co. Clare. Enlisted in Glasgow while living in Ballymaclure, Co. Clare. Son of Patrick and Margaret Hayes, of Ballymacloon, Quin, Co. Clare.

Grave or memorial reference: I. B. 10. Cemetery: Dozinghem Military Cemetery in Belgium.

HAYNES, HARRY EDGAR:
Rank: Sergeant. Regiment or service: West Yorkshire Regiment. Unit: 15th Battalion. Date of death: 3 May 1917. Age at death: 22. Service No.: 15/440. Killed in action.

Supplementary information: Born in Ballybhon, Co. Clare. Enlisted in Leeds while living in Carlisle. Son of James and Mary Ann Haynes, of No. 32 Norfolk Road, Southampton.

Grave or memorial reference: He has no known grave but is listed in Bay 4 on the Arras Memorial in France

HEAVY, THOMAS: Served as BARLOW, THOMAS. Rank: Private.
Regiment or service: Royal Army Service Corps. Date of death: 8 April 1919. Age at death: 36. Service No.: DM2/225827. This man is only recorded

in the Commonwealth War Graves Commission database.

Grave or memorial reference: In the south corner of the west part. Cemetery: Ennistymon Cemetery, Co. Clare.

HEGARTY, PATRICK: Rank: Lance Sergeant. Regiment or service: Irish Guards. Unit: 3rd Battalion. Date of death: 23 February 1920. Age at death: 30. Service No.: 3178.

Supplementary information: Husband of Margaret Hegarty. Patrick also appears in the list of wounded in the *Clare Journal*, June 1916. This man is only recorded in the Commonwealth War Graves Commission database.

Grave or memorial reference: In East part. Cemetery: Ennistymon Cemetery, Co. Clare.

HENN, EDWARD HENRY LOVETT: Rank: Second Lieutenant. Regiment or service: Rifle Brigade (The Prince Consort's Own). Unit: 9th Battalion. Date of death: 29 May 1915. Age at death: 23. Killed in action.

Supplementary information: Son of Edward Lovett-Henn and Margaret Agnes Vaughan Henry, of Campagne Sidi-Merzoug, El-Biar, Algiers. Educated at Freiburg University, Baden, and Trinity College, Cambridge BA, 1913. Qualified for entry to Foreign Office (second in competition), August, 1914. Volunteered September, 1914, and went to France in August, 1915.

From the *Clare Journal*, October 1915:

Lieutenant E. L. Henn
Lieutenant Eric Lovett Henn, 9th Rifle Brigade, reported Killed in action in France was the only son of

Lieut. E. H. L. HENN,
9th Rifle Brigade.

Second Lieutenant Edward Henn.

Mr and Mrs Edward Lovett Henn, of Sidi Mirrong, El Biar, Algeria, and grandson of the late Thomas Rice Henn, K.C, D. L., of Paradise, Co. Clare, for many years Recorder of Galway, and the late Mitchell Henry, of Kylemore Castle and Stratheden House, London, S. W., formerly M. P., for Co. Galway.

Lieutenant Eric Lovett Henn was born in 1890, and educated at Freiburg, Germany, and Trinity College, Cambridge, of which University he was a graduate. He had taken a high place in the examination for the diplomatic service, but gave it up to join the New Army. He spoke French and German fluently, and was in the first instance given a commission as interpreter, which he relinquished to join a fighting unit.

Grave or memorial reference: Panel 46-48 and 50. Memorial: Ypres (Menin Gate) Memorial in Belgium.

HICKEY, JOHN JOSEPH: Rank: Private. Regiment or service: Australian Infantry, AIF. Unit: 60th Battalion. Date of death: 27 January 1918. Age at death: 23. Service No.: 1699. Death due to shock and haemorrhage resulting from being struck by a train

Supplementary information: Occupation on enlistment: Foreman Mason at Murray Bridge. Son of Johanna Jones, of No. 43 Tarragon Street, Mile End. Nephew of Thomas Hickey, of Ballybrack, Kilmore, Limerick. Born, Port Melbourne, Victoria. Age on enlistment: 21 years 7 months. Next of kin Mr John Patrick Hickey (father), of 240 Ross Street, Port Melbourne. Victoria. Place and date of enlistment: Melbourne, 16 February 1916. Weight: 14st 9lbs. Complexion: Medium. Eyes: Blue. Hair: Brown. Received gun shot wounds to the hands in July 1916 and embarked on board *St David* to England

for treatment. Returned to his unit and suffered shell-shock in November, 1917.

Death due to shock and haemorrhage resulting from being struck by a train. Compound fracture, right arm, right femur, nasal bones, parietal bone. Accident occurred at Newbridge Station. Died in Edgy Curragh Military Hospital, Dublin (*sic*).

The deceased soldier was interred privately. The remains were taken by road from Limerick. All arrangements incidental to the funeral ceremony were conducted by deceased's Uncle. Uncle and Aunt, 4 cousins and about 25 friends of deceased were present.

Administrative Headquarters, A.I.F., London, were represented at the funeral. An oak cross, bearing the deceased's regimental particulars, one taken from London by the A.I.F. representative, and was erected on the grave after the burial ceremony. Relatives present expressed their grateful satisfaction to the A.I.F. for the arrangements made from London. The coffin was made of good polished oak. Interred on 31 January, 1918 at 4.45 p.m.

Names and addresses of relatives, T. Hickey (uncle), Ballybrack, Clonlara, Co. Clare, Ireland.

Grave or memorial reference: East of church. Cemetery: Bridgetown Catholic Churchyard, Co. Clare.

The above image is from 'War Illustrated'.

HICKEY, JOHN: Rank: Private. Regiment or service: Royal Irish Regiment. Unit: 7th Battalion. Date of death: 28 October 1918. Service No.: 25370. Formerly he was with the South

Irish Horse where his number was 1698. Died of wounds.

Supplementary information: Born in Kilrush, Co. Clare. Enlisted in Limerick while living in Kilrush, Co. Clare.

Grave or memorial reference: IV. N. 13. Cemetery: Tournai Communal Cemetery Allied Extension in Belgium.

HICKMAN, POOLE HENRY:

Rank: Captain (TP) Regiment or service: Royal Dublin Fusiliers. Unit: 7th Battalion. Date of death: 15 August 1915. Age at death: 35. Killed in action.

Supplementary information: Son of Francis William Hickman and Elizabeth B. Gore Hickman, of No. 23 Earlsfort Terrace, Dublin.

From *Our heroes* 1916:

Captain Poole Henry Hickman, who fell in action at Gallipoli on August 15th last, was one of the many members of the Irish Bar who on the outbreak of the war joined the 7th Battalion, Royal Dublin Fusiliers. He was called to the Bar in 1900, and was Hon. Secretary of the Munster Circuit. His short professional career was full of promise, and he was highly esteemed by his collegues. Captain Hickman was a son of Mr F. W. Hickman, D. L., Kilmore, Knock, and was educated at Tipperary Grammar School and Trinity College.

From the *Clare Journal*, September 1914:

Clare Barrister Volunteers for the Front

About 120 of the Irish Rugby Union Volunteers for the front left Dublin yesterday amid much enthusiasm, for Kildare, for training before going to the front.

There were five Barristers in the ranks, one being Mr Poole Hickman, B. L., the Hon. Secretary to the Munster Bar, son of Mr E. G. Hickman, D. L., Kilmore, West Clare.

From *Wigs and Guns*, 2005:

Born 8 June 1880. Parents; Francis William Gore Hickman, duty lieutenant, gentleman, and Elizabeth O'Brien. Address, Family; Kilmore, Knock, near Kilrush, Co. Clare. Self; 25 South Frederick Street, Dublin, Vaughans Hotel, 29 Rutland (now Parnell) Square, and 23 Earlsfort Terrace, Dublin. Religion; Church of Ireland. School; The Abbey, Tipperary Grammar School. University; Dublin, TCD. BA, Hiemalis, 1902. Legal Career; King's Inns, Dublin. Admitted as student; 1906. Called to Bar; Easter term, 1909. Legal Practice; Awarded an exhibition at King's Inns, and medal for legal debate at the Law Students Debating Society. Some of his extended family were solicitors, practicing as Kerrin and Hickman, Ennis. He was honorary secretary and treasurer of the Munster Bar. 'His short legal career was full of promise and he was highly esteemed by his colleagues', according to Our Heroes; Mons to the Somme, supplement to Irish Life (24 September 1916). Army career; Enlisted in September

1914. Unit D Company (Pals), 7th Battalion, Royal Dublin Fusiliers, 10th (Irish) Division, 30th Brigade, rank captain. Service' Gallipoli. Member of DU OTC, TCD; gazetted as lieutenant, 7th Dublins and promoted captain in January, 1915. As commanding officer of D Company, pals, 7th Dublins, he led them as they marched from Royal (Collins) Barracks to the ferry at North Wall, Dublin on 30 April, 1915 en route to Gallipoli. His brothers, Thomas and Norman, also served with the Dublin pals. Died; Killed in action on 16 August, 1915, aged 35, in Gallipoli when leading a bayonet charge at Kiretch Tepe/Kirectepe ridge during the gallant stand and subsequent fall of the Dublins. Well out in front of his wavering men, waving his revolver he shouted, 'On Dublins!', according to Michael McDonagh, 'The Irish at the Front' (London, 1916), p. 95. Memorials; named at; Four Courts, Dublin, TCD, WDL, no. 212; IMR; Helles memorial, Turkey, CWGC ref. MR 4. 6, Dublins' panels 190-96; 'Our Heroes', p. 126; roll of honour, Free and Accepted masons of Ireland, lodge 60, Ennis Co. Clare; roll of honour, in R. W. Walker, 'To what end did they die; officers died at Galipoli', Hanna, The Pals at Suvla Bay; PRO, WO 339/12366; Dublin Book of Honour, 2003.

From *The Irish at the Front*, 2009:

The first line was led by Captain Poole Hickman, of D company, who came of a well-known Clare family and was a barrister by profession. He never returned from the charge. As the Dublins appeared at the summit there was a splutter of fire along the opposite ridge, which was lined by Turkish marksmen. The men wavered and swayed uncertainly for a minute or two before the shower of bullets. Hickman was well in front, waving his revolver and shouting "On, Dublins!" That was the last that was seen of him alive.

The famous D company of the 7th Dublins, led by Captain Poole Hickman and Captain Tobin, was practically wiped out. It was composed altogether of young men distinguished in football and cricket and other forms of sport. Many of them had ample Private means, all belonged to the professional middle class of Dublin, and they felt it a high honour to serve in the rank and file of the Army.

Sir Bryan Mahon, the General in command of the 10th Division, sent a message to his troops saying that Ireland should be proud to own such soldiers. Ireland, indeed, is proud, though what happened was no more than what she expected. When the 7th Dublins were congratulated upon the stand they had made, their answer was: "And what the blank, blank, did you think we would do?" But with all her exultation in the valour of her sons, Ireland cannot close her ears to the cry of the Colonel of the 7th Munsters on seeing the few officers who returned from the fray: "My poor boys! My poor boys!"

From the *Clare Journal*, 2 September 1915:

Vivid Story of Irish Gallantry
Clare Officer tells how the advance
was made from Suvla Bay

The following account of the operations of the 7th Royal Dublin Fusiliers in the Dardanelles between the 6th and 14th August was written by our gallant Captain Poole H. Hickman, who commanded the D Company, and was killed on the 15th inst. It is as vivid a picture as has been given by anyone yet from the firing lines—

We left Mitylene at 3 p.m. on Friday, August 6th, and arrived here at 4 a.m, on Saturday morning. We carried our rations with us—a sandwich for the voyage, and two days iron rations, consisting (each day's ration) of a tin of bully beef, tea, sugar, biscuits, and Oxo tablets. From 2 o'clock in the morning we could see the flashing of the big guns and hear the rattle of musketry, the first indication to us that we were within the war zone. Our first two boats, consisting of A and C Companies, started landing at 5.30 a.m., but did not get ashore without mishap as a shrapnel struck the boat, killing one man and wounding eleven. Amongst the wounded was one of our officers, Second Lieutenant Harvey. We landed a short time later, but escaped without being hit, and then about 8 a.m, we commenced a general advance. It was allotted to us and to another Irish Regiment to take a certain hill, which was 3 ¼ miles from where we landed.

We had not advanced one hundred yards when we were greeted with a perfect hail of shrapnel. And shrapnel is not a pleasant thing. You hear a whistle through the air, then a burst, and everything within a space of 200 yards from where the shrapnel burst is liable to be hit. The wounds inflicted are dreadful—deep, big irregular gashes, faces battered out of recognition, limbs torn away.

"An open target to the enemy"

We got some protection under cover of a hill, and steadily continued our advance in a line parallel to the enemy's position. We had to change direction and advance in a direct line on a position at a small neck of land, and the crossing of this neck was awe-inspiring but ghastly. The enemy guns had got the range to a yard, and a tornado of high explosives and shrapnel swept the place. Your only chance was to start immediately after a burst, and run as fast as you could across the place, as there was some cover at the other side. We lost heavily at this particular place, and from then on commenced the serious business. The enemy were strongly entrenched on a line of hills about two miles from the neck of land. The right of the attack had to get over a bare, sandy sweep, but there was some cover, such as it was for the left. The heat was intense and the going very heavy. We advanced in long lines, with two paces between each man, and about eight such lines altogether at the start; of course, by the time we got to the hill the supports and reserves had closed up with the firing line. Meanwhile we presented an open target to the enemy, but, though we advanced through a regular hail of bullets and shrapnel, our casualties were not heavy. Major Harrison was in command of the first line, and was marvellously good. About 3 o'clock in the afternoon we were within 600 yards of the hill, which was fairly high—a network of trenches, and sides covered with furze and thorny scrub, which afforded cover from view. When we got to the foot of the hill, A and D Companies, led by Major Harrison, were in the first line, about a platoon of each, with some Enniskillings and a few stragglers.

"At the point of the bayonet"
They took the hill at the point of the bayonet, the Turks fleeing in all directions. It was a magnificent performance, and we have been personally congratulated on it, and we called the hill Fort Dublin. Our casualties were over 100, including Major Tippett, shot dead, and Lieutenant Julian, who has, I hear, since died. D Company lost 22 altogether, and only one killed outright, though I am afraid some of the others will not recover. It was just disk when the hill fell, and then we had to go and get water for the men, who were parched with the thirst This was a long job, and we had to go some miles back to a well. Meanwhile we had established ourselves in the trenches on the hill, and at 1. 30 on Sunday morning I ate a biscuit, which was my first food since breakfast the previous morning. The enemy counterattacked during the night, but were easily driven off.

All Sunday morning and afternoon a furious fight was going on the ridge to our right, where our forces had the advantage. Meanwhile, all day shrapnel and high explosives were spoiling our day's rest, and the place was full of snipers. These snipers—unreadable—, and it is very hard to spot them. We captured some, including a woman, and a man dressed in green to resemble the tree he was in, and shot several more. On Monday there was a tremendous fight for the hill on our left by an English division. The brigade on the right rant out of ammunition, and D Company were called upon to supply them. I sent 40 men, under Captain Tobin, to bring uo 20, 000 rounds to the supports, and took 80 men myself with 40, 000 rounds, which were further away, to the same place, but with orders from the Colonel to come back immediately, as our side of the hill was very weakly held. When I got up I found that Tobin and twelve of his party had gone on further, as the ammunition was very urgently needed. I dumped down our ammunition with the supports, and came back to the hill, as ordered. Meanwhile Tobin and his party got into the firing line, and one of my best sergeants, Edward Millar, was killed … He died gallantly, and his name has been sent forward for recognition.

"Waiting to go forward again"

The next few days were uneventful, save that we got no sleep, as we had to stand to arms about six times each night; and the incessant din of howitzers and heavy guns allowed no rest whatsoever. Finally, on Thursday night, or rather Friday morning, at 1.30 a. m., we were relieved, and were not sorry to leave a hill which none of us will forget, and the taking of which was an achievement which will add lustre to the records of even the Dublin Fusiliers. D Company's casualties amounted to 40 out of 188 men landed on Saturday morning. I forgot to say that we discarded our packs at the landing (and have never seen them again), and all this time we never had even our boots off, a shave, or a wash, and even the dirtiest water was greedily drunk on the hill, where the sun's rays beat pitilessly down all day long, and where the rotting corpses of the Turks created a damnably offensive smell. That is one of the worst features here—unburied bodies, and flies, but the details and more gruesome, some than my pen can depict. Well, we marched out at 1.30 on Friday morning, a bedraggled and want of sleep tired body, and marched seven miles back to a rest camp. Several of the men walked back part of the way in their sleep, and when we arrived at 4. 30 on Friday morning everyone threw himself down where we was and fell asleep. But our hopes of a rest were short-lived, as we were ordered out again at four the next day, and here we are now on the side of a hill waiting to go forwardd again and attack. Meanwhile it is soothing for us to know that we have achieved something which has got us the praise of all the Staff and big men here, but I dare say you will hear all about it in despatches from the front.

From the *Clare Leader*, 27 August 1915:

Another Clare Officer Killed Ennis, Wednesday night. News reached his father, Mr Gore Hickman, D. L., of the death of another gallant young Clare man, Captain Poole Henry Hickman, of the 7th Battalion, Royal Dublin Fusiliers, who was Killed in action in the fighting in the Dardanelles on August 15th. Captain Hickman was a prominent and promising member of the Munster Bar, being secretary of the Munster Circuit at the time he joined, soon after the outbreak of the war. He was one of the first of the Irish Bar to enlist He received a commission in a short time, and received command of D Company in December last He played in Dublin University first fifteen at Rugby, and after leaving the University, joined the Wanderers F. C., and became captain of its first fifteen in 1903. He was second son of Mr Francis William Gore Hickman, D. L., Kilmore, Co. Clare. Two other sons of Mr Hickman are in the Dublins, Norman Gore Hickman and Thomas Gore Hickman, while another son is Mr F. W. Gore Hickman, Solr., Ennis. Lieut. Henn, who has been wounded, was a cousin of Captain Hickmans.

From the *Clare Journal*, August 1915:

Death of Gallant Young Clare
Officer
Captain Poole H Hickman

We deplore the death, news of which reached his father on Monday evening, of another gallant young Clareman, Captain Poole Henry Hickman, who fell in action in Gallipoli on Sunday, August 15. Remarkably enough, his College comrade and Bar colleague, Captain Robin H Cullinan, was killed the previous Sunday in the new landing on this peninsula of bloody memories. Captain Hickman was 35 years only. He was educated at the Abbey, Tipperary, and entered Dublin University in 1897 or 1898. He played in the University's first fifteen at Rugby football, and after leaving the University, he joined the well-known Wanderers Football Club, for which he played for several years, being captain of the first fifteen in 1908. He was called to the Bar at the Easter Sittings of 1909, and joined the Munster Circuit. He was Secretary of the Munster Circuit at the time he joined the Army. On the outbreak of war our gallant young countryman enlisted in D Company of the 7th Battalion of the Royal Dublin Fusiliers, in which battalion he received a Commission in a very short time, and was eventually promoted Captain, and received command of the D Company in December, 1914. He was the second son of Mr Francis William Gore-Hickman, D. L., of Kilmore, Co. Clare. Two other brothers are serving in the D Company of the Royal Dublin Fusiliers, Norman Gore-Hickman, and Thomas Gore-Hickman. A third brother is Mr F. W. Gore-Hickman, Solr, Bindon Street.

The deceased officer was one of the most popular and promising members of our Barm when he unhesitatingly and unselfishly gave up his prospects in his profession at the call of duty. May the grass grow green on his grave—unfortunately not a lonely one-far from the County he loved so well.

Grave or memorial reference: Panel 190 to 196. He has no known grave but is listed on the Helles Memorial in Turkey.

HIGGINS, MICHAEL: Rank: Lance Corporal. Regiment or service: Irish Guards. Unit: 2nd Battalion. Date of death: 15 September 1916. Service No.: 7493. Killed in action.

Supplementary information: He won the Military Medal and is listed in the London Gazette. Born in Liscannor, Co. Clare. Enlisted in Ennis.

From the *Munster Express*:

Roll of Honour
In fond memory of Corporal Michael Higgins (Military Medal), Irish Guards, Killed on September 15, 1916. Son of the late — Higgins, Solicitor, Seamount House, Liscannor, Co. Clare. "He died that we may live".

Grave or memorial reference: Pier and Face 7D. Memorial: Thiepval Memorial in France.

HILL, TOM/THOMAS: Rank: Corporal. Regiment or service: Royal Dublin Fusiliers. Unit: 8th Battalion. Date of death: 7 September 1916. Service No.: 16234. Killed in action.

Supplementary information: Born in Miltown Malbay, Co. Clare. Enlisted in Liverpool while living in Limerick. Son of the late Dr John Hill, of Glendine House, Milltown Malbay, Co. Clare.

From the *Clare Journal*, September 1916:

Roll of Honour
Death of Mr Tom Hill, Junior,
Miltown Malbay
The relatives and friends of the late Dr John Hill, for many years the popular and well-known Medical Officer of Miltown Malbay and district, and of Mrs Hill, formerly of Glendine House, Miltown Malbay, who in years gone by took a prominent part in social matters in Miltown, will be very sorry to hear that their youngest son, Tom, has been Killed in action, with the Expeditionary Force on the Western Front.

Mr Thomas Hill endeared himself to a wide circle of friends during his boyhood's days, by his sunny, happy and unselfish disposition, and his cheery word for everybody.

He was abroad at the time of the outbreak of the war and immediately hastened home to join the Army, and do a manly man's part in the cause of freedon and liberty.

His sad death has been communicated to his sorrowing mother by his superior officer, captain White Bell, who wrote that her son,

Sergeant T. Hill, "had been Killed in action on the 6th, September." He added that "he was a very gallant soldier, and had been promoted to the rank of sergeant only a short time previously, that he was a great loss to him (Captain White Bell) and that he was having forwarded to her his Rosary beads and wrist watch."

There is no doubt had Tom Hill been spared, a brilliant career in the army lay before him, but Providence in His Wisdom willed it otherwise. All deeply regret the death of this gallant young Clareman, and tender to his relatives and friends their sincere sympathy.

Grave or memorial reference: XIV. I. 8. Cemetery: Guillemont Road Road, Guillemont, France.

HOARE, JOHN JOSEPH: Rank: Driver. Regiment or service: Royal Field Artillery. Unit: D Battery, 98th Brigade. Date of death: 26 October 1918. Age at death: 33. Service No.: 75728. Died in Salonika.

Supplementary information: Born in Drumcliffe, Co. Clare. Enlisted in Ennis. Stepson of Bridget Hoare, of Clare Road, Ennis, Co. Clare. In his will, dated 6 July 1917, his personal effects and property were received by Mrs Bridget Hoare (stepmother), Clare Road, Ennis, Co. Clare.

Grave or memorial reference: 675. Cemetery: Mikra British Cemetery, Kalamaria in Greece.

HOGAN, FRANK: Rank: Gunner. Regiment or service: Canadian Field

Artillery. Unit: 4th. Date of death: 1 November 1918. Age at death: 34. Service No.: 874831.

Supplementary information: Son of Michael Henry and F.M. Hogan, of 'Kincora', No. 33 Street Mary's Road, Llandudno UK. Born in Killaloe, Co. Clare. Next of kin listed as Mrs M.H. Hogan (mother), 'Kincora', St Marys Road, Llandudno. Place of birth: Norfolk, England. Date of birth: 30 July 30 1884. Occupation on enlistment: Book keeper. Place and date of enlistment: Winnipeg, 17 March 1916. Address on enlistment: No. 536 William Street, Winnipeg. Height: 5ft 11in. Complexion: Fair. Eyes: Grey. Hair: Fair.

Grave or memorial reference: M. 66. Cemetery: Llandudno (Great Orme's Head) Cemetery, UK.

HOGAN, NELLIE: Rank: Nurse. Regiment or service: No military or naval connection. Date of death: 10 October 1918.

Supplementary information: Drowned when the packet SS RMS *Leinster* was torpedoed and sunk by German submarine U-123 on 10 October 1918. Originally from Newmarket-on-Fergus.

Grave or memorial reference: Civilian nursing casualties are not commemorated in any of the First World War dead databases.

HOGAN, PATRICK: Rank: Lance Corporal. Regiment or service: Lancashire Fusiliers. Unit: 11th Battalion. Date of death: 16 May 1916. Age at death: 28. Service No.: 7127 and 7727. Killed in action.

Supplementary information: Born in Limerick. Enlisted in Salford in Lancashire while living in Killaloe, Co. Clare. Son of Mary Hogan, of Newtown, Killaloe, Co. Clare, and Thomas Hogan.

Grave or memorial reference: Bay 5. Memorial: Arras Memorial in France.

HOLMES, WILLIAM J.: Rank: Lance Corporal. Regiment or service: Irish Guards Unit: 1st Battalion. Date of death: 31 December 1915. Age at death: 21. Service No.: 5816. Killed in action.

Supplementary information: Born in Killaloe, Co. Clare. Enlisted in Kilkenny. Son of Abel and Rebecca Holmes, of Great Oak, Callan, Kilkenny.

Grave or memorial reference: I. E. 15. Cemetery: Rue-du-Bacquerot No. 1 Military Cemetery, Laventie in France.

HONAN, JOHN: Rank: Corporal. Regiment or service: Royal Munster Fusiliers. Unit: 2nd Battalion. Date of death: 9 May 1915. Age at death: 24. Service No.: 4319. Killed in action.

Supplementary information: Born in Kilrush, Co. Clare. Enlisted in Kilrush, Co. Clare while living in Kilrush, Co. Clare. Son of Michael Honan and Honor Honan, of Russells Lane, Kilrush, Co. Clare. Also commemorated in the 'List of Kilrush Men engaged in the War from August 1914', Grace Street. This pamphlet lists the Kilrush men who were involved in the First World War until 11 November 1918.

Grave or memorial reference: Panel 43 and 44. Memorial: Le Touret Memorial in France.

HOPE, FRANK: Rank: Private. Regiment or service: Royal Army Medical Corps. Date of death: 28 November 1918. Service No.: 54355. Died at home after discharge.

Supplementary information: His personal effects and property were sent to Miss E. Hope, Abbeyview, Killaloe, Co. Clare, Ireland.

Grave or memorial reference: unknown.

HOUGH, JOHN: Rank: Able Seaman. Regiment or service: Mercantile Marine. Unit: SS *Gretaston* (Glasgow) Date of death: 11 April 1917. Age at death: 39.

Supplementary information: Born in Co. Clare The 3,395 ton SS *Gretaston* was a cargo/transport vessel was supposedly sunk by German mine-laying submarine UC-72 with the loss of twenty-nine lives. The sinking could also have been due to bad weather. She was *en route* from Heulva to Garston and lies at a depth of 48m with her cargo of copper ore.

Grave or memorial reference: Tower Hill Memorial, UK.

HOULIHAN, MICHAEL: Rank: Private. Regiment or service: Irish Guards. Unit: 2nd Battalion. Date of death: 18 September 1916. Age at death: 29. Service No.: 7835. Died of wounds.

Supplementary information: Born in Kilrush, Co. Clare. Enlisted in Limerick. Son of Thomas and Mary Houlihan, of Crofton Street, Kilrush, Co. Clare. Also commemorated in the 'List of Kilrush Men engaged in the War from August 1914'. This pamphlet lists the Kilrush

men who were involved in the First World War until 11 November 1918. He was also commemorated in the 'List of Employees of Messrs. M. Glynn and Sons. Flour and Meal Millers and Steamship Owners. Kilrush, Co. Clare, who took part in the War, 1914 to 1918. Dated 11 November 1918'.

Grave or memorial reference: I. D. 40. Cemetery: Grove Town Cemetery, Meaulte, France

HOURIGAN, PATRICK: Rank: Private. Regiment or service: Royal Munster Fusiliers. Unit: 2nd Battalion. Date of death: 21 March 1918. Service No.: 6871. Killed in action.

Supplementary information: Born in Corofin, Co. Clare. Enlisted in Ennis, Co. Clare while living in Corofin, Co. Clare.

Grave or memorial reference: He has no known grave but is listed on Panels 78 and 79 on the Pozieres Memorial in France.

HOURIGAN, WILLIAM: Rank: Private. Regiment or service: Machine Gun Corps. Unit: Infantry, 17th Battalion. Date of death: 18 December 1916. Service No.: 22784. Formerly he was with the Royal Munster Fusiliers where his number was 4079. Died in Wimereux, France.

Supplementary information: Born in Newmarket-on-Fergus, Co. Clare. Enlisted in Limerick while living in Newmarket-on-Fergus, Co. Clare. In his will, dated 16 January 1916, his personal effects and property were received by Mrs J. Hourigan (mother), Ralahine, Newmarket-on-Fergus, Co. Clare, Ireland.

Grave or memorial reference: II. B.9A. Cemetery: Wimereux Communal Cemetery, Pas-De-Calais, France.

HOWARD, JOHN: Rank: Private. Regiment or service: Royal Munster Fusiliers. Unit: 1st Battalion. Date of death: 19 October 1915. Service No.: 6175. Killed in action in Gallipoli.

Supplementary information: Born in Ennistymon, Co. Clare. Enlisted in Ennis while living in Miltown Malbay, Co. Clare.

From the *Clare Journal*, November 1915:

Another Miltown Malbay Man
killed at the Dardanelles.
The following letter has been received in Miltown Malbay –
26th Brigade, 27th Division.
Mediterranean Force.
19-10-15.
Dear Martin O'Loughlin, --Just a few lines, hoping you are getting on well and in good health, just the same as myself and willie Loftus are at present, thanks God. Poor John Howard was killed by shrapnel on the 19th October. You can give his name to the parish priest. Myself and Loftus were down to see him. It was a sad death, but the poor fellow died in peace. We felt in a terrible way, but could do nothing for him. You can tell his sister of his sad death. How is Martin getting on in France? Tell him in your next I am asking for him. No more to say, from 6134. Pte C Gleeson.

The sad event records the fourth young man from Miltown Malbay who has lost his life during the war.

There are others who have been seriously wounded with shrapnel and gas.

In his will, dated 3 June 1915, his personal effects and property were received by Mary Howard (sister), Ennistymon Road, Miltownabbey, Co. Clare.

Grave or memorial reference: II. G. 11. Cemetery: Azmak Cemetery in Suvla, Turkey.

HOWARD, THOMAS: Rank: Corporal. Regiment or service: Royal Munster Fusiliers. Unit: 2nd Battalion. Date of death: 4 February 1915. Service No.: 4437. Died of wounds.

Supplementary information: Born in Milton Malbay, Co. Clare. Enlisted in Limerick while living in Milton Malbay. his personal effects and property were sent to Mrs Howard, Miltown, Malbay, Co. Clare, Ireland.

From the *Clare Journal*, February 1915:

Death of Miltown Malbay Man
from Wounds
The sad intelligence has reached the young widow and her two children of the death of Sergeant Thomas Howard from wounds received in action in the trenches on 4th Feb. The deceased was Sergeant in the 5th Royal Munster Fusiliers. The following correspondence nurse speaks well of this young soldier.

At Mass on Sunday, the Very reverend Canon Hannon, P. P., in asking the prayers of the people for the repose of his soul, said he had known this young man for close on three years, living as he was opposite the Chapel gate, and during that time he had never heard his voice on the streets, or at home. He prayed that God would have mercy on him.

His captain writes:

Madam, It is my painful duty to inform you that a report this day has been received from the War Office, notifying the death of No. 4437, Sergeant Thomas Howard, of the 5th Royal Munster Fusiliers, which occurred at Bologne on the 4th Feb-1915, and I am to express to you my sympathy and regret of the Army Council at your loss. The cause of death was from wounds received in action. Any application you may wish to make regarding the late soldier's effects should be addressed to the Secretary, War Office, Whitehall.

14th General Hospital.
Bologne Base.
British Imperial Force
Dear Mrs Howard, – You will probably have been informed of the sad news before this reaches you. I regret very much to have to tell you that your husband died on yesterday morning about 10 o/c. He was going on splendidly, and we all thought he might recover, but I believe he had a relapse about 7 o/c. I had visited him every day for some time and was with him at 8. 30, a short time before he died. I gave him the last Sacraments and the last blessing. He was not I any pain, and was quite conscious. He spoke of you, and, indeed, the only trouble he had was the thought of the sorrow to you his loss would be.

Then he grew weaker and wanted to sleep, and he died quietly in his sleep. I pray God to give you the strength to bear your great loss.
With all sympathy.
Francis Day.
Chaplain to the Forces.

Letter from his Nurse
February 4th 1915
Dear Mrs Howard, – I am, indeed, sorry to send you the sad news, and had hoped it would be good news. I have now to tell you of the saddest Your husband passed away this morning at 9 o/clock, am. He had a good night, and was very easy, and was then taken suddenly worse. The officers were there, and did all they possibly could for him. I am glad to say he did not suffer, and regained consciousness for a short time, during which he saw the priest, who gave him the last rites. He will be buried, I believe, to-morrow. His Rosary and Queen Mary's Box you will receive in time. Your letter arrived the night before and he was feeling all right, so well, that he thoroughly enhoyed reading it himself, and was pleased to hear from you.
Yours etc,
Sister G. M. Morris.
P. S. – We shall miss him in the ward, he was so bright and pleasing to all.

Lord Kitchener's letter:
The King commands me to assure you of the true sympathy of his Majesty and the Queen in your sorrow.
Kitchener.

Grave or memorial reference: I. C. 27A. Cemetery: Wimereux Communal Cemetery, Pas-De-Calais, France.

HOWE, DANIEL: Rank: Private. Regiment or service: Tank Corps. Unit: 6th Battalion. Date of death: 11 August 1918. Age at death: 26. Service No.: 308723. Formerly he was with the Royal Munster Fusiliers where his number was 3767. Died of wounds.

Supplementary information: Born in Clarecastle, Co. Clare. Enlisted in Limerick. Son of James Howe.

From the *Saturday Record* and *Clare Journal*, August 1918:

Roll of Honour
The War Office has just informed Mrs J Howe, Claremount, Clarecastle, of the death of her son, Daniel, son France. Reverend Bullock, C. F., Chaplain, writes that the poor young man received the last Sacraments of Mother Church and all the rites of burial. His belongings were to be forwarded home.

Reverent Captain M. J. Pickett, Chaplain, writes that he was a "good boy, a brave and courageous soldier—a boy to be proud of."

Grave or memorial reference: II. AA. 9. Cemetery: Villers-Bretonneux Military Cemetery in France.

HOWLEY, THOMAS: Rank: Sergeant. Regiment or service: Royal Munster Fusiliers. Unit: 2nd Battalion. Date of death: 19 April 1917. Service No.: 4170. Formerly he was with the Royal Irish Regiment where his number was 1720. Died of wounds.

Supplementary information: He won the DCM. Born in Twoclay, Co. Clare. Enlisted in Cashel, Co. Tipperary.

Grave or memorial reference: V. B. 9. Cemetery: Niederzwehren Cemetery in Germany.

HUSSEY, JAMES: Rank: Private. Regiment or service: Royal Welsh Fusiliers. Unit: 1st Battalion. Age at death: 30. Date of death: 16 May 1915. Service No.: 6203. Killed in action.

Supplementary information: Born in Farkel, Co. Clare. Enlisted in Merthyr, Wales. Son of John Hussey, of Annagh, Feakle, Co. Clare.

Grave or memorial reference: Panel 13 and 14. Memorial: Le Touret Memorial in France.

HYNES, JAMES and daughter **CLARE HYNES**: Rank: Civilian. Regiment or service: No military or naval connection. Date of death: 10 October 1918.

Supplementary information: Drowned returning to Manchester from Tulla Co. Clare when the packet SS RMS *Leinster* was torpedoed and sunk by German Submarine U-123 on 10 October 1918.

From the *Saturday Record*, November, 1918:

A Tulla Victim
High Mass was celebrated in the Parish Church, Tulla, on Wednesday, for the repose of the souls of Mr James Hynes and his daughter, Miss Clare Hynes, who were lost in the 'Leinster' disaster.

Mr Hynes was a native of Tulla, but had his home in Manchester, where he resided for a number of years. He was educated at the old College at Springfield, Ennis, and was one of the original boarders, having turned up at the opening day, April 15th 1866.

His very tragic end will be much regretted by his old school-fellows who still survive him.

The Loss of the "Leinster"
Vigorous Denunciation
Interesting Discussion at Clare
Asylum

At the monthly meeting of the Committee of Management of the Clare Lunatic Asylum on Monday, Rev. A. Clancy, P.P., Chairman, presiding, the sinking of the Leinster was refered to. Mr J. Lynch said he considered their first dury should be to pass a resolution, not only sympathising with the relatives and friends of the people who had gone down in the ill-fated ship, but they should also condemn the outrage committed upon the men and women who were whirled so unexpectedly into eternity. There were a good many people from Clare who were, unfortunatley, on the Leinster, and who were, he was sorry to say, drowned. For that reason their resolution on these lines would be quite in order. It was certainly not warfare to murder innocent and defenceless women travelling by a passenger boat. Mr Culloo said as far as could be learned, there were some people from Tulla on the Leinster. Their names were Hynes, a father and daughter, who were natives of Tulla, but were resident in England. Their

was no account of them up to the present, so it was presumed they were drowned with the vessel. The outrage was a cruel act on defenceless people. If it were a naval boat conveying soldiers it would, perhaps, be an act of warfare. But in the present circumstances it was real murder on the part of the perpetrators of such a cowardly crime. The Chairman said all warfare was cruel, but in the present case there was really nothing extraordinary in what occurred. There was a vessel containing troops, and it was an act of warfare, and any person who went in to that vessel ran the risks in their journey across to England. There was no use in attacking the Germans for cruelty; that was fair warfare to sink a vessel containing troops, and munitions. Those who travelled by such a boat ran the risks of war. He was in favour of expressing their sympathy with the friends of those people who had gone down, and he lamented their deaths, but further than that he would not go. (SR, 1918, James Hynes and his daughter Clare Hynes, from Tulla with an address in Manchester drowned on the "Leinster".)

Grave or memorial reference: These civilian casualties are not commemorated in any of the First World War dead databases.

HYNES, MICHAEL: Rank: Private. Regiment or service: Royal Munster Fusiliers. Unit: 8th Battalion. Date of death: 20 June 1916. Age at death: 30. Service No.: 4677.

Supplementary information: Born in Drumcliffe, Co. Clare. Enlisted in Ennis, Co. Clare while living in Ennis, Co. Clare. Killed in action. Son of Thomas and Eliza Hynes, of Ennis, Co. Clare. In his will, dated 14 March 1916, his personal effects and property. were received by Mrs Eliza Hynes (mother), 4 Fergus Row, Ennis, Co. Clare, Ireland.

From the *Saturday Record* and *Clare Journal*, July 1916:

A Credit to the Co. Clare and to the Munsters

Private Michael Hynes, who responded to the call of his country at the outbreak of the war, has had his name added to the roll of honour, and it has been creditably recorded of him that he was a "credit to his Co. and to the Munsters", to which regiment he belonged. The sad news of his having fallen on the field was conveyed to his mother, Mrs Eliza Hynes, 4 Fergus Row, Ennis, by Major L. Roche, commanding A Company, 8th R. M. F. who write as follows—"It is with the greate4st possible regret that I have to inform you of the death of your son, Private. M. Hynes, of A Company. He was Killed in action on the 19th June, and had an absolutely painless death. He fell facing the enemy like a brave and true Irish soldier to his regiment and to Ireland. Officers and men of A Company send you their deepest sympathy. "

Grave or memorial reference: I. E. 1. Cemetery: Street Patrick's Cemetery, Loos in France.

HYNES, MICHAEL: Rank: Unknown. Regiment or service: Royal Irish Regiment. Date of death: February 1919. This man is not in any of the databases and the only information I can find is in the newspaper article below.

From the *Saturday Record*, February 1919:

Ex-Army Man's Sudden Death

A very sudden death occurred in Ennis this week, the victim being an ex-Army man named Michael Hynes, who lived in the Turnpike. He had been recently discharged and had seen service in Gallipoli, Egypt and France in the Royal Irish Regiment. He had previously served with the 8th King's Liverpool Regiment. His funeral on Wednesday partook of a military character, the coffin being borne through the town by soldiers who happened to be home on furlough.

HYNES, TERENCE: Rank: Rifleman. Regiment or service: Royal Irish Rifles. Unit: 2nd Battalion. Date of death: 16 December 1914. Service No.: 7233. Killed in action.

Supplementary information: Born in Burrin, Co. Clare. Enlisted in Ashton-under-Lyne, Lancashire.

Grave or memorial reference: He has no known grave but is listed on Panel 40 on the Ypres (Menin Gate) Memorial in Belgium.

I

IVIS/IVES/IRIS, JOSEPH: Rank: Private. Regiment or service: Royal Army Medical Corps. Unit: Date of death: July 1917. Age at death: 30. Service No.: 63319. Died of disease in London.

Supplementary information: Joseph is listed in the online census as IRIS and IVIS. In his records he is IVIS. Enlisted in Aldershot on 19 August 1915. Occupation on enlistment: Fisherman. Next of kin: William and Louisa, of Canal Bank, Killaloe. Eyes: Hazel. Hair: Black. Reported ill in Alexandria 12 December 1916 with tuberculosis of the spine. Disease between the third and fourth vertebrae. 'Patient is wasted looking.' Invalided to England 29 June 1916. Discharged 26 July 1916 'no longer fit for war service'.

Entitled to the Victory Medal and the British War Medal.

Grave or memorial reference: Burial Plot, Templechally, Ballina, Co. Clare.

Medal entitlement card from Joseph Ivis' records showing he was discharged due to illness.

J

JOHNS, SAMUEL: Rank: Private. Regiment or service: Royal Army Service Corps. Unit: 7th Division. M.T. Company. Date of death: 5 November 1918, a week before the war ended. Service No.: M/347903.

Supplementary information: Born in Ballyvaughan, Co. Clare. Enlisted in Dublin while living in the Curragh Camp.

Grave or memorial reference: IV. B. 29. Cemetery: Mazargues War Cematery, Marseilles in France.

JOHNSON, EDWIN ERNEST: Rank: Sapper. Regiment or service: Corps of Royal Engineers. Unit: 560th (Hants) Army Troops Company. Date of death: 7 June 1917. Age at death: 23. Service No.: 519428. Killed in action.

Supplementary information: Born in Southsea. Enlisted in Porstmouth while living in Southsea. Son of John and Victoria Johnson; husband of Nellie Beatrice Naish (*née* Johnson), of No. 36, Princes' Street, Mile End, Portsmouth.

From De Ruvigny's Roll of Honour:

Johnson, Edwin Ernest, Sapper, No 519428, R. E. Second son of John Johnson, by his wife, Victoria, daughter of William (and Jane) Daverage, of Exmouth, Co., Devon. Born in Kilkee, Co. Clare, 27 January 1894. Educated at Portsmouth, was a Plumber and Gas Fitter. Joined the R. E. in October, 1915. Served with the Expeditionary Force in France and Flanders from September, 1916 and was Killed in action near Vimy Ridge, 7th June 1917.

Captain S. Chater wrote; "Your husband has left a splendid record of devotion to duty and good work, besides having given his life for his country. During these trying times we have recently been through he showed splendid courage and endurance, and we all, officers and men, are very grieved at his loss."

He married at St Mary's Parish Church, Portsmouth, 15 April, 1916, Nellie (48 Aningdon Road, Southsea) daughter of Frank Durtnell, and had a son, Ernest, born 28th March, 1917.

Soldiers who Died in the Great First World War show he was born in Southsea and De Ruvignys Roll of Honour show he was born in Kilkee. He is not in the 1911 census for Clare but he is in the 1911 census in Devon living with his mother Victoria and father, John, aged 48 a Church Caretaker and pensioner. It also says that he was born in Kilkee, Ireland.

Grave or memorial reference: I. F. 12. Cemetery: Aix-Noulette Communal Cemetery Extension in France.

JOHNSON, WILLIAM: Rank: Private. Regiment or service: Royal Dublin Fusiliers. Unit: 1st Battalion. Date of death: 1 March 1917. Service No.: 25771. Killed in action.

Supplementary information: Born in Kilrush, Co. Clare. Enlisted in Dublin while living in Kilrush, Co. Clare. Son of the late John and Bridget Johnson (*née* Cronin). Also commemorated in the 'List of Kilrush Men engaged in the War from August 1914'. This pamphlet lists the Kilrush men who were involved in the First World War until 11 November 1918.

Grave or memorial reference: Pier and Face 16 C. Memorial: Thiepval Memorial in France.

JONES, ANDREW: Rank: Pioneer. Regiment or service: Royal Engineers. Unit: 12th Labour Battalion. Date of death: 24 June 1916. Service No.: 163594. Died at home.

Supplementary information: Born in Cahir, Co. Tipperary. Enlisted in Ennis. Brother of P. Jones, of Upper Jail Street, Ennis, Co. Clare. Patrick and his brother Andrew Jones show up in the 1911 census with the Piggott family in No. 6 Fahey's Lane, Ennis, as boarders. There were four other boarders in the same house, as well as four others at that time. Patrick and Andrew were general labourers. In 1911. Andrew was 42 and Patrick, his brother, was 39. They were both born in Clare and were single men. It was a four-roomed house and the oldest member of living in it was 80 years old and she was a boarder also.

Grave or memorial reference: Near south boundary. Cemetery: Ennis (Clare Abbey) Cemetery, Co. Clare.

K

KANE, ROBERT ROMNEY GODRED: Rank: Lieutenant Colonel. Regiment or service: Royal Munster Fusiliers. Unit: 1st Battalion. Date of death: 1 October 1918. Age at death: 29. Died of wounds.

Supplementary information: Son of Judge R.R. Kane and Eleanor Coffey, of No. 4 Fitzwilliam Place, Dublin and Glendree, Co. Clare. Educated at the Oratory School, Edgbaston and Sandhurst. Born 11 October 1888. Listed in the *London Gazette*, 8 October 1915 and 18 April 1916.

From *Who Was Who 1916-1930*:

Entered army 1908. Joined the 1st Battalion Royal Munster Fusiliers in 1908 at Rawalapindi and served in India and Burma (where his sister also lived) until 1914. Present at the Gallipoli landings until 13 July 1915. Wounded in action 4 May 1915, (DSO; Chevalier, Legion of Honour; despatches) Address, 201 Ashley Gardens, SW. member of the Army and Navy Club. Recreations, hunting, polo, big and small game shooting.

Grave or memorial reference: III. E. 20. Cemetery: Sunken Road Cemetery, Boiusleux Street Marc in France.

KEANE, CHRISTOPHER: Rank: Private. Regiment or service: Highland Light Infantry. Unit: 18th Battalion (4th Glasgow). Date of death: 4 June 1918. Service No.: 43505. Killed in action.

Supplementary information: Born in Clareabbey, Co. Clare. Enlisted in Ennis while living in Clarecastle, Co. Clare.

Grave or memorial reference: I.D. 40. Cemetery: Martinsart British Cemetery in France.

KEANE, JOHN: Rank: Private. Regiment or service: Royal Munster Fusiliers. Unit: 1st Battalion. Date of death: 27 August 1917. Service No.: 9407. Died in India.

Supplementary information: Born in Ballyvaughan, Co. Clare. Enlisted in Limerick while living in Lisdoonvarna, Co. Clare.

Grave or memorial reference: Cemetery: Taukkyan War Memorial in Burma.

KEANE, JOHN: Rank: Private. Regiment or service: Royal Munster Fusiliers. Unit: 1st Battalion. Age at death: 20. Date of death: 9 September 1916. Service No.: 4612. Killed in action.

Supplementary information: Born in Kilrush, Co. Clare. Enlisted in Kilrush, Co. Clare while living in Kilrush, Co. Clare. He won the Military Medal and is listed in the *London Gazette*.

Son of Patrick and Mary Keane, of Burton Street, Kilrush, Co. Clare. Also commemorated in the 'List of Kilrush Men engaged in the War from August 1914 until November 1918'. This pamphlet lists the Kilrush men who were involved in the First World War until 11 November 1918.

From the *Clare Journal*, March 1917: The death is announced of a brave Kilrush soldier, Private J Keane, of the 1st Royal Munster Fusiliers, who was killed in action. He received the Military Medal and parchment certificate for bravery. Deceased is son of Mr and Mrs Pat Keane, Burton Street.

Grave or memorial reference: Pier and Face 16C. Memorial: Thiepval Memorial in France.

KEANE, JOHN: (Alias – True name is **SAVAGE, JOHN**) Rank: Private. Regiment or service: Leinster Regiment. Unit: 2nd Battalion. Date of death: 14 July 1915. Service No.: 4892. Killed in action.

Supplementary information: Born in Drumcliffe, Co. Clare. Enlisted in Drogheda, Co. Louth. His personal effects and property were sent to Mr P. Savage (father), Ennis, Co. Clare.

Grave or memorial reference: BI. 9. Cemetery: Potijze Burial Ground Cemetery in Belgium.

KEANE, MICHAEL: Rank: Private. Regiment or service: Royal Munster Fusiliers. Unit: 1st Battalion. Date of death: 26 April 1915. Service No.: 5835. Killed in action in Gallipoli.

Supplementary information: Born in Kilrush, Co. Clare. Enlisted in Kilrush, Co. Clare while living in Kilrush, Co. Clare. Son of Patrick and Mary Keane, of Glen Street, Kilrush, Co. Clare.

From the *Clare Journal*, November 1914:

Five sons in the Army
In reference to his Majesty's congratulations to Mr Wm Slade,

commercial porter at Reading, for having six sons in his Majesty's Forces, we may call attention to the fact that Mr Pat Keane, Kilrush, Co. Clare, has five gallant sons serving in his Majesty's Forces.

Grave or memorial reference: Panel 185 to 190. Memorial: Helles Memorial in Turkey.

KEANE, PATRICK: Rank: Corporal. Regiment or service: Leinster Regiment. Unit: 2nd Battalion. Date of death: 20 October 1914. Service No.: 6460. Killed in action.

Supplementary information: Born in Kilkeling, Co. Clare. Enlisted in London.

Grave or memorial reference: Panel 10. Memorial: Ploegsteert Memorial in Belgium.

KEANE, THOMAS: Rank: Private. Regiment or service: Connaught Rangers. Unit: 1st Battalion. Date of death: 23 November 1914. Age at death: 25. Service No.: 8696. Killed in action.

Supplementary information: Born in Ennis, Co. Clare. Enlisted in Gort, Co. Galway. Son of the late James and Bridget Keane, of Clarecastle, Co. Clare.

Grave or memorial reference: Panel 43. Memorial: Le Touret Memorial in France.

KEANE, THOMAS: Rank: Unknown. Regiment or service: Irish Volunteer Corps. Age at death: 20. Died of wounds. The only information I have on this man is contained in the newspaper article below. He is not in any of the War Dead Databases.

From the *Saturday Record*, March 1916:

The Fatal Accident to Irish Volunteer
At Target Practice

Our Kilrush correspondent writes that a shooting accident occurred on Sunday at Cross, in the Carrigaholt district, as a result of which a young man named Thomas Keane, aged 20 years, of Kiltrellig. Lost his life. It would appear that a number of the Irish Volunteer Corps were at target practice, and that a stray bullet from the rifle of Edmond Crotty, aged 16, of Ross, struck the deceased, who expired almost immediately. Crotty was subsequently taken into custody.

Another account:

On Sunday evening, about 5 o'clock, while a crowd of Irish Volunteers, after a route march from Carrigaholt to Kilbaha, were engaged at rifle practice in the village of Cross, a young man named Keane was accidentally killed by a rifle bullet fired by a young man named Crotty, aged about 16 years. The rifle in some unaccountable way turned aside in the hands of young Crotty, and the bullet entered the neck of Keane ho was quite close.

Father Culligan, C. C., who happened to be near at hand, administered the last sacraments. Dr Studdert was soon on the scene, but deceased was beyond human aid.

Much sympathy is felt for the young man's family, as well as for Crotty, who was the innocent cause of the fatal accident, and much indignation is expressed at the indiscriminate use of firearms in the hands of irresponsible youths.

Grave or memorial reference: Unknown. Cemetery: Unkown.

KEANELLY, PATRICK: Rank: Private. Regiment or service: North Staffordshire Regiment. Unit: 1st Battalion. Date of death: 5 Jaunuary 1915. Age at death: 38. Service No.: 7504. Killed in action.

Supplementary information: Born in Kilkee, Co. Clare. Enlisted in Limerick while living in Kilkee, Co. Clare. Son of Mrs Nora Keanelly, of Lisdeen, Co. Clare.

Grave or memorial reference: Panel 8. Memorial: Ploegsteert Memorial in Belgium.

KEARNEY, MICHAEL: Rank: Private. Regiment or service: Royal Munster Fusiliers. Unit: 1st Battalion. Date of death: 1 May 1915. Age at death: 30. Service No.: 7500. Killed in action in Gallipoli.

Supplementary information: Born in Drumcliffe, Co. Clare. Enlisted in Ennis, Co. Clare while living in Clonloun, Co. Clare. Son of Mrs Anne Kearney, of Drumbiggle Road, Ennis, Co. Clare.

Grave or memorial reference: Panel 185 to 190. Memorial: Helles Memorial in Turkey.

KEATING, PATRICK: Rank: Private. Regiment or service: Australian Infantry, AIF. Unit: 51st

Battalion. Date of death: 27 September 1917. Age at death: 32. Service No.: 5413. Died of wounds received in action (gun shot wounds to the hip and shoulder).

Supplementary information: Son of Patrick and Mary Keating, of Ballyblood, Tulla, Co. Clare, Ireland. Born, Co. Clare, Ireland. Occupation on enlistment: Labourer. Age on enlistment: 26 years 9 months. Next of kin: Mary Keating (mother), Tulla, Co. Clare, Ireland. Place and date of enlistment: Queensland, 24 January 1916. Weight: 11st. Complexion: Dark. Eyes: Blue. Hair: Black. Wounded in May 1915 by being buried in a shell explosion (sprained ankle). His received a pension of 20s per fortnight from December 1917.

Grave or memorial reference: XXIII. A. 10A. Cemetery: Lijssenthoek Military Cemetary in Belgium.

KELLY, JOHN: Rank: Private. Regiment or service: Royal Dublin Fusiliers. Unit: 8th Battalion. Date of death: 10 August 1917. Age at death: 38. Service No.: 41232. Formerly he was with the Royal Munster Fusiliers where his number was 7018. Killed in action.

Supplementary information: Born in Garteen, Co. Clare. Enlisted in Limerick. Son of Patrick and Bridget Kelly of Shannakyle; husband of Alice Kelly, of Shannakyle, Limerick. Grave or memorial reference: Panel 44 and 46. Memorial: Ypres (Menin Gate) Memorial in Belgium.

Notification of the death of Private P. Keating.

KELLY, MORTIMER: Rank: Sergeant. Regiment or service: Royal Dublin Fusiliers. Unit: 9th Battalion. Date of death: 1 July 1916. Service No.: 14822. Died of wounds.

Supplementary information: Born in Ennis, Co. Clare. Enlisted in Dublin.

Grave or memorial reference: V. F. 22. Cemetery: Bethune Town Cemetery in France.

KELLY, PATRICK: (Served as **CONSIDENE, PATRICK**). Rank: Private. Regiment or service: Leinster Regiment. Unit: 2nd Battalion. Date of death: 20 October 1914. Age at death: 35. Service No.: 6205. Killed in action.

Supplementary information: Born in Drumcliffe, Co. Clare. Enlisted in Ennis, Co. Clare. Son of Patrick Kelly, of Lifford, Ennis, Co. Clare.

Grave or memorial reference: Panel 10. Memorial: Ploegsteert Memorial in Belgium.

KELLY, P.J.: Rank: Lieutenant. Regiment or service: Royal Field Artillery. The only information I can find on this man is from the *Clare Journal* below. I cannot find him in any other reference work.

From the *Clare Journal*, October 1916:

Lieutenant P. J. Kelly, R. F. A.
Lieutenant P. J. Kelly, R. F. A., whose death is reported from Athlone, where he had been in the legal business before getting his commission, was a prominent member of the Athlone Boat Club. He was a Clare man, being, we understand, son of Mr P. Kelly, Caher, Feakle, East Clare.

KELLY, THOMAS: Rank: Private. Regiment or service: Royal Munster Fusiliers. Unit: 1st Battalion. Date of death: 9 September 1916. Service No.: 9373. Killed in action.

Supplementary information: Born in Tulla, Co. Clare. Enlisted in Ennis while living in Tulla.

From the *Clare Journal*, November 1914:

Clareman's Letter from the Front
Mr T Kelly, Clarecastle, has received the following letter from his son, Corporal T Kelly, who was one of the 500 or 600 Munster Fusiliers taken prisoners on August 27. It is dated "France, 31 August-1914," and from the tone one can understand why it was let through so soon. A German censor was not far away when it was written.
"… Of course I told you I was going to the war in France. Well I left on 13th August along with my regiment. I was 14 days in France, and on 27th August the Munster Fusiliers had a great battle with the Germans, where we lost a few men, but there was a lot of us captured by the Germans, about 500 men, and I was lucky to be amongst them. Of course I cannot give you any information. Tell the Hynes in Ennis that their son is all right. A brother of Paddy Moroney's that works at Howard's in Ennis, is all right also. We are kept as prisoners of war by the Germans until the war is over. The German soldiers are very nice people. They are giving us all the privileges they can, and plenty to eat. I will be sorry to leave them,

I think, when we are leaving ... But wont I be delighted when I am on the boat for England again. Pray for my safe return, soon, and sound. You can imagine what it is to be a prisoner of war. I shall laugh when I'll be telling ye by word of mouth ... I have a terrible story to tell ye when I get home, I can't give ye any address, being a prisoner. Cheer up as I am as happy and cheerful as can be. "

Grave or memorial reference: Pier and Face 16 C. Memorial: Thiepval Memorial in France.

KELLY BLAKE, JOHN: (Served as **KELLY, JOHN**). Rank: Private. Regiment or service: Manchester Regiment. Unit: 13th Battalion. Date of death: 9 Jaunuary 1918. Age at death: 29. Service No.: 7800. Killed in action in Salonika.

Supplementary information: Born in Clare, Ireland. Enlisted in Manchester while living in Hull, Yorkshire. Son of Bat and Jane Kelly Blake, of Corry's Lane, Kilkee, Co. Clare.

Grave or memorial reference: III. F. 5. Cemetery: Doiran Military Cemetery in Greece.

KENNEALLY, JOHN: Rank: Private. Regiment or service: Irish Guards. Unit: 1st Battalion. Date of death: 26 September 1916. Service No.: 9495. Died of wounds.

Supplementary information: Born in Tulla, Co. Clare. Enlisted in Limerick while living in Carrahan, Co. Clare.

Grave or memorial reference: I. E. 12. Cemetery: Grove Town Cemetery, Meaulte, France.

KENNEDY, JOSEPH: (Served under the alias, **MORONEY, JAMES**). Rank: Private. Regiment or service: Royal Munster Fusiliers. Unit: 1st Battalion. Date of death: 3 January 1919. Service No.: 8084.

From the *Saturday Record*, January 1919:

Moroney—On January 3rd-1919, at Rouen, France, after release as prisoner of war in Germany, James (Sonny) fifth son of the late Charles Moroney, Mill Street, Ennis, R. I. P.

Another Hun Victim

We see by our obituary columns to-day that Private. James (Sonny) Moroney, R. M. F., died a victim to Hun brutality, at Rouen Hospital, France, on Friday last He was taken prisoner at the opening of the big German "Push", on March 22, and was kept a prisoner in Germany until the armistice. He was released on November-29th, but was so prostrated from bad treatment and starvation, that he had to be sent to hospital at once in France, being unable to travel home, and never rallied. He had been badly wounded in August-1917, but recovered and rejoined his regiment.

Grave or memorial reference: S. IV. J. 13. Cemetery: St Sever Cemetery Extension, Rouen in France.

KENNY, CECIL STACKPOOLE: Rank: Second Lieutenant. Regiment or service: Shropshire Light Infantry. Date of death: 11 November 1915. Died on active service at sea.

Supplementary information: This man is not listed in Soldiers Died in the Great War.

From *Our Heroes*, 1916:

Lieutenant Cecil Stacpoole Kenney, King's Shropshire Light Infantry, was drowned at sea, on active service on November 11th, 1915. he was the youngest son of Mr Thomas Hugh Kenney, Indianville, Limerick, and Louisa M. Stacpoole Kenney. Leiutenant Stacpoole Kenny graduated in Trinity College in 1912 and was called to the Irish Bar in the same year. In August, 1915, he was gazetted to the king's Shropshire Light Infantry and was in his 25th year.

From *Wigs and Guns*, 2005:

Born; 20 October 1891 (also shown as 1888), Limerick. Parents; Thomas Hugh Kenny, solicitor, and Loiuse Stacpoole/Dunne, author of fiction and hagriography. Address; 55 George Street, Limerick, and Indiaville, Corbally. School; Private study. Unicersity; Dublin, TCD. Scholar; BA, Hiemalis, 1912. Legal career; King's Inns. Admitted as student; 1909. Called to Bar; Michaelmas term, 1912. Army career; Enlisted August 1915. Unit: 9th Battalion, King's Shropshire Light Infantry, no. 3 (b), Young Officers Company. Rank; 2nd Lt.

He left his regiment on leave, pending resignation, apparently due to trauma or mental illness. While travelling back by troopship, SS *Greenore*, he fell overboard and was drowned. Pte McDonnell, 5th Bn, Connaught Rangers, who was travelling on furlough to Brook Street, Ballina, reported the tragic incident; the body could not be found. Died; Accidentally drowned at sea, between Holyhead, Wales, and Kingstown/Dun Laoghaire, Co. Dublin, 11 November 1915, aged 25. Memorials; Named at; Four Courts; TCD, WDL no. 235; IMR; Hollybrook memorial, in cemetery at Shirley, Southampton, Hants, England, CWGC. Ref. MR 40; 'Our heroes', p. 216; PRO, WO 339/38456.

From the *Clare Journal*, November 1915:

Lieutenant Cecil Stacpoole Kenny, B.A.,B.L.

A Gallant scion of old Clare Stock
It is feared in Limerick and Clare that the owner of the luggage unclaimed on the Holyhead to Dublin steamer on the morning of the 11th November and marked "Lieutenant C. S. Kenny, 9th (King's) Shropshire Light Infantry," is an Irish Barrister, Mr Cecil Stacpoole Kenny, the youngest son of Mr Thomas H Kenny, Indianaville, Limerick, and of Moymore House, Co. Clare. Lieutenant Kenny was called to the Irish Bar in Michaelmas Term, 1912, passing out of Trinity College, and the B. A. Degree T. C. D. conferred

on him in Hilary Term, 1913. It was known that he was returning home from England, where he had been on duty since he was given a commission last August, and as nothing has been heard of him, grave fears are felt for his safety.

Pte McDonnell, 5th Connaught Rangers, saw a young officer lean over the rail of the SS *Greenore*, who was very ill, and in a paroxysm of seasickness, he, it is believed, fell overboard. There is great sympathy with his relatives. He was aged about twenty-five.

The tragic occurrence will have a peculiarly melancholy interest for Clare folk, for Mr Kenny was connected with the county by the closest family ties. He was a son of Mr Thomas H Kenny, one of the most esteemed members of the legal profession in Limerick, himself a grandson of the late Mr William Kenny, of Cragleigh, Ennis, who was so well known to the older generation of Ennis residents. The Lieutenants mother is Mrs Louise M. Stacpoole Kenny, whose high literary attainments will be familiar to and appreciated by all interested in current Irish literature. Again, to still further show the close association, this gifted lady is granddaughter of the late Mr Matthias Stacpoole. of Moymore, while the late Mr George Stacpoole, of Cragbrien, and Captain John MacNamara, of the Doolin branch of that family, were great-grandfathers, whose sad death is so widely lamented, was an ardent lover of our county. and its traditions, and

a keen student of its past history and records, all reliable information about which he was indefatigable in collecting, connected as he was with the Stacpooles, MacNamaras, Lysaghts and Davorens. He had a special fondness for Moymore and the cliff-bound coast adjacent, whose praises he was never weary of sounding, and the tenants on the property were one and all devoted to him, and sent numerous touching expressions of sympathy and condolence to his bereaved parents.

From the *Clare Journal*, November 1915:

Lieutenant Cecil Stacpoole Kenny,
B. L., Limerick
Very general regret and sympathy have been called forth by the sad occurrence on the Holyhead to Dublin steamer on Thursday last Some luggage was found on board the vessel, marked "Lieutenant C. S. Kenny, King's Shropshire Light Infantry," and not being asked for, it was presumed a mishap had befallen the owner. The luggage was detained in Kingstown, and on inquiries being made it was ascertained that the missing officer was the younger son of Mr Thomas H. Kenny, Solr., Limerick. He had been under training with one of the service battalions of the Shropshire Regiment, and was coming home for a few days holiday. The steamers now doing the journey from Holyhead to Dublin make the night passage to and from without lights on deck, owing to the war, and it is thought that this may have con-

tributed to the sad accident which is presumed to have taken place. The melancholy occurrence is a very distressing and painful on to his relatives and friends. He was quite a young man, only 27 years, just entering, practically, on a promising officer career. Lieutenant Kenny was called to the Irish Bar in Michaelmas Term of 1912, and it is but a few months since he joined the Army with some other young barristers.

Grave or memorial reference: He has no known grave but is listed on the Hollybrook Memorial, Southampton UK.

KEOGH, FREDERICK BERTRAM: Rank: Captain. Regiment or service: Tank Corps. Unit: 4th Battalion. Date of death: 8 August 1918. Killed in action with his orderly, Gunner Henry Smith while with the 1st Battalion.

Supplementary information: Born in Birchfield, Liscannor, Co. Clare.

From the *London Gazette* Supplement, 28 October 1915, and 20 August 1917, and in the *Edinburgh Gazette*:

2nd Lt. Frederick Keogh, Connaught Rangers, Special Reserve attached to the Machine Gun Corps. His citation: 'For conspicuous gallantry and devotion to duty. When his tank was broken down, he kept in action for twenty-four hours, working all his guns and giving the greatest assistance to the infantry in repelling two counter-attacks at a critical time. When the situation was safe, he withdrew,

handing over his guns to the infantry. He had been for several hours without infantry support.'

He is also in the *London Gazette* Supplement, 28 October 1915. Formerly he was with the Connaught Rangers.

From the *Saturday Record* and *Clare Journal*:

Captain F. Bertram Keogh, attached to Tanks' Corps, Killed in action, was a son of the late Cornelious A. Keogh, of Birchfield, Co. Clare, and a brother of Mrs Glendedding Ness, of Dublin. He had seen considerable service with the Connaught Rangers, and was awarded the M. C., for gallantry. He was on leave in Dublin a few weeks ago, and had only recently returned to France.

Grave or memorial reference: V.A. 18. Cemetery: Bouchoir New Cemetery in France.

KEOGH JOHN: Rank: Lieutenant. Regiment or service: Leinster Regiment. Unit: 3rd Battalion. Attached to 2nd Battalion. Date of death: 22 March 1918. Killed in action. Age at death: 24.

Supplementary information: Son of Mrs Keogh, of The Cottage, Killaloe, Co. Clare. Brother of William Gerard Keogh (*see* below). Also listed in the Blackrock College Roll of Honour where he attended 1908 to 1912.

Grave or memorial reference: I. A. 10. Cemetery: Ste. Emilie Valley Cemetery, Villers-Faucon, in France.

KEOGH, WILLIAM GERARD:
Rank: Lieutenant(TP). Regiment or service: Leinster Regiment. Unit: 6th Battalion, attached to the 2nd/4th Battalion. Date of death: 12 October 1918. Died of wounds received in Mesopotamia. Killed in action.

Supplementary information: Born in Killaloe. Son of Doctor John Keogh and Emily Sullivan, brother of John Keogh

Grave or memorial reference: I. A. 12. Cemetery: Khartoum War Cemetery, Sudan.

KIELY, CHRISTOPHER: Rank: Private. Regiment or service: Royal Irish Regiment. Unit: 7th Battalion. Date of death: 4 February 1917. Service No.: 25469. Formerly he was with the South Irish Horse where his number was 1696. Killed in action.

Supplementary information: Born in St John's, Limerick. Enlisted in Limerick while living in Kilrush, Co. Clare.

Grave or memorial reference: Pier and Face 3A. Memorial: Thiepval Memorial in France.

KILDEA, MICHAEL: Rank: Private. Regiment or service: Royal Munster Fusiliers. Unit: 1st Battalion. Date of death: 19 October 1916. Age at death: 18. Service No.: 4483. Killed in action.

Supplementary information: Born in Drumcliffe, Co. Clare. Enlisted in Ennis, Co. Clare while living in Miltown Malbay, Co. Clare. Son of Annie Kildea (*née* Doherty), of Ennistymon Road, Miltown Malbay, Co. Clare.

From the *Clare Journal*, November 1916:

Another Young Clareman Killed in action

It is with feelings of deep regret his friends have heard of the death of Private. Michael Kildea, Killed in action in France. He was a son of Mrs Michael Doherty, Miltown Malbay, and a cousin of the local newsagent, martin Whyte, of the same place.

Joining at the outbreak of hostilities, he spent most of his time in France. Splendid in physique, and handsome and manly in appearance, as a boy of 18 years of age, he carried an irreproachable character to the blood-stained fields of France. Since God bestowed upon him the use of reason, he was a good an faithful Catholic, always attentive and exacting in his religious duties, and now that the end has come, many friends are left to deplore his loss. In the course of a letter written to his cousin, Martin Whyte, he said; "I go into battle, after saying a few fervent prayers, with a light heart."

Grave or memorial reference: VII. C. 3. Cemetery: La Laiterie Military Cemetery in Belgium.

KILLEEN THOMAS: Rank: Private. Regiment or service: Royal Munster Fusiliers. Unit: 2nd Battalion. Date of death: 4 October 1918. Service No.: 7443. Killed in action.

Supplementary information: Born in Doonbeg, Co. Clare. Enlisted in Cork while living in Mallow, Co. Cork.

Grave or memorial reference: I. H. 41. Cemetery: Templeux-Le-Guerard British Cemetery in France.

KILLEEN, TIMOTHY: Rank: Guardsman. Regiment or service: Irish Guards. Date of death: 31 July 1919. Service No.: 10511.

Supplementary information: Brother of George Killeen, of Doonbeg, Co. Clare. This man is only in the Commonwealth War Graves database.

Grave or memorial reference: Between entrance and church. Cemetery: Doonbeg Catholic Cemetery, Co. Clare.

KING, PATRICK: Rank: Private. Regiment or service: South Lancashire Regiment. Unit: 2nd Battalion. Age at death: 27. Date of death: 2 February 1915. Service No.: 7330. Died of wounds.

Supplementary information: Born in Kildysart, Co. Clare. Enlisted in Ennis, Co. Clare, Kilmale Co. Clare (*sic*). Son of George and Alice King; husband of Mary Anne King, of Turnpike, Ermis, Co. Clare. In the 1911 census he was living with the Murphy family in Lack, West, Kilmihil and he is listed as a farm servant. In his will, dated 13 August 1914, his personal effects and property were received by: Mrs P. King, Turnpike, Ennis, Co. Clare, Ireland.

Grave or memorial reference: H. 5. Cemetery: Bailleul Communal Cemetery (Nord) in France.

KING, THOMAS CHRISTOPHER: Rank: Private. Regiment or service: Royal Scots Fusiliers. Unit: 6th/7th Battalion. Date of death: 22 July 1917. Age at death: 39. Service No.: 23631. Died of wounds.

Supplementary information: Born in Parsonstown, Ireland. Enlisted in Glasgow while living in Kilrush, Co. Clare. Son of George and Alice King, of No. 7 Black Street, Townhead, Glasgow. Born in Birr, Co. Offaly

Grave or memorial reference: II. F. 21. Cemetery: Mendinghem Military Cemetery in Belgium.

KINSLEY, FRANCIS: Rank: Able Seaman. Regiment or service: Royal Navy. Unit: HMS *Monmouth*. Date of death: 1 November 1914. Age at death: 26. Service No.: 212039.

Supplementary information: On this day HMS *Monmouth* received a 8.2in shell from the SMS *Gneisenau* which almost blew her to pieces. She limped away and later that day was sent to the bottom by SS *Nurnberg*. There were no survivors.

Son of the late Peter and Maria Kinsley, of Coast Guard Station, Seafield, Co. Clare.

Grave or memorial reference: 1. Memorial: Plymouth Naval Memorial, UK.

KINSLEY, MICHAEL: Rank: Corporal. Regiment or service: Royal Munster Fusiliers. Unit: 2nd Battalion. Date of death: 9 May 1915. Service No.: 5572. Killed in action.

Supplementary information: Born in Fothera, Co. Clare. Enlisted in Ennis, Co. Clare while living in Corss Carrigaholt, Co. Clare.

Grave or memorial reference: Panel 43 and 44. Memorial: Le Touret Memorial in France.

L

LAHIFFE, MICHAEL: Rank: Private. Regiment or service: Royal Munster Fusiliers. Unit: A Company. 2nd Battalion. Date of death: 9 May 1915. Age at death: 30. Service No.: 5530. Killed in action.

Supplementary information: Born in Killimer, Co. Clare. Enlisted in Ennis, Co. Clare while living in Tiermaclane, Co. Clare. Son of Patrick and Mary Lahiffe, of Island Avana, Tiermaclane, Ennis, Co. Clare. In his will, dated 8 April 1915, his personal effects and property were received by, Mr Patrick Lahiffe (father), Islandarana, Tuam Clare Post Office, Near Ennis, Co. Clare, Ireland.

Grave or memorial reference: Panel 43 and 44. Memorial: Le Touret Memorial in France.

LARKIN, JAMES: Rank: Private. Regiment or service: Royal Irish Regiment. Unit: 2nd Battalion. Date of death: 24 May 1915. Service No.: 8120. Died of wounds.

Supplementary information: Born in Killaloe, Co. Clare. Enlisted in Wexford while living in Sallystown, Co. Wexford.

From an article in the *Enniscorthy Guardian*:

Private James Larkin, Son of Mr John Larkin, D. C., Sallystown, Murrintown, was the victim of gas poisoning in an engagement near Ypres on 24th of May. He died while being removed to the Base Hospital on the same day. Larkin joined the Royal Irish Regiment about 12 years ago and after service of about seven years, the greater part of which was spent in India, he retired and subsequently emigrated to Australia.

Being still attached to the reserve he was called up at Brisbane on the outbreak of hostilities. He afterwards took part in the New Guinea Campaign and came to Clonmel in January whence he proceeded to the front. At the time he paid a brief visit to his parents at Murrintown. Private Larkin, who was scarcely 29 years old was of fine physical stature. The deepest sympathy is felt for his parents and relatives in their great loss.

Grave or memorial reference: III. B. 6. Cemetery: Vlamertinghe New Military Cemetery in Belgium.

LARKIN, JOHN: Rank: Private. Regiment or service: Australian Infantry, AIF. Unit: 45th Battalion. Date of death: 14 December 1917. Service No.: 3659. Died of tubercular meningitis at Bedford Park Sanatorium, Port Lyttleton.

Supplementary information: Born, Killaloe, Co. Clare. Age on enlistment: 40 . Occupation on enlistment: Carter. Next of kin listed as Mrs Margaret Larkin (wife), of No. 247 Underwood Street, Sydney. He had four children, Michael Patrick, Kathleen Mary, Margaret May and Mary Josephene.

A letter from the wife of Private John Larkin.

Previous Military Experience: 5 years, 2nd Regiment, N.S.W. Date and location of enlistment: 5 April 1917, East Sydney. Height: 5ft 9in. Complexion: Fresh. Eyes: Blue. Hair: Fair/Grey.

The following letter was found with his records:

'Gladstone', 7 Grosvenor Street
Woolahra, Sydney
19/11/19.

Dear Sir.

Am writing to you for a little advice concerning my father. He enlisted in the beginning of 1917. He went away, but only England and took ill, was sent back home but died at Adelaide, the military sent for my stepmother but send me no word I am his daughter, an orphan, my stepmother gets my father's pension and so much for each of her children. Still I have not got anything, not even a badge. Don't you think that I am at least entitled to a badge?. I have to earn my own living. I have no home, my father's second wife has that, but his orphan girl has nothing only what I earn, don't you think that you could get me a badge given to women of Australia. I am only 20 years of age and had to leave my home at 18 to earn my living because my stepmother was never kind to me. My brother died in 1916 at the age of 19 and I have been alone ever since. So dear Sir, would you try to see if you could do anything in my favour so that the military will give me a badge. My fathers name was John Larkin, he enlisted in the infantry.

Signed, Nellie Larkin
A. A. G.
2nd Military District

Referred for favour of attention and reply to writer direct. Formal acknowledgement has been sent.

Grave or memorial reference: Western. 0. 129. (GRM/5★). Cemetery: Adelaide (West Terrace) Cemetery, Adelaide, South Australia.

LEAHY, JOHN: Rank: Private. Regiment or service: Royal Munster Fusiliers. Unit: 1st Battalion. Date of death: 1 May 1915. Age at death: 30. Service No.: 7310. Killed in action in Gallipoli.
Supplementary information: Born in Drumcliffe, Co. Clare. Enlisted in Tralee, Co. Kerry, while living in Corrovorin, Co. Clare. Son of Mrs Hannah Leahy, of Causeway, Ennis, Co. Clare.
Grave or memorial reference: Panel 185 to 190. Memorial: Helles Memorial in Turkey.

LEAHY, WILLIAM: Rank: Private. Regiment or service: Irish Guards. Unit: 1st Battalion. Date of death: 6 November 1914. Service No.: 4155. Killed in action.
Supplementary information: Born in Dysart, Co. Clare. Enlisted in Limerick, Co. Limerick while living in Erinagh, Co. Clare. Son of John Leahy, of Erinagh, Fountain Cross, Ennis, Co. Clare.

Grave or memorial reference: Panel 11. Memorial: Ypres (Menin Gate) Memorial in Belgium.

LEFROY, GERALD: Rank: Second Lieutenant. Regiment or service: Royal Munster Fusiliers. Unit: 5th Battalion, attached to the 2nd Battalion. Date of death: 24 August 1916. Killed in action.
Supplementary information: Born in 1896. Son of Mr J.A.G. Lefroy, Japan and grandson of the late Henry Maunsell Lefroy, of Ferns Hollow, Killaloe. Mentioned in despatches, *London Gazette*, January 1916. Listed in Burke's *Landed Irish Gentry* on p. 434. His grandfather from Ferns Hollow, died in the Yokohama earthquake of 1923.
Grave or memorial reference: Pier and Face 16 C. Memorial: Thiepval Memorial in France.

LEGGATT, EDWARD: Rank: Engine Room Artificer 1st Class (Pensioner). Regiment or service: Royal Navy. Unit: HMS *Good Hope*. Age at death: 44. Date of death: 1 November 1914. Service No.: 159975.
Supplementary information: Edward Leggatt died before the sinking of the *Good Hope*. Son of George and Mary Ann Leggatt, of Kilrush, Co. Clare.
From an article in the *Enniscorthy Guardian*:

The British crusier *Monmouth* was sunk in a naval action in the Pacific Ocean, off the coast of Chili, South America. The crusiers *Good Hope* and *Glasgow* were severely damaged, but apparently escaped with an auxiliary cruiser. A message from Otranto (Italy) says that three German warships are now in Valpariso Bay, Chili. Five more warships and auxiliaries are outside the bay. The *Mounmouth* was an armoured cruiser of 9, 800 tons built at Glasgow at a cost of £979,000. She belonged to what is known as the County Class, and carried a crew of 537 men.

Her armoured belt was 4.2 in of Krupp steel and her 14.6 in guns were protencted by 5.4 in of steel and her secondary guns by 4 in. She was fitted with two torpedo tubes and had a speed of nearly 23 knots. The *Good Hope* is also and armoured cruiser, but much more heavily armoured and armed than that the *Monmouth*. Her belt is 6 in of Krupp steel. And her 9.2in guns are protected by 6.5 in. She also carries 16, 6-inch guns and 15 quickfirers. Her speed is over 23 knots and she has a crew of 900 men. The *Monmouth* was commissioned in July, 1914, under the command of Captain Frank Brandt. The *Good Hope* was commissioned in 1912, and carried the flag of Sir Christopher Cradock, K. C.V. O.

From De Ruvigny's Roll of Honour:

Leggatt, Edward, E. R. A., 1st Class (Pensioner), 159975, HMS, *Good Hope*; lost in action off Coronel, on the coast of Chile, 1 November 1914.

Grave or memorial reference: 3. Memorial: Portsmouth Naval Memorial, UK.

LENANE, JAMES: Rank: Private. Regiment or service: Royal Munster Fusiliers. Unit: 2nd Battalion. Date of death: 2 November 1914. Service No.: 5271. Died of wounds.

Supplementary information: Born in Lisdoonvarna, Co. Clare. Enlisted in Tralee while living in Lisdoonvarna, Co. Clare.

Grave or memorial reference: I.L. 48. Cemetery: Poperinghe Old Military Cemetery Belgium.

LENDRUM, A.C.: Rank: Captain. Regiment or service: Royal Inniskilling Fusiliers. Date of death: 27 October 1920. Age at death: 34.

Supplementary information: Son of George and Netta Lendrum, of Corkill, Kilskeery. He won the Military Cross and bar and is listed in the *London Gazette*. Resident Magistrate in Co. Clare.

From the *Saturday Record*, 9 October 1920:

Missing Clare R. M.'s Fate
The mystery of the fate of Captain A. C. Lendrum, M. C., the West Clare Resident Magistrate, who has been missing since September 22, was solved on Friday morning by the discovery of the dead body at the side of the West Clare Railway near Kilmurry station. There were two bullet wounds on the head, and the remains were contained in a rudely constructed coffin, and were labelled "Kilkee; identified." Indications on the body suggest that it had been in the water, whether a bog hole or the sea is not, of course, known. All the clothing was

gone, and the body was wrapped in a sheet. Written on the coffin, which was found by railway workers, in blue pencil was a statement; "He died for a foreign Hunnish Government, and his body is given up, regardless of threatened reprisals." Military motor lorries conveyed the remains to Kilkee police barrack. Later they were removed, pending the arrival of relatives, to kilrush military barrack. The cortege included the Catholic and Protestant clergy, wimitary, police, and the principal residents.

Captain Lendrum was Resident Magistrate at Kilkee, and left there by his motor alone on September 22nd, to attend petty sessions court, it is said, at Ennistymon. He was attacked on the journey, as news of an ambush reached Kilkee some hours after his departure. As Captain Lendrum did not reach his destination, troops and police made an unavailing search of the district.

Captain Lendrum served with distinction in the late war, and was five times wounded.

An official report issued from Dublin Castle stated that investigations, continued during succeeding days, revealed evidences of an ambush at one point along the road beyond the forge at Caherfeenick. The hedge was loopholed and the grass behind it trampled down. Tracks of a motorcar having been driven on to the grass at the roadside and back were discovered.

It will be remembered that a few days after the Press reported threats of reprisal by burnings unless Captain Lendrum's whereabouts were made known to the police within forty-eight hours. Official steps were at once taken to prevent any such unauthorised acts, but apparently those responsible for the murder thought it best in the circumstances to reveal the truth, and Captain Lendrum's body was placed in a position where it must be discovered.

An inquiry was held at the military barracks, Kilrush, on Friday evening and next morning, and the remains were brought to Ennis on their way for internment in Co. Fermanagh.

This newspaper article predates his death as recorded by the Commonwealth War Graves Commission Database, also, he was not buried in Fermanagh but in Tyrone.

This man is only in the Commonwealth War Graves database. Grave or memorial reference: West of Church. Cemetery: Kilskeery Church of Ireland Churchyard in Co. Tyrone.

LENNANE, FRANK: Rank: Private. Regiment or service: Royal Warwickshire Regiment. Unit: 15th Battalion. Date of death: 4 October 1917. Age at death: 35. Service No.: 32733. Killed in action. Formerly he was with the Dragoons where his number was 6271.

Supplementary information: Born in Clare, Ireland. Enlisted in Aldershot, Hampshire while living in Dublin. Son of the late Patrick and Susan Lennane.

Grave or memorial reference: Panel 3 to 28 and 163A. Memorial: Tyne Cot Memorial in Belgium.

LENNON, THOMAS: Rank: Private. Regiment or service: Connaught Rangers. Unit: 1st Battalion. Date of death: 12 November 1914. Age at death: 20. Service No.: 10135. Killed in action.

Supplementary information: Born in Kilrush, Co. Clare. Enlisted in Ennis, Co. Clare while living in Kilrush, Co. Clare. Son of George Henry and Margaret Lennon, of Boultydoolin, Kildysart, Co. Clare. Native of Ennis, Co. Clare. Son of Margaret Lennon, Burton Street, Kilrush, Co. Clare, Ireland.

Grave or memorial reference: I. A. 11. Cemetery: Rue-du-Bacquerot No. 1 Military Cemetery, Laventie in France.

LERNAN, RONALD: Rank: Private. Regiment or service: Royal Irish Regiment. Unit: 1st Battalion. Date of death: 27 August 1918. Service No.: 5467. Killed in action.

Supplementary information: Born in Newtown Forbes, Co. Longford Enlisted in Liverpool, Lancashire while living in Clonawhite, Co. Clare. In his will, dated 7 May 1915, his personal effects and property were received by Mrs Lernan (mother), Dunbeg, Co. Clare, Ireland.

Grave or memorial reference: IV. E. 20. Cemetery: Mory Abbey Military Cemetery, Mory in France.

LEYDEN/LYDEN, MARTIN: Rank: Lance Corporal. Regiment or service: Royal Irish Regiment. Unit: 2nd

Battalion. Date of death: 19 December 1916. Age at death: 42. Service No.: 5054. Died at home.

Supplementary information: Born in Killuran, Co. Clare. Enlisted in Ennis, Co. Clare while living in O'Callaghan's Mills, Co. Clare. Son of Denis and Bridget Leyden, of Iragh, O'Callaghan's Mills, Co. Clare. Served on the north-west frontier of India 1895 and 1897-8. A repatriated Prisoner of War.

Grave or memorial reference: 501. Cemetery: Whalley (Queen Mary's Hospital) Military Cemetery, Lancashire, UK.

LOFTUS, PETER: Rank: Private. Regiment or service: Royal Munster Fusiliers.
Unit: Y Company, 1st Battalion. Date of death: 19 May 1915. Age at death: 19. Service No.: 9483. Died of wounds in Gallipoli.

Supplementary information: Born in Ennistymon, Co. Clare. Enlisted in Ennis while living in Ennistymon, Co. Clare. Son of W. and Annie Loftus. He was awarded the Distinguished Conduct Medal (DCM).

Grave or memorial reference: H. 94. Cemetery: Alexandria (Chatby) Military and War memorial Cemetery in Egypt.

LOONEY, JAMES: Rank: Private. Regiment or service: Irish Guards. Unit: 1st Battalion. Date of death: 2 June 1918. Age at death: 23. Service No.: 10138. Killed in action.

Supplementary information: Born in Kilmurray, Co. Clare. Enlisted in Dublin while living in Miltown Malbay, Co. Clare. Son of James and Mary J. Looney, of Knockanalban, Miltown Malbay, Co. Clare.

Grave or memorial reference: XIX. C. 8. Cemetery: Bienvillers Military Cemetery in France.

LUCITT, EDWARD: Rank: Private. Regiment or service: Irish Guards. Unit: 1st Battalion. Date of death: 14 September 1914. Age at death: 30. Service No.: 2225. Died of wounds.

Supplementary information: Born in Labasheeda, Co. Clare. Enlisted in Cork while living in Tralee, Co. Kerry. Son of E. Lucitt and Margaret Falvey Lucitt, of No. 3 Bridge Street, Tralee.

Grave or memorial reference: III. 1. Cemetery: Guards Grave, Villers Cotterets Forest in France.

LUCITT, JOHN: Rank: Lance Corporal. Regiment or service: Irish Guards. Unit: 1st Battalion. Date of death: 6 November 1914. Service No.: 3947.

Supplementary information: Born in Labasheeda, Co. Clare. Enlisted in Tralee, Co. Kerry. Killed in action.

Grave or memorial reference: Panel 11. Memorial: Ypres (Menin Gate) Memorial in Belgium.

LYNCH, JAMES: Rank: Private. Regiment or service: Royal Irish Fusiliers. Unit: 7th/8th Battalion. Date of death: 7 June 1917. Age at death: 22. Service No.: 43181. Formerly he was with the Connaught Rangers where his number was 6303.

Supplementary information: Son of Peter and Ellen Lynch, of Feenagh, Sixmilebridge, Co. Clare. Born in Sixmilebridge, Co. Clare. Enlisted in

Limeick while living in Sixmilebridge, Co. Clare. Killed in action.

Grave or memorial reference: Panel 42. Memorial: Ypres (Menin Gate) Memorial in Belgium.

LYNCH, MARTIN: Rank: Private. Regiment or service: Manchester Regiment. Unit: 19th Battalion. Age at death: 21. Date of death: 23 July 1916. Service No.: 26713. Killed in action.

Supplementary information: Born in Miltown Malbay, Co. Clare. Enlisted in Manchester while living in Miltown Malbay, Co. Clare. Son of Thomas Lynch, of Main Street, Milltown Malbay, Co. Clare.

Grave or memorial reference: Pier and Face 13 A and 14 C. Memorial: Thiepval Memorial in France.

LYNCH, MICHAEL: Rank: Private. Regiment or service: Royal Munster Fusiliers. Unit: 1st Battalion. Date of death: 1 May 1915. Service No.: 9548. Killed in action in Gallipoli.

Supplementary information: Born in Kilrush, Co. Clare. Enlisted in Tralee, Co. Kerry while living in Tralee. Also commemorated in the 'List of Kilrush Men engaged in the War from August 1914'. This pamphlet lists the Kilrush men who were involved in the First World War until 11 November 1918.

Grave or memorial reference: Panel 185 to 190. Memorial: Helles Memorial in Turkey.

LYNCH, PATRICK: Rank: Private. Regiment or service: Australian Pioneers Unit: 4th Pioneers. Date of death: 6 August 1916. Age at death: 34. Service No.: 1660.

A letter concerning Private P. Lynch.

Supplementary information: Son of Patrick and Catherine Lynch, of Lisdoonvarna, Clare, Ireland. Born in Kilmoon, Lisdoonvarna, Co. Clare. Occupation on enlistment: Butcher. Age on enlistment: 28 years. Next of kin: Joseph Lynch, The Square, Lisdoonvarna, Co. Clare. Place and date of enlistment: Broadmeadows, Victoria, 21 February 1915. Weight: 13st 5lbs. Height: 6ft. Complexion: Fair. Eyes: Blue. Hair: Brown. Buried north of Becourt Military Cemetery, 1½ miles East of Albert, 2/05-17.

From the *Clare Journal*, August 1916:

Gallant Young Clare Man Killed in action

We hear with much regret of the death at the front of Private. Patrick Lynch, second son of the late Mr Pat Lynch, Lynch's Hotel, Lisdoonvarna, and brother of Mr Joe Lynch. He was attached to the Pioneer Battalion, Australian Infantry brigade. He came from Australia with the first contingent, and took part in the two landings in Gallipoli, at Sedal Bahr, and Suvla, without being wounded.

His brother has received the following notification of his death—

France, 7-8-'16

Dear Sir—It is with very deep regret that I now confirm the death of your brother, Private. P. Lynch, (No. 1660). He was killed on the morning of the 6th August, while returning from duty in the front line of trenches. Death was instantaneous. He will be greatly missed by both officers and men, as he was a general favourite with everyone with whom he came in contact. Again expressing my deepest sympathy.

I am, yours faithfully,

J. B. Calder, Lieutenant.,

D Company, 4th Pioneer Battalion.

From the *Saturday Record* and *Clare Journal*, August 1916 (Obituary):

Death

Lynch—August 6, 1916, Killed in action in France, Patrick Lynch, Pioneer battalion, Australian Infantry Brigade, second son of the late Patrick Lynch, Lynch's Hotel, Lisdoonvarna. Sadly mourned by his children, mother, sisters and brothers. R. I. P.

Grave or memorial reference: Villers-Bretonneux Memorial. Villers-Bretonneux Military Cemetery in France.

LYNCH, THOMAS JOSEPH/ JOHN: Rank: Sapper. Regiment or service: Royal Engineers: Unit: 11th Field Company. Date of death: 16 May 1915. Age at death: 32. Service No.: 13419. Died of wounds.

Supplementary information: Born in Deerpark, Co. Clare. Enlisted in Fermoy, Co. Cork. Son of John and Bridget Lynch (*née* Hickey), of Doora, Quin, Co. Clare.

Grave or memorial reference: Panel 1. Memorial: Le Touret Memorial in France.

LYNCH, THOMAS: Rank: Able Seaman. Regiment or service: Royal Navy. Unit: HMS *Vivid III*. The HMS *Vivid III* was a shore establishment and part of the Naval Base at Devonport. Date of death: 28 June 1917. Age at death: 43. Service No.: 155798.

Supplementary information: (RFR/ Dev/A/4105). Son of Mr E. and Mrs J. Lynch, of Kilcredane, Carrigaholt, Co. Clare; husband of Catherine Lynch, of No. 4 Clifton Terrace, Falmouth.

Grave or memorial reference: K. E. 32. Cemetery: Falmouth Cemetery, Cornwall, UK.

LYONS, PATRICK: Rank: Private. Regiment or service: Royal Munster Fusiliers. Unit: 1st Battalion. Date of death: 3 March 1915. Service No.: 8505. Killed in action in Gallipoli.

Supplementary information: Born in Newmarket-on-Fergus, Co. Clare. Enlisted in Ennis, Co. Clare while living in Newmarket-on-Fergus, Co. Clare.

Grave or memorial reference: Panel 185 to 190. Memorial: Helles Memorial in Turkey.

LYSAGHT, THOMAS: Rank: Lieutenant.

Supplementary information: This man is not in any of the War Dead databases. The only references I can find are the two newspaper articles below and some additional snippets from his family.

Information provided by his family (Cathal McLysaght) show that he went to Rugby College. In November 1914 he mentions, in letters, training with thirty-two other men with the Quakers at Jordan's Camp Beaconsfield. The EE. Lysaght bwlow was his brother, Edward Edgeworth Lysaght. Lieutenant Lysaght died in an accident on 19 December 1914 and was buried 6 Juanuary 1915 in Cimetiere de La Madeleine in Amiens, France.

Brave Kilrush Man

The promotion of a young Clareman for repeated acts of bravery in front of the enemy, is announced. Thomas Lysaght, Corporal, C Battery, Royal Horse Artillery, has been given a Lieutenant's commission in the Royal Field Artillery, No 2 general base reinforcements, British Expeditionary Forces. He is 24 years of age and a native of Kilrush, and the commission dates from 14th December. Lieutenant Lysaght's promotion has given great satisfaction to his friends.

The Late Lieutenant Lysaght, I. N. V.

We have been sent the following correspondence for publication:

I, N, V. Barracks.
Raheen Manor
11th Jan 1915.

Dear Captain Lysaght, --It is with feelings of the greatest sorrow that the officers of the national Volunteers of the National Volunteers Barracks, Raheen manor, have heard of the death of your brother, and I tender on behalf of them and myself our deepest sympathy with you and Mrs Lysaght in your bereavement. Believe me to be

Yours faithfully,

Charles Philips.

Captain I. N.V.

Raheen Manor. Tuamgraney.

Co. Clare.

1st Jan 1915

Dear Captain Philips—Please accept yourself, and express to the members of the officers mess, my gratitude for the kind note of sympathy I have received. I appreciate it very much.

I propose to carry on the camp as usual to-morrow. I hope everything will go on just as usual, my brother having been a keen member of the INV.

I think, perhaps, we might break up the camp on Wednesday instead of Thursday, if the officers and men are satisfied.

Yours very truly.

E. E. Lysaght.

From the *Limerick Leader*, January 1915:

The promotion of a young Clareman for repeated acts of bravery in front of the enemy is announced. Thomas Lysaght, Coproral, C Battery, Royal Horse Artillery, has been given a Lieutenant's commission in the Royal Field Artillery, No 2 General Base Reinforcements, British Expeditionary Forces. He is 24 years of age, and the commission dates from the 14th December. Lieutenant Lysaght's promotion has given great satisfaction to his friends.

M

MACLAURIN/McLAURIN, JOHN HENRY: Rank: Flight Cadet. Regiment or service: Royal Air Force. Unit: 1st TDS. Date of death: 20 September 1918.

Supplementary information: Son of the late Revd R. T. McLaurin. Born in Ennis, Co. Clare. Killed when his aircraft crashed and burst into flames at Wittering Areodrome near Stamford.

From the *Saturday Record*, October 1918:

Death of Flight Cadet MacLaurin
We sincerely regret to hear of the death, as a result of a flying accident, on Sunday, of Flight Cadet J. H. MacLaurin, the only son of Rev. Canon R. T. MacLaurin. The Rectory, Ennistymon. He had not yet reached his nineteenth year, and had not long been in the ranks of the gallant force, which has sent forth so many fine young spirits to offer up the final sacrifice for their country, against a foreign enemy. He was exceedingly popular with all his comrades, who deeply mourn the sudden end to a highly promising career.

The remains were brought to Ennis by the last train on Wednesday night, and the internment took place at Drumcliffe on the next day. There was a special service at the Parish Church, where the remains had lain overnight, and at the close the coffin was bourne from the building to the hearse by a party of the Royal Welsh Fusiliers, of whom about fifty marched in the cortege, under Lieutenants. Llewellyn and Townsend. Major Langford and Lieutenants Ellard and McCall were also present. The chief mourners were the bereaved parents, Canon and Mrs MacClaurin ... After the final prayers at the graveside, the last salute was fired by a party of the Welsh Fusiliers.

From De Ruvigny's Roll of Honour:

... only son of the Revd Robert Twiss MacLaurin, M. A., Rural Dean of Kilfenora, Canon of Killaloe, and rector of Kilmanaheen, Ennistymon, Co. Clare, by his wife, Maud Dolmage, 2nd daughter of the Revd Julius H. Griffith, D. D., Rector of Ennis. Born in Ennis, Co. Clare, 25 November, 1899. Educated at Tipperary Grammar School, and Campbell College, Belfast. Was in the employ of Messrs Hawthare & Leslie, Newcastle-on-Tyne, and while there served in the 1st Volunteer Battalion, Northumberland Fusiliers, 22 July 1917 to 7 January 1918. Joined the R.A.F. as Flight Cadet, 7 January 1918. Trained at Oxford (Brasenose College), Uxbridge and Stamford, obtaining his pilot's Certificate, and was accidentally killed while flying at Wittering Aerodrome, Stamford, 29 September 1918. Buried in Drumcliffe Cemetery, Ennis.

His Flight Commander wrote; "He was a qualified Pilot, and one of the best they had," and his Captain and Adjutant; "I may say I you're your son to be a very promising Pilot, with plenty of courage and sound judgment." Some of his brother officers also wrote; He was thought a great deal of by all who knew him; his loss is a big blow to his flight, as he was a good Pilot and knew no fear."

Grave or memorial reference: The north part of the old ground. Cemetery: Ennis (Drumcliffeo Cemetery) Cemetery, Co. Clare.

MACNAMARA, FRANCIS (FRANK) JOSEPH:

Rank: Sergeant. Regiment or service: King's African Rifles. Unit: 2nd. Date of death: 8 July 1917. Age at death: 25. Service No.: 11565.

Supplementary information: Son of William and Anne Macnamara. Born at Kilrush, Co. Clare, Ireland. Also commemorated in the 'List of Kilrush Men engaged in the War from August 1914'. This pamphlet lists the Kilrush men who were involved in the First World War until 11 November 1918.

Grave or memorial reference: 2. B. 12. Cemetery: Dar Es Salaam War Cemetery in Tanzania.

MACNAMARA, GEORGE:

Rank: Major. Regiment or service: Wiltshire Regiment. Unit: 2nd Battalion. Secondary Regiment: North Staffordshire Regiment Secondary. Unit: Attached to 2nd Battalion. Date of death: 27 May 1917. Age at death: 27. Died of wounds.

Major George Macnamara.

Supplementary information: Son of Henry V. and Elizabeth Edith Macnamara (*née* Cooper), of Ennistymon House, Co. Clare. He was mentioned in Despatches by F. M. Sir Douglas Haig (*London Gazette*, 25 May 1917), for gallant and distinguished service in the field.

From De Ruvigny's Roll of Honour:

Macnamara, George, Major, 2nd Battalion, (99th Foot) The Duke of Edinburgh's (Wiltshire Regiment). Youngest son of Henry Valentine Macnamara, of Doolin, and Ennistymon House, Co. Clare, by his wife, Elizabeth Edith, daughter of Sir Daniel Cooper, K. C. M. G. ; Born in Dublin, 23 May, 1890. Educated in Clifton College, at West Wratting Park, County Cambridge, and at the Royal Military College, Sandhurst. Gazetted 2nd Lieutenant, 5th October 1910. promoted

Lieutenant, 17th April 1913, Captain, 25th February, 1915, and Major, 9th July-1916. Served with the Expeditionary Force in France and Flanders from October 1914, when his regiment was overwhelmed by immensely superior numbers near Ypres on 24th October. As Transport Officer, and, unaccompanied, he bravely attempted to get up to its assistance. He was fired at by ten Germans who occupied an eminence about 300 yards from him, and was eventually wounded, a bullet passing through his body, was invalided home, but though far from recovered in health, took up home duty in Febraury 1915. In June 1916, he was sent out to France and posted to his battalion, which he commanded for over two months. Was subsequently attached to a unit of the North Staffordshire Regiment as Second in Command, and was Killed in action at Hill 70 near Loos, 25 May 1917. Buried in the British Cemetery, Noeux-les-Mines.

The General of the Division wrote; "He met his death at the conclusion of a most successful enterprise carried out by the battalion, and for the success of which he was largely instrumental. I deplore exceedingly the loss of this valuable officer, in whom I had the most complete confidence, and who was loved and respected in his battalion."

Grave or memorial reference: I. L. 22. Cemetery: Noeux-les-Mines Communal Cemetery in France.

MACNAMARA, MACCON JOHN: Rank: Second Lieutenant. Regiment or service: Royal Dublin Fusiliers. Unit: 2nd Battalion. Date of death: 26 March 1918. Age at death: 20. Killed in action

Supplementary information: Son of George Uthank Macnamara and Frances Jane Macnamara, Baunkyle, Corofin.

From the *Saturday Record* and *Clare Journal*, May 1918.

Roll of Honour
Liutenant Macken Macnamara, son of Dr G U Macnamara, Corofin, is, we regret very much to hear, reported missing after the late severe fighting.

Grave or memorial reference: Panel 79 and 80. Memorial: Pozieres Memorial in France.

MACNAMARA, PATRICK FRANCIS: Rank: Private. Regiment or service: Canadian Infantry (Quebec Regiment). Unit: 42nd Battalion. Date of death: 4 March 1919. Service No.: 3080114.

Supplementary information: Son of Mrs MacNamara, of Quarry Road, Thomond Gate, Limerick. Next of kin listed as Mrs Isabel Owens (aunt), No. 114 Sawyer Avenue, Dorchester, Mass, USA. Place of birth: Limerick, Ireland. Date of birth: 20 January 1885. Occupation on enlistment: Male Nurse. Place and date of enlistment: Montreal, 5 October 1917. Address on enlistment: 10 Assasabet Street, Dorchester, Mass, USA. Height: 5ft, 9½in. Complexion: Fair. Eyes: Green. Hair: Dark brown.

Grave or memorial reference: In north-east corner. Cemetery: Kilquane Cemetery, Co. Clare.

MACNAMARA/McNAMARA, WILLIAM: Rank: Private. Regiment or service: Royal Munster Fusiliers. Unit: 8ᵗʰ Battalion. Date of death: 18 June 1916. Service No.: 5716. Killed in action.

Supplementary information: Born in Whitegate, Co. Clare. Enlisted in Tomgraney, Co. Clare while living in Whitegate.

Grave or memorial reference: I.E. 1. Cemetery: St Patrick's Cemetery, Loos in France.

MADIGAN, JOHN: Rank: Private. Regiment or service: Royal Munster Fusiliers. Unit: 2ⁿᵈ Battalion. Date of death: 10 July 1917. Age at death: 24. Service No.: 4596. Killed in action.

Supplementary information: Born in Kilrush, Co. Clare. Enlisted in Ennis, Co. Clare while living in Kilrush, Co. Clare. Son of Michael and Nora Madigan, of Kiltrellig, Kilbaha, Co. Clare.

Grave or memorial reference: I. E. 26. Cemetery: Coxyde Military Cemetery in Belgium.

MAGEE/McGEE, MICHAEL: Rank: Private. Regiment or service: Royal Munster Fusiliers. Unit: 1ˢᵗ Battalion. Date of death: 26 April 1915. Age at death: 36. Service No.: 9792. Killed in action in Gallipoli.

Supplementary information: Born in Ballina, Co. Mayo. Enlisted in Limerick while living in Scarriff, Co. Clare. Son of Micaheal and Johanna McGee, of John's Street, Killaloe, Co. Clare. His personal effects and property were sent to Johanna McGee (mother), Green, Killaloe, Co. Clare, Ireland.

Grave or memorial reference: Panel 185 to 190. Memorial: Helles Memorial in Turkey.

MAHER, MICHAEL: Rank: Private. Regiment or service: Connaught Rangers. Unit: 1ˢᵗ Battalion. Date of death: 11 August 1917. Service No.: 7759 and 7799. Born in Portroe Co. Tipperary. Died of wounds in Mesopotamia.

Supplementary information: Enlisted in Killaloe while living in Killaloe Co. Clare. In his will, dated 20 November 1916, his personal effects and property were received by: Mrs Bridget Maher (mother), of, Townlough, Ballina, Killaloe, Co. Clare. Will witnessed by: J. Tracey CQMS, Military Barracks Kinsale. 2/9644, D McAuliffe, The Connaught Rangers. The Military Barracks, Kinsale.

Also commemorated in the 'List of Kilrush Men engaged in the War from August 1914', Malt House Lane. This pamphlet lists the Kilrush men who were involved in the First World War until 11 November 1918.

He has no known grave but is listed on Panel 40 and 64 on the Basra Memorial in Iraq.

MAHONEY/MAHONY, JOHN: Rank: Private. Regiment or service: Royal Munster Fusiliers. Unit: 2ⁿᵈ Battalion. Date of death: 16 July 1915. Service No.: 5334. Died of wounds.

Supplementary information: Born in Kilrush, Co. Clare. Enlisted in Kilrush while living in Kilrush, Co. Clare. Also commemorated in the 'List of Employees of Messrs. M. Glynn and Sons. Flour and

Meal Millers and Steamship Owners. Kilrush, Co. Clare, who took part in the War, 1914 to 1918. Dated 11 November 1918'. In his will, dated 10 February 1915, his personal effects and property were received by Mrs Mahoney (mother), Crafton Street, Kilrush, Co. Clare, Ireland.

From the *Clare Journal*, 10 August 1916:

Ennis Men Killed
News has been received of the deaths of two Ennis men at the front, Private. McCormack, and Private. John Mahony, of the Munster Fusiliers.

Of the latter Major Laurence Roche, writes to his wife—"It is with greatest possible regret that I have to announce the death of your brave husband, he was killed in action early this morning, and fell side by side with his gallant officer, Lieutenant Fitzpatrick. We buried both today with full military honours. On behalf of officers and men of old D Company, I again tender to you our very deep sympathy. We have lost a brave and gallant soldier, and we shall miss him very much."

Grave or memorial reference: IV. D. 12. Cemetery: Bethune Town Cemetery in France.

MAHONEY, MYLES: Rank: Chief Petty Officer (CG). Regiment or service: Royal Navy. Unit: HM Coastguard Station, Seafield near Sunderland, UK. Date of death: 23 May 1916.
Supplementary information: Husband of Annie Mahoney, of No. 36 Appach Road, Brixton Hill, London.

Grave or memorial reference: New Ground. 1. 1. 9. Cemetery: Kildeema Burial Ground, Co. Clare.

MAHONEY, PATRICK: Rank: Lance Corporal. Regiment or service: Canadian Infantry (Quebec Regiment). Unit: 14th Battalion. Date of death: 9 April 1917. Age at death: 27. Service No.: 448723.
Supplementary information: Son of the late Thomas Mahoney; husband of Minnie M. Mahoney, of Manor Farm, Brandon, Suffolk, England. Next of kin listed as his wife Minnie Mary Mahoney of No. 5 Artillery Street, Quebec. Place of birth: Kilrush, Co. Clare. Date of birth: 13 March 1890. Occupation on enlistment: Labourer. Date of enlistment: 27 October 1915. Height 5ft 4in. Complexion: Fair. Eyes: Blue-grey. Hair: Brown. Also commemorated in the 'List of Kilrush Men engaged in the War from August 1914'. This pamphlet lists the Kilrush men who were involved in the First World War until 11 November 1918.

Grave or memorial reference: VI. C. 15. Cemetery: Ecoivres Military Cemetery Mont-Street Eloi in France.

MAHONY, JOHN: Rank: Private. Regiment or service: Royal Munster Fusiliers. Unit: 8th Battalion. Date of death: 29 July 1916. Service No.: 3761. Killed in action.
Supplementary information: Born in Drumcliffe, Co. Clare. Enlisted in Limerick while living in Ennis, Co. Clare. His personal effects and property were sent to Mrs J O'Mahoney (wife), of Old Mill Street, Ennis, Co. Clare, Ireland. Also commemorated in the 'List of Kilrush Men engaged in the War from

August 1914'. This pamphlet lists the Kilrush men who were involved in the First World War until 11 November 1918.

From the *Clare Journal*, November 1916:

Honouring Memory of Ennis Soldier

Major General W.B. Hickie, Comanding the 16th Irish Division, has caused the following to be issued in reference to the late Pte J Mahony, Ennis, 8th Royal Munsters, who was, sad to say, killed soon after its receipt – "I have read with much pleasure the reports of your regimental Commander and Brigade Commander, regarding your gallant conduct and devotion to duty in the field in July 28th, 1916, and have ordered your name and deed so be entered in the record of the Irish Division."

From the *Clare Journal*, August 1916:

Comrade's Tribute to Dead Ennis Soldier

Following the letter of Major L Roche, R. M. F., announcing the death of Pte John Mahony, of Old Mill Street, which we published last week, comes another tribute from a comrade soldier, Pte Martin Woods, now wounded in hospital in Essex, says—"I cannot believe about John Mahony, for I am looking at the papers every day, and I cannot see anyone's names from the town, either killed or wounded, so I hope it is not true about him, for he did a good turn to me the night I was wounded, and I should never forget it for him—he came over a mile with me along a narrow trench, and I on his back, and he never left me till he saw me alright and dressed."

Grave or memorial reference: I. C. 12. Cemetery: Mazingarbe Communal Cemetery Extension in France.

MALONEY / MOLONEY, CORNELIUS: Rank: Corporal. Regiment or service: Leinster Regiment. Unit: 2nd Battalion. Date of death: 14 March 1915. Age at death: 32. Service No.: 3592. Killed in action.

Supplementary information: Born in Feakle, Co. Clare. Enlisted in Ennis, Co. Clare. Son of Pat and Kate Moloney, of Carheen, Flagmount, Co. Clare.

Grave or memorial reference: A. 21. Cemetery: Ferme Buterne Military Cemetery, Houplines in France.

MALONEY / MOLONEY, MICHAEL: Rank: Private. Regiment or service: Royal Munster Fusiliers. Unit: 5th Battalion. Date of death: 13 August 1914. Age at death: 18. Service No.: 5889. Died at home.

Supplementary information: Born in O'Brien's Bridge, Co. Clare. Enlisted in Limerick while living in O'Brien's Bridge, Co. Clare. Son of M. Maloney, of Fairyhall, Montpelier, O'Brien's Bridge, Limerick. Alternative Commemoration – buried in Cork Military Cemetery.

Grave or memorial reference: Cemetery: Special Memorial, Grangegorman (Cork) Memorial Headstones.

MALONEY, THOMAS: *see* **MOLONEY, TOM / THOMAS.**

MANNING, PATRICK: Rank: Driver. Regiment or service: Royal Field Artillery. Unit: 76th Battery. Date of death: 10 September 1916. Age at death: 25. Service No.: 53082. Died in Turkey.

Supplementary information: Born in Kilrush, Co. Clare. Enlisted in Kilrush, Co. Clare. Son of Patrick and Maria Manning, of No. 9 Pound Street, Kilrush, Co. Clare. Also commemorated in the 'List of Kilrush Men engaged in the War from August 1914'. This pamphlet lists the Kilrush men who were involved in the First World War until 11 November 1918. It says Manning, P.J., R.F.A., prisoner in Turkish hands. Patrick also appears in the list of wounded in the *Clare Journal* June, 1916.

Grave or memorial reference: XXI. E. 16. Cemetery: Baghdad (North Gate) War Cemetery in Iraq.

MANNIX, PATRICK: Rank: Trooper. Regiment or service: Auckland Mounted Rifles, NZEF. Date of death: 5 November 1917. Age at death: 40. Service No.: 36118. Killed in action in Palestine.

Supplementary information: Son of Mary O'Grady (*née* Mannix), of Ballyvaughan, Co. Clare, and the late Michael Mannix. Occupation on enlistment: Miner. Next of kin: Michael Mannix (father), Queensland, Australia. Embarked with the 25th Reinforcements, Mounted Rifles. New Zealand Expeditionary Force on 31 May 1917 in Wellington, New Zealand aboard the *Moeraki* bound for Suez, Egypt.

Grave or memorial reference: A. 21. Cemetery: Beersheba War Cemetery in Israel.

MARKHAM, THOMAS: Rank: Private. Regiment or service: Royal Munster Fusiliers. Unit: 2nd Battalion. Date of death: 21 March 1918. Age at death: 25. Service No.: 7020. Killed in action.

Supplementary information: Born in Meelick, Co. Clare. Enlisted in Limerick while living in Meelick, Co. Clare. Son of Michael and Catherine Markham, of Meelick, Cratloe, Co. Clare.

Grave or memorial reference: Panel 78 and 79. Memorial: Pozieres Memorial in France.

MARTIN, HARRY: Rank: Private. Regiment or service: Suffolk Regiment. Unit: 5th Battalion. Date of death: 21 August 1915. Service No.: 1346. Killed in action in Gallipoli

Supplementary information: Born in Clare. Enlisted in Clare – I am unsure if this is Co. Clare or some other Clare. Rather than pass it by I include it for your reference.

Grave or memorial reference: Panel 46 and 47. Memorial: Helles Memorial in Turkey.

MAUNSELL, GEORGE WYNDHAM: Rank: Second Lieutenant. Regiment or service: Indian Army Reserve of Officers. Unit: Attached to 2nd Queen Victoria's Own Sappers and Miners. Date of death: 23 February 1917. Age at death: 28.

Supplementary information: Son of Richard and Elizabeth Maunsell, of Islandmore, St Kevin's Park, Dartry, Dublin.

From De Ruvigny's Roll of Honour:

Maunsell, George Wyndham, 2nd Lieutenant, 2nd Queen Victoria's

Own Sappers and Miners, Indian Army. Eldest son of Richard Maunsell, of the Island, Clarecastle, Co. Clare by his wife, Elizabeth, daughter of the Reverend John Twamley, of Timolin Rectory, Co. Kildare. Born, The Island, Clarecastle, 20 October, 1889. Educated, Grammer School, The Abbey, Tipperary, and Trinity College, Dublin, where he graduated B.A. in October, 1911. Was a Civil Engineer, and in October 1913, went to India to take up an appointment under the Public Works department. Was gazetted 2nd Lieutenant, Queen Victoria's Own Sappers and Miners in September 1916. Served with the Indian Expeditionary Force in Mesopotamia from December 1916 and was Killed in action at the Shamran Bend on the River Tigris 23 Febraury 1917, and buried there.

His Commanding Officer, major Pemberton, wrote; "Your son was killed on the morning of 23 February whilst working with my company of Sappers on the crossing of the Tigris River at Shamran bend. We were working the centre of three ferries under very heavy shell and machine-gun fire. Your son was out on the exposed beach with the men, and with my other subalterns, organising the Sapper rowing parties embarking men of the 9th Gurkhas in the pontoons doing splendid work, when he was hit through the heart and died instantly. I was near by at the time and can testify to this. He was buried, together with officers and men of the British regiments who also gave their lives

that memorable day, close to the site of the srossing. Previous to this he had done most gallant service with my company since joining in December-1916. For all the assistance he gave me I wish to thank you. He reconnoitred the crossing and led the column out during the night of 22 February. He was a first-class soldier. He always carried out my orders to the minutest detail and wit perfect satisfaction. He gave his life on a day which will always be remembered as one of the most successful during the campaign."

From the *Clare Journal*, March 1917:

Death of Clare Officer
We deeply regret to notice by the list of casualties the death in action at Kut, Mesopotamia, of second lieutenant George Wyndham Maunsell, of the Indian Reserve of Officers, the only surviving son of Mr Richard and Mrs Maunsell, of island McGrath, Clarecastle. This gallant young officer, who was only 28 years, was a graduate B.A. of T. C.D., and was afterwards Executive Engineer, P.W.D., India. There is very deep and sincere sympathy with his parents on the death of this fine young officer.

From the *Clare Journal*, March 1917:

The Death of 2nd Lieutenant
George Wyndham Maunsell
We briefly noticed in our last issue, with deepest regret, the death of 2nd Lieutenant G.W. Maunsell. He was the eldest and only surviv-

ing son of Richard Maunsell, The Island, Clarecastle. The following telegram from the War Office has been received;-

"Deeply regret to state your son Second Lieutenant G. W. Maunsell, Indian Army Reserve, attached 12th Company, 2nd Sappers and Miners, officially reported from Persian Gulf Killed in action on February 23 Road"

Lieutenant Maunsell was educated at The Abbey School, Tipperary. He took his Degree B. A. I, T. C. D., in October, 1911. He was appointed an Executive Engineer, Public Works Dept, India, in October, 1913. In 1914 he volunteered for active service, and obtained his commission in 1916. After training he was sent to Mesopotamia, where he was killed in action on the Tigris. With reference to his death, Mr Chamberlain wired—"I desire to express sincere sympathy with you in the death of this gallant officer—
Signed Military Sec., India. "

Lieutenant Maunsell was well known in this county, and universally popular wherever he went. The greatest sympathy is felt for his bereaved family by all classes in the community. His short life of 28 years has ended, but he died nobly in the cause of his King and country, and is now numbered with that glorious army who "counted not their lives dear unto them."

From the *Carlow Sentinel*, March 1917:

2nd Lieutenant George Wyndham Mansell

The sad intelligence has been received that this young officer, 12th Company, Queen Victoria's Own Sappers and Miners, Indian Army Reserve, was killed in action on the Tigris on February 23rd last aged 28 years. He was eldest and only surviving son of R. Mansell, Esq. The Island, Clarecastle, and cousin of Reverend J. R. Kellett, B.A, Carlow. He was educated at the Abbey School, Tipperary. Obtained his degree B.A. I. T.C.D., October, 1911. Was appointed to the position of Executive Engineer, Public Works Department, India, October 1913. Volunteered for Active Service 1914, obtained his Commission 1916, and after training was drafted to Mesopotamia.

Grave or memorial reference: He has no known grave but is listed on Panel 43 and 65 of the Basra memorial in Iraq.

McAULEY, JOHN. Rank: Private. Regiment or service: Royal Munster Fusiliers. Unit: 6th Battalion. Date of death: 3 October 1916. Service No.: 6347. Killed in action in Greek Macedonia.

Supplementary information: Born in Drumbiggle, Co. Clare. Enlisted in Ennis while living in Ennis.

Grave or memorial reference: III. D. 7. Cemetery: Struma Military Cemetery in Greece.

McAULIFFE, The Reverend, CORNELIUS: Also know as Fr Raphael, OFM. Rank: Chaplain/Reverend/Franciscan Friar. Regiment or service:

Army Chaplains Department. Date of death: 6 October 1916. Died of wounds.

From the *Saturday Record* and *Clare Journal*, October 1916:

Death of Army Chapalin

The death is announced from wounds, in his 30th year, of Rev Father Raphael, O. F. M. Abbeyfeale. Deceased, who was ordained in Rome six years ago, was nephew of three well known and highly respected priests of the same Order, the Late C. Begley, Father Peter Begley, O. F. M. of Ennis, and Rev. J Begley. After his instination [?] he was stationed in Athlone, and later in Cork and Limerick. He volunteered as Army Chaplain, and ministered at different periods in Egypt, Salonika and France. He died on his way home from France, and the remains reached Limerick on Wednesday, and were received with military honours.

Grave or memorial reference: 30861. Cemetery: Limerick (St Lawrence's) Catholic Cemetery, Limerick.

McCANN, JOHN: *see* **GALLAGHER, JOHN.**

McCARTHY, JOHN: Rank: Lance Corporal. Regiment or service: Royal Munster Fusiliers. Unit: 2nd Battalion. Date of death: 9 May 1915. Service No.: 6596. Killed in action.

Supplementary information: Born in Drumcliffe, Co. Clare. Enlisted in Ennis while living in Ennis.

Grave or memorial reference: Panel 43 and 44. Memorial: Le Touret Memorial in France.

McCARTHY, JOSEPH: Rank: Private. Regiment or service: Leinster Regiment. Unit: 1st Battalion. Date of death: 21 April 1915. Service No.: 4195. Killed in action.

Supplementary information: Born in Clare, Co. Clare. Enlisted in Nenagh Co. Tipperary while living in Nenagh.

He has no known grave but is listed on Panel 44 on the Ypres (Menin Gate) Memorial in Belgium.

McCARTHY, MICHAEL: Rank: Private. Regiment or service: Royal Munster Fusiliers. Unit: 2nd Battalion. Date of death: 21 December 1914. Age at death: 25. Service No.: 5360. Killed in action.

Supplementary information: Born in Kilrush, Co. Clare. Enlisted in Ennis, Co. Clare while living in Kilrush, Co. Clare. Son of John and Bridget McCarthy, of Grace Street, Kilrush, Co. Clare. Also commemorated in the 'List of Kilrush Men engaged in the War from August 1914'. This pamphlet lists the Kilrush men who were involved in the First World War until 11 November 1918.

Grave or memorial reference: Panel 43 and 44. Memorial: Le Touret Memorial in France.

McCLINTOCK, RICHARD: Rank: Private. Regiment or service: Highland Light Infantry. Unit: 2nd Battalion. Date of death: 14 July 1920. Age at death: 20. Service No.: 76512.

Supplementary information: Son of William and Agnes McClintock, of Greenock.

Grave or memorial reference: In south-east corner. Cemetery: Kilrush (Shanakyle) Cemetery, Co. Clare.

McCONVILLE, PETER REGINALD: Rank: Rifleman. Regiment or service: New Zealand Rifle Brigade Unit: A Company. 3rd Battalion. Date of death: 18 June 1917. Age at death: 25. Service No.: 20202. Died of wounds.

Supplementary information: Son of Ellen and Michael McConville, of Co. Clare, Ireland. Next of kin listed as Mrs E. McConville (mother), of No. 61 O'Neill Street, Ponsonby, Auckland, New Zealand. Occupation on enlistment: Accountant. Address on enlistment: Ponsonby. Embarked with the 10th Reinforcements Wellington Infantry Battalion, B Company of the New Zealand Rifle Brigade on 19 August 1916 in Wellington, New Zealand; aboard the *Aparima* bound for Devonport, England.

Grave or memorial reference: A. 17B. Cemetery: Bois Guillaume Communal Cemetery Extension France.

McCORMACK, ALFRED: Rank: Stoker 1st Class. Regiment or service: Royal Navy. Unit: HMS/M. E-36. Date of death: 19 Jaunuary 1917. Age at death: 28. Service No.: 231071

Supplementary information: Born on 5 April 1888 in Limerick. Son of James and Margaret McCormack, of Fairy Hall, O'Brien's Bridge, Co. Clare. The E-36 was a British submarine on patrol in the North Sea. She left Harwick to patrol around Terschelling and was struck by another British submarine, E-43. After it sank nothing of the Submarine or her crew was ever heard of again. The wreck was never located.

Grave or memorial reference: 22. Memorial: Plymouth Naval Memorial, UK.

McCORMACK, CHRISTOPHER: Rank: Driver. Regiment or service: Royal Horse Artillery and Royal Field Artillery. Unit: 19th Division Ammunition Col. Date of death: 23 July 1916. Service No.: 100572. Died of wounds.

Supplementary information: Born in Ennis, Co. Clare. Enlisted in Ennis.

From the *Clare Journal*, 10 August 1916:

Ennis Men Killed
News has been received of the deaths of two Ennis men at the front, Private McCormack, and Private John Mahony, of the Munster Fusiliers.

Of the latter Major Laurence Roche, writes to his wife—"It is with greatest possible regret that I have to announce the death of your brave husband, he was killed in action early this morning, and fell side by side with his gallant officer, Lieutenant Fitzpatrick. We buried both today with full military honours. On behalf of officers and men of old D Company, I again tender to you our very deep sympathy. We have lost a brave and gallant soldier, and we shall miss him very much."

Grave or memorial reference: II. B. 64. Cemetery: Heilly Station Cemetery, Mericourt-L'Abbe in France.

McCORMACK, PATRICK: Rank: Private. Regiment or service: Connaught Rangers. Unit: 1st Battalion. Date of death: 19 June 1915. Service No.: 10755. Killed in action.

Supplementary information: Born in Ennis, Co. Clare. Enlisted in Ennis while living in Ennis.

Grave or memorial reference: Panel 43. Memorial: Le Touret Memorial in France.

McCREADY, WILLIAM: Rank: Master. Regiment or service: Mercantile Marine. Unit: *Keeper*. Date of death: 20 June 1917. Age at death: 31.

Supplementary information: Son of James and Catherine McCready, of Glenarm, Co. Antrim; husband of Delia Murphy McCready, of Clarecastle, Co. Clare. SS *Keeper* was built in 1906 and owned by J. Bannatyne & Sons Ltd, Limerick. She was torpedoed and sunk possibly by German submarine UC-66 during a voyage from Belfast to Limerick. Twelve seamen were lost including four Clare men; **CONSIDINE, ARTHUR**; **COLE, RICHARD**; **McCREADY, WILLIAM** and **McMAHON J**.

Grave or memorial reference: Tower Hill Memorial, UK.

McDONAGH, MICHAEL: Rank: Private. Regiment or service: Royal Irish Fusiliers. Unit: 1st Garrison Battalion. Date of death: 21 September 1918. Service No.: 28279, and G/28279. Formerly he was with the Royal Dublin Fusiliers where his number was 26134. Died in India.

Supplementary information: Born in Clare, Co. Clare. Enlisted in Naas while living in Dublin.

Grave or memorial reference: Cemetery: Taukkyan War Memorial in Burma.

McDONALD, JAMES: Rank: Private. Regiment or service: Royal Irish Regiment. Unit: 2nd Battalion. Date of death: 25 May 1915. Age at death: 35. Service No.: 8189. Died of wounds.

Supplementary information: Born in Kilrush, Co. Wexford Ireland's Memorial Records states that he was born in Kilrush, Co. Clare. Enlisted in Wexford while living in Ferrybank, Co. Kilkenny. Husband of Mary Anne McDonald of Glasshouse, Ferrybank, Waterford.

Grave or memorial reference: I. F. 75. Cemetery: Bailleul Communal Cemetery Extension (Nord) in France.

McDONALD, MICHAEL: Rank: Private. Regiment or service: Royal Irish Regiment. Unit: 2nd Battalion. Date of death: 24 May 1915. Service No.: 7015. Killed in action.

Supplementary information: Born in Drumcliffe, Co. Clare. Enlisted in Ennis while living in Kilmaley.

Grave or memorial reference: Panel 33. Memorial: Ypres (Menin Gate) Memorial in Belgium.

McDONNELL, JOHN: Rank: Private. Regiment or service: Royal Munster Fusiliers. Unit: 8th Battalion. Date of death: 14 October 1916. Service No.: 4337. Died of wounds at home.

Supplementary information: Born in Kilrush, Co. Clare. Enlisted in Kilrush while living in Kilrush, Co. Clare. Also commemorated in the 'List of Kilrush Men engaged in the War from August 1914'. This pamphlet lists the Kilrush men who were involved in the First World War until 11 November 1918.

From the *Clare Journal*, October 1916:

Gallant Kilrush Man Dies in Hospital

There has just been laid to rest in the Cemetery of Kilrush, a son of the old town who was one of the bravest of the gallant Munsters, who have brought such lustre on the old flag of Ireland. This was Private John McDonnell, who was one of the Irish Brigade, and had taken part in over twelve months strenuous fighting against the Huns. Among the actions in which he took part in France and Flanders were Festubery, Neuve Chapelle, Le Bassee, lens, Loos, Guinchey, Richburg, Vimy, Hulluch, Vermeilles, the Brickfields, Ypres, Arras and Contelmaison; and Guillemont, Ginchy, Combles and Espinal, in the big battles of the Somme. He was wounded in the latter battle, and died of his wounds in Cardiff Hospital. The gallant young Munster leaves a wife and child, also a mother and sisters. The remains were brought by his friends to his native place, and laid lovingly to rest by the Shannon's shore, which he loved so well.

Grave or memorial reference: Near the north-east corner of the Chapel. Cemetery: Kilrush Church of Ireland Churchyard, Co. Clare.

McEVOY, MICHAEL: Rank: Private. Regiment or service: Army Service Corps. Unit: 596th Mechanical Transport Company. Date of death: 4 July 1916. Age at death: 18. Service No.: DM2/162831. Died in Mesopotamia.
Supplementary information: Born in Killaloe, Co. Clare. Enlisted in Nenagh while living in Killaloe, Co. Clare. Son of Mrs J. McEvoy, of Canal Bank, Killaloe, Co. Clare.

Grave or memorial reference: V. Q. 10. Cemetery: Basra War Cemetery in Iraq.

McGANN, THOMAS: Rank: Private. Regiment or service: Irish Guards. Unit: 1st Battalion. Date of death: 6 November 1914. Age at death: 30. Service No.: 3356. Killed in action.
Supplementary information: Born in Ennistymon, Co. Clare. Enlisted in Ennis Co. Clare. Son of Patrick and Jane McGann.

Grave or memorial reference: Panel 11. Memorial: Ypres (Menin Gate) Memorial in Belgium

McGEE, MICHAEL: *see* **MAGEE MICHAEL.**

McGEE, PATRICK: Rank: Private. Regiment or service: Royal Munster Fusiliers. Unit: 9th Battalion. Date of death: 28 April 1916. Service No.: 4435. Killed in action.
Supplementary information: Born in Killaloe, Co. Clare. Enlisted in Limerick while living in Killaloe, Co. Clare.

Grave or memorial reference: II. F. 20. Cemetery: Dud Corner Cemetery, Loos in France.

McGRATH, JOHN: Rank: Private. Regiment or service: Royal Munster Fusiliers. Unit: 2nd Battalion. Date of death: 9 May 1915. Service No.: 5788. Killed in action.
Supplementary information: Born in Kilrush, Co. Clare. Enlisted in Ennis while living in Kilrush, Co. Clare. Also commemorated in the 'List of Kilrush

Men engaged in the War from August 1914'. This pamphlet lists the Kilrush men who were involved in the First World War until 11 November 1918. Also commemorated in the 'List of Employees of Messrs. M. Glynn and Sons. Flour and Meal Millers and Steamship Owners. Kilrush, Co. Clare, who took part in the War, 1914 to 1918. Dated 11 November 1918.'

Grave or memorial reference: XXIX. B. 24. Cemetery: Cabaret-Rouge British Cemetery, Souchez in France.

McGRATH, MARTIN: Listed in Ireland's Memorial Records as McGRATH, PATRICK. Rank: Private. Regiment or service: Royal Irish Regiment. Unit: 5th Battalion. Date of death: 17 August 1915. Service No.: 3435. Died of wounds at Sea.

Supplementary information: Born in Kilrush, Co. Clare. Enlisted in Ennis while living in Kilrush, Co. Clare.

Grave or memorial reference: Panel 55. Memorial: Helles Memorial in Turkey.

McGRATH, MARTIN: Rank: Private. Regiment or service: Royal Munster Fusiliers. Date of death: 15 September 1916. Age at death: 24. Service No.: 5/6372 and 6372. Died of wounds at home.

Supplementary information: Born in Kilrush, Co. Clare. Enlisted in Limerick while living in Kilrush, Co. Clare. Son of Martin McGrath, of Pella Road, Kilrush, Co. Clare. Also commemorated in the 'List of Kilrush Men engaged in the War from August 1914'. This pamphlet lists the Kilrush men who were involved in the First World War until 11 November 1918.

Grave or memorial reference: R. C. 887. Cemetery: Netley Military Cemetery, Hampshire, UK.

McGREEN, PATRICK: Rank: Private. Regiment or service: Royal Munster Fusiliers. Unit: 8th Battalion. Date of death: 30 June 1916. Service No.: 4375. Died of wounds.

Supplementary information: Born in Kilkee, Co. Clare. Enlisted in Limerick while living in Kilkee, Co. Clare. Patrick also appears in the list of wounded in the *Clare Journal*, June 1916 where he is listed under McGrinn.

Grave or memorial reference: V. F. 11. Cemetery: Bethune Town Cemetery in France.

McILROY, H.: Rank: Private. Regiment or service: Highland Light Infantry. Unit: 2nd Battalion. Date of death: 14 July 1920. Service No.: 74786.

Supplementary information: One of four British soldiers drowned at Carrigaholt on that day.

Grave or memorial reference: In South-East corner. Cemetery: Kilrush (Shanakyle) Cemetery, Co. Clare.

McINERNEY, JOHN: Rank: Private. Regiment or service: Royal Munster Fusiliers. Unit: 2nd Battalion. Date of death: 10 November 1917. Age at death: 21. Service No.: 5899. Killed in action.

Supplementary information: Born in Killaloe, Co. Clare. Enlisted in Killaloe, Co. Clare while living in Killaloe, Co. Clare. Son of Annie McInerney, of John Street, Killaloe, Co. Clare, and Michael McInerney.

Grave or memorial reference: Panel 143 to 144. Memorial: Tyne Cot Memorial in Belgium.

McINERNEY, MARTIN: Rank: Driver. Regiment or service: Royal Field Artillery. Unit: 1st Reserve Brigade. Date of death: 22 December 1916. Age at death: 51. Service No.: 89623. Killed in action.

Supplementary information: Born in Kilmurrysbricken, Co. Clare. Enlisted in Ennis. Son of Martin and Mary McInerney (*née* Stack); husband of Catherine McInerney, of Quilty West, Co. Clare.

Grave or memorial reference: W. U. 452. Cemetery: Newcastle-Upon-Tyne (St Andrews and Jesmond) Cemetery, UK.

McINERNEY, MICHAEL: Rank: Private. Regiment or service: Royal Munster Fusiliers. Unit: 2nd Battalion. Date of death: 22 March 1918. Age at death: 22. Service No.: 6456. Died of wounds.

Supplementary information: Born in Meelick, Co. Limerick. Enlisted in Limerick while living in Meelick. Son of Timothy and Annie McInerney (*née* Garry), of Derramore, Meelick, Co. Clare.

Grave or memorial reference: Panel 78 and 79. Memorial: Pozieres Memorial in France.

McINERNEY, PATRICK: Rank: Private. Regiment or service: Irish Guards. Unit: 1st Battalion. Date of death: 15 April 1916. Age at death: 21. Service No.: 4078. Killed in action.

Supplementary information: Born in Meelick, Co. Limerick. Enlisted in

Limerick while living in Derrymeelick, Co. Clare. Son of Timothy McInerney, of Derrymore, Meelick, Limerick.

Grave or memorial reference: XX. K. 8. Cemetery: Hooge Crater Cemetery Zillebeke, Belgium.

McINERNEY, THOMAS: Rank: Private. Regiment or service: Leinster Regiment. Unit: 2nd Battalion. Date of death: 16 May 1915. Service No.: 8719. Killed in action

Supplementary information: Born in Arklow, Co. Wicklow. Enlisted in Sheffield. Son of Mrs M. McInerney, of Killwran, Broadford, Co. Clare.

Grave or memorial reference: C. 10. Cemetery: Ferme Buterne Military Cemetery in France.

McKEOGH, J.: Rank: Second Lieutenant. Regiment or service: Unknown.

From the *Saturday Record* and *Clare Journal*, May 1918:

> Roll of Honour
> Second Lieut. J McKeogh, son of
> the late Dr McKeogh, Killaloe, has,
> we regret t hear, died of wounds.

This man is not in any of the databases. The only reference to him is in the snippet above.

McKIERNAN, MICHAEL VINCENT: Rank: Second Lieutenant. Regiment or service: Connaught Rangers. Unit: 6th Battalion. Date of death: 11 May 1918. Age at death: 22. Died of wounds.

Supplementary information: He won the Military Medal and bar and is listed in the *London Gazette*. He won the Military Medal and not the Military Cross. This would indicate that he rose through the ranks as the Military Medal is not issued to officers.

Son of James and Anna Maria McKiernan, of Clooney, Quin, Co. Clare. Native of Moycullen, Co. Galway.

Grave or memorial reference: Officers, B. 7. 3. Cemetery: Street Sever Cemetery, Rouen in France.

McKNIGHT, STEPHEN: Rank: Private. Regiment or service: Royal Munster Fusiliers. Unit: 1st Battalion. Date of death: 22 March 1918. Service No.: 3622. Killed in action.

Supplementary information: He won the Military Medal and is listed in the *London Gazette*. Also awarded two Parchment certificates. Born in Kilrush, Co. Clare. Enlisted in Limerick while living in Kilrush, Co. Clare. Son of Patrick and Ellen McKnight, of Hector Street, Kilrush, Co. Clare. Also commemorated in the 'List of Kilrush Men engaged in the War from August 1914'. This pamphlet lists the Kilrush men who were involved in the First World War until 11 November 1918.

Grave or memorial reference: Panel 78 and 79. Memorial: Pozieres Memorial in France.

McKNIGHT, THOMAS: Rank: Sergeant. Regiment or service: Irish Guards. Unit: 2nd Battalion. Date of death: 13 September 1916. Service No.: 3198. Killed in action.

Supplementary information: Born in Mullough, Co. Clare. Enlisted in Cork, Co. Cork while living in Moylesky, Co. Clare.

Grave or memorial reference: Pier and Face 7 D. Memorial: Thiepval Memorial in France.

McLAURIN, JOHN HENRY: *see* **MACLAURIN, JOHN HENRY.**

McMAHON, AGNES: Rank: Worker. Regiment or service: Royal Munster Fusiliers. Unit: Attached to the Officer's Cadet School, Kildare. Date of death: 27 October 1918. Age at death: 22. Service No.: 18691.

Supplementary information: Born in Sixmilebridge, Co. Clare. Daughter of Mrs Mary McMahon, of No. 14 Prospect, Rossbrien, Limerick.

Grave or memorial reference: 32180. Cemetery: Limerick (St Lawrence's) Catholic Cemetery, Limerick.

McMAHON, CHARLES: Rank: Private. Regiment or service: Royal Munster Fusiliers. Unit: 2nd Battalion. Date of death: 9 May 1915. Service No.: 5879. Killed in action.

Supplementary information: Born in Kilrush, Co. Clare. Enlisted in Kilrush while living in Kilrush. Also commemorated in the 'List of Kilrush Men engaged in the War from August 1914', Malt House Lane. This pamphlet lists the Kilrush men who were involved in the First World War until 11 November 1918.

Grave or memorial reference: Panel 43 and 44. Memorial: Le Touret Memorial in France.

McMAHON, CHRISTOPHER: Rank: Private. Regiment or service: Royal Irish Fusiliers. Unit: 5th Battalion. Date of death: 16 August 1918. Service No.: 16182. Killed in action.

Supplementary information: Born in Ennis, Co. Clare. Enlisted in Salford, Manchester while living in Dublin.

Grave or memorial reference: Panel 178 to 180. Memorial: Helles Memorial in Turkey.

McMAHON FREDERICK: Rank: Private. Regiment or service: Royal Dublin Fusiliers. Unit: 1st Battalion. Date of death: 22 October 1916. Age at death: 38. Service No.: 43088. Died of wounds.

Supplementary information: Born in Drumeliffe (*sic*), Co. Clare. Enlisted in Ennis, Co. Clare. Formerly he was with the Royal Munster Fusiliers where his number was 6724. Husband of Mary McMahon, of Lifford, Ennis, Co. Clare.

Grave or memorial reference: V. C. 7. Cemetery: Heilly Station Cemetery, Mericourt-L'Abbe in France.

McMAHON J.: Rank: Fireman. Regiment or service: Mercantile Marine. Unit: SS *Keeper* (Limerick). Date of death: 10 June 1917.

Supplementary information: Husband of Mrs McMahon, of Clarecastle, Co. Clare. SS *Keeper* was built in 1906 and owned by J. Bannatyne & Sons Ltd, Limerick. She was torpedoed and sunk possibly by German submarine UC-66 during a voyage from Belfast to Limerick. Twelve seamen were lost including four Clare men: **CONSIDINE, ARTHUR**; **COLE, RICHARD**; **McCREADY, WILLIAM** and **McMAHON J.**

Grave or memorial reference: Tower Hill Memorial, UK.

McMAHON JAMES: Rank: Private. Regiment or service: Irish Guards. Unit: 2nd Battalion. Date of death: 27 September 1915. Age at death: 26. Service No.: 6650. Killed in action.

Supplementary information: Born in Tomgraney, Co. Clare. Enlisted in Dublin, Co. Dublin while living in Tomgraney, Co. Clare. Son of Thomas and Mary McMahon, of Tomgraney, Co. Clare. Volunteered from the Royal Irish Constabulary in 1914. His personal effects and property were sent to Thomas McMahon (father), Tomgraney, Co. Clare. Will was witnessed by Maurice Cahill, Coolmagort, Co. Kerry. James Connolly, Moate Westmeath, R.E. Sasson Medical officer.

Grave or memorial reference: VI. C. 6. Cemetery: Cabaret-Rouge British Cemetery, Souchez in France

McMAHON, JAMES: Rank: Private. Regiment or service: Royal Munster Fusiliers. Unit: 9th Battalion. Date of death: 15 May 1916. Service No.: 4625. Killed in action.

Supplementary information: Enlisted in Ennis, Co. Clare while living in Clarecastle, Co. Clare. Son of Mrs Anne McMahon, of Craggaun, Clarecastle, Co. Clare.

From the *Saturday Journal*, July 1916:

A credit to the County Clare and
To the Munsters
Another of our brave young Claremen, Private. Thomas Browne, who responded to the call of his country, and has it creditably recorded of him that he was a credit

to his country and to the Munsters, to which regiment he belonged. The sad news of his having fallen on the field of battle, was conveyed to his sister. Mrs McMahon, of Ballygreene, Newmarket-on-Fergus, by Lieutenant Hugh M. V. O'Brien, who wrote as follows—

"I am extremely sorry to have to tell you of the death of your brother, Pte Thomas Browne, C Company, 8th R. M. F. he was killed by a German shell on the 21st of this month in the front trench, and has been buried in a soldier's graveyard He was a very good boy, and we shall all kiss him. Sergeant O'Connor, of Newcastle West, who was his platoon Sergeant, tells me he would sooner have lost a brother. He was killed instantly, and so suffered no pain. He was a credit to the Co. Clare, and the Munsters."

Mrs McMahon's husband also received a similar communication apprising him of the death of his brother, Pte Jim McMahon, of the Munsters, who belonged to Clarecastle.

Grave or memorial reference: Addenda Panel. Memorial: Loos Memorial in France.

McMAHON, JOHN: Rank: Gunner. Regiment or service: Royal Garrison Artillery. Date of death: 26 April 1917. Age at death: 42. Service No.: 292979. Killed in action.

Supplementary information: Born in Dublin. Enlisted in Dublin while living in Kilmaley, Co. Clare. Formerly he was with the 138th Hampstead Heavy Battery where his number was 1608. Son of John and Mary Ann McMahon, of Kildogher, Kilmaley. Brother of Thomas Francis McMahon, AIF. who was also killed in action in the Dardanelles (*see* McMahon, John Francis).

Grave or memorial reference: VI. G. 5. Cemetery: Vermelles British Cemetery in France.

McMAHON, JOHN: Rank: Private. Regiment or service: Royal Munster Fusiliers. Unit: 2nd Battalion. Date of death: 2 June 1917. Service No.: 6718.

Supplementary information: Born in Kilrush, Co. Clare. Enlisted in Kilrush while living in Kilrush, Co. Clare. Died at home. His personal effects and property were sent to Michael McMahon, Grace Street, Kilrush, Co. Clare.

Grave or memorial reference: In the south-west corner. Cemetery: Kilrush Church of Ireland Churchyard, Co. Clare.

McMAHON, JOHN: Rank: Drummer. Regiment or service: King's Own Scottish Borderers. Unit: 2nd/5th Battalion. Date of death: 7 July 1917. Service No.: 31043. Died at home.

Supplementary information: Born in Luton, Bedfordshire. Enlisted in Luton, Bedforshire while living in Luton, Bedfordshire.

Grave or memorial reference: South-East part of new ground. Cemetery: Ennis (Drumcliff) Cemetery, Co. Clare.

McMAHON, MARTIN: Rank: Private. Regiment or service: Irish Guards. Unit: 1st Battalion. Date of death: 10 October 1917. Service No.: 1128. Killed in action.

Supplementary information: Born in Killmurry McMahon (*sic*), Co. Clare. Enlisted in Ennis, Co. Clare.

Grave or memorial reference: Panel 10 and 11. Memorial: Tyne Cot Memorial in Belgium.

McMAHON MICHAEL: Rank: Lance Corporal. Regiment or service: Royal Munster Fusiliers. Unit: 2ⁿᵈ Battalion. Date of death: 10 October 1915. Age at death: 23. Service No.: 6004. Died of wounds.

Supplementary information: Born in Kilrush, Co. Clare. Enlisted in Kilrush, Co. Clare while living in Kilrush, Co. Clare. Son of Thomas and Margaret McMahon, of Burton Street, Kilrush, Co. Clare. Also commemorated in the 'List of Kilrush Men Engaged in the War from August 1914', Malt House Lane. This pamphlet lists the Kilrush men who were involved in the First World War until 11 November 1918.

Grave or memorial reference: I. G. 23. Cemetery: Chocques Military Cemetery in France.

McMAHON, MICHAEL: Rank: Private. Regiment or service: Royal Dublin Fusiliers. Unit: 1ˢᵗ Battalion. Date of death: 20 August 1917. Age at death: 25. Service No.: 40124. Formerly he was with the Royal Munster Fusiliers where his number was 7049. Died of wounds.

Supplementary information: Born in Sixmilebridge, Co. Clare. Enlisted in Ennis, Co. Clare while living in Clarecastle, Co. Clare. Son of Pat and Kate McMahon, of Newmarket-on-Fergus; husband of Mary McMahon, of Main Street, Clarecastle, Co. Clare.

Grave or memorial reference: Panel 144 to 145. Memorial: Tyne Cot Memorial in Belgium.

McMAHON PATRICK: Rank: Private. Regiment or service: Royal Munster Fusiliers. Unit: 1ˢᵗ Battalion. Date of death: 22 March 1918. Age at death: 20. Service No.: 6714. Killed in action.

Supplementary information: Born in Kilfinanae (*sic*) Co. Clare. Enlisted in Limerick while living in Ennis, Co. Clare. Son of James and Margaret McMahon, of Cahercon, Shanahea, Ennis, Co. Clare.

Grave or memorial reference: I. A. 12. Cemetery: Ste. Emilie Valley Cemetery, Villers-Faucon, in France.

McMAHON, PATRICK: Rank: Private. Regiment or service: Royal Munster Fusiliers. Unit: 2ⁿᵈ Battalion. Date of death: 9 May 1915. Service No.: 6323. Killed in action.

Supplementary information: Born in Drumcliffe, Co. Clare. Enlisted in Ennis while living in Ennis.

From the *Clare Journal*, 1915:

Claremen lost at the Front

News reached his wife on Thursday that Pte Pat McMahon, of the Royal Munster Fusiliers, a native of Ennis, was killed in the late severe fighting.

Captain Filgate writes—"I deeply sympathise with you in your great loss. It may be a little consolation to you to know that the regiment was the only one in the Brigade to reach the German trenches, and behaved in a very gallant manner. We are all proud of the many gallant officers and men that fell, and they succeeded in adding to the honour and name of the Regiment, which I know always came first with them."

Grave or memorial reference: Panel 43 and 44. Memorial: Le Touret Memorial in France.

McMAHON, PATRICK: Rank: Private. Regiment or service: South Lancashire Regiment. Unit: 2nd Battalion. Date of death: 31 January 1915. Service No.: 9464.
Supplementary information: Born in Ennis, Co. Clare. Enlisted in Galway.
Grave or memorial reference: Panel 37. Memorial: Ypres (Menin Gate) Memorial in Belgium.

McMAHON, PATRICK SENON/ STAN: Rank: Second Lieutenant. Regiment or service: Royal Munster Fusiliers. Unit: 8th Battalion. Date of death: 29 December 1915. Age at death: 28. Died of wounds at Bethune Hospital.
Supplementary information: Son of John McMahon, of Knocknagun House, Newmarket-on-Fergus, Co. Clare. Wounded in action by a stray bullet while with a working party on reserve trenches. He was the first casualty of the 8th Battalion and the 16th Irish Division.
From *Our Heroes*, 1916:

Second Lieutenant Patrick Stan McMahon, 8th Royal Munster Fusiliers, was the son of Mr John McMahon, Knocknagarm House, Newmarket-on-Fergus, Co. Clare. He enlisted in the Cadet Company,

7th Leinster Regiment on the outbreak of the war, and from thence obtained his commission in the 8th Royal Munster Fusiliers. He died on December 29th in France, of wounds received in action on the night of December 24th.

From the *Clare Journal*, December 1915:

Young Clare Officer Dead
Second Lieutenant P. S. McMahon
Second Lieutenant Patrick S. McMahon who die din France from wounds received in action, was son of Mr John McMahon, Knocknagun House, Newmarket-on-Fergus, Clare. When the country needed men he enlisted into the Cadet Company, 7th Leinster Regiment, from which he obtained his commission in the 8th Royal Munster Fusiliers, and he accompanied the battalion on field service. Second Lieutenant McMahon was a well-known athlete. Quite recently we won the open 100 yards at the 47th, (Irish) Brigade Sports at Fermoy, and later distinguished himself at Lansdowne at the D. M. P. Sports. He was a very popular young officer, and his loss is deeply deplored by Lieutenant Colonel Williamson and all ranks of the battalion.

Grave or memorial reference: II. L. 7. Cemetery: Bethune Town Cemetery in France.

McMAHON, THOMAS: Rank: Lance Corporal. Regiment or service: West Riding Regiment. Unit: 2nd Battalion. Date of death: 11 November

1914. Service No.: 3/9910. Killed in action

Supplementary information: Born in Madras, India. Enlisted in Huddersfield while living in Ennis.

Grave or memorial reference: Addenda panel 57. Memorial: Ypres (Menin Gate) Memorial in Belgium.

McMAHON, THOMAS FRANCIS: Rank: Private. Regiment or service: Australian Infantry, AIF. Unit: 2nd Battalion. Date of death: 20 May 1915. Age at death: 29. Service No.: 1602. Killed in action in Gallipoli.

Supplementary information: Son of John and Mary Ann McMahon, of Kilmaley, Ennis, Co. Clare, Ireland. In his records his mother is listed as Margaret McMahon. Born, Kilmaley, Ennis, Co. Clare. Occupation on enlistment: Labourer. Age on enlistment: 28 years 5 months. Previous military experience: 8 years; Royal Dubin Fusiliers, time expired. Next of kin: Mrs Mary Anne McMahon (mother),

Kilmaley, Ennis, Co. Clare. Place and date of enlistment: Liverpool, N.S.W. 29 Decemeber 1914. Weight: 11st 6lbs. Complexion: Ruddy. Eyes: Grey. Hair: Ruddy. His mother received a pension of 22s per fortnight from August 1915. His brother John was killed in the past when he was with the Royal Garrison Artillery, 22 April 1917 (*see* McMahon, John, No. 4625).

Grave or memorial reference: II. C. 6. Cemetery: Lone Pine Cemetery, Anzac in Turkey.

McNAMARA, CHARLES: Rank: Private. Regiment or service: Scottish Rifles. Unit: 2nd Battalion. Date of death: 23 October 1916. Service No.: 6893. Killed in action.

Supplementary information: Born in Kilrush, Co. Clare. Enlisted in Glasgow while living in Kilrush, Co. Clare. Also commemorated in the 'List of Kilrush Men engaged in the War from August 1914'. This pamphlet lists the Kilrush men who were involved in the First

The notification of the death of Private T. McMahon.

World War until 11 November 1918 and states that he was 'missing'.

Grave or memorial reference: Pier and Face 4 D. Memorial: Thiepval Memorial in France.

McNAMARA, EDWARD JAMES:
Rank: Rifleman. Regiment or service: Royal Irish Rifles. Unit: 1st Battalion. Date of death: 16 January 1918. Service No.: 47462. Killed in action.

Supplementary information: Born in Drumcliffe, Co. Clare. Enlisted in Boulogne, France while living in Ennis.

Grave or memorial reference: Panel 138 to 140, and 162 to 162A and 163A. Memorial: Tyne Cot Memorial in Belgium

McNAMARA, FRANCIS: Rank:
Private. Regiment or service: Royal Irish Regiment. Unit: 7th Battalion. Date of death: 27 September 1918. Age at death: 21. Service No.: 25565. Formerly he was with the South Irish Horse where his number was 1901. Killed in action.

Supplementary information: Born in Ennis, Co. Clare. Enlisted in Ennis, Co. Clare. Son of Joseph McNamara, of Turnpike Road, Ennis, Co. Clare.

From the *Saturday Record*, November 1918:

Roll of Honour
Among the casualties recorded this week is the death of Pte Frank McNamara, son of Mr J. McNamara, tailor, Ennis, who fell in recent fighting.

Grave or memorial reference: VII. G. 7. Cemetery: Queant Road Cemetery, Buissy, Pas-De-Calais in France.

McNAMARA, FRANCIS JOSEPH:
Rank: Private. Regiment or service: Wellington Regiment, NZEF. Date of death: 8 October 1920. Age at death: 46. Service No.: 68303. Died after discharge from the NZEF from wounds inflicted or disease contracted while on active service

Supplementary information: Son of Daniel and Susan McNamara. Born in Co. Clare, Ireland. Next of kin listed as J. McNamara (brother), No. 140 High Street, Christchurch, New Zealand. Occupation on enlistment: Fitter. Embarked with the 37th Reinforcements, B Company, NZEF on 9 May 1918 in Wellington, New Zealand aboard the *Maunganui* bound for Liverpool, England.

Grave or memorial reference: H. 16. (S). Cemetery: Wellington (Karori) Cemetery, New Zealand.

McNAMARA, JOHN: Rank: Private.
Regiment or service: Royal Munster Fusiliers. Unit: 1st Battalion. Date of death: 1 May 1915. Service No.: 8720. Died of wounds in Galipoli.

Supplementary information: Born in Drumcliffe, Co. Clare. Enlisted in Ennis while living in Ennis.

Grave or memorial reference: Panel 185 to 190. Memorial: Helles Memorial in Turkey.

McNAMARA JOHN: Rank: Private.
Regiment or service: Royal Munster Fusiliers. Unit: 8th Battalion. Date of death: 27 July 1916. Service No.: 4464. Died of wounds.

Supplementary information: Born in Carnaghclogan, Co. Clare. Enlisted in Limerick while living in Ennis, Co. Clare. Son of Martin McNamara, of Carnaclohy, Crusheen, Co. Clare.

Grave or memorial reference:V. G. 36. Cemetery: Bethune Town Cemetery in France.

McNAMARA, JOSEPH: Rank: Private. Regiment or service: Irish Guards. Unit: 2nd Battalion. Date of death: 15 September 1916. Age at death: 29. Service No.: 7259. Killed in action.

Supplementary information: Born in Kilmihil, Co. Clare. Enlisted in Ennis, Co. Clare. Son of Michael and Mary McNamara, of Knockalough, Ennis, Co. Clare.

Grave or memorial reference: Pier and Face 7 D. Memorial: Thiepval Memorial in France.

McNAMARA, MICHAEL FRANCIS: Rank: Staff Sergeant Major. Regiment or service: Royal Army Service Corps. Unit: GHQ Baghdad. Date of death: 20 January 1918. Age at death: 38. Service No.: S/13074. Formerly he was with the 5th Royal Munster Fusiliers where he was awarded the Medaille D'Honneur and Diploma. Died in Mesopotamia.

Supplementary information: Born in Newcastle West, Co. Limerick. Enlisted in Ennis while living in Brownstown. Husband of Margaret Mary McNamara, of Brownstown Road, Curragh Camp, Co. Kildare.

From the *Clare Journal*, 2 September 1915:

French Decoration for Ennis Man Ennis Family well represented at the front.

We learn from official documents that First Class Staff Sergeant Major, Michael McNamara, A. S. C., son of Mr P McNamara, Market Street, Ennis, has had the Bronze Medal, for an act of courage and devotion to duty, conferred on him by the French Government. The presentation was made by the French Minister of Foreign Affairs. Sergenat Major McNamara comes of a stalwart family, of which his father may well be proud. His elder brother, John, who is 6ft 3in, in height, and is in the Guards, fought in the South African War, and came on to Europe for the present war. The Sergeant major is 6ft 1in. John [*sic*], a third brother, who is 6ft, is in the R. G. A., and the fourth, Peter, is in the A. S. C. He is 5ft 9ins. All are at the front.

Grave or memorial reference: XVI. J. 1. Cemetery: Baghdad (North Gate) War Cemetery in Iraq.

McNAMARA, PATRICK: Rank: Chief Stoker. Regiment or service: Royal Navy. Unit: HMS *Pylades* This ship survived the First World War and was scrapped in 1921. Date of death: 15 May 1917. Age at death: 38. Service No.: 292326.

Supplementary information: Son of Michael and Ellen McNamara, of Killispuglinane, Ennistymon, Co. Clare.

Grave or memorial reference: General T. 4. 33. Cemetery: Ford Park Cemetery (Formerly Plymouth Old Cemetery) (Pennycomequick), UK.

McNAMARA, PATRICK: Rank: Private. Regiment or service: Royal Munster Fusiliers. Unit: 2nd Battalion. Date of death: 10 November 1917. Age at death: 21. Service No.: 6872. Killed in action.

Supplementary information: Born in Corofin, Co. Clare. Enlisted in Corofin, Co. Clare while living in Corofin, Co. Clare. Son of Nora McNamara, of Back Street, Corofin, Co. Clare.

Grave or memorial reference: Panel 143 to 144. Memorial: Tyne Cot Memorial in Belgium.

McNAMARA, RODY: Rank: Gunner. Regiment or service: Royal Field Artillery. Unit: 50th Reserve Brigade. Date of death: 27 March 1916. Age at death: 34. Service No.: 36589. Died at home.

Supplementary information: Born in Scarrip (*sic*), Co. Clare. Enlisted in Dublin. Son of Daniel and Catherine McNamara, of Waterpark, Scariff.

Grave or memorial reference: South East of ruins. Cemetery: Scariff (Moynoe) Cemetery, Co. Clare.

McNAMARA/MACNAMARA, WILLIAM: Rank: Private. Regiment or service: Royal Munster Fusiliers. Unit: 8th Battalion. Date of death: 18 June 1916. Service No.: 5716. Killed in action.

Supplementary information: Born in Whitegate, Co. Clare. Enlisted in Tomgraney, Co. Clare while living in Whitegate.

Grave or memorial reference: I.E. 1. Cemetery: St Patrick's Cemetery, Loos in France.

MEADE, MICHAEL: Rank: Company Quartermaster Sergeant. Regiment or service: Royal Munster Fusiliers. Unit: 1st Battalion. Date of death: 21 August 1915. Age at death: 35. Service No.: 5817. Killed in action in Gallipoli.

Supplementary information: Born in Kilrush, Co. Clare. Enlisted in Kilrush while living in Kilrush, Co. Clare. Husband of Annie Kearen Dwyer (*née* Meade), of No. 15 Ballymullen Road, Tralee, Co. Kerry. Also commemorated in the 'List of Kilrush Men engaged in the War from August 1914'. This pamphlet lists the Kilrush men who were involved in the First World War until 11 November 1918.

Grave or memorial reference: Panel 185 to 190. Memorial: Helles Memorial in Turkey.

MEANEY, JAMES: Rank: Private. Regiment or service: Royal Munster Fusiliers. Unit: 1st Battalion. Date of death: 2 April 1918. Age at death: 18. Service No.: 6759. Killed in action.

Supplementary information: Born in Thurles. Enlisted in Limerick while living in Kilkee Co. Clare. Son of Martin and Ellen Meaney, of Ballaney Lane, Kilkee, Co. Clare.

Grave or memorial reference: VI. E. 2. Cemetery: Villers-Bretonneux Military Cemetery in France.

MEEHAN, DANIEL: Rank: Private. Regiment or service: Royal Irish Regiment. Unit: 7th Battalion. Date of death: 17 October 1918. Service No.: 25602. Formerly he was with the South Irish Horse where his number was 2140.

Supplementary information: Born in Clonlara, Co. Clare. Enlisted in Newcastle West, Co. Limerick.

Grave or memorial reference: IV. D. 18. Cemetery: Hautmont Communal Cemetery in France.

MESCAL, MARK S.: Rank: Lance Corporal. Regiment or service: Irish Guards. Unit: 1ˢᵗ Battalion. Date of death: 1 December 1917. Age at death: 23. Service No.: 11452. Killed in action.

Supplementary information: Born in Kilrush, Co. Clare. Enlisted in Dublin while living in Kilrush, Co. Clare. Son of Michael Mescal, of Vandeleur Street, Kilrush, Co. Clare. Also commemorated as 'Mark Mescall' of Vandeleur Street in the 'List of Kilrush Men engaged in the War from August 1914'. This pamphlet lists the Kilrush men who were involved in the First World War until 11 November 1918.

Grave or memorial reference: Panel 2 and 3. Memorial: Cambrai Memorial, Louveral, Nord in France.

MILICAN, PATRICK: Rank: Sailor. Regiment or service: Mercantile Marine. Unit: SS *Huntsvale* (London) Date of death: 4 November 1916. Age at death: 19.

Supplementary information: Son of the late Michael and Bridget Milican. Born at Kilrush. The 5,609 ton British cargo/transport SS *Huntsville* was torpedoed and sunk by German submarine UB-43, 200 miles east of Malta *en route* from Salonika to Algiers. Seven men were lost.

Grave or memorial reference: Tower Hill Memorial, UK.

MINETER, MARTIN: Rank: Private. Regiment or service: Australian Infantry, AIF. Unit: 48ᵗʰ Battalion. Date of death: 5 August 1916. Service No.: 473.

Supplementary information: Born, Moyne/Moynoe, Scarriff, Co. Clare. Occupation on enlistment: Tailor. Age on enlistment: 41 years 6 months. Next of kin: Catherine Robertson (sister), of No. 53 Church Street, Whittlesea, Peterborough, England; later changed to Mr P. Mineter (brother), of No. 232 Queens Road, Manchester, England. Later his brother's address and his sister's addres were the same, No. 53 Church Street, Whittlesea. Place and date of enlistment: Perth, Western Australia, 6 March 1915. Weight: 11st 10lbs. Height: 5ft 10in. Complexion: Fair. Eyes: Blue. Hair: Very dark brown.

Grave or memorial reference: Villers-Bretonneux Memorial. Villers-Bretonneux Military Cemetery in France.

MINOGUE, JOHN: Rank: Company Sergeant Major. Regiment or service: Royal Munster Fusiliers. Unit: 7ᵗʰ Battalion. Date of death: 17 August 1915. Service No.: 2460. Died of wounds in Gallipoli.

Supplementary information: Born in Feakle, Co. Clare. Enlisted in Bradford, Yorkshire.

Grave or memorial reference: Panel 185 to 190. Memorial: Helles Memorial in Turkey.

MINOGUE, JOHN O'BRIEN (CMG): Rank: Lieutenant Colonel. Regiment or service: West Yorkshire Regiment. Unit: 3ʳᵈ Battalion, attached to the 9ᵗʰ Battalion. Date of death: 26 October 1916.

The Officer in Charge,
        Base Records,
                Victoria Barracks,
                MELBOURNE.
                ———————— Victoria.

Dear Sir,

                re No. 473 Private M. Miniter,
                48th Battalion A.I.F.(decd.)
        ————————————————————

        The Curator of Intestate Estates handed us
your letter of the 12th ultimo and in reply we advised
that we are administrators of the above deceased soldier's
Estate and that his next of kin are Edward Patrick
Miniter of No. 232 Queens Road, Cheetham, Manchester,
England and Mrs. Catherine Robertson of Church Street,
Whittlesey, Peterborough, England a brother and sister
respectively of the above soldier.   There is another
sister Mary Miniter who went to America and has not been
heard of for over thirty years.

                Yours faithfully,

                U/ AnKetell

                Pro. Secretary.

Next of kin for Private M. Miniter is listed in this document from records.

Supplementary information: Husband of A. Minogue (later Mrs Bannister), of Cleve Lodge, No. 40 Hyde Park Gate, London.

From the *Clare Journal*, February 1916:

> The following Officer is a casualty
> Distinguished Clare Officer
>
> In the last list of honours for military services in the field, appears the following—To be additional member of the Third Class for Companions of the most distinguished Order of St Michael and St George—Lieutenant Colonel John O'Brien Minogue, reserve of officers, late West Yorkshire Regiment, commanding service battalion Lieutenant Colonel Minogue, is an East Clare man, from the Scariff district. He has had a brilliant career, rising from the ranks.

From the *Clare Journal*, November 1916:

> Death of Clare Officer
>
> Lieutenant Colonel John O'Brien Minogue, C.M.G., West Yorkshire Regiment, died on October 6th, at 9 Berkeley Square, London. Born in 1861, he entered the Army in May 1886, and received his majority in

March, 1905. He first saw active service with the Burmese Expedition in 1885-89, being mentioned in despatches and receiving the medal with two clasps. In 1889-90 he took part in the Chin-Lushai Expedition, and was mentioned in despatches and awarded the clasp. He held the Star for the Ashanti Expedition, 1895-96, and in 1903-04. He served as D.A A.G. in Tibet, being present at the action at Niani, the operation at and around Gyantee, and the march to Lhassa. He was mentioned in despatches, and received the medal with clasp. In 1908 he took part in the operations in the Mohamand country, including the engagement of Matta (medal with clasp). Colonel Minogue, who retired in October, 1909, was appointed to the command of a battalion of the West Yorkshire Regiment in March, 1915 He was a native of the Scariff district.

Grave or memorial reference: A 34. Cemetery: Mortlake (St Mary Magdalen) Roman Catholic Churchyard in Surrey.

MITCHELL, JAMES: Rank: Second Lieutenant. Regiment or service: Royal Flying Corps. Unit: 18th Squadro. Secondary. Unit: and 5th Canadian Infantry Brigade HQ. Date of death: 26 April 1916. Age at death: 34.

Supplementary information: Son of James and Ellen Mitchell, of Cappa, Kilrush, Co. Clare.

Grave or memorial reference: A. 10. Cemetery: Bruay Communal Cemetery Extension in France.

MOLONEY, JAMES EDWARD: Rank: Sergeant. Regiment or service: Auckland Mounted Rifles, NZEF. Date of death: 8 August 1915. Age at death: 22. Service No.: 13/555. Killed in action.

Supplementary information: Son of Edmond and Catherine McMerney Moloney, of Market Street, Ennis, Co. Clare, Ireland. Next of kin listed as E.J. Howley (stepbrother), Auburn, Sydney, New South Wales, Australia. Embarked with the Auckland Mounted Rifles (Main body) 16 October 1914 in Auckland, New Zealand aboard the *Star of India* or the *Waimana* bound for Suez, Egypt.

Grave or memorial reference: 1. Memorial: Chunuk Bair (New Zealand) Memorial in Turkey.

MOLONEY/MOLONY, JOHN: Rank: Private. Regiment or service: Royal Munster Fusiliers. Unit: 1st Battalion. Date of death: 21 March 1918. Age at death: 21. Service No.: 6792. Killed in action.

Supplementary information: Born in Kildysart, Co. Clare. Enlisted in Ennis while living in Kildysart, Co. Clare. Son of Simon and Katie Molony, of Derrylea, Kildysart, Co. Clare.

Grave or memorial reference: IV.A. 5. Cemetery: Ste. Emilie Valley Cemetery, Villers-Faucon, in France.

MOLONEY, JOHN: Rank: Private. Regiment or service: Royal Munster Fusiliers. Unit: 1st Battalion. Date of death: 1 May 1915. Age at death: 33. Service No.: 6346. Killed in action in Gallipoli.

Supplementary information: Born in Kilrush, Co. Clare. Enlisted in Limerick while living in Kilrush, Co. Clare. Husband of Johannah Moloney, of

Crofton Street, Kilrush, Co. Clare. Also commemorated as 'Jack Molony' in the 'List of Kilrush Men engaged in the War from August 1914'. This pamphlet lists the Kilrush men who were involved in the First World War until 11 November 1918. Also commemorated in the 'List of Employees of Messrs M. Glynn and Sons. Flour and Meal Millers and Steamship Owners. Kilrush, Co. Clare, who took part in the War, 1914 to 1918. Dated 11 November 1918'.

Grave or memorial reference: Panel 185 to 190. Memorial: Helles Memorial in Turkey.

MOLONEY, JOHN: Rank: Company Quartermaster Sergeant. Regiment or service: Rifle Brigade. Unit: 23rd Battalion. Date of death: 4 February 1917. Service No.: T/205316. Formerly he was with the 3rd/5th Liverpool Regiment where his number was 22891. Died in India.

Supplementary information: Enlisted in Liverpool while living in Liverpool. Son of Andrew and Mary Moloney, of Ennis, Co. Clare Irish Republic. Memorial: Karachi 1914-1918 War Memorial in Pakistan.

MOLONEY, JOHN: Rank: Private. Regiment or service: Royal Dublin Fusiliers. Unit: 8th Battalion. Date of death: 9 September 1916. Service No.: 20351. Killed in action.

Supplementary information: Born in Clonlara, Co. Clare. Enlisted in Bray, Co. Wicklow.

Grave or memorial reference: Pier and Face 16 C. Memorial: Thiepval Memorial in France.

MOLONEY, MARTIN: Rank: Seaman. Regiment or service: Royal Naval Reserve. Unit: HMS *Laurentic*. Date of death: 25 Jaunuary 1917. Age at death: 40. Service No.: 5237B.

Supplementary information: Long Service and Good Conduct Medal. Son of Marcin and Ellen Moloney (*née* Brown); husband of Bridget Moloney, of Quilty West, Miltown Malbay, Co. Clare.

Grave or memorial reference: 23. Memorial: Memorial: Plymouth Naval Memorial, UK.

MOLONEY, MICHAEL: Rank: Private. Regiment or service: Royal Inniskilling Fusiliers. Unit: 7th Battalion. Date of death: 27 April 1916. Age at death: 18. Service No.: 26452. Killed in action.

Supplementary information: Born in Kuilty, West Clare. Enlisted in Ennis while living in Kuilty, Co. Clare. Formerly he was with the Royal Munster Fusiliers where his number was 4137. Son of Martin and Bridget Moloney, of Quilty West, Miltown Malbay, Co. Clare.

Grave or memorial reference: I. C. 11. Cemetery: Philosophe British Cemetery, Mazingarbe in France.

MOLONEY, PATRICK: Rank: Private. Regiment or service: Royal Irish Regiment. Unit: 2nd Battalion. Date of death: 26 October 1915. Age at death: 23. Service No.: 4856. Killed in action.

Supplementary information: Born in Cappawhite Co. Tipperary. Enlisted in Tipperary while living in Cappawhite. In his will, dated 18 June 1915, his personal effects and property were received by Bridget Shannon (mother),

Croveghan, Kildysent Cottage, Co. Clare, Ireland. Son of John and Bridget Shannon, of Kildysart, Co. Clare.

Grave or memorial reference: I. A. 7. Cemetery: Auchonvillers Military Cemetery in France.

MOLONEY, PATRICK: Rank: Private. Regiment or service: Royal Munster Fusiliers. Unit: 2nd Battalion. Date of death: 24 August 1916. Service No.: 4921. Killed in action.

Supplementary information: Born in Kilrush, Co. Clare. Enlisted in Limerick while living in Kilrush, Co. Clare.

Grave or memorial reference: Pier and Face 16 C. Memorial: Thiepval Memorial in France.

MOLONEY, PETER: Rank: Private. Regiment or service: Machine Gun Corps (Infantry). Unit: 3rd Company. Age at death: 21. Date of death: 12 March 1916. Service No.: 19414. Formerly he was with the Royal where his number was 9858. Killed in action.

Supplementary information: Born in Drumcliffe, Co. Clare. Enlisted in Ennis, Co. Clare. Son of John and Alice Moloney, of Cloghleigh Road, Ennis, Co. Clare.

Grave or memorial reference: I. D. 1. Cemetery: Maroc British Cemetery, Grenay in France.

MOLONEY, SIMON: Rank: Gunner. Regiment or service: Royal Garrison Artillery. Unit: 2nd Battalion. Date of death: 3 August 1916. Service No.: 57579. Died in Mesopotamia.

Supplementary information: Born in Kilrush, Co. Clare. Enlisted in Limerick while living in Kilrush, Co. Clare. In his

will, dated 22 Janury 1916, his personal effects and property were received by Mrs Susan Moloney (mother), Grace St, Kilrush, Co. Clare, Ireland. Also commemorated as 'SINON MOLONEY' in the 'List of Kilrush Men engaged in the War from August 1914', Grace Street. This pamphlet lists the Kilrush men who were involved in the First World War until 11 November 1918.

Grave or memorial reference: VI. N. 5. Cemetery: Basra War Cemetery in Iraq.

MOLONEY/MALONEY, TOM/ THOMAS: Rank: Company Sergeant Major. Regiment or service: Royal Irish Regiment. Unit: 7th Battalion. Date of death: 2 September 1918. Age at death: 26. Service No.: 5608. Killed in action.

Supplementary information: Born in O'Gonnelloe, Co. Clare. Enlisted in Dublin while living in O'Gonnelloe, Co. Clare. He won the Military Medal and is listed in the *London Gazette*. There seems to be a duplicate entry for this man in *Soldiers Died in the Great War* but it gives his rank as Private, his place of birth as Killaloe and his place of enlistment as Dublin. All other details are the same.

Son of Mr and Mrs Patt Moloney, of New Chapel, O'Gonnelloe, Killaloe, Co. Clare. In his will, dated 17 November 1916, his personal effects and property were received by Mr Patrick Maloney, (father), New Chapel, Ogonnellooe, Killaloe, Co. Clare, Ireland. Will was witnessed by C. Strudwick CQMS Sergeant Belmont Hutments, Queenstown, 6th Battalion, The Royal Irish Regiment. M. Kavangh Corporal, Belmont Hutments, Queenstown, 6th Battalion, The Royal Irish Regiment.

The Commonwealth War Graves Commisssion only have one entry for him. Grave or memorial reference: V. E. 19. Cemetery: Wulverghem-Lindenhoek Road Military Cemetery in Belgium.

MOLONY, BERTRAM WELDON:

Rank: Captain. Regiment or service: East Lancashire Regiment. Unit: 1st Battalion. Date of death: 28 February 1915. Age at death: 26. Killed in action.

Supplementary information: Son of Weldon Charles and Eleanor A. Molony, of No. 5 Upper Fitzwilliam Street, Dublin.

From the *County Offaly Chronicle*, March 1915:

Captain Bertram, Weldon Molony, East Lancashires, Killed, belonged to the well known Molony's of Kiltanon, County Clare, and was born in May 1888. He joined the East Lancahsire Regiment when he was 20, got his lieutenancy in 1911, and was made Captain last November.

From *Our heroes*, 1916:

Captain Bertam Weldon Moloney was gazetted to the 2nd Battalion of the East Lancashire regiment in 1908, was promoted to Lieutenant in January, 1911, and got his Captaincy last November. He was in his 27th year when he was killed. He belonged to a well-known County Clare family, the Moloneys of Kiltannon, of which Captain William Beresford Moloney is the representative.

Grave or memorial reference: I. A. 8. Cemetery: Lancashire Cottage Cemetery, Comines-Warneton, Hairaut, Belgium.

MOLONY, CHARLES FREDERICK: Rank: Rifleman.

Regiment or service: King's Royal Rifle Corps. Unit: D Company, 8th Battalion. Date of death: 5 March 1916. Age at death: 24. Service No.: R/15572. Killed in action.

Supplementary information: Born in Dublin. Enlisted in London while living in Ennis, Co. Clare. Son of Patrick Considine Molony, J. P., and Mrs M. J.W.M. Molony (*née* Molyneux), of No. 78 Kenilworth Square, Rathgar, Dublin.

Grave or memorial reference: XVII. L. 29. Cemetery: Cabaret-Rouge British Cemetery, Souchez in France.

MOODY, THOMAS: Rank: Lance Corporal. Regiment or service: Irish Guards. Unit: 2nd Battalion. Date of death: 27 November 1917. Age at death: 25. Service No.: 10156. Died at home.

Supplementary information: Born in Ennis, Co. Clare. Enlisted in Dublin while living in Ennis. Son of Mrs Frances Moody, of Waterpark, Ennis, and the late William Moody.

Grave or memorial reference: East side of new ground. Cemetery: Ennis (Drumcliffe) Cemetery, Co. Clare.

MORAN, WILLIAM: Rank: Able Seaman. Regiment or service: Royal Navy. Unit: (RFR/DEV/B/1925), HMS *Majestic*. Date of death: 6 October 1914. Age at death: 39. Service No.: 181311.

Supplementary information: At the time of William's death the *Majestic* was accompanying the First Canadian Troop Convoy. It was later torpedoed by U-21 off the Gallipoli Peninsula on 27 May 1915 and sunk with the loss of forty-nine men.

Son of Patrick and Margaret Hannah Moran, of Scattery Island, Co. Clare; husband of Annie Moran, of Cappath, Kilrush, Co. Clare. Also commemorated in the 'Kilrush Men belonging to or who joined the Naval Service since commencement of the War. This pamphlet lists the Kilrush men who were involved in the First World War until 11 November 1918.

Grave or memorial reference: 1. Memorial: Memorial: Plymouth Naval Memorial, UK.

MORGAN, MARTIN: Rank: Private. Regiment or service: Connaught Rangers. Unit: 1st Battalion. Date of death: 23 November 1914. Service No.: 5230. Killed in action.

Supplementary information: Born in Ennis, Co. Clare. Enlisted in Ennis while living in Sixmilebridge.

Grave or memorial reference: VIII. H. 14. Cemetery: Brown's Road Military Cemetery, Festubert in France.

MORONEY, JAMES: Rank: Private. Regiment or service: Leinster Regiment. Unit: 1st Battalion. Date of death: 16 August 1918. Service No.: 8220. Died in Egypt.

Supplementary information: Born in Derrynaveigh, Co. Clare. Enlisted in Limerick. His personal effects and property were sent to his brother Michael. Will was witnessed by Margaret Moroney (sister), Derrynaveigh,

Oatfield, Sixmilebridge, Co. Clare, W Wilson Lynch JP, Belvoir, Sixmilebridge, Co. Clare.

Grave or memorial reference: C. 88. Cemetery: Alexandria (Hadra) War memorial Cemetery in Egypt.

MORONEY, JAMES: *see* **KENNEDY, JOSEPH.**

MORONEY, JAMES (SONNY): Rank: Private. Regiment or service: Unknown. Date of death: 3 January 1919.

Supplementary information: The only information I can find on this casualty is contained in the newspaper article below.

From the *Saturday Record*, January 1919:

Moroney—On January 3rd-1919, at Rouen, France, after release as prisoner of war in Germany, James (Sonny) fifth son of the late Charles Moroney, Mill Street, Ennis, R. I. P.

Another Hun Victim

We see by our obituary columns to-day that Private. James (Sonny) Moroney, R. M. F., died a victim to Hun brutality, at Rouen Hospital, France, on Friday last He was taken prisoner at the opening of the big German "Push", on March 22, and was kept a prisoner in Germany until the armistice. He was released on November-29th, but was so prostrated from bad treatment and starvation, that he had to be sent to hospital at once in France, being unable to travel home, and never rallied. He had been badly wounded in August-1917, but recovered and rejoined his regiment.

Grave or memorial reference: Unknown at this time.

MORONEY, MARTIN: Rank: Sergeant. Regiment or service: Machine Gun Corps (Infantry). Unit: 99th Company. Date of death: 27 July 1916. Age at death: 20. Service No.: 12070. Formerly he was with the Manchester Regiment where his number was 2865. Killed in action.

Supplementary information: Born in Miltown Malbay, Co. Clare. Enlisted in Cork while living in Miltown Malbay, Co. Clare. Son of Martin and Bridget Moroney, of Main Street, Miltown Malbay, Co. Clare. According to a letter from his Commanding Officer, expressing his sympathy, Sergeant Moroney was killed on 29 July in the field. In his will, dated 24 April 1916, his personal effects and property were received by his mother Mrs M. Moroney, of Main Street, Miltown, Malbay, Co. Clare.

From the *Clare Journal*, August 1916:

Another Brave Clareman Killed in action
Our Miltown Malbay correspondent wires—The sad intelligence has reached here, by the mid-day mail, from his company's officer, that Sergeant Martin Moroney, the only child of Mr and Mrs Martin Moroney, General merchant, Main Street, Miltown Malbay, was killed while bravely leading his men. The greatest sympathy of the townspeople, and their numerous friends is extended to their sorrowing parents on the death of their only son.

From the *Saturday Record* and *Clare Journal*, September 1916:

The Death of Miltown Malbay
Man at the Front
The following letter has been received by Mr Martin Moroney, Miltown Malbay, from Colonel Lynch, M. P., on the death of his son in action–

House of Commons.
4th Sept., 1916.
Dear Mr Moroney—I read in the Record the news of the sad loss you have sustained, and I write a few words to say how much I feel for you and all your family. It must be a consolation to you to think that your son met his death bravely leading on his men and that everyone in Miltown Malbay will sympathise most deeply with you. will you please offer my condolence to Mrs Moroney also, and believe me. Sincerely yours.
ARTHUR GEORGE.

Grave or memorial reference: Pier and Face 5 C and 12 C. Memorial: Thiepval Memorial in France.

MORRIS, JOHN: Rank: Lance Sergeant. Regiment or service: Royal Munster Fusiliers. Unit: 8th Battalion. Date of death: 4 May 1916. Age at death: 21 Service No.: 5797. Killed in action.

Supplementary information: Born in Glenvickee, Co. Kerry. Enlisted in Limerick while living in Glencar, Co. Kerry. Son of Francis N. and Mary Morris, of Glenmackee, Glencar, Co.

Kerry. Volunteered for active service from RIC. Kilmihill, Co. Clare.

Grave or memorial reference: I. A. 5. Cemetery: Philosophe British Cemetery, Mazingarbe in France.

MORRISSEY, PATRICK: Rank: Private. Regiment or service: US Army. Unit: 165th Infantry, H Company. Date of death: 18 July 1918. Age at death: 23. Killed in action.

From the *Saturday Record*, 1919:

Roll of Honour

Mr Pat Morrissey, the ever-popular Guard on the South Clare Railway, has received the sad intelligence of the death of his son, Pat, aged 23, who was killed at the second battle of the Marne, on July 18th. Young Morrissey, who was a teacher in the Catholic Protectory Schools, Bronx, New York, was a member of Company H of the 165th Infantry (the famous old 69th Regiment) and enlisted in the outfit at the outbreak of the war. Visitors and residents alike extend their sympathy to is father in the loss of his gallant son.

Grave or memorial reference: Unknown.

MORRISSEY/MORRISEY, WALTER GEORGE: Rank: Staff Sergeant. Regiment or service: Connaught Rangers. Unit: 1st Battalion, attached to the Indian Ordance Department. Date of death: 6 May 1916. Age at death: 34. Service No.: 5358. Died in India.

Supplementary information: Born in Ennis, Co. Clare. Enlisted in Sheffield while living in Sheffield. Son of the late Timothy and Rachel Morrissey; husband of Louisa Mary Morrissey, of Lyndhurst, Winster, Matlock, Derbyshire.

Grave or memorial reference: He has no known grave but is listed on Panel 40 and 64 on the Basra Memorial in Iraq.

MUIR, ALBERT: Rank: Private. Regiment or service: Irish Guards. Unit: 2nd Battalion. Date of death: 16 September 1916. Service No.: 6481. Killed in action.

Supplementary information: Enlisted in Dublin while living in Killaloe, Co. Clare. In his will, dated 3 August 1915, his personal effects and property were received by Isabella (sister), Killaloe, Co. Clare, Ireland. Will was witnessed by Michael Legis, Ballyorgan Kilfinane, Co. Limerick, Ireland and executed by Michael Legier, 6475 Irish Guards Warley Barracks.

Grave or memorial reference: Pier and Face 7 D. Memorial: Thiepval Memorial in France.

MUIR, WILLIAM A.: Rank: Private/ Lance Corporal. Regiment or service: Royal Irish Regiment. Unit: 6th Battalion. Date of death: 12 April 1917. Age at death: 40. Service No.: 9864. Died of wounds.

Supplementary information: Born in Ballycoyney, Co. Clare. Enlisted in Roscrea while living in Leeds.

Grave or memorial reference: III. B. 83. Cemetery: Bailleul Communal Cemetery (Nord) in France.

MULCAHY, PATRICK: Rank: Private. Regiment or service: Royal

Army Medical Corps. Unit: 108th Field Ambulance. Date of death: 10 October 1917. Age at death: 20. Service No.: 54186. Died of wounds.

Supplementary information: Born in Bindon Street Ennis, Co. Clare. Enlisted in Limerick while living in Bindon Street, Ennis, Co. Clare. Son of Maurice Michael and Mary Isabella Mulcahy, of Wyndham Square, Plymouth.

Grave or memorial reference: F. 3. Cemetery: Ruyaulcourt Military Cemetery in France.

MULCAHY, PATRICK: Rank: Sergeant. Regiment or service: South Lancashire Regiment. Unit: 1st Battalion. Date of death: 12 August 1917. Age at death: 33. Service No.: 6887. Died of fever in Quetta, Pakistan.

Supplementary information: Born in Newmarket, Co. Clare. Enlisted in Birr, Co. Offaly. Soldiers died in the Great War gives his place of death as India. Son of John and Julia Mulcahy, of No. 4 Pound Street, Birr, Offaly, Ireland. Buried in Quetta – Quetta Government Cemetary 2304.

From the *Midland Tribune*, August 1917:

Sergeant Mulcahy, son of Mr J Mulcahy, Pound Street, Birr, has died of fever in India. A brother has been invalided having lost his leg on active service. In all there were seven brothers in the army.

Patrick had five other brothers who served and survived the war. They were John, Peter, and Daniel all in the 2nd Leinsters. Stephen, Leinsters and Michael in the South Lancashire Regiment. They were all sons of John Mulcahy, painter, Pound Street.

There is a photograph of Peter Mulcahy in the Kings Co. Chronicle in 1916 beside Martin O'Meara V. C.

Grave or memorial reference: Panel 44. Cemetery: Delhi (India Gate) Memorial in India.

MULDOON, THOMAS: Rank: Acting Sergeant. Regiment or service: Royal Munster Fusiliers. Unit: C Company, 1st Battalion. Date of death: 9 September 1916. Service No.: 7857. Killed in action.

Supplementary information: He won the Military Medal and is listed in the *London Gazette*. Born in Karachi, India. Enlisted in Limerick while living in Feakle, Co. Clare. Son of the late Mr Thomas Muldoon. Served on the North Western Frontier of India.

Grave or memorial reference: He has no known grave but is listed on Pier and Face 16C of the Thiepval Memorial in France.

MULLINS, MICHAEL: Rank: Gunner. Regiment or service: Royal Garrison Artillery. Unit: 246th Siege Battery. Age at death: 27. Date of death: 1 July 1918. Service No.: 159378. Died in Egypt.

Supplementary information: Born in Enagh, Sixmilebridge, Co. Clare. Enlisted in Limerick while living in Sixmilebridge, Co. Clare. Son of Edmond and Margaret Mullins, of Enagh, Belvoir, Sixmilebridge, Co. Clare.

Grave or memorial reference: C. 173. Cemetery: Kantara War Memorial Cemetery in Egypt.

MULQUEEN, JACK: Rank: Private. Regiment or service: Irish Guards. Unit: 1st Battalion. Date of death: 15 September 1916. Service No.: 8565. Killed in action.

Supplementary information: Born in Kilfenora, Co. Clare. Enlisted in Ennistymon, Co. Clare. In his will, dated 1 July 1916, his personal effects and property were received by Mrs Harry Mulqueen (mother), Kilginora, Co. Clare, Ireland.

Grave or memorial reference: XVI. D. 6. Cemetery: Delville Wood Cemetery, Longueval in France.

MUNGOVAN, PATRICK: Rank: Private. Regiment or service: Canadian Infantry (Saskatchewan Regiment) Unit: 46th Battalion. Date of death: 27 September 1918. Age at death: 36. Service No.: 466539.

Supplementary information: Brother of Mary J. Mungovan of No. 78 Parnell Street, Ennis, Co. Clare, Ireland. Next of kin listed as Timothy McInerney (friend), Maple Creek, Sask. Place of birth: Co. Clare, Ireland. Date of birth: 18 September 1881. Occupation on enlistment: Labourer. Date of enlistment: 12 July 1915. Height: 5ft 8in. Complexion: Medium. Eyes: Grey. Hair: Dark brown.

Grave or memorial reference; I. A. 35. Cemetery, Quarry Wood Cemetery, Sains-Les-Marquion, Pas-De-Calais, France.

MURCHIE, WILLIAM: Rank: Private. Regiment or service: Black Watch (Royal Highlanders). Unit: 1st Battalion. Date of death: 15 September 1914. Age at death: 25. Service No.: 984. Killed in action.

Supplementary information: Born in Glasgow, Lanarkshire. Enlisted in Glasgow. Son of William and Margaret Murchie, of No. 15 Lambhill Street, Glasgow; husband of Ellen Murchie, of Sixmilebridge, Co. Clare.

Grave or memorial reference: La Ferte-Sous-Jouarre Memorial in France.

MURPHY, CHARLES: Rank: Private. Regiment or service: Yorkshire Regiment. Unit: 6th Battalion. Date of death: 14 September 1916. Service No.: 11398. Killed in action.

Supplementary information: Born in Skibbereen, Co. Clare. Enlisted in South Shields while living in Cork.

Grave or memorial reference: Pier and Face 3 A and 3 D. Memorial: Thiepval Memorial in France.

MURPHY, JAMES: (Served as **CLARKE, JAMES**) Rank: Private. Regiment or service: Leinster Regiment. Unit: 1st Battalion. Date of death: 14 May 1915. Age at death: 29. Service No.: 7208. Killed in action.

Supplementary information: Born in Ennis, Co. Clare. Enlisted in Birr, Co. Offaly. Husband of Mrs Annie Sullivan (*née* Murphy), of Ordnance House, Ennis, Co. Clare. In his will, his personal effects and property were received by Mrs Annie Murphy (wife), Old Mill Street, Ennis, Co. Clare, Ireland.

Grave or memorial reference: Panel 44. Memorial: Ypres (Menin Gate) Memorial in Belgium.

MURPHY, MICHAEL: Rank: Private. Regiment or service: Royal Dublin Fusiliers. Unit: 2nd Battalion. Date of death: 30 December 1914. Age at death: 30. Service No.: 9542. Born in Kilrush, Co. Wexford. Killed in action.

Supplementary information: Enlisted in Carlow while living in Ryland Road, Bunclody (address from the *Enniscorthy Guardian*). Son of Michael and Bridget Murphy of No. 2 Ryland Road, Newtownbarry, Co. Wexford.

Grave or memorial reference: I. C. 2. Cemetery: Prowse Point Military Cemetery in Belgium.

MURRAY, ALFRED: Rank: Private. Regiment or service: Norfolk Regiment. Unit: 8th Battalion. Date of death: 19 July 1916. Service No.: 13091. Killed in action.

Supplementary information: Born in Clare, Co. Clare, Ireland. Enlisted in Norwich, Norfolk.

Grave or memorial reference: Pier and Face 1C and 1 D. Memorial: Thiepval Memorial in France.

MURRAY, JAMES JOSEPH: Rank: Private. Regiment or service: East Yorkshire Regiment. Unit: 11th Battalion. Date of death: 23 September 1915. Service No.: 11/373. Born in Kilrush, Co. Clare. Enlisted in Hull while living in Kilrush, Co. Clare. Died at home.

Grave or memorial reference: V. C. 4. Cemetery: Hamburg Cemetery in Germany.

MURRAY, MICHAEL: Rank: Rifleman. Regiment or service: Royal Irish Rifles. Unit: 3rd Battalion. Date of death: 4 December 1915. Service No.: 8998. Died at home.

Supplementary information: Born in Ennis, Co. Clare. Enlisted in Ballinasloe,

Co. Galway while living in Ennis. Son of Michael Murray, of Harmony Row, Ennis.

From the *Clare Journal*, December 1915:

The Late Mr M. J. Murray, Junr., Ennis. The funeral of the above young townsman, whose tragic death has aroused such profound sympathy with the afflicted parents, took place in Dublin, with full military honours, on Wednesday.

The cortege left King George's Hospital, where the remains lay, at 11 o'clock, for Glasnevin. It was headed by the brass band of the Royal Irish Rifles, after which came the gun carriage bearing the coffin. On either side of the carriage, marched three pall-bearers, carrying wreaths, and immediately behind walked the chief mourners, Mr M.J. Murray, Ennis, father and Edward V. Murray, National Bank, Boyle, brother; Martha and Clare, sisters; Mr P J Murray, uncle; Miss and John Murray, cousins; Gertie, Emily, Kathleen, May and Aggie, cousins, and Mr T Considine, Ennis. Then marched the company to which the deceased belonged, about a hundred men, under Captain Began and other officers. Following these came the mourning carriages, containing Mrs Murray, and other relatives and friends.

The route of the cortege from the Hospital was through the North Circular Road, and Glasvevin Road, to Glasnevin Church, where the coffin was left for some ten minutes, when it was blessed by the Chaplain of the Barracks, and prayers recited for the repose of the soul of the deceased. The coffin was then borne as before through the walks to the grave, where the final service for the dead was recited, and when the remains were reverently laid in their last resting place the firing party discharged the usual salvoes over the grave of their departed comrade.

The wreaths which were laid on the grave included the following

"With Heartfelt Sympathy," from his loving cousins in Dublin; "With Deepest Sympathy," from the officers of his company; "With Deepest regret to Dearest Michael." from the N. C. O's of his company, and two beautiful wreaths, "In Fond and Loving Memory of Dear Mick." From his old companions in Ennis.

From the *Clare Journal*, December 1915:

A Dead Son
Young soldier's sad death in Dublin
Barrack
A Verdict against a Lance Corporal
Dr Louis A. Byrne, Dublin City Coroner, held an inquest on Tuesday on the body of Michael Joseph Murray, Rifleman, F Company, 3rd R. I. Rifles, who died on the 4th inst, at George V. Hospital, following injuries received at Portobello Barracks the same day.

Inspector Gray, represented the D. M. P. authorities.

Mr M. J. Murray, organist and professor of music, father of the deceased boy, who had proceeded to Dublin on receiving intimation of the deplorable occurrence, identified the remains. Deceased was aged 16 ½ years.

The Coroner said that on Saturday last the boy received a blow on the head which ended fatally.

Private Quill deposed that he and deceased had returned to their room after morning parade and were directed by Lance-Corporal James Anderson, to settle up their beds properly before inspection of the bedrooms. The deceased's rifle was equipment were on the bed. The corporal told him to take them off. Deceased said he would in a minute. The corporal said a minute wont do, and that he would make him do it. Deceased said he would not be able to make him. The corporal shoved the deceased, and deceased struck him on the face. The corporal, who had been a sweeping brush in his hands, staggered back, and in turning round and regaining his balance the brush struck the deceased.

Replying to Inspector Gray—He had the brush in his hand the whole time, and when he got the blow in the face he (Anderson) staggered back, and when regaining his balance the brush came round in his hand and struck the deceased on the head. After about half a minute deceased fell on his knees beside the bed. The corporal had the brush on his shoulder. Deceased and Corporal Anderson, so far as witness knew, were on the same terms as the other men, and there was no ill-feeling against deceased.

To the foreman of the jury — He used good force in swinging round.

The Coroner — A moment ago you said there was no force? The swing round made the force. There was no blow. I could not explain how the man was struck on the head.

Mr Murray (deceased's father)— Simply tell the truth about my son and how the corporal struck him.

When the corporal staggered did the brush fall off? No.

Was it after my son hitting him that he made a strike to put off or keep away young Murray? I could not say.

Did he strike him on the side of the temple? He did.

Then it was not the fall off the shoulder? No.

What position was my son in? He was standing near the bed, and I think he put up his hand, but it was too late.

The boy's equipment was on the bed, and the corporal asked him to remove it and make up his bed? Yes, and your son said "I'll do it this minute." The corporal said: "This minute won't do; you'll have to do it immediately, or I'll make you."

Mr Murray—Now that is a very strong word for a young man in charge to use. My son was a quiet and honorable boy—

The Coroner—You must remember that in another place that is will be tried.

Mr Murray—I'll say that in another place; my son would say, "you would not make me," or words to that effect.

Inspector Gray—The guardroom would be the place then.

The Coroner—His evidence at first gave us to understand that the brush on the corporal's shoulder when he turned round, hit deceased. But there must have been some force to fracture the boy's head and rupture a blood vessel. I am sorry the accused is not present, but he is under confinement.

Dr Kirwin, of the R.A.M.C., described the minutes from which deceased suffered, and expressed the view that death was caused by shock and fracture.

Questioned by the Coroner he said that violence, but not extreme violence, must have been used.

Captain Regan, who commanded the F Company, was asked by the Coroner if a Lance-Corporal had a right to shove a man, and he replied that that was a question of civil law.

The Coroner—We are dealing with military law now. Has he power to shove a man?

Captain Regan—Supposing—

The Coroner—I can't take any supposition at all. I have asked you a simple question and I must get a simple answer. Has a Lance-Corporal power to shove a man—I want "yes" or "No. "?

Captain Regan—He would not be allowed to shove a man.

The Coroner—I would be surprised if it was otherwise.

The jury found that death was caused by the injuries described, caused by a violent blow given by Lance-Corporal James Anderson. They expressed the opinion that there was no premeditation on the part of the Lance-Corporal, and tendered their sympathy to the parents of the deceased.

The father exclaimed that he lad lost a dear son, who was only three weeks in the regiment, "but," he added, "I forgive the boy that caused his death, though he must have been struck with violence."

The Coroner said that Mr Murray had met with a terrible affliction but bore it like a man.

Captain Regan, on behalf of the military, joined in the expression of sympathy with the parents.

The court case that followed is covered in detail in the *Clare Journal*. It found the cause of death was due to an accident and the accused was discharged.

Grave or memorial reference: South FC. 36. Cemetery: Glasnevin (or Prospect) Cemetery in Dublin.

MYLNE, EDWARD GRAHAM:
Rank: Captain. Regiment or service: Irish Guards. Unit: 1st Battalion. Date of death: 12 June 1915. Age at death: 32. Died of wounds.

Supplementary information: Born at Bombay. Son of Louis George and Amy Frederica Mylne. Mentioned in Despatches.

From the *Clare Journal*, July 1915 and *Our Heroes*, 1916:

Captain Edward Graham Mylne, 1st Irish Guards, who died in No. 11, Red Cross Hospital, Rouen, on June 12, of wounds received on May 13, was the eldest son of the Right Rev. L. G. Mylne, Rector of Alvechurch, Worcestershire, formerly Bishop of Bombay. He ran for Oxford against Cambridge in the 100 Yards in 1905. In the same year he received an appointment in the Royal Irish Constabulary, in which he served with distinction, obtaining special good service pay and other honours.

The Late Captain E. G. Mylne, Irish Guards.

Resolution of Clare Magistrates
Reference was made at the late Sixmilebridge Petty Sessions to the late Captain E. G. Mylne, who had been D. I. in that district for some time. On the outbreak of the war Mr Mylne volunteered, and as a Captain in the Irish Guards, spent months in the very severe fighting around Ypres. He was shot through the chest, and although he survived for some weeks, his wound, unfortunately, proved fatal. Captain Mylne was a first class athlete, and had not reached his 50th year. Coming to Clare shortly after joining the R. I. C., he soon became popular among the people of the district, and although an Englishman, he had a real and sympathetic interest in Ireland, as is shown by the fact that the Irish Guards was the regiment in which he chose to serve. Had he been Irish-born, his sympathy might have been more demonstrative, but that it as real, is proved by the pathetic incident related by Head Constable Tobin, in Court, who stated that a few days ago he received a letter from a deceased's mother saying that by his will he had left a legacy to the

man who acted as his servant at Sixmilebridge some years ago. The Head Constable also stated that the deceased was a most efficient and popular officer and a very brave man. He has proved this my making the supreme sacrifice in laying down his life for his country. The sadness which the death of such a fine and manly man – in the very heyday of his youth – must cause to all who knew him, and above all, to his poor mother, will surely be tempered by the thought that he died as he had lived-doing his duty in that fearless, unselfish way so characteristic of him. His friends around Sixmilebridge trust that it will be some small consolation to the relations of deceased to be thus assured that the memory of him is, and will, remain green in the hearts of his friends in old Ireland.

The following resolution was proposed by Mr Wilson Lynch, and seconded by Mr Loftus Studdert;-

"The magistrates of Sixmilebridge (Co. Clare) Petty Sessions have learned with sincere regret of the death, from wounds received in action in Flanders, of Captain E. G. Mylne, of the Irish Guards, who was for some time District-Inspector of R. I. C., in this district, where he earned the good will and respect of all classes, and we hereby tender our sincere condolence to his relatives."

The resolution was supported by Dr Fross, Mr McElroy, R. M., and Head-Constable M. Tobin, and of whom referred in very eulogistic terms to the good qualities of deceased.

In addition to Captain Mylne, there are two others, formerly D. I. 's in Sixmilebridge District, now serving at the front, viz.;- Major G, De M, Rodwell, and Captain F. Jackson.

From *La Bassée to Laventie* by Rudyard Kipling:

No. 2 Company, on the right flank, had reached its objective and dug itself in under bursts of raking machine-gun and rifle-fire directed against the dykes and bridges, which unfortunately wounded both Captain Mylne and Lieutenant Kemp, and the company command devolved on 2nd Lieutenant S. G. Tallents … Captain Mylne and 2nd Lieutenant H. Marion-Crawford went home for a week's leave—for that wonderful experience of "first leave" was now available.

Grave or memorial reference: Officers, A. 1. 5. Cemetery: St Sever Cemetery, Rouen in France.

N

NASH, MICHAEL: Rank: Pioneer. Regiment or service: Corps of Royal Engineers. Unit: 12th Labour Battalion. Date of death: 11 June 1916. Age at death: 63. Service No.: 163287. Died at home.

Supplementary information: Enlisted in Dublin while living in Newmarket-on-Fergus, Co. Clare. Also commemorated in the 'List of Kilrush Men engaged in the War from August 1914'. This pamphlet lists the Kilrush men who were involved in the First World War until 11 November 1918 and adds that he died after two years in France. There is a Private Patrick Nash of the Royal Munster Fusiliers in the same pamphlet but he survived.

Grave or memorial reference: R.C. 487. Cemetery: Grangegorman Military Cemetery in Dublin.

NELSON, JOHN: Rank: Private. Regiment or service: Gloucestershire Regiment. Unit: 8th Service Battalion. Date of death: 3 July 1916. Service No.: 13582.

Supplementary information: Born in Ennis, Co. Clare. Enlisted in Gloucester. Killed in action.

Grave or memorial reference: Pier and Face 5A and 5B. Memorial: Thiepval Memorial in France.

NEVIN, PATRICK: Rank: Lance Corporal. Regiment or service: Royal Munster Fusiliers. Unit: 9th Battalion. Date of death: 28 April 1916. Service No.: 5578. Killed in action.

Supplementary information: Born in Kilkee, Co. Clare. Enlisted in Limerick while living in Kilkee, Co. Clare.

From the *Saturday Journal*, June 1916:

> Kilkee Fatality at the Front
> Events at the front in France have been painfully brought for the past few weeks to several families in Kilkee. Private P. Nevin of the Munsters was killed in the trenches.

Grave or memorial reference: I. G. 6. Cemetery: Dud Corner Cemetery, Loos in France.

NEYLON, MICHAEL: Rank: Private. Regiment or service: Royal Army Medical Corps. Unit: 2nd Field Ambulance. Date of death: 2 November 1914. Service No.: 3675. Died of wounds.

Supplementary information: Born in Ennis, Co. Clare. Enlisted in Manchester. Son of Patrick and Anne Neylon, of Skagh, Inagh, Ennis, Co. Clare.

Grave or memorial reference: Panel 56.

NEYLON, SIMON/SINON: Rank: Private. Regiment or service: Royal Munster Fusiliers. Unit: 5th Battalion. Date of death: 22 July 1916. Service No.: 6832. Died of compression of the brain due to a fall. He never regained consciousness.

Supplementary information: Unmarried. Born in Ennistymon, Co. Clare. Enlisted in Ennis while living in Lahinch, Co. Clare.

The following snippets are taken from the Court report in the *Clare Journal*, March 1917. The complete article is too big to reproduce here:

Before My Justice Dodd and a special Jury on Friday afternoon, a record suit was heard in which John Neylon, a farmer living near Lahinch, and his wife Margaret, claimed £500 damages from the Great Southern and Western Railway Co. for the loss of his son, Sinon Neylon, who was at the time a Private. in the Munster Fusiliers, and was proceeding from Limerick to the Curragh in charge of a military escort when he fell from the train near Lisnagry station.

Sinon Neylon joined the Munster Fusiliers and after five moths training was given a some leave. He overstayed his leave by a few days and was arrested as an absentee. He was taken to Limerick Jail. Later an escort of one N. C. O. and two Privates from the Munsters was sent from the Curragh to collect him. Pte Neylon had been sick for a few days prior to this and said so to the Corporal. After the train had passed Lisnagry station where it did not stop, Pte Neylon felt very sick and leaned out of the carriage door window to prevent vomiting in the carriage. The door opened, and as Pte Neylon was falling out one of the escort caught him but had to let him go or they would have gone with him. He fell on the track and sustained injuries from which he later died.

Grave or memorial reference: In the west part, south of the ruin. Cemetery: Ennistymon Cemetery, Co. Clare.

NEYLON/NAYLON, THOMAS:
Rank: Private. Regiment or service: Australian Infantry, AIF. Unit: 25th Battalion. Date of death: 29 July 1916. Age at death: 42. Service No.: 192. Killed in action at Pozieres.

Supplementary information: Occupation on enlistment: Storeman. Was a farmer in Ireland before he went to Australia aged 17. Next of kin: Mr P. Naylon (brother). Son of Lawrence and Eliza Naylon. Born at Kilshanny, Co. Clare, Ireland. Age on enlistment: 41 years 1 months Place and date of enlistment: Brisbane, Queensland; 8 January 1915. Weight: 9st 10lbs. Height: 5ft 7in. Complexion: Dark. Eyes: Brown. Hair: Black. Reported missing, later changed to Killed in action.

Grave or memorial reference: Villers-Bretonneux Memorial. Villers-Bretonneux Military Cemetery in France.

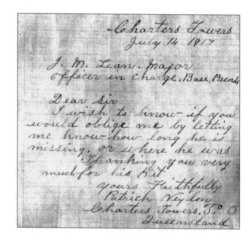

A letter from the brother of Thomas Neylon.

NIALL, PATRICK JOSEPH: Rank: Corporal. Regiment or service: King's Own (Royal Lancaster Regiment). Unit: 1st Battalion. Date of death: 21 March 1918. Age at death: 29. Service No.: 24635. Killed in action.

Supplementary information: Born in Killaloc, Ireland. Enlisted in Birkinhead. Husband of Rosa Niall, of No. 7 Baytree Road, Higher Tranmere, Birkenhead. Born in Co. Clare.

Grave or memorial reference: VII. B. 9. Cemetery: Faubourg D'Amiens Cemetery, Arras in France.

NIGHTENGALE, EDWIN ARTHUR: Rank: Private. Regiment or service: Hampshire Regiment. Unit: 2nd/5th (TF) Battalion. Date of death: 10 April 1918. Service No.: 240214. Killed in action in Egypt.

Supplementary information: Born in Plymouth, Devon. Enlisted in Southampton while living in Ennis, Co. Clare.

Grave or memorial reference: He has no known grave but is listed on the Jerusalem Memorial on panel 28 and 29.

NOLAN, JOHN MICHAEL: Rank: Private. Regiment or service: Australian Infantry, AIF. Unit: 9th Battalion. Date of death: 3 June 1918. Age at death: 42. Service No.: 2194. Wounded by gas, died the same day.

Supplementary information: Son of Margaret Mahoney (*née* Nolan), of Knockerra, Killimer, Co. Clare, Ireland, and John Nolan. Born, Tumut, N. S. W. Tumut. Place and date of enlistment: Townsville, Queensland, 1 March 1915. Occupation on enlistment: Plumber.

Age on enlistment: 38 years 1 month. Apprenticeship: 5 years to H. Smith. Weight: 8st 12lbs. Height: 5ft, 6in. Complexion: Fresh. Eyes: Hazel. Hair: Dark brown.

In November 1916 received a shell wound to the head, treated and returned to his unit. In May 1917 he was hospitalised with the after-effects, discharged 4 weeks later.

He was Court Martialled in March 1917. It shows that he was a prisoner in a cell when a riot broke out outside. The reports are contained in 19896 and A471 in the Australian National Archives. He was wounded in August 1916 with a gunshot to the shoulder and arm. There seems to have been a question regarding his identity as there were two men with this name and number.

After his death his personal effects were sent to Mr John Strathie, Railway Hotel, Townsville, Queensland.

Grave or memorial reference: I. P. 19. Cemetery: Ebblinghem Military Cemetery in France.

NOONAN, FRANCIS: Rank: Private. Regiment or service: Royal Munster Fusiliers. Unit: B Company, 2nd Battalion. Date of death: 9 May 1915. Age at death: 20. Service No.: 5900. Killed in action.

Supplementary information: Born in Killaloe, Co. Clare. Enlisted in Killaloe, Co. Clare while living in Killaloe, Co. Clare. Son of Francis and Mary Noonan, of No. 6 Cottage, Newtown, Killaloe, Co. Clare.

Grave or memorial reference: Panel 43 and 44. Memorial: Le Touret Memorial in France.

NOONAN, JOSEPH: Rank: Private. Regiment or service: Irish Guards. Unit: 1st Battalion. Date of death: 17 June 1915. Service No.: 3017. Killed in action.

Supplementary information: Born in Killaloe, Co. Clare. Enlisted in Dublin while living in Killaloe, Co. Clare. His personal effects and property were sent to Mrs Noonan, Canal Bank, Killalaoe, Co. Clare.

Grave or memorial reference: E. 38. Cemetery: Cambrin Churchyard Extension in France.

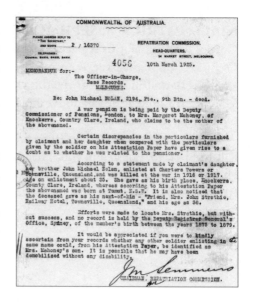

A letter concerning the war pension of Private J. Nolan.

O

O'BRIEN DANIEL JOSEPH:
Rank: Second Lieutenant. Regiment or
service: Royal Munster Fusiliers. Unit:
B Company, 3rd Battalion. Attached
to 2nd Battalion. Date of death: 10
November 1917. Age at death: 33. Killed
in action during the attack on Tounont
farm, Passchendale.

Supplementary information: Son of
Mrs Margaret O'Brien, of Clare Abbey
House, Clarecastle, Co. Clare.

Grave or memorial reference:
Panel 143 to 144. Memorial: Tyne Cot
Memorial in Belgium.

**O'BRIEN, The Hon. DESMOND
D.:** Rank: Flight Lieutenant. Regiment
or service: Royal Naval Air Service.
Date of death: 16 February 1915. Age at
death: 19.

Supplementary information: Son of
the late Edward Donough O'Brien,
14th Baron Inchiquin, of Dromoland
Castle, Co. Clare, Ireland (where he was
born), and Lady Inchiquin. Educated at
Charterhouse College.

From the *Clare Journal*, March 1915:

Missing Clare Man
No tidings have yet been received,
says the 'Morning Post,' of the Hon.
Desmond O'Brien, flight Lieutenant,
who is missing since the Belgian
coast air raid. Lieutenant O'Brien is
half brother to Lord Inchiquin.

Grave or memorial reference: 12.
Memorial: Chatham Naval Memorial,
UK.

O'BRIEN, GEORGE: Rank: Private.
Regiment or service: Royal Munster
Fusiliers. Unit: 1st Battalion. Date of
death: 25 April 1915. Service No.: 6642.
Died of wounds in Gallipoli.

Supplementary information: Born
in Drumcliffe, Co. Clare. Enlisted in
Ennis while living in Castleconnell, Co.
Limerick. Son of Mr Martin O'Brien,
The Upper Market.

Grave or memorial reference: Panel
185 to 190. Memorial: Helles Memorial
in Turkey.

O'BRIEN, JOHN: Rank: Private.
Regiment or service: Royal Munster
Fusiliers. Unit: 1st Battalion. Date of
death: 15 June 1915. Service No.: 9667.
Died in Gallipoli.

Supplementary information: Born in
Doonbeg, Co. Clare. Enlisted in Kilrush,
Co. Clare while living in Doonbeg.

Grave or memorial reference: XI.
E. 16. Cemetery: Twelve Tree Copse
Cemetery, Gallipoli.

O'BRIEN MARTIN: Rank: Private.
Regiment or service: Royal Munster
Fusiliers. Unit: 2nd Battalion. Date of
death: 9 May 1915. Age at death: 18.
Service No.: 6015. Killed in action.

Supplementary information: Born in
Kilkee, Co. Clare. Enlisted in Kilrush, Co.
Clare while living in Kilkee, Co. Clare.
Son of Michael and Mary O'Brien, of
Ball Alley Lane, Kilkee, Co. Clare.

Grave or memorial reference: VI. J.
20. Cemetery: Guards Cemetery, Windy
Corner, Cuinchy in France.

O'BRIEN, MARTIN: Rank: Private. Regiment or service: Royal Munster Fusiliers. Unit: 1st Battalion. Date of death: 28 June 1915. Service No.: 6002. Killed in action in Gallipoli.

Supplementary information: Born in St Michael's, Limerick. Enlisted in Ennis, Co. Clare while living in Kildysart, Co. Clare.

Grave or memorial reference: Panel 185 to 190. Memorial: Helles Memorial in Turkey.

O'BRIEN, MICHAEL: Rank: Gunner. Regiment or service: Royal Garrison Artillery. Date of death: 4 September 1914. Age at death: 35. Service No.: 3641. Died at home.

Supplementary information: Born in Ennis, Co. Clare. Enlisted in Ennis.

Grave or memorial reference: South part of old ground. Cemetery: Ennis (Drumcliffe) Cemetery, Co. Clare.

O'BRIEN, MICHAEL JOSEPH: Rank: Private. Regiment or service: The King's (Liverpool Regiment). Unit: 1st/8th Battalion. Date of death: 18 July 1917. Service No.: 307325 (CWGC) 237235 (SDGW). Died of wounds.

Supplementary information: Born in Kilkee, Co. Clare. Enlisted in Liverpool while living in Liverpool. Son of Frank and Mary O'Brien, of No. 330 Knight Street, Providence, Rhode Island, USA. Born Caherfinick, Co. Clare, Ireland.

Grave or memorial reference: XVI. D. 10A. Cemetery: Lijssenthoek Military Cemetery in Belgium.

O'BRIEN, PATRICK: Rank: Private. Regiment or service: Connaught Rangers. Unit: 6th Battalion. Date of death: 21 March 1918. Service No.: 18132. Formerly he was with the Royal Sussex Regiment where his number was 5424. Killed in action.

Supplementary information: Born in Killaloe, Co. Clare. Enlisted in Chelsea while living in Chelsea.

Grave or memorial reference: II. D. 5. Cemetery: Templeux-Le-Guerard British Cemetery in France.

O'BRIEN, PETER: Rank: Private. Regiment or service: Irish Guards. Unit: 2nd Battalion. Date of death: 27 November 1917. Service No.: 10048. Killed in action.

Supplementary information: Born in Inch, Co. Clare. Enlisted in Ballinasloe, Co. Galway while living in Ennis, Co. Clare.

Grave or memorial reference: Panel 2 and 3. Memorial: Cambrai Memorial, Louveral, Nord in France.

O'BRIEN, THOMAS: Rank: Leading Seaman. Regiment or service: Royal Naval Reserve. Unit: SV *Mary Fanny*. Date of death: 15 September 1918. Age at death: 39. Service No.: 3720C.

Supplementary information: Son of Thomas and Mary O'Brien, of Killard, Doonbeg; husband of Bridget O'Brien, of Killard, Doonbeg, Co. Clare.

Grave or memorial reference: 29. Memorial: Memorial: Plymouth Naval Memorial, UK.

O'BRIEN, THOMAS: Rank: Private. Regiment or service: Royal Welsh Fusiliers. Unit: 9th Battalion. Date of death: 8 November 1915. Service No.: 13264. Killed in action.

Supplementary information: Born in Kilmurrybricam, Co. Clare. Enlisted in Tonypandy while living in Shandrum.

From an article in a Wexford newspaper:

Wexford Soldier Killed

It has been officially announced that Private. Thomas O'Brien, of the Welsh Fusiliers, a brother of Mr James O'Brien, merchant, South Main Street, Wexford, has been Killed in action in France. He resided in Wales for some years and joined the colours after the outbreak of war. Much sympathy is felt with his relatives. His medal index card show he first entered the French theatre of war on 19 July 1915 and was entitled to the 1914 15 Star, the victory medal and the war medal.

Grave or memorial reference: Panel 50 to 52. Memorial: Loos Memorial in France.

O'CONNELL, PATRICK: *see* **CONNELL, PATRICK.**

O'CONNOR, JOHN: Rank: Private. Regiment or service: Royal Munster Fusiliers.
Unit: 2nd Battalion. Date of death: 27 August 1914. Age at death: 29. Service No.: 6137. Killed in action.
Supplementary information: Born in Liscannon, Co. Clare. Enlisted in Ennistymon while living in Ennistymon, Co. Clare.
Grave or memorial reference: I. 13. Cemetery: Etreux British Cemetery, Aisne, France.

O'CONNOR, MICHAEL: Rank: Private. Regiment or service: Royal Munster Fusiliers. Unit: 2nd Battalion. Date of death: 24 September 1916. Age at death: 30. Service No.: 6377. Killed in action.
Supplementary information: Born in Doolin Co. Clare. Enlisted in Limerick while living in Ennistymon, Co. Clare. Son of Austin and Mary O'Connor, of New Church, Ennistymon; husband of Ellen O'Connor, of Church Hill, Ennistymon, Co. Clare.
Grave or memorial reference: Pier and Face 16 C. Memorial: Thiepval Memorial in France.

O'CONNOR, MICHAEL: Rank: Chief Steward. Regiment or service: Mercantile Marine Reserve. Unit: HMS *Redbreast*. Date of death: 15 July 1917. Age at death: 33.
Supplementary information: Son of John and Catherine O'Connor, of Music Hill, Co. Clare; husband of Margaret McCourt O'Connor, of No. 93 Battlefield Avenue, Langside, Glasgow. The 1,313 ton HMS *Redbreast* was a British transport/passenger steamship and was torpedoed by German submarine UC-38 in the Aegean Sea.
Grave or memorial reference: 26. Memorial: Memorial: Plymouth Naval Memorial, UK.

O'CONNOR, THOMAS: *see* **CONSIDINE, WILLIAM.**

O'DEA, DANIEL JOSEPH: Rank: Private. Regiment or service: Royal Irish Regiment. Unit: 7th Battalion. Date of death: 12 December 1917. Age at death: 22. Service No.: 25665.

Supplementary information: Enlisted in Cahir, Co. Tipperary. Son of Thomas and Bridget O'Dea, of Ballynacally, Co. Clare.

Grave or memorial reference: II. H. 28. Cemetery: Templeux-Le-Guerard British Cemetery in France.

O'DEA, DANIEL: Rank: Private. Regiment or service: Royal Dublin Fusiliers. Unit: 1st Battalion. Date of death: 3 April 1918. Age at death: 19. Service No.: 20961. Formerly he was with the South Irish Horse where his number was 2851. Killed in action.

Supplementary information: Born in Kilmigil, Co. Clare. Enlisted in Ennis. Only son of Daniel and Maria O'Dea (*née* Daly), of Knockmore, Kilmihil, Co. Clare.

Grave or memorial reference: Panel 79 and 80. Memorial: Pozieres Memorial in France.

O'DEA, PATRICK JOHN: Rank: Private. Regiment or service: Australian Infantry, AIF Unit: 48th Battalion. Date of death: 8 August 1916. Service No.: 1792.

Supplementary information: Born, Clare, Ireland. Occupation on enlistment: Labourer. Age on enlistment: 36 years 5 months. Next of kin: Mrs Anne O'Dea (mother), of No. 153 Gilbert Street West, Adalaide, S.A. Place and date of enlistment: Adalaide, 28 August 1915. Previous military experience: Irish Corps, Adelaide, 2½ years – resigned. Weight: 10st 6lbs. Height: 5ft 10½in. Complexion: Fresh. Eyes: Blue. Hair: Dark. Reported missing in action, later changed to killed in action. At the Battle of Pozieres he was last seen by his

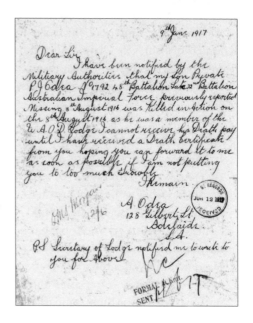

A letter from the mother of Private O'Dea.

mates just before the battle. His mother was granted a pension of £2 per fortnight from 8 October 1916

Grave or memorial reference: He has no known grave but is listed on the Villers-Bretonneux Memorial in France.

O'DEA, TIMOTHY: Rank: Lance Corporal. Regiment or service: Irish Guards. Unit: 2nd Battalion. Date of death: 27 November 1917. Age at death: 39. Service No.: 10251(CWGC) 10231(SDGW). Killed in action.

Supplementary information: Enlisted in Dublin, Co. Dublin while living in Tullabrack, Co. Clare. He won the Military Medal and is listed in the *London Gazette*. Son of Michael and Honor O'Dea, of Tullabrack, Cooraclare, Co. Clare.

Grave or memorial reference: Panel 2 and 3. Memorial: Cambrai Memorial, Louveral, Nord in France.

O'DELL, MARTIN: Rank: Private. Regiment or service: Australian Infantry, AIF. Unit: 16th Battalion. Date of death: 30 April 1915. Service No.: 116. Killed in action on the Gallipoli Peninsula.

Supplementary information: Born, O'Gonnelloe, Co. Clare. Occupation on enlistment: Lumper. Age on enlistment: 33 years 6 months. Next of kin: Mrs Moran (sister), Bayley Street, Coolgardie, later changed to Mrs M. O'Dell (mother), Corhula, Killaloe, Co. Clare. Place and date of enlistment: Helena Vale, W.A. 16 October 1914. Weight: 9st 12lbs. Height: 5ft 7¼in. Complexion: Dark. Eyes: Blue. Hair: Black.

Temporarily 'Buried at right of Popes Hill by Rev F. W. Wray, 9 June 1915.' Grave or memorial reference: A. 26. Cemetery: Quinn's Post Cemetery, Anzac, Turkey.

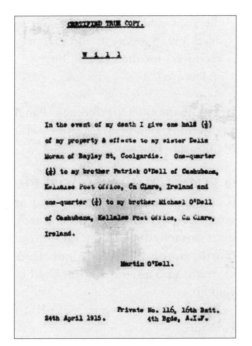

The will of Private M. O'Dell.

O'DONNELL, PHILIP: Rank: Private. Regiment or service: Royal Munster Fusiliers. Unit: 3rd Battalion. Date of death: 5 November 1918. Age at death: 21. Service No.: 9983. Died at home from wounds received in France.

Supplementary information: Born in Kilrush, Co. Clare. Enlisted in Kilrush, Co. Clare while living in Kilrush, Co. Clare. Son of Philip and Mary O'Donnell, of Kilrush, Co. Clare.

Grave or memorial reference: D. 11. Cemetery: Edinburgh (Comely Bank) Cemetery, UK.

O'DONOGHUE, CORNELIUS: Rank: Private. Regiment or service: Royal Munster Fusiliers. Unit: 2nd Battalion. Date of death: 12 November 1914. Age at death: 32. Service No.: 6641. Killed in action.

Supplementary information: Born in Kilkisheen, Co. Clare. Enlisted in Ennis, Co. Clare while living in Clarecastle, Co. Clare. Son of Mrs Catherine Murphy, of Clarecastle, Co. Clare.

I include the following article for your reference as they may be related. From the *Clare Journal*, May 1915:

Interesting Letter from the Front.
From Clarecastle Man.
'Pals' not Divided in Death.
Bdr John O'Donohue, of the 61st Battery, R. F. A., who belongs to Clarecastle, has sent a letter to his mother in that place, the date being a very recent one, from which we extract the following:

One of the cruellest incidents of the war happened yesterday. One of the gunners was sent back from the firing line to bring our letters from the supply depot. On his way back he was killed by a shrapnel shell.

I was one of a party sent to bury him, and we had to take him to a cemetery near a big town. Just as we came near the gate four terrible big shells came tearing through the air and burst right in the burying ground, bursting open graves, and sending tombstones flying in the air. A civilian and his horse were killed and several of our men were wounded. I dropped flat on the ground, with several others, and this saved me from flying fragments of shell. We had hardly recovered from this shock when I could hear another salvo tearing through the air. At this time I had hold of the stretcher with another man, and was trying to get under cover with the poor corpse, when crash came the shells. This time I thought I must get hit as fragments flew all around us. But God spoke before the Germans. He was protecting the bearers of the dead. They [the Germans] continued to shell the cemetery, and we had to postpone the burying until night. We were all sent back to our lines, except six men left behind as a burying party, and amongst them was the dead man's 'best pal', as we say in the army, who remained to pay a last token of respect to his old friend. Well, at 6 o'clock, pm, they took the body to the cemetery, and were just putting the last sod on the grave when they heard the buzzing noise that there was no mistaking.

They all dropped flat, except the dead man's pal, who ran to take shelter under a wall, but he was too late. The shell burst, a piece struck him, and he was dead. To-day we buried him side by side with his friend—'pals' in death, as they were in life. Such tragic incidents happen out here every day. The Germans have no respect over the dead.

In the cemetery the family vaults are all blown to bits. Churches and convents are everywhere levelled to the ground. I am proud to see by the papers that our countrymen are doing their share at this critical time. The more that give a hand, the sooner the War will be over, and peace restored to Europe once more. I would like you to put this in the "Record" I would like you to have a Mass said for me by the Friars, and ask everyone to pray for the poor soldiers who are facing death every moment, and giving their lives for the cause of liberty and justice."

Grave or memorial reference: Panel 44. Memorial: Ypres (Menin Gate) Memorial in Belgium.

O'FLYNN, MICHAEL JOSEPH: Rank: Lieutenant (TP). Regiment or service: Royal Army Medical Corps. Unit: attached to the 1st Battalion Northamptonshire Regiment. Date of death: 24 September 1918. Died of wounds:

From De Ruvigny's Roll of Honour:

... so of James Flynn, of Sixmile Bridge, Co. Clare, Mill Owner, by his wife, Margaret, daughter of [-] O'Halloran. Born at Sixmile Bridge, Co. Clare, 26 November 1879. Educated at Blackrock, Dublin, and at the National University of Ireland, where he graduated M. D. in 1903. Subsequently practiced in Neath, Co. Glamorgan. Gazetted Temporary Lieutenant. Royal Army Medical Corps, 20 November 1917. Served with the Expeditionary Force in France and Flanders from the following December, being attached to the 1st Battalion Northamptonshire Regiment, and died near Peronne, 24 September 1918, from wounds received while attending the wounded near Peronne. Buried at Poeuilly.

The A.D.M.S. wrote; "We all mourn a gallant, cheery and brave comrade, who always did his duty." He married at St George's Church, Neath, Co. Glamorgan, 2 January 1910, Florence E. (22, London Road, Neath), daughter of G. H. Davey, of Woodside, Briton-Ferry, J. P., and had four children. Patrick, born November 1910; Garrett, born November 1913; Geoffrey, born December 1917; and Margaret, born May 1915.

Grave or memorial reference: I. K. 8. Cemetery: Roisel Communal Cemetery Extension, Somme, France.

O'GORMAN, JOHN: Rank: Captain. Regiment or service: Mercantile Marine. Unit: SS *Jessie*. Date of death: 2 November 1917. Age at death: 35.

Supplementary information: Son of John and Bridget O'Gorman; husband of Catherine O'Gorman, of The Bay, Glenariffe, Co. Antrim. Born at Carrigaholt, Co. Clare. The British cargo/transport SS *Jessie* was raked with gunfire from German submarine U-35, 3 miles north of Flamborough Head. She stayed afloat and later ran aground. Four men died and the ship was scrapped.

Grave or memorial reference: A. 61. Cemetery: Carnlough (Cavalry) Roman Catholic Cemetery, Co. Antrim.

O'GRADY, MARGARET and **MARY:** Rank: Both Nurses. Margaret worked at the Isolation Hospital, Mitcham, England. Date of death: 10 October 1918. Drowned when the Packet SS RMS *Leinster* was torpedoed and sunk by German Submarine U-123 on 10 October 1918.

Supplementary information: Daughters of Francis O'Grady, Manse, Quin, Co. Clare. They are also listed as from Newmarket-on-Fergus. Mary's sister Margaret was also on the Leinster. Both were returning from holidays to nursing duties. In *Torpedoed! The R.M.S. Leinster Disaster* (Periscope Publishing Ltd, 2005), Mary is listed as May. Margaret is not commemorated in any of the First World War dead databases.

Grave or memorial reference: Buried at Quin Abbey.

O'HALLORAN, THOMAS: Rank: Guardsman. Regiment or service: Scots Guards. Unit: 1st Battalion. Date of death: 11 November 1914. Service No.: 6607. Killed in action.

Supplementary information: Born in Ennis, Co. Clare. Enlisted in Edinburgh while living in Kildysart, Co. Limerick.

Grave or memorial reference: Panel 11. Memorial: Ypres (Menin Gate) Memorial in Belgium.

O'HALLORAN, THOMAS:

Rank: Private. Regiment or service: Connaught Rangers. Unit: 5th Battalion. Date of death: 30 November 1915. Service No.: 6137. Killed in action in Salonika.

Supplementary information: Born in Kilkee, Co. Clare. Enlisted in Kilrush while living in Moyasta, Co. Clare. This man is only in Soldiers Died in the Great War database. No burial information is available from the CWGC. He has however a medal index card that shows he had two names and two numbers. Thomas Nevils, No. 28488 who did not die and was discharged to the reserve in 1919. The other card says his name is O'HALLORAN who went to the Balkans four weeks before he was supposed to have been killed in action and although he is not in the Commonwealth War Graves Database he is, in fact, listed on the Doiran memorial in Greece under his serial number 6137. The name on the memorial is scheduled to be deleted with about 60 others as they were found (since the end of the First World War) to be buried elsewhere.

O'KEEFE, PATRICK:

Rank: Private. Regiment or service: Auckland Regiment, NZEF. Unit: 2nd Battalion. Date of death: 30 March 1918. Service No.: 49736. Killed in action.

Supplementary information: Son of Mrs E. O'Keefe, of Broadford, Co. Clare. Next of kin listed as Mrs Martin Murphy (aunt), Eureka, New Zealand. Occupation on enlistment: Railway labourer. Embarked with the 26th Reinforcements Auckland Infantry Regiment, A Company, NZEF on 9 June 1917 in Wellington, New Zealand aboard the *Willochra* bound for Suez, Egypt.

Grave or memorial reference: He has no known grave but is listed on the Grevillers (New Zealand) Memorial in France.

O'LEARY, MICHAEL:

Rank: Private. Regiment or service: Connaught Rangers. Unit: 5th Battalion. Date of death: 5 July 1916. Service No.: 2878. Died in Salonika.

Supplementary information: Enlisted in Galway while living in Ennis.

From the *Clare Journal*, 1915:

Letter from an Ennis Soldier Private O'Leary, The Connaughts, from whom we published a letter while he was lying wounded in the Versailles Hospital, has sent another note to a friend in Ennis. Writing from Havre he says:

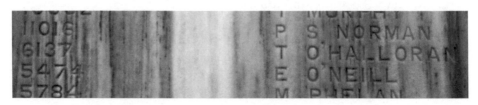

Thomas O'Halloran on the Doiran Memorial, soon to be deleted.

"I am now out of hospital and am at the base of operations, but I don't know whether I will be at the front on not, as there is a bullet still in my side and the muscles are badly injured. I am out of hospital since before Christmas, and I met a lot of chaps from Ennis going up to the front. They are leaving in thousands every day here for the front. Let me know if Jack [a brother] was killed, as a chap of the Leinsters told me he was killed on Xmas Eve. He was in the Maxim gun section. I would be glad if you send a paper. We don't see any here. This war is fearful slaughter, and I hope it will soon be over."

Grave or memorial reference: 193. Cemetery: Salonika (Lembet Road) Military Cemetery in Greece.

O'LOUGHLIN, JOHN P.: Rank: Acting Bombardier. Regiment or service: Royal Horse Artillery and Royal Field Artillery. Unit: 46th Brigade. Date of death: 25 April 1915. Age at death: 21. Service No.: 51134. Killed in action.

Supplementary information: Born in Clare, Ireland. Enlisted in Milford Haven, Pembroke. Son of Joseph and Margaret O'Loughlin, of Telegraph Cottage, Milford Haven. Born in Ireland.

Grave or memorial reference: IV. F. 2. Cemetery: Vieille-Chapelle New British Cemetery, Lacouture in France.

O'LOUGHLIN JOHN: Rank: Sapper. Regiment or service: Royal Engineers. Unit: 56th Field Company. Date of death: 14 Jaunuary 1915. Age at death: 32. Service No.: 4827. Killed in action.

Supplementary information: Born in Ennistymon, Co. Clare. Enlisted in Ennistymon, Co. Clare. Husband of Catherine O'Loughlin, of Bogberry, Ennistymon, Co. Clare.

From the *Clare Journal*, February 1915:

Volunteer Instructor Killed
The Ennistymon Volunteers have learned with the deepest regret of the recent death at the front in Belgium of their late instructor, Sapper John O'Loughlin, who was attached to the Royal Engineers. The commanding officer in communicating news of the death to the bereaved widow of the deceased, under date the 15th January, wrote: "It is with the deepest regret that I report to you the death of your husband. He was killed last night when doing his duty at the front. Only two weeks ago it was my very great pleasure to mention his name in despatches for the very good work he had done on previous occasions in face of the enemy. His loss is very deeply felt by the officers and men of the company. With greatest sympathy in your terrible loss."

A native of Ennistymon, the deceased was only 35 years of age, and besides his widow, leaves four little ones, varying from four months to six years of age to mourn his loss. The greatest sympathy is felt with the bereaved wife and children in their sad loss. The local Volunteer Corps, for whom the late Sapper did so much during his period as instructor, have arranged for a Memorial Mass to be offered for him.

Grave or memorial reference: IV. B. 13. Cemetery: Wytschaete Military Cemetery in Belgium.

O'LOUGHLIN/O'LOUGHLEN, PATRICK JOSEPH:
Rank: Private. Regiment or service: Australian Infantry, AIF. Unit: 3rd Battalion. Date of death: 18 September 1917. Age at death: 29. Service No.: 7048.

Supplementary information: Son of Mary O'Brien (*née* O'Loughlen), of Corkscrew Hill, Ballyvaughan, Co. Clare, Ireland, and the late Martin O'Loughlen. Place and date of enlistment: Molong, 22 October 1915. Weight: 13 stone. Height: 6ft. Complexion: Medium. Eyes: Light brown. Hair: Black. His records say he was discharged as medically unfit after 16 days on 29 November 1915. Born, Ballyvaughan, Co. Clare. Occupation

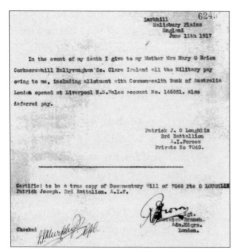

The will of Private P. O'Loughin.

on enlistment: Labourer. Age on enlistment: 27 years 8 months. Address on enlistment: Tattersalls Hote, Gilgaindra. N.S.W. Next of kin: Mrs Mary O'Brien (mother), Corkscrew Hill, Ballyvaughan, Co. Clare.

This man enlisted in 1915 and after 16 days was discharged as medically unfit. Later he rejoined at a different location (Dubbo, N. S. W.) and according to his second set of enlistment documents he had grown another ¾in taller. His only crime in the army was being AWOL in Waterford and 'attempting to escape from escort by jumping from a train whilst in motion.' He was fined 30 days pay.

His mother received a pension of 15s per fortnight from 29 November 1917.

Grave or memorial reference: Panel 7 - 17 - 23 - 25 - 27 - 29 - 31. Memorial: Ypres (Menin Gate) Memorial in Belgium.

O'LOUGHLIN, THOMAS:
Rank: Acting Sergeant. Regiment or service: Royal Munster Fusiliers. Unit: 2nd Battalion. Date of death: 9 May 1915. Age at death: 29. Service No.: 5816. Killed in action.

Supplementary information: Born in Miltown Malbay, Co. Clare. Enlisted in Ennis while living in Miltown Malbay, Co. Clare. Son of the late Martin and Katie O'Loughlin. His personal effects and property were sent to Mr Martin O'Loughlin (father), Ennistymon Road, Miltown, Malbay, Co. Clare, Ireland

From the *Clare Journal*, 1915:

Miltown Malbay Man Killed at the Front
The sad news reached Miltown Malbay on Saturday in a letter to the

father sent by his second son, Martin, that Sergeant Thomas O'Loughlin, Royal Munster Fusiliers, has been Killed in action.

A carpenter by trade, in the employment of Mr Michael Moroney, contractor and builder, Miltown Malbay, he volunteered at the beginning of the war. In the early days of March he arrived home suffering from frost bite contracted in the trenches. Remaining home only a few weeks to recuperate, he again went to the front, having volunteered to accompany his brother Martin, who belonged to the same company, and had been ordered to the front, having completed his home service. He was a splendid athletic young fellow, and had been one of the famous "St Joseph's football team". He also was one of the first organisers of the Volunteer Corps, and was their early instructor, and was most popular with all his comrades in the ranks. His brother had been a short time previously relieved in the trenches, and on returning to them poor Tom was found dead in the same portion of the trench.

At the eight o'clock Mass yesterday morning, the Rev. Fr Enright, C. C. in asking the prayers of the congregation for the repose of his soul, feelingly referred to the sad event. This death was the second at the front of Miltown Malbay men.

The greatest sympathy from all is extended to the bereaved father, sister and only brother at home.

From the *Clare Journal*, 2 September 1915:

Letter from the Dardanelles

Sergeant J. O'Shea, of the Royal Munster Fusiliers, writes to his uncle, who lives in the Flag Road, Miltown Malbay—

"I suppose you will be surprised to receive a letter from me. I read in the 'Cork Examiner' of Tommy O'Loghlen's death in France. Are there any more Miltown lads knocked out? The fighting here is very severe, as you can judge from Sir Ian Hamilton's despatch, and the Munsters are badly smashed up. Very few have escaped the fighting for the past four months, and the area of operations here is so confined that we are always under shell-fire no matter where we go. The Turks have some mobile batteries on the Asiatic side which give us a great deal of trouble as they are very difficult to locate. The French have wonderful artillery—75's. It is a splendid sight to see the French infantry advancing under their fire. They are practically covered from the enemy's view by a screen of shells. It is wonderful to think of the many different races fighting in this small piece of ground—Algerians, Gurkhas, British, Turkos, Turks, Arabs, and the many different races of the French Foreign Legion. There never was so many in any war up to the present. When you reply to this letter send me some news, as I never have a letter from willie. Show this letter to Alie McKenzie. I know he would like to know how I am progressing."

Grave or memorial reference: Panel 43 and 44. Memorial: Le Touret Memorial in France.

O'MEEHAN, The Revd ISIDORE JAMES:
Rank: Chaplain 4th Class. Regiment or service: Army Chaplains' Department. Date of death: 19 December 1919. Age at death: 52.

Supplementary information: Son of Thomas and Catherine O'Meehan (*née* Dwyer). Born at Ennis, Co. Clare.

Grave or memorial reference: XII. E. 3. Cemetery: Amara War Cemetery in Iraq.

O'NEILL, MICHAEL:
Rank: Private. Regiment or service: Irish Guards. Unit: 1st Battalion. Date of death: 6 November 1914. Age at death: 26. Service No.: 2960. Killed in action

Supplementary information: Born in Kilkerrin, Co. Clare. Enlisted in Ennis, Co. Clare. Son of John and Mary O'Neill, of Kilkerrin, Labasheeda, Co. Clare.

Grave or memorial reference: Panel 11. Memorial: Ypres (Menin Gate) Memorial in Belgium.

O'NEIL/O'NEILL, MICHAEL:
Rank: Private. Regiment or service: Australian Infantry, AIF. Unit: 21st Battalion. Date of death: 18 May 1917. Age at death: 24. Service No.: 6073.

Supplementary information: Son of Patrick and Ellen O'Neill (*née* Melican), of Lismuse, Lisdeen, Co. Clare. Born, Kilkee, Co. Clare. Occupation on enlistment: Labourer. Age on enlistment: 23 years 6 months. Next of kin: Mr Patrick O'Neill (father), Lismore, Lisdeen, Co. Clare. Place and date of enlistment:

Receipt for Private O'Neill's personal effects signed by his father.

Bathurst; 29 February 1916, while living at No. 40 Elizabeth Street, Redfern, N.S.W. Height: 5ft 8½in. Complexion: Dark. Eyes: Blue. Hair: Dark brown. His records seem to insist that his name be spelled with only one L. Died of gunshot wounds to his back at No. 9 General Hospital, Rouen, France.

Grave or memorial reference: P. II. O. 2A. Cemetery: St Sever Cemetery Extension, Rouen in France.

O'NEILL, PATRICK:
Rank: Private. Regiment or service: Royal Munster Fusiliers. Unit: 8th Battalion (SDGW) 1st Battalion (CWGC). Date of death: 9 September 1916. Age at death: 26. Service No.: 5571. Killed in action.

Supplementary information: Enlisted in Ennis while living in Feakle, Co. Clare. Son of William O'Neill, of Ballylongford, Co. Kerry.

Grave or memorial reference: A. 26. Cemetery: Queant Communal Cemetery British Extension in France.

ORMROD, OLIVER HUGH:
Rank: Captain/Temporary Captain. Regiment or service: Royal Field Artillery. Unit: Attached to the Royal Flying Corps. Date of death: 12 September 1916. Killed in action.

From De Ruvigny's Roll of Honour:

Ormrod, Oliver Hugh. Captain, Royal Flying Corps, formerly Royal Field Artillery. Eldest son of Oliver Ormrod, Pickhill Hall, Co. Denbigh, J. P., for Co. Flint and Co. Denbigh. High Sheriff for Co. Denbigh 1916-17, and Major and Hon. Lieut-Col. (retired 1903) of the Denbighshire Hussars, by his wife, Emily Westropp Harrison, daughter of the late W.J.H. Moreland, of Rahecus Manor, Tomgraney, Co. Clare, LL. D.; and brother to Captain L. M. Ormrod, M. C. (q.v.). Born, Holt Co. Denbigh, 3 October 1885.

Educated at Sandroyd and Eton. After leaving school he studied Farming and Land Agency;

Captain O. Ormrod.

was in the Denbighshire Hussars. Retired as Lieutenant; went out to Canada, and entered into business in Vancouver, British Columbia. On the outbreak of war he returned home. Obtained a commission in the Royal Field Artillery. Was gazetted Lieutenant, October 1914. Promoted Captain, February 1915. Served with the Expeditionary Force in France and Flanders from July 1915 as Adjutant to the 87th Brigade, Royal Field Artillery. Contracted enteric fever in December 1915, and was invalided home in February 1916. On his recovery he transferred to the Royal Flying Corps, May 1916. Obtained his wings, and was about to return to France as Pilot when he was killed in a flying accident at Gosport, Co. Hants, 12 September 1916. Buried at Bangor Isycoed, Co. Flint. His Commanding Officer wrote; "He was a very able and plucky pilot, and to be relied on in everything," and his Commanding Officer in the Field Artillery; "He was a smart officer and a good fellow all round" When at Eton he was captain of his house football for two years.

Grave or memorial reference: In the south east part. Cemetery: Bangor Monachorum (St Dunawd) Churchyard in Flintshire.

O'SHEA J.: Rank: Private. Regiment or service: Royal Dublin Fusiliers. Unit: 2nd Battalion. Date of death: 13 March 1920. Age at death: 20. Service No.: 31339.

Supplementary information: Son of Mrs Sarah O'Shea, of Turnpike, Ennis, Co. Clare. This man is only in the Commonwealth War Graves database.

Grave or memorial reference: I. K. 1. Cemetery: Haidar Pasha Cemetery in Turkey.

O'SHEA, MICHAEL: Rank: Bombardier. Regiment or service: Royal Horse Artillery and Royal Field Artillery. Unit: 97th Battery. Date of death: 29 June 1915. Service No.: 57329. Died of wounds in Gallipoli.

Supplementary information: Born in Birdhill, Co. Clare. Enlisted in Limerick. Son of Patrick and Catherine O'Shea, of No. 4 Clare Street, Limerick.

Grave or memorial reference: Panel 21 and 22. Memorial: Helles Memorial in Turkey.

O'SHEA, PAT: *see* **SHEA, PATRICK.**

O'SHEA, T.: *see* **SHEA, PATRICK.**

O'SHEA, T.: Rank: Gunner. Regiment or service: Royal Garrison Artillery. Date of death: 3 Jaunuary 1919. Service No.: 283002.

Supplementary information: Husband of Ellen O'Shea, of Kilrush, Co. Clare.

This man is only in the Commonwealth War Graves database. Grave or memorial reference: Near the West boundary. Cemetery: Labasheeda (Killofin) Cemetery, Co. Clare.

O'SULLIVAN, JOHN: Rank: Private. Regiment or service: Royal Munster Fusiliers. Unit: 2nd Battalion. Date of death: 3 June 1915. Age at death: 23. Service No.: 5795. Died of wounds.

Supplementary information: Born in Ennistymon, Co. Clare. Enlisted in Ennis, Co. Clare while living in Ennistymon, Co. Clare. Son of Stephen and Margaret O'Sullivan, of Church Hill, Ennistymon, Co. Clare.

Grave or memorial reference: 1320. Cemetery: Fort Pitt Military Cemetery in Kent, UK.

P

PARKE, WILLIAM HENRY: Rank: Captain/Temporary Captain. Regiment or service: Connaught Rangers. Unit: 6th Battalion. Date of death: 15 October 1916. Killed in action.

From the *Saturday Record* and *Clare Journal*, October 1916:

> Captain William H. Parke
> A telegram has been received announcing that captain william. H. Parke had been killed at the front. Captain Parke was a brother of the late Surgeon-Major T. H. Parke, Medical Officer of the Stanley Expedition across Africa, whose statue stands in the Leinster Lawn, Dublin, and also of Mr B. Parke, formerly of the provisionl Bank, Ennis. Captain Parke, gave up his position as Sub Sherriff of the Co. of Sligo in order to go to the front.

Lieutenant R Parker.

Grave or memorial reference: D. 3. Cemetery: Kemmel Chateau Military Cemetery, Heuvelland, West-Vlaanderen, Belgium.

PARKER, RONALD ELPHINSTONE: Rank: Lieutenant. Regiment or service: Royal Horse Artillery and Royal Field Artillery. Unit: D Battery. Date of death: 9 September 1914. Age at death: 28. Killed in action.

From De Ruvigny's Roll of Honour:

Parker, Ronald Elphinstone, Lieutenant, D Battery, Royal Horse Artillery. Youngest son of Robert Gabbett Parker, of Bally Valley, Killaloe, Co. Clare, J. P., by his wife, Louisa, daughter of John C ... Whitty, of Broadwater Down, Tunbridge Wells. Born in Baly Valley, aforesaid, 5th January 1886. Educated at the Abbey, Tipperary, and Clifton College. Joined the Clare Artillery, 11 February 1907 and posted to the 87th Howitzer Battery. Promoted Lieutenant, 25 May 1910. Went to

France, 16 August 1914 and was Killed in action at the Battle of the Marne, 8th September following. Four guns of D Battery, R. H. A., were supporting the 3rd Cavalry Brigade in the advance to the Marne. The Germans brought back some 12 guns against them, but the battery held its ground, and eventually the enemy drew off. The battery lost its Major, wounded, and both its subalterns, killed. He was un., and was buried at the Hotel de Bois, Jonarre, Meaux. His brigade commander wrote; "He died like a man, fighting his guns at great odds to the last." The officer commanding his R.H.A. battery wrote;

"He was indefatigable, undaunted even in the darkest moments; his good temper and high spirits were worth anything to us all"; and the officer commanding his R. H. A. battery; "In 20 years I have never met a better subaltern and a keener sportsman, in both of which capacities he won my complete respect and affection, as he did that of every man or horse that came into his care." Lieutenant Parker excelled at all field sports and was a fine horseman and whip.

From the *Clare Journal*, 1914:

Sympathy of Killaloe Magistrates
At the last Killaloe Petty Sessions, the magistrates present being Mr W.J. Hardy, RM (in the chair), Mr J.M. Galwey-Foley and Mr T. Hogan.

The Chairman said he wished to express his sympathy and that of the Bench with one of their colleagues, Mr Parker, in the loss he had sustained by the death of his son, who was killed at the front, while another of his sons was wounded. Since the war broke out many lives were lost, and he hoped it would end in victory for their army, for which so many had bravely parted with their lives.

Mr Galwey-Foley, in associating himself with the vote of sympathy, will be heard a great deal spoken in Nenagh of Mr Parker's great loss, whose son was killed whilst fighting ruthless savages.

Mr Shannon, solicitor, on behalf of himself and his profession, joined in the vote of sympathy.

District Inspector McClelland, on behalf of himself and the police, and Mr Hassett, C. P. S., also associated themselves with the vote of sympathy.

From the *Clare Journal*, September 1914:

Clare Officer Killed
Lieutenant Parker
There is great sympathy with Mr R. G. Parker, J.P., Ballyvalley, Killaloe, and Mrs Parker, whose youngest son, Lieutenant R.E. Parker, Royal Horse Artillery, was killed at the front a few days ago. Lieutenant Parker was well known in Clare and Limerick, and was a general favourite.

The article below concerns Lieutenant Parker's brother, from *Our Heroes*, 1916:

Major R. G. Parker, King's Own Lancaster Regiment, who has been mentioned in Sir John French's despatches, is the son of Mr R.G. Parker, J.P., of Ballyvalley, Killaloe, Co. Clare. He served in the South African War, being present at nearly all the important engagements during the campaign. He was mentioned in despatches twice, and received the Queen's Medal with 6 clasps and the King's Medal with 2 clasps.

Also from *Our Heroes*, 1916:

Lieutenant Ronald Elphinstone Parker, Royal Horse Artillery, killed in a action. He was the youngest son of Mr R.G. Parker, J.P., and Mrs Parker, of Ballyvalley, Killaloe, Co. Clare. Gazetted to the R. H. A. on the 25th May, 1907, and beame Lieutenant on 25th May, 1910. Lieutenant Parker was well known in Limerick, where he was very popular.

From *Bond of Sacrifice*, Volume 1:

Lieutenant Ronald Elphinstone Parker, D Battery, Royal Horse Artillery, was the third son of Robert Gabbett and Louisa Parker, of Bally Valley, Killaloe, Co. Clare, Ireland, and was born there on the 5th January, 1886. His brother, Major R.G. Parker, D.S.O., is serving in the King's Own (Royal Lancaster Regiment). Lieutenant Parker was educated at The Abbey, Tipperary; and at Clifton College. He joined the Clare Artillery Militia, and, taking first place in the Militia Competitive Ezmination, was gazetted to the Royal Artillery in May, 1907, being posted to the 87th Howitzer Battery, Royal Field Artillery. He was promoted Lieutenant in 1910, and served on the Staff of the Brigadier-General Commanding Artillery, 1st Divisdion, Aldershot, in 1912-13. In June, 1911, he was posted to D Battery, Royal Horse Artillery, with which he was serving in France when he was killed in the Battle of the Marne on the 8th September, 1914. At the time his battery was closely supporting the 3rd Cavalry Brigade in the advance to the Marne when the Germans brought back twelve guns against them. D Battery lost its Major wounded and both Subalterns killed. The Officer Commanding his Royal Horse Artillery Brigade wrote; "He died like a hero, fighting his gun at great odds to the last" Lieutenant Parker excelled in all field sports, was a fine horseman, keen rider to hounds, and an excellent whip. He also was a first-rate shot and a good fisherman.

Grave or memorial reference: I. B. 44. Cemetery: Perreuse Chateau Franco British National Cemetery, Seine-et-Marne, France.

PEACOCKE, HERBERT PARKER: Rank: Second Lieutenant. Regiment or service: South Lancashire Regiment. Unit: 8th Battalion. Date of death: 3 July 1916. Age at death: 20. Killed in action.

Supplementary information: Son of Twiss and Mary E.M. Peacocke, of Kilrush, Co. Clare.

Grave or memorial reference: Pier and Face 7 A and 7 B. Memorial: Thiepval Memorial in France.

PEPPER, GEORGE: Rank: Private. Regiment or service: Royal Inniskilling Fusiliers. Unit: 2nd Battalion. Date of death: 16 May 1915. Service No.: 4364. Killed in action.

Supplementary information: Born in Tullagh, Co. Clare. Enlisted in Limerick.

Grave or memorial reference: Panel 16 and 17. Memorial: Le Touret Memorial in France.

PERRY, GEORGE: Rank: Sergeant. Regiment or service: Royal Munster Fusiliers. Unit: 6th Battalion. Date of death: 19 August 1915. Service No.: 4308. Died of wounds in Gallipoli.

Supplementary information: Born in Tulla, Co. Clare. Enlisted in Ennis, Co. Clare while living in Ennis.

Grave or memorial reference: II. G. 117. Cemetery: East Mudros Military Cemetery in Greece.

PERSSE, DUDLEY EYRE: Rank: Captain. Regiment or service: Royal Dublin Fusiliers. Unit: 4th Battalion. Attached to 2nd Battalion. Age at death: 22. Date of death: 1 February 1915. Died of wounds.

Supplementary information: Son of Alfred Lovaine Persse and Florence G. Persse, of Cragmoher, Corofin, Co. Clare.

From De Ruvigny's Roll of Honour:

Captain D. Persse.

Persse, Dudley Eyre, Captain, (4th Reserve) Attached to the 2nd (103rd Foot), Battalion, The Royal Dublin Fusiliers. Only son of Alfred Loubaine Persse, of Rose Park, Gort, Co. Galway, by his wife, Florence Geraldine, youngest daughter of the late Canon Richard Booth Eyre, of Eyrecourt, Co. Galway; and grandson of the late Dudley Persse, or Rocborough, Co. Galway, D.L. Born at Ormonde View, Ballycrissan, Co. Galway, 14 August 1892. Educated at Chesterfirld, Birr, and Galway Grammar School. Gazetted 2nd Lieutenant, 4th Dublin Fusiliers, 20 April 1911, and promoted Lieutenant, 20 April 1912, and Captain, 4 December 1914. Served with the Expeditionary Force in France, attached to the

2nd Battalion of his Regiment from 19 December 1914, and died in No. 2 Casualty Clearing Station, at Bailleul, 1 February 1915, from wounds received in action. From a letter received by his parents it appears that "he saw some Germans going into a wood some distance off and wanted to telephone to the General. There was no telephone in his trench, so he ran 80 yards across the open in a hail of bullets and telephoned from another trench. The General ordered the wood to be shelled at once, and commended him for what he had done. He also found that the Germans were mining the trench, and started counter-mining, which stopped the enemy's game, so he did all he could bravely, poor boy." His Commanding Officer, Lieutenant Colonel A. Loveband wrote; "His death is very sad, and your son was doing well indeed in the trenches; keen, and taking great interest in his work, and always ready to go out to do work in front of the trenches at night." He possessed marked literary ability, and many beautiful poems written by him were found after his death. As a sportsman he had proved himself an expert at shooting. Riding and fishing, qualities inherited from both sides of his house, his mother being one of the Eyres of Eyrecourt, East Galway, a well-known sporting family.

From *Our Heroes*, 1916:

Captain Dudley Eyre Persse, 4th Battalion, Dublin Fusiliers, who died from wounds received in active service in France in February last, was the son of Mr Alfred Lovain Persse and Mrs Persse, late of Rose Park, Co. Galway, and grandson of the late Mr Dudley Persse, of Roxborough, Co. Galway. He was gazetted Second Lieutenant in April, 1911, was promoted Lieutenant in 1912 and Captain in February, 1915. His father has received a telegram from their Majesties expressing their regret and sympathy in the loss he has sustained on the death of his son.

From the *Clare Journal*, February 1915:

Death of Gallant young Officer
The late Captain Dudley Eyre Persse, aged 22, who died February 1st, of wounds received in active service, was the only son of Mr A.L. Persse and Mrs Persse, late of Rose Park, Co. Galway, and Grandson of the late Dudley Persse, of Roxborough, Co. Galway.

Captain D. E. Persse was granted Second Lieutenant 4th Batt, Royal Dublin Fusiliers on April-20th-1911. He was promoted Lieutenant Aptil-20th-1912.

He was attached to the 2nd batt, R. D. F., when he went to active service last year, and was promoted Captain on Feb 7th this year. His parents have received a message of condolence from The King and Queen.

Captain Persse was interred with full military honours on February 4th.

Grave or memorial reference: F. 6. Cemetery: Bailleul Communal Cemetery (Nord) in France.

PERSSE, RODOLPH ALGERNON: Rank: Second Lieutenant. Regiment or service: Rifle Brigade. Unit: Attached to the 2nd Battalion, K.R.R.C. Date of death: 1 January 1915. Age at death: 22. Killed in action.

Supplementary information: Mentioned in Despatches. Son of the late Algernon Persse and the Hon. Mrs Persse, of Lough Cutra Castle, Co. Galway.

From De Ruvigny's Roll of Honour:

Second Lieutenant R. Persse.

Persse, Rodolph Algernon, 2nd Lieut, Reserve Battalion, The Rifle Brigade, attached to the 2nd Battalion, King's Rifle Corps. Only son of the late Robert Algernon Persse, of Creg Clare, Co. Galway, J.P., by his wife, the Hon. Eleanor Laura Jane, neé Gough (Creg Clare, Ardrahan, Co. Galway), only surviving daughter of George Stephens, 2nd Viscount Gough and grandson of the late Dudley Persse, of Roxborough, Co. Galway. Born in Roxborough, aforesaid, 12 May, 1892. Educated at Eton and Magdalen College Oxford, where he had just completed his second year when war broke out. Obtained a commission in the Rifle Brigade on 26 August 1914, joining the Reserve Battalion at Sheerness. Went to France, 16 October 1914. Was there attached to the 2nd Battalion, King's Royal Rifle Corps, and was Killed in action at Cuinchy, 1 January following during a night attack. Buried there. He was mentioned in F.M. Sir John (now Lord) French's Despatch of 14 January 1915.

His commanding officer wrote; "He had taken his platoon to attack a position early on the morning of 1 January, and after the position was taken it was found to be untenable, and the whole force was ordered back to their trenches. It was here that poor Persse was killed. He was an extremely gallant bay, and we shall miss him very much. I had already submitted his name for his gallant behaviour near Ypres."

A brother officer also wrote; "What a splendid, brave, cool officer he was. He never flinched or wavered in his most gallant spirit, and his absolute fearlessness and pluck were grand; and were of the greatest value to his men. He will, indeed, be sadly missed, for he made himself so popular with all ranks"; and another; "He was without exception the bravest officer I have ever seen, and the best His men would do anything for him. This is not only my own opinion, for I know that it was shared by every officer in the mess." He was a fine all-round athlete and a first rate shot. He played in the Eton eleven in July-1911. At Oxford he did well in the Freshmen's sports of 1913; won the Magdalen Grind; rode in the Intervarsity point-to-Point, and was whip to the Magdalen Beagles. The President of Magdalen wrote of him; "He is indeed a loss to us here, your bright, vivid daring, high-spirited chivalrous personality had endeared him to us all."

Grave or memorial reference: He has no known grave but is listed on Panel 44 on the Le Touret Memorial in France.

PIERCE, MICHAEL: Rank: Private. Regiment or service: Royal Munster Fusiliers. Unit: 7th Battalion. Date of death: 16 August 1915. Age at death: 33. Service No.: 3519. Killed in action in Gallipoli.

Supplementary information: Born in Drumcliffe, Co. Clare. Enlisted in Limerick while living in Ennis, Co. Clare. His personal effects and property were sent to Mrs Bridget Pierce (mother), Old Mill Street, Ennis, Ireland. Will was witnessed by Private James Pierce 7th RMF. Pound Lane, Ennis, Co. Clare Laurence Roche, Justice of the Peace, Major Royal Munster Fusiliers.

Grave or memorial reference: Panel 185 and 190. Memorial: Helles Memorial in Turkey.

POTTER, CHARLES: Rank: Private. Regiment or service: South Staffordshire Regiment. Unit: 3rd Special Reserve Battalion. Date of death: 15 January 1918. Service No.: 11328. Died at home

Supplementary information: Born in Belturbet, Co. Clare. Enlisted in Wolverhampton.

Grave or memorial reference: 18423. Cemetery: Wolverhampton Borough Cemetery, Staffordshire, UK.

POWER, JOHN: Rank: Private. Regiment or service: Royal Dublin Fusiliers. Unit: A Coy. 10th (Pals) Battalion. Date of death: 13 November 1916. Age at death: 25 Service No.: 26017. Killed in action.

Supplementary information: Born in Dublin. Enlisted in Dublin while living in Clarecastle, Co. Clare. Son of Patrick Power (Coal Importer), of Clarecastle, Co. Clare.

From the *Clare Journal*, January 1917:

Death of Private Power
Clarecastle
We much regret to hear of the death in action in France, of Private. Power, son of Mr Patrick Power, Clarecastle, to whom sincere sympathy goes out in full measure on the loss of his gallant son. He joined the "Pals" Battalion of the Dublin Fusiliers, soon after its formation, and had taken part I many engagements. He was promising career before him in the service.

Grave or memorial reference: Pier and Face 16 C. Memorial: Thiepval Memorial in France.

PURTELL/PURTILL, MICHAEL: Rank: Private. Regiment or service: Royal Munster Fusiliers. Unit: 6th Battalion. Date of death: 10 September 1916. Age at death: 34. Service No.: 483. Killed in action in Greek Macedonia.

Supplementary information: Born in Kilrush, Co. Clare. Enlisted in Limerick while living in Kilrush, Co. Clare. Son of Thomas and Mary Madigan, of Moor Street, Kilrush, Co. Clare. Listed as H. Purtell in the casualty list, *Clare Journal*, November 1916.

Grave or memorial reference: II. B. 1. Cemetery: Struma Military Cemetery in Greece.

Q

QUAILE, FRANCIS: Rank: Private. Regiment or service: Royal Irish Regiment. Unit: 1ˢᵗ Battalion. Date of death: 14 November 1914. Service No.: 8925. Died in India.

Supplementary information: Born in Killaloe, Co. Clare. Enlisted in Carrick-on-Suir, Co. Tipperary.

Grave or memorial reference: Face 4. Memorial: Kirkee 1914-1918 Memorial in India.

QUINLIVAN, ALFRED: Rank: Private. Regiment or service: Royal Munster Fusiliers. Unit: 1ˢᵗ Battalion. Date of death: 15 August 1917. Age at death: 33. Service No.: 4549. Killed in action.

Supplementary information: Born in Drumcliffe, Co. Clare. Enlisted in Ennis, Co. Clare while living in Ennis, Co. Clare. Son of Mrs Mary Quinlivan, of Market Street, Corofin, Co. Clare.

Grave or memorial reference: Panel 44. Memorial: Ypres (Menin Gate) Memorial in Belgium.

QUINN, JOHN: Rank: Private. Regiment or service: Royal Munster Fusiliers. Unit: 1ˢᵗ Battalion. Date of death: 23 February 1918. Service No.: 5897. Died of wounds.

Supplementary information: He won the Military Medal and is listed in the *London Gazette*. Enlisted in Ennis while living in Lahinch, Co. Clare.

Grave or memorial reference: IV. F. 17. Cemetery: Tincourt New British Cemetery in France.

R

REDMOND, WILLIAM HOEY KEARNEY: Rank: Major. Regiment or service: Royal Irish Regiment. Unit: 6th Battalion. Date of death: 7 June 1917. Age at death: 56. Died of Wounds received in an attack at Wytschaete Wood in Belgium after being injured by a shell.

Supplemenary information: Mentioned in Despatches. Husband of Eleanor Redmond. Nationalist Member of Parliament for Wexford since 1884. Also MP for Clare East 1892-1917. Awarded the Legion of Honour (France). Redmond was one of the rare people to be buried abroad during the First World War in a coffin.

Information taken from his records (WO339/19182) by Jimmy Taylor:

Served as an officer in the Wexford Militia and the 3rd (Militia) Battalion, Royal Irish regiment from 24 December 1879 till 11 January 1882. Temporary commission as captain in 6th (Service) Battalion, Royal Irish Regiment 22 February 1915. Home address Glenbrook, Delgany, Co. Wicklow and Palace Manshions, Kensington, London. Wife was Eleanor Mary. War Office telegram to wife 8 June 1917 reports Died of wounds 7 June 1917 and expresses sympathy. Death report dated 10 June 1917 shows died of wounds, 7 June 1917, 6th Royal Irish Regiment attached 16th Divisional Company.

Undated War Office memo reports burial "at the south end of the garden of the hospice, Locre,

SW of Ypres". Letter to HQ Horse Guards Whitehall 21 June 1917 requests buglers of one Battlion Brigade of Guards to attend St Mary's Catholic Church, Clapham (London SW) 23rd June at 10a.m. to sound Last Post at requiem Mass for Major Redmond. "All expenses incurred will be refunded Privately." (Irish Guards preffered). Estate valued at £4018.2.9., against which there were debts of £1885.3.2 Whole estate to widow. Personal effects were taken directly to Mrs Redmond by the Reverend M. O'Connell, S.C.F. 16th Division, whilst on leave.

Mentioned in Despatches, *London Gazette*, 4 January 1917. French Legion d'Honeur (Chevalier) London Gazette 14 July 1917. 1914-15 Star, British War Medal and Victory Medals, with oak leaf (MID).

Grave or memorial reference: Close to path leading to the Cemetery. Cemetery: Locre Hospice Cemetery in Belgium.

REGAN, JOHN: Rank: Private. Regiment or service: Royal Munster Fusiliers. Unit: 1st Battalion. Date of death: 3 May 1915. Service No.: 6353. Killed in action in Gallipoli during the landings at the Dardanelles.

Supplementary information: Born in Kilrush, Co. Clare. Enlisted in Ennis while living in Ennis.

From the *Clare Journal*, June 1915:

Ennis Man's Letter from the
Dardanelles
How he killed the Turk
Ennis Men Killed

Mr Joseph Kennedy, Ennis, has just had a letter from Private Gormley, of the Munsters, from the Military Hospital, Port Said, Egypt, where he lies, recovering from wounds received in the Dardanelles. We take the following extract from it –

"I happened to get wounded while up the Dardanelles. My wound is progressing favourably. We had a very warm time of it up in Gallipoli, most of my regiment being knocked over. This hospital is situated down on the seashore, so we are in quite a healthy spot, with plenty of sea breezes, etc. We are getting well treated, so have no cause to complain. I have one consolation in knowing that I killed my opponent. I was coming from the firing line with a wounded comrade. I brought him to the first dressing station, about four miles from Aki Baba. Returning again to the firing line, I had to pass a battery of howitzers on my right, when the Major of the battery called me and asked me if I was going back to the firing line. I told him I was, so he told me to look out for snipers. I went almost 150 yards from the battery. I stood against a tree to have a drink when I heard noises. I got closer to the tree, from where I could see the bayonet and part of the rifle of a Turk protruding from behind the tree. Unfortunately, I did not have my rifle with me, having left it in the trenches. I made a grab for his rifle, and he fired, wounding me in the right hand. I made a grab with the left hand and caught hold of his rifle. I then forced the rifle upwards. He tried to wrench the rifle from me, but I still held on. I watched my opportunity and kicked him in the groin. He then dropped, letting go of the rifle. With his struggles, I gave him another kick, this time in the jaw. This knocked him unconscious for a time. I then pointed the bayonet at his stomach and putting my weight on the butt drove the point home. During the affair the Major of the battery heard the report, on which he came up with four men and asked me if I were much hurt. He bandaged my hand up with my field dressing, there being a constant flow of blood. He congratulated me, and took my name, number, and regiment. When I said it was the Munsters, he said he thought so. So that it is the only one I can account for. I can tell you it is no picnic up there. I regret to say Jack Regan was killed by my side on May 2nd and Pat Frawley and young Burley.

Grave or memorial reference: Panel 185 and 190. Memorial: Helles Memorial in Turkey.

REID, JAMES: Rank: Private. Regiment or service: Royal Irish Regiment. Unit: 2nd Battalion. Date of death: 6 November 1914. Age at death: 30. Service No.: 7963. Killed in action.

Supplementary information: Born in Dublin. Enlisted in Dublin while living in Dublin. Husband of Kate Reid, Phoenix Park, Dublin

From De Ruvigny's Roll of Honour:

... 3rd son of John Reid, of Cabra, by his wife, Margaret, daughter of John Carbara. Born in Cabra, Co. Dublin, 24 September 1884. Educated in the Phoenix Park National School. Enlisted in September 1903. Served eight years with the colours, including four years in India and three years on the Reserve; was called up on mobilisation 5 August 1914. Went to France on the 12th, and was killed in action there 6 November following. He married at St Patrick's Church, Galay, Catherine (Kennedy's Cottages, Black Horse Lane, Dublin), daughter of Thomas O'Connor, of Spancilhill, Co. Clare, and had a daughter, Nora, born 23 June 1907.

Grave or memorial reference: Panel 42. Memorial: Ypres (Menin Gate) Memorial in Belgium.

REIDY, J.: Rank: Private. Regiment or service: Royal Inniskilling Fusiliers. Date of death: 5 July 1919. Age at death: 31. Service No.: 24444.

Supplementary information: Son of Mrs Margaret Reidy, of Bogberry, Ennistymon. This man is only in the Commonwealth War Graves database.

Grave or memorial reference: South of gate leading from West to East Cemetery: Ennistymon Cemetery, Co. Clare.

REIDY, MICHAEL: Rank: Private. Regiment or service: Royal Irish Regiment. Unit: 2nd Battalion. Date of death: 19 July 1918. Service No.: 6194. Died of wounds.

Supplementary information: Formerly he was with the Leinster Regiment where his number was 4594. Born in Leitreim (*sic*), Co. Clare. Enlisted in Kilrush, Co. Clare while living in Cooraclare, Co. Clare. In his will, dated 6 April 1918, his personal effects and property were received by Miss Nano Reidy, Cooraclare, Co. Clare, Ireland.

Grave or memorial reference: Plot 1, Row E, Grave 11. Cemetery: Louvencourt Military Cemetery in France.

REILLY, JOHN: Rank: Private. Regiment or service: Irish Guards. Unit: 1st Battalion. Date of death: 31 July 1917. Service No.: 3754. Killed in action.

Supplementary information: Born in Drumcliffe, Co. Clare. Enlisted in Lancaster, Lancs while living in Phillipstown, Mon. Grave or memorial reference: I. A. 16. Cemetery: Artillery Wood Cemetery in Belgium.

REILLY, JOHN: Rank: Driver. Regiment or service: Royal Horse Artillery and Royal Field Artillery. Unit: Northern Command Depot. Date of death: 6 May 1918. Age at death: 21. Service No.: 100920 (SDGW) 100929 (CWGC). Died at Home.

Supplementary information: Born in Athy Co. Clare. Enlisted in Naas, Clare (*sic*). Son of James and Bridget Reilly, of Levitstown, Athy, Co. Kildare.

Grave or memorial reference: G. 128. Cemetery: Ripon Cemetery, Yorkshire, UK.

REYBAULD, WILLIAM: Rank: Private. Regiment or service: Royal Munster Fusiliers. Unit: 8th Battalion. Date of death: 3 September 1916. Service No.: 4675. Killed in action.

Supplementary information: Born in Drumcliffe, Co. Clare. Enlisted in Ennis while living in Ennis.

Grave or memorial reference: Pier and Face 16 C. Memorial: Thiepval Memorial in France.

REYNOLDS, JAMES: Rank: Corporal. Regiment or service: Royal Munster Fusiliers. Unit: 2nd Battalion. Date of death: 9 May 1915. Age at death: 23. Service No.: 5514. Killed in action.

Supplementay information: Born in Corrovorrin, Co. Clare. Enlisted in Ennis, Co. Clare while living in Ennis, Co. Clare. Son of James and Margaret Reynolds, of Corovorin, Ennis, Co. Clare. In his will, dated 20 October 1914, his personal effects and property were received by Mrs Margret Reynolds (mother), Corsovorren, Ennis, Co. Clare, Ireland.

Grave or memorial reference: Panel 43 and 44. Memorial: Le Touret Memorial in France.

REYNOLDS, PETER: Rank: Private. Regiment or service: AIF. Unit: A Company, 35th Battalion. Date of death: Unknown. Service No.: 1685.

Supplementary information: Born, Kilrush, Co. Clare. Occupation on enlistment: Seaman. Age on enlistment: 21 years 8 months. Next of kin: Mrs Bridget Reynolds (mother), of No. 8 Moore Street, Kilrush, Co. Clare, Ireland. Later changed to Mr william Reynolds (father), of No. 8 Moore Street, Kilrush, Co. Clare. Place and date of enlistment: Newcastle, N.S.W.; 26 February 1916. Weight: 10st. Height: 5ft 5½in. Complexion: Fresh. Eyes: Brown. Hair: Brown. Address on enlistment: Boat Hotel, Stocton.

Declared an illegal absentee from Larkhill at a Court of Enquiry held in London on 26 September 1916. Discharged from the AIF., 21 July 1920. Served 213 days total of which 143 days of this service was abroad. Commemorated in the 'List of Kilrush Men engaged in the War from August 1914'. This pamphlet lists the Kilrush men who were involved in the First World War until 11 November 1918. It adds that he was wounded in France and died in Africa. He is also commemorated in a different section to Kilrush men of the Mercantile Marine where its adds; Wounded, France, August-1917, died Secondee, Gold Coast, West Africa, September 1918. Admiralty ship *Pantiotis*'.

Grave or memorial reference: No burial details are available at this time.

RIORDAN, JOSEPH: Rank: Private. Regiment or service: Royal Inniskilling Fusiliers. Unit: 1st Battalion. Date of death: 29 November 1917. Age at death: 26. Service No.: 26467. Formerly he was with the Royal Munster Fusiliers where his number was 3845. Killed in action.

Supplementary information: Born in Ennistymon, Co. Clare. Enlisted in Limerick while living in Clare.

Son of J. Riordan (late of Royal Irish Constabulary). In his will, dated 3 July 1916, his personal effects and property were received by Michael Riordan (brother), Ennistymon, Co. Clare.

Grave or memorial reference: Panel 5 and 6. Memorial: Cambrai Memorial, Louveral, Nord in France.

RIORDAN, PATRICK: Rank:
Private. Regiment or service: Australian Infantry, AIF. Unit: 25th Battalion. Date of death: 20 May 1916. Age at death: 29. Service No.: 3300. Died of wounds (gunshot to the breast) received in action.

Supplementary information: Born in Ennistymon, Co. Clare. Location of death, near Armentieres. Next of kin: Michael Riordan (brother), Ennistymon, Co. Clare. Went to Australia when he was 27. Occupation on enlistment: Bootmaker. Son of John and Johanna Riordan, of Church Street, Ennistymon, Co. Clare, Ireland. Born, Co. Clare, Ireland. Age on enlistment: 25 years. Place and date of enlistment: Ennogera, Queensland. 28 December 1915. Weight: 10st 7lbs. Height: 5ft 5in. Complexion: Fair. Eyes: Grey. Hair: Fair.

Grave or memorial reference: I. G. 12. Cemetery: Ration Farm Military Cemetery, La Chapelle-Darmentieres, Nord in France.

ROBERTSON-GLASGOW, ARCHIBALD WILLIAM: Rank:
Captain. Regiment or service: Indian Army. Unit: 2nd Battalion, 39th Garhwal Rifles. Date of death: 13 November 1914. Age at death: 34.

Supplementary information: Son of Mr R.B. Robertson-Glasgow, of Montgreenan, Ayrshire; Husband of

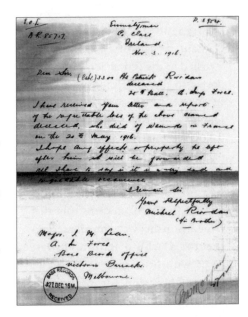

Philadelphia C. Violet Fraser Giles (*née* Robertson-Glasgow). Served in the Somaliland Campaign (1901).

From De Ruvigny's Roll of Honour:

Robertson-Glasgow, Archibald William, Captain, 2nd Battalion, 39th Garhwal Rifles, Indian Army. Youngest son of the late Robert Bruce Robertson-Glasgow of Mountgreenan Co. Ayr, J.P., D.L., formerly 74th Highlanders, by his wife, Deborah Louisa Grace, 2nd daughter of Simon George Purdon of Tinerana, Co. Clare. Born at Mountgreenan aforesaid on 24 May 1880. Educated at Wellington House School, Westgate-on-Sea (September 1891 to July 1894). Marlborough College (September 1894 to December 1897), and at the Royal Military College, Sandhurst (January to December 1898). Gazetted 2nd Lieutenant to the unattached List for the Indian Army, 25 January 1899 and promoted

Lieutenant, 25 April 1901 and Captain, 25 Janaury 1908, he was attached to the Royal Scots, and was posted to the 16th Bombay Infantry in April, 1901, and appointed Double Company Officer, 1 August, following, and the same year took part in the operations against the Ogaden Somalis in Jubaland, British East Africa, and receive the medal with clasp. On his return from this expedition he was transferred to the 39th Garhwal Rifles. He left India with his regiment in the 7th Meerut Division for France, 21 September 1914, and on arrival was detailed Railway Transport Officer until early in November, when he rejoined his regiment in the trenches. He was Killed in action at Bethune a few days later, 13-14 Nov, 1914. Numerous letters from his brother officers all bear witness to his splendid qualities. His Colonel wrote; "He had charged right up most valiantly to the enemy's trench and in a yard or two more would have been in it ... The regiment has suffered a double loss in losing a first-rate officer and generous hearted friend," and a brother officer:

"I spent a good time on the afternoon of that disastrous night attack with him. He was as cheery as ever, and told me all about the exciting time he had digging out some men who had been buried by the exploding of a heavy German shell. The trench was knocked in and cover practically nil, so the operation had to be carried out in full view of the Germans who put a lot of shrapnel over him and his men. Of course, he joked about it, but poor old---said it was a very fine show and one needing a great deal of pluck. I am sure his coolness and pluck then must have been a good example to the men, and just the sort of example they needed in the early days when everything was new and very terrifying to them." He married at St Peter's, Cranley Gardens, London, 19-January-1911, Philadelphia Constance Violet Flora MacDonald, daughter of Major Francis Fraser, of Tornaveen, Aberdeenshire, and has a son, Archibald Francis Colin, born 31-July-1914.

From the British Roll of Honour 1914-1916:

It is only thirty-five years since Captain Robertson-Glasgow, son of the late R. B. Robertson-Glasgow, sq., D.L., of Montgreenan, Ayrshire, formerly in the Highland Light Infantry, was born at Montgreenan, but his life was diversified and of a thrilling nature, experiences of a most varied character having been crowded into it. Born on May 24th, 1880, he was educated at Wellington House School, Westgate-on-Sea, 1889-94; Marlborough College, 1894-97; and at the Royal Military College, Sandhurst, January, 1898 – December, 1898. On January, 19th, 1911, he married Violet, elder daughter of major Francis Fraser, of Tornaveen, Torphins, Aberdeenshire, and had issue a son, Archibald Colin. Captain A. W. Robertson-Glasgow was a good and keen sportsman—

a first class shot, both with gun and rifle, and a fine fisherman. During his two years garrison duty in Chitral he made many successful shooting trips and secured some very fine heads of various kinds. He also did some shooting in East Africa when on duty there. He was in command of his Battalion Machine Gun Detachment for some time, and was recognised as an authority on matters connected with machine guns. He Captained his Battalion's shooting team for the Empire Day Challenge Cup, two years. A near relative of captain Robertson-Glasgow was Colonel J.G. Robertson-Glasgow, of the Suffolk regiment, who was a brother of our subject's father. As Captain Robertson-Glasgow's education would signify, he was early destined for a military career. He was gazetted Second-Lieutenant on January 25th, 1899, being attached to the Royal Scots, then serving in India. After a year's service he joined the 16th Bombay Infantry. His promotion to Lieutenant was dated April 25th, 1901, in which year he saw service with the East African Jubaland Expeditionary Force, and for his services was awarded the medal with clasp. After the return of the Expeditionary Force he transferred to the 2nd battalion, 39th Garwal Rifles, and was promoted Captain on January 25th, 1908. He left India on September 21st, 1914, and went to France with his regiment in the Meerut Division. He was last seen leading a local attack on the night of November 13th, 1914, But his body was not recovered until Christmas Day. It was found on a German parapet, by one of his brother officers, during an informal armistice which ensued that day. The exact circumstances of captain Robertson-Glasgow's death are unknown; but his coolness and presence of mind under extreme danger were very real, as will be gathered from an extract from the letter of a fellow officer, who, relating an episode which occurred a few days before the gallant Officer's end, wrote:

"I spent a good time on the afternoon of that disastrous night attack with him. He was a cheery as ever, and told me all about the exciting time he had had digging out some men who had been buried by the exploding of a German shell. The trench was knocked in, and cover practically nil; so the operation had to be carried out in full view of the Germans, who put a lot of shrapnel over him and his men. Of course he joked about it, but poor old---said it was a very fine show, and one needing a great deal of pluck; and I am sure his coolness and pluck then must have been a good example to the men, and just the sort of example they needed in the early days, when everything was new and very terrifying to them."

Another Officer testified that:

"He was full of courage, and always ready to take on the most dangerous job."

Keen soldier and active sportsman, Captain Robertson-Glasgow was endeared to his brother-officers and friends by his good nature, cheeriness, and gallantry. His death is widely regretted, but he lived and died like a soldier, and was an example to all about him.

Grave or memorial reference: I. B. 10. Cemetery, Le Touret Military Cemetery, Richebourg-L'Avoue in France.

ROCHFORD, WILLIAM: Rank: Private. Regiment or service: Royal Munster Fusiliers. Unit: 8th Battalion. Date of death: 4 September 1916. Age at death: 30. Service No.: 5749. Killed in action.

Supplementary information: Born in Drumbiggle, Co. Clare. Enlisted in Ennis, Co. Clare while living in Ennis, Co. Clare. Son of Patrick and Margaret Rochford, of Drumbiggle, Ennis, Co. Clare.

Grave or memorial reference: Pier and Face 16 C. Memorial: Thiepval Memorial in France.

RONAN, MICHAEL: Rank: Private. Regiment or service: Australian Infantry, AIF. Unit: 50th Battalion. Date of death: 17 October 1917. Age at death: 27. Service No.: 1582. Killed in action.

Supplementary information: Born in Kilshanny, Co. Clare. Age on enlistment: 23 years 3 months. Occupation on enlistment: Labourer. Next of kin: Thomas Ronan (uncle), Carrowkeel, Kilshanny, Co. Clare. Place and date of enlistment: Oaklands, South Australia; 1 December 1914. Weight: 11st. Height: 5ft 7½in. Complexion: Fair. Eyes: Blue. Hair: Dark. Previous military experience: 2 years with the Connaught Rangers. Was wounded in June 1917, gunshot to the head and hospitalised

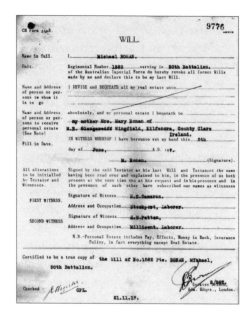

The will of Private M. Ronan.

in Boulogne. Rejoined his unit in September, 1917.

Grave or memorial reference: Originally he was buried at the military cemetery in Broodseinde but now he has no known grave but is listed on Panel 7 - 17 - 23 - 25 - 27 - 29 - 31 on the Ypres (Menin Gate) Memorial in Belgium.

ROUGHAN, EDWARD: Rank: Private. Regiment or service: Royal Dublin Fusiliers. Unit: 10th Battalion. Date of death: 11 October 1916. Service No.: 26292. Killed in action.

Supplementary information: Born in Tulla, Co. Clare. Enlisted in Ennis while living in Cragg, Tulla.

Grave or memorial reference: II. R. 4. Euston Road Cemetery, Colincamps in France.

ROWAN, THOMAS: Rank: Petty Officer. Regiment or service: Royal

Navy. Unit: HMS/ME-10. The E-10 was a British Submarine which struck a sea mine and sank just off Heligoland. Date of death: 21 Jaunuary 1915. Age at death: 34. Service No.: 181381.

Supplementary information: Son of James Rowan of Kilrush, Co. Clare; husband of Theresa Rowan of No. 5 Shelford Road, Milton, Portsmouth.

Grave or memorial reference: 7. Memorial: Portsmouth Naval Memorial, UK.

ROY, JOHN ROBIN: Rank: Private. Regiment or service: Royal Army Medical Corps. Unit: 98th Field Ambulance. Date of death: 2 October 1918. Age at death: 38. Service No.: 112046. Died of wounds.

Supplementary information: Born in Ipswitch, Suffolk. Enlisted in Southampton. Son of Mary Bertha Roy, of Masonic Hall, Ennis, Co. Clare; husband of Bertha Roy, of No. 13 Highland Road, Itchen, Hampshire.

From the *Saturday Record*, 1918:

Roll of Honour

Roy;October 2nd 1918. Private John Robin Roy (Dick), R.A.M.C., youngest son of Mrs Dean, Masonic Hall, Ennis, and the late Mr J. R. Roy, Ordnance Survey, Ennis, aged 38 years. Inserted by his sorrowing mother.

Grave or memorial reference: VI. A. 1. Cemetery: La Kreule Military Cemetery, Hazebrouck in France.

RUSSELL, HAROLD WALTER: Rank: Private. Regiment or service: Corps of Royal Engineers. Unit: 59th Field Company. Date of death: 1 August 1918. Age at death: 23. Service No.: 28886. Killed in action.

Supplementary information: Born in Clare. Enlisted in Woolwich while living in Southampton. Co. Clare. Son of William. and A. Russell, of Upswell, Nr. Wisbech, Norfolk.

Grave or memorial reference: Plot 5 Row B. Grave 1. Cemetery: Tannay British Cemetery, Thiennes, France.

RUSSELL, JAMES: Rank: Private. Regiment or service: Royal Munster Fusiliers. Unit: 2nd Battalion. Date of death: 22 March 1918. Service No.: 6938. Killed in action.

Supplementary information: Enlisted in Cork while living in Ennis.

Grave or memorial reference: Panel 78 and 79. Memorial: Pozieres Memorial in France.

RUSSELL, PETER: Rank: Private. Regiment or service: Royal Munster Fusiliers. Unit: 2nd Battalion. Date of death: 4 October 1918. Age at death: 31. Service No.: 5755. Killed in action.

Supplementary information: Born in Kilkee, Co. Clare. Enlisted in Kilkee, Co. Clare while living in Kilkee, Co. Clare. Son of Martin and Annie Russell, of Dunlickey Road, Kilkee, Co. Clare. Peter also appears in the list of badly wounded in the Clare Journal, June, 1916.

Grave or memorial reference: Special Memorial. Cemetery: Le Catelet Churchyard, Aisne in France.

RUSSELL, THOMAS: Rank: Lance Corporal. Regiment or service: Royal Munster Fusiliers. Unit: 1st Battalion.

Date of death: 15 August 1917. Age at death: 21. Service No.: 6825. Killed in action.

Supplementary information: Born in Kilmaley, Co. Clare. Enlisted in Ennis, Co. Clare while living in Kilmaley, Co. Clare. Son of John and Catherine Russell, of Culleen, Kilmaley, Ennis, Co. Clare.

Grave or memorial reference: Panel 44. Memorial: Ypres (Menin Gate) Memorial in Belgium.

RUSSELL, THOMAS: Rank: School Teacher. Date of death: November 1918.

From the *County Offaly Chronicle*, November 1918:

Death from bayonet wound
Mr Thomas Russell, a teacher, who received a bayonet wound in the back in a conflict with the military, who made a bayonet charge in clearing a room at Carrigaholt on Sunday week, where a Sin Fein Club meeting was being held, succumbed to the injury at St Joseph's Hospital, Kilrush, on Wednesday evening.

At the inquest held on Thursday, Mr John Murphy, National Teacher, Corbally, near Kilkee, identified the deceased, who was a native of Kerry.

Mr Thomas Lillis, J.P., applied to have summonses issued for the presence at the inquest of the commander of the military at Carrigaholt on the day of the occurrence; also Captain Glass, who was in charge of the military, and the sergeant and men who made the charge; and further, of Dr Studdert, of Carrigaholt, who examined the deceased first after the injury. The Coroner gave the necessary order. The inquest was adjourned until this Thursday.

Grave or memorial reference: not available at this time.

RYAN, AUSTIN FRANCIS: Rank: Private. Regiment or service: Royal Munster Fusiliers. Unit: 11th Battalion. Date of death: 9 June 1916. Age at death: 22. Service No.: 6740. Died at home.

Supplementary information: Born in Ballyvaughan, Co. Clare. Enlisted in Llanelly, Carmarthenshire while living in Llanelly. Son of Mrs Ryan, of Fanore, Ballyvaughan, Co. Clare.

Grave or memorial reference: C. 24. 54. Cemetery: Cobh Old Church Cemetery in Co. Cork.

RYAN, JAMES: Rank: Private. Regiment or service: Royal Munster Fusiliers. Unit: 8th Battalion. Date of death: 28 July 1916. Service No.: 8/3951. Died at home

Supplementary information: Born in St Munchin's, Limerick. Enlisted in Limerick while living in Clarecastle, Co. Clare. Husband of M. Ryan, of Clarecommons, Clarecastle, Co. Clare.

From the *Saturday Journal*, August 1916:

Clare Soldier's Sad End
A Fatal Plunge
The body of a Private soldier, presumed to be the one reported to have jumped from Baal's Bridge into the Abbey river late on Friday

night, was recovered from the river early on Tuesday, and conveyed to the new Barracks, Limerick. The deceased is stated to be a young man named Ryan, a native of Clarecastle, and to have been passing through Limerick on his way to rejoin at Tralee the depot companies of the Munster Fusiliers, to which Regiment he belonged. Before taking what proved to be a final leap from the bridge, the soldier gave his khaki overcoat to some person about the place at the time, so it is said, and the statement seems to be borne out by the fact that the Mary Street Police had a soldier's overcoat handed in to them when the man did not return to claim it, as, it is reported, he said he would. There was very little water in the Abbey river at the time the soldier is stated to have jumped from the bridge.

Mr J. F. Barry, City Coroner, and a jury held an inquest on Wednesday at the New Barracks as to the cause of death of Private James Ryan, 8th Battalion, Royal Munster Fusiliers, whose body was recovered from the river on Tuesday forenoon.

Sergeant McCarthy, William Street station, conducted the inquiry on behalf of the Crown.

Evidence was given by Roger Ryan, brother of the deceased, who stated that he saw deceased at six o'clock on last Friday, and deceased was perfectly sober, on good humour and spirits. The deceased was 12 months in the army, was wounded, and home on sick leave.

Mrs B [sic] Ryan, wife of deceased, deposed that her husband left Clare Cadtle on Friday last perfectly sober.

Tim Tobin, boatman, stated that his attention was directed to a body floating in the water at about five minutes past eleven. He put a rope under the deceased's arms and brought the body down to the ferry slip. He identified the body as the one he brought in.

Mahor J. P. Murohy, R.A.M.C., deposed that there were no marks of violence, and that death was due to drowning.

The jury returned a verdict of death due to drowning.

The following resolution was proposed by Mr Kenny, B. C., foreman of the jury—"That we tender to his widow, brother, and family, our sincere sympathy, and as the deceased had been at the front, wounded, and home on sick leave, we recommend his widow and family to the kind consideration of the War Office and respectfully ask Major C. P. Murphy to have same forwarded to the propped authority.

The Coroner said—I knew Ryan perfectly well, and he was a respectable, hard-working man. I fully endorse all that was said by Mr Kenny, and I heartily agree with the resolution which the jury has just passed. I hope your resolution will have god effect with the War Office. It is a case in which compensation of some sort should be made, if there is such a fund available, as this man leaves a wife and eight helpless children wholly, unprovided for, whose ages average from 2 to 12 years. I sincerely trust, under the very painful circumstances connected with the case that the War Office will see their way to make this poor widow a grant that will help her bring up her eight helpless children.

Grave or memorial reference: Addenda Panel (Screen Wall). Memorial: Grangegorman Memorial, Dublin. Alternative Commemoration - buried in Limerick (Street Lawrence) Catholic Cemetery, Co. Limerick.

RYAN, JAMES: Rank: Private. Regiment or service: Royal Irish Regiment. Unit: 2nd Battalion. Date of death: 5 July 1916. Service No.: 8117. Killed in action.

Supplementary information: Born in Ballina Co. Tipperary. Enlisted in Nenagh while living in Killaloe Co. Clare.

Grave or memorial reference: VII. C. 6. Cemetery: Flatiron Cemetery: Flatiron Copse Cemetery. Mametz in France.

RYAN, JOHN PATRICK: Rank: Private. Regiment or service: Royal Munster Fusiliers. Unit: 1st Battalion. Date of death: 1 July 1918. Age at death: 21. Service No.: 6840. Died of wounds.

Supplementary information: Born in Lissycasey, Co. Clare. Enlisted in Ennis, Co. Clare while living in Kildysart, Co.

Clare. Son of Thomas and Mary Ryan, of Effeman, Kildysart, Co. Clare.

Grave or memorial reference: III. E. 29. Cemetery: Bagneux British Cemetery, Gezauncourt in France.

RYAN, THOMAS JOSEPH: Rank: Private. Regiment or service: Royal Munster Fusiliers. Unit: 2nd Battalion. Date of death: 19 May 1916. Age at death: 17. Service No.: 6543. Killed in action.

Supplementary information: Born in Newmarket-on-Fergus, Co. Clare. Enlisted in Limerick while living in Newmarket-on-Fergus, Co. Clare. Son of Patrick and Mary Ryan, of Newmarket-on-Fergus, Co. Clare.

Grave or memorial reference: I. E. 2. Cemetery: Maroc British Cemetery, Grenay in France.

RYAN, WILLIAM: Rank: Private. Regiment or service: Irish Guards. Unit: 1st Battalion. Date of death: 9 October 1917. Age at death: 27. Service No.: 10592. Killed in action.

Supplementary information: Born in Castletown, Co. Tipperary. Enlisted in Nenagh while living in Killaloe, Co. Clare. Son of Matthew and Mary Ryan, of Cloneybrien, Killaloe, Co. Clare.

He has no known grave but is listed on Panels 10 to 11 on the Tyne Cot Memorial in Belgium.

S

SAUNDERS, FRANCIS: Rank: Private. Regiment or service: Royal Irish Regiment. Unit: 2nd Battalion. Date of death: 19 October 1918. Age at death: 17. Service No.: 7357. Died of wounds at home.

Supplementary information: Born in Clare Abbey, Co. Clare. Enlisted in Ennis while living in Newmarket-on-Fergus, Co. Clare. Son of the late Robert and Mary Saunders. Born at Clarecastle, Co. Limerick. In his will, dated 8 July 1918, his personal effects and property were received by Mrs Mary Burke (aunt), The Green, Newmarket-on-Fergus, Co. Clare. Will was witnessed by, CQMS Colgan of No. 8 Durrington Camp Sailsbury. Percy Webster Lt, O/c B Company 4th Royal Irish Regiment. No 8 Durrington Camp, Salisbury.

Grave or memorial reference: Screen Wall, 03259. Cemetery: Notingham General Cemetery, UK.

SAVAGE, JOHN: *see* **KEANE, JOHN.**

SCANLAN, MARTIN: Rank: Bombardier. Regiment or service: Royal Field Artillery. Date of death: 9 February 1916. Age at death: 28. Service No.: 3778. Died of disease contracted while on service.

Supplementary information: Son of Mrs Mary Scanlan, of Moore Street, Kilrush. Also commemorated in the 'List of Kilrush Men engaged in the War from August 1914'. This pamphlet lists the Kilrush men who were involved in the First World War until 11 November 1918. This man is only in the Commonwealth War Graves database.

Grave or memorial reference: Near North boundary. Cemetery: Kilrush Church of Ireland Churchyard, Co. Clare.

SCANLAN, PATRICK: Rank: Private. Regiment or service: Royal Munster Fusiliers. Unit: 1st Battalion. Date of death: 20 November 1917. Service No.: 6750. Killed in action.

Supplementary information: Born in Kilrush, Co. Clare. Enlisted in Limerick while living in Caherconlish, Co. Limerick.

Grave or memorial reference: I. C. 22. Cemetery: Croiselles Railway Cemetery in France.

SCANLAN, THOMAS: Rank: Private Regiment or service: Labour Corps Secondary Regiment: Royal Munster Fusiliers Secondary. Unit: Formerly (G/4627). Date of death: 19 March 1920. Age at death: 33. Service No.: 382893.

Supplementary information: Son of Mrs Mary Scanlan, of Moore Street, Kilrush. This man is only in the Commonwealth War Graves database.

Grave or memorial reference: Near North boundary. Cemetery: Kilrush Church of Ireland Churchyard, Co. Clare.

SCULLEY/SCULLY, MARTIN: Rank: Private. Regiment or service: Royal Dublin Fusiliers. Unit: 2nd Battalion. Date of death: 17 October 1914. Service No.: 7465.

Supplementary information: Born in Limerick. Enlisted in Dublin while living in Kilkee, Co. Clare.

Grave or memorial reference: H. 3. 9. Cemetery: Nantes (La Bouteillerie) Cemetery, in France.

SCULLY, MICHAEL: Rank: Private. Regiment or service: Irish Guards. Unit: 1st Battalion. Date of death: 1 November 1914. Age at death: 23. Service No.: 4460. Killed in action.

Supplementary information: Born in Clarecastle, Co. Clare. Enlisted in Ennis, Co. Clare Son of Patrick and Mary Scully, of Tiermaclane, Ennis, Co. Clare. In his will, dated 5 August 1914, his personal effects and property were received by, Mrs Mary Scully (mother), Buneratty, Ennis, Co. Clare, Ireland. Will was witnessed by, John Cullen?, Irish Guards. James Egan, Irish Guards

From the *Clare Journal*, 1914:

Clare Victims of the War
News has reached Ennis that Pte John Copeland, Scots Guards; Pte Michael Scully (Ballyea), Irish Guards; and Pte Murphy, Clarecastle, Irish Guards, have been Killed in action.

From the *Clare Journal*, 1914:

Death of Killaloe Man at the Front
A letter from the War Office has been received by Mrs Behan, Atlantic View, Kilkee, stating that her youngest brother, Martin Scully, had been killed at the front. He was a man of splendid physique and height, and went through the South African war, where he was wounded, having volunteered for service there out of the R. I. C., which he had originally joined. He again volunteered for service with Lord Kitchener's Expeditionary Force. He was a brother of District Inspector, J Scully, R. I. C.

Grave or memorial reference: Panel 11. Memorial: Ypres (Menin Gate) Memorial in Belgium.

SEXTON, MICHAEL: Rank: Staff Quartermaster Sergeant. Regiment or service: Royal Army Service Corps. Date of death: 26 Jaunuary 1919. Age at death: 40. Service No.: S/13182.

Supplementary information: Son of James and Mary Sexton; husband of Ellen Sexton, of No. 128 Maryland Road, Wood Green, London. Born at Miltown Malbay, Co. Clare.

This man is only in the Commonwealth War Graves database. Grave or memorial reference: F. 1177. Cemetery: New Southgate Cemetery in Hertfordshire, UK.

SHANK, JOSEPH: Rank: Driver. Regiment or service: Royal Horse Artillery and Royal Field Artillery. Unit: 62nd Battery. Date of death: 8 May 1915. Service No.: 49252. Killed in action.

Supplementary information: Born in Ennis, Co. Clare. Enlisted in Aldershot.

Grave or memorial reference: XXX. G. 5. Cemetery: New Irish Farm Cemetery in Belgium.

SHANNON, EDWARD: Rank: Seaman. Regiment or service: Royal Naval Reserve. Unit: SS *Zelo*. Date of death: 16 June 1918. Age at death: 26. Service No.: 5287/A.

Supplementary information: Son of James and Susan Shannon, of Quilty East, Miltown Malbay, Co. Clare.

Grave or memorial reference: F. R.C. 205. Cemetery: Cardiff (Cathays) Cemetery, Glamorganshire, UK.

SHANNON, EDWARD: Rank: Private. Regiment or service: Royal Munster Fusiliers. Unit: 2nd Battalion. Date of death: 20 December 1916. Age at death: 25. Service No.: 5/6720 and 6720. Killed in action.

Supplementary information: Born in Kingstown, Co. Dublin. Enlisted in Kilkee, Co. Clare while living in Kilkee, Co. Clare. Son of Edward and Mary Shannon, of No. 8 O'Connell Street, Kilkee, Co. Clare.

Grave or memorial reference: VIII. A. 12. Cemetery: Warlencourt British Cemetery in France.

SHARRY/SHERRY, THOMAS: Rank: Rifleman. Regiment or service: Royal Irish Rifles. Unit: 1st Battalion. Date of death: 9 May 1915. Age at death: 27. Service No.: 2511. Killed in action.

Supplementary information: Born in Burrin, Co. Clare. Enlisted in Liverpool Co. Clare. Son of Michael and C. Sharry, of New Quay, Burrin, Co. Clare.

Grave or memorial reference: Panel 9. Memorial: Ploegsteert Memorial in Belgium.

SHARRY, THOMAS: Rank: Private. Regiment or service: Royal Dublin Fusiliers. Unit: 1st Battalion. Date of death: 28 February 1917. Service No.: 40092. Formerly he was with Hussars where his number was 24716. Killed in action.

Supplementary information: Born in Drumcliffe, Co. Clare. Enlisted in Ennis.

Grave or memorial reference: Pier and Face 16 C. Memorial: Thiepval Memorial in France.

SHAUGHNESSY, JAMES: Rank: Gunner. Regiment or service: Royal Garrison Artillery. Unit: 143rd Heavy Battery. Date of death: 15 December 1917. Service No.: 280990. Died in Salonkia.

Supplementary information: Born in Inagh, Co. Clare. Enlisted in Ennis. His personal effects and property were sent to, Mrs Robert Stack, Lysaght Lane, Ennis. His Nuncupative (or missing) will was witnessed by, Michael Hallinan, Lysaghts Lane, Ennis Co. Clare. Mr P. Moran, Lysaghts Lane, Ennis, Co. Clare. Patrick J. Hogan Adm, The Presbytery, Ennis.

Grave or memorial reference: III. C. 16. Cemetery: Lahana Military Cemetery in Greece.

SHAUGHNESSY, MICHAEL: Rank: Private. Regiment or service: Royal Irish Regiment. Unit: 7th Battalion. Date of death: 21 March 1918. Age at death: 21. Service No.: 25771. Formerly he was with the South Irish Horse where his number was 2355. Killed in action.

Supplementary information: Born in Drumcliffe, Co. Clare. Enlisted in Ennis. Son of Frederick and Ellen Shaughnessy.

Grave or memorial reference: Panel 30 and 31. Memorial: Pozieres Memorial in France.

SHAW, BASIL CLAUDE: Rank: Private. Regiment or service: Monmouthsire Regiment (Territorial Force). Unit: 1st Battalion. Date of death: 4 June 1918. Service No.: 226237. Died at Sea.

Supplementary information: Born in Clare, Ireland. Enlisted in Newport, Monmouthshire. On this day HMS *Monmouth* received a 8.2in shell from the SMS *Gneisenau* which almost blew her to pieces. She limped away and later that day was sent to the bottom by SS *Nurnberg*. There were no survivors.

Grave or memorial reference: II. F. 10. Cemetery: Pernes British Cemetery in France.

SHAW, CHARLES: Rank: Private. Regiment or service: Royal Welsh Fusiliers. Unit: 1st Battalion. Date of death: 13 March 1915. Age at death: 20. Service No.: 10587. Killed in action

Supplementary information: Born in Ennis, Co. Clare. Enlisted in Wrexham while living in Newport, Monmouthshire. Son of Donald Robert Clark Shaw and Mary Shaw, of No. 1 Riverside East Usk Road, Newport, Monmouthshire.

Grave or memorial reference: Panel 13 and 14. Memorial: Le Touret Memorial in France.

SHEA, BATT: Rank: Petty Officer Stoker. Regiment or service: Royal Navy. Unit: HMS *Good Hope*. Date of death: 1 November 1914. Age at death: 36. Service No.: 284107.

Supplementary information: Born in Trough Co. Clare. Son of John and Margaret Shea, of Droum, Glenbeigh, Co. Kerry.

From an article in the *Enniscorthy Guardian*:

The British crusier *Monmouth* was sunk in a naval action in the Pacific Ocean, off the coast of Chili, South America. The crusiers *Good Hope* and *Glasgow* were severely damaged, but apparently escaped with an auxiliary cruiser. A message from Otranto (Italy) says that three German Warships are now in Valpariso Bay, Chili. Five more Warships and auxiliaries are outside the bay. The *Monmouth* was an armoured cruiser of 9, 800 tons built at Glasgow at a cost of £979, 000. She belonged to what is known as the County Class, and carried a crew of 537 men. Her armoured belt was 4.2in of Krupp steel and her 14.6in guns were protenced by 5.4in of steel and her secondary guns by 4in.

She was fitted with two torpedo tubes and had a speed of nearly 23 knots. The *Good Hope* is also and armoured cruiser, but much more heavily armoured and armed than that the Monmouth. Her belt is six in of Krupp steel. And her 9.2in guns are protected by 6.5in. She also carries 16, 6in guns and 15 quickfirers. Her speed is over 23 knots and she has a crew of 900 men. The *Monmouth* was commissioned in July, 1914, under the command of Captain Frank Brandt. The *Good Hope* was commissioned in 1912, and carried the flag of Sir Christopher Cradock, K.C.V.O.

Grave or memorial reference: 3. He has no known grave but is listed on the Plymouth Naval Memorial, UK.

SHEA, MICHAEL J.: Rank: Corporal. Regiment or service: US Army. Unit: 165th Infantry Regiment: 42nd Division. Date of death: 1 August 1918. Service No.: Unknown. Died of wounds.
Supplementary information: see **SHEA, THOMAS** (brother).
Grave or memorial reference: Plot A, Row 9, Grave 25. Cemetery: Aisne-Marne American Cemetery, Belleau, France.

SHEA, PATRICK: Rank: Private. Regiment or service: Irish Guards. Unit: 2nd Battalion. Date of death: 29 April 1916. Service No.: 7430. Killed in action.
Supplementary information: Born in Cappamore, Co. Limerick (census says, born in Co. Clare). Enlisted in Drogheda, Co. Louth while living in Ashton-in-Makefield, Lancashire. His medal index card shows that he first entered the theatre of war (France) on 17 August 1915 and he enlisted under Patrick Shea and that he was KIA on 29 April 1916. SDGW shows he was the only man who died with the Irish Guards on that day and the 1901 census shows he lived at Flag Road, Miltown Malbay. CWGC has him incorrectly listed under Shea, T.

From the *Saturday Record*, May 1916:

Miltown-Malbay Man Killed at the Front
The following sympathetic letter has been received from the chaplain of the Irish Guards, by the mother of Pte Pat O'Shea, Miltown Malbay, killed at the front—

May 1st, 1916.
Dear Mrs O'Shea, --I am the chaplain to the 2nd Irish Guards, and it is with much sorrow that I write to inform you, that God in His infinite wisdom and love has seen fit to accept the sacrifice which your son made of his life in coming out here to do his duty to his country and to his God. He was killed when holding the trenches against the enemy on April 29. His death was painless and merciful. Nor need you fear that because his death was sudden he was unprepared. Only a few days before, the men of the Battalion attended the services of Holy Week and received Absolution, Holy Communion and the Holy Father's Blessing and Plenary Indulgence.

I know that this cannot prevent you feeling very terribly the loss of your dear boy. He was a good soldier, esteemed by officers as well as by his comrades. But it is much that to your sorrow for his loss you need not add anxiety for his soul, which has gone to God. May that comfort and console you in the hope of meeting your holy boy once again in heaven, and may Our Blessed Lady; the consoler of the afflicted, be with you in your grief.
With all sympathy.
Yours sincerely in Jesus Christ
S. S. Knapp, Chaplain.

The announcement of Pat O'Shea's death caused much regret in his native town, Miltown-Malbay. He was a son of the late Head Constable O'Shea, R. I. C., and grandson of Mrs James Comyn. He first served as telegraph messenger, from whence he was sent as rural postman at an early age, to Athenry, being scarcely 16 years of age. In the Co. Galway, while in the discharge of his duty there we was sent by his officials to take up duty, which was rather unpleasant for a boy of his years, and he received some injuries. The story of his short time there is now well known to the people of that district. He spent some months in the Co. Hospital of Galway, until, fully recovered from the effects of the injuries he received in the discharge of his duty, his chiefs again recognised the worth of the young official, and transferred him to Drogheda, where he was for some months, and on the Postmaster General's circular inviting postal carriers to join the ranks, he was one of the first in his centre to join.

(I contacted the CWGC and got them to check the entry for Private Shea, and they said the original entry gave his initial as T but it may be a typesetters error in which case it will be corrected after military records are consulted – Author).

Grave or memorial reference: I. H. 8. Cemetery: White House Cemetery, St Jean-Les-Ypres in Belgium.

SHEA, THOMAS: Rank: Sergeant. Regiment or service: US Army. Unit: G Company, 9th Infantry. Date of death: 18 July 1918. Age at death: 29. Service No.: Unknown. Killed in action.

Supplementary information: Enlisted in New York.

From the *Saturday Record*, November 1918:

Gallant Clare Man Dead
Sergeant Thomas Shea Dies in
France

It is with regret we announce the death of Sergeant Thomas Shea, Co, G., 9th Infantry, who was Killed in action on July, 18th. It will be recalled that the 9th Infantry flanked the Marines in their recent victory at Chateau Thierry, and no doubt it was in the battle he received the fatal wound. Born scarcely 29 years ago at Ruan, Co. Clare, Sergeant Shea was one of the first to answer his country's call; he enlisted in April 191--, and arrived in France the following August. He was true specimen of Irish manhood, with a heart as true as steel, loved by all who knew him, and was one of the staunchest of friends. He had sacrificed his life for his country, and died a noble death so that others may enjoy the liberty he prized so much. Greater love than this no man can show.

His brother, Michael J. Shea is also in France with the colours. He joined the 69th, now the 165th, Infantry, Company G in May, 1917.

Grave or memorial reference: No burial details available at this time.

SHIPLEY JOHN PHILIP:
Rank: Private. Regiment or service: Manchester Regiment. Unit: $1^{st}/7^{th}$ Battalion. Date of death: 16 October 1915. Age at death: 32. Service No.: 2243. Killed in action in Gallipoli.

Supplementary information: Born in Manchester. Enlisted in Manchester while living in Ennis, Co. Clare. Husband of A.K. Shipley, of Claureen, Ennis, Co. Clare.

Grave or memorial reference: Sp. Mem. C. 3. Cemetery: Twelve Tree Copse Cemetery, Gallipoli.

SIMMS, ARTHUR: Rank: First Mate. Regiment or service: Mercantile Marine. Unit: SS *Lewisham* (London) Date of death: 17 May 1917. Age at death: 26.

Supplementary information: Son of Antonia Simms, of Moorlands, Banbridge, Co. Down, and the late David Simms. Born at Killaloe. The 2, 810 ton British SS *Lewisham* was torpedoed by a German submarine off Fastnet. Twenty-four men died.

Arthur had two brothers who also died in the First World War. They were **SIMMS, GORDON LUTWITCH,** Mercantile Marine, died on the S. S. *Isleworth* in 1918 and **SIMMS, JOHN EDWARD**, born in Canada, killed in Ypres in 1917. John was a Private. in the Australian Infantry.

Grave or memorial reference: He has no known grave but is listed on the Tower Hill Memorial, UK.

SLATTERY, FRANCIS JAMES:
Rank: Captain. Regiment or service: Royal Engineers. Unit: 8th Field Company. Date of death: 9 January 1919.

Supplementary information: Son of Thomas Slattery, of Fergus View, Darragh, Ennis.

From the *Saturday Record*, February 1919:

The Late Captain Slattery, R.E. The remains of the above much lamented young officer, whose death we have already noticed, were removed from London for internment in the family burial place at Kilchreest, Ballynacally. They were removed from the train at Clarecastle, and were placed in the Parish Church on Friday night, 15th inst; and there was a Solemn Requiem Mass the following morning.

The celebrant was Rev M. McGrath, C.C., and the deacon and sub deacon, Rev John McMahon, Ennis, and Rev Fr Donnellyy, Cranny. Tehre were also pesent Very rev Canon Burke, P.P.; Very Rev Canon O'Dea, The College; and Rev M Crowe, C. C., Doora.

Mr Thomas Slattery, Fergus View, Darragh, has received the following telegram from Buckingham Palace, London—

"The King and Queen deeply regret the loss that you and the army have sustained by the death of your son in the service of his country. Their Majesties truly sympathise with you in your sorrow."

Grave or memorial reference: In North-East part. Cemetery: Ballynacally (Kilchreest) Cemetery, Co. Clare.

SMYTH, SIMON: Rank: Lance Corporal. Regiment or service: Royal Munster Fusiliers. Unit: 1st Battalion. Date of death: 21 August 1915 (SDGW); 7 July 1915 (CWGC). Service No.: 9683. Died of wounds in Gallipoli.

Supplementary information: Born in Lisgreen, Co. Clare. Enlisted in Limerick while living in Lisgreen, Co. Clare.

Grave or memorial reference: D. 83. Cemetery: Lancashire Landing Cemetery in Turkey.

SOMERS, CYRIL DERMOTT FOUACE: Rank: Second Lieutenant. Regiment or service: Royal Inniskilling Fusiliers. Unit: 1st Battalion. Date of death: 20 May 1917. Died of wounds.

Supplementary information: Son of Mr S.H. Somers, of The Rectory, Mount Shannon Co. Clare.

Grave or memorial reference: III. N. 17. Cemetery: Duisans British Cemetery, Etrun in France.

SOMERS, THOMAS CHRISTOPHER: Rank: Private. Regiment or service: South Irish Horse. Unit: Attached to the Dorsetshire Yeomanry. Date of death: 22 November 1918. Service No.: 73492.

Supplementary information: Born in Newmarket, Co. Clare. Served with the British Expeditionary Force.

Grave or memorial reference: DD. 29. Cemetery: Ramleh War Cemetery in Israel.

SPARROW, FRANK EDWARD: Rank: Lieutenant (TP). Regiment or service: Corps of Royal Engineers. Unit: 129th Field Company. Date of

death: 13 August 1918. Age at death: 37. Died of wounds.

Supplementary information: Son of Edward and Annie Sparrow, of No. 55 Palmerston Road, Dublin. Junior Architect, Local Government Board (Ireland), MRIAI.

From the *Clare Journal*, August 1916:

Second Lieutenant F.E. Sparrow, killed on August 13, was a L.G.B Inspector and was the elder son of the late Mr E. Sparrow, 55 Palmerstown Road, Dublin. He was in charge of the Ennis district at the time he volunteered.

From De Ruvigny's Roll of Honour:

Sparrow, Frank Edward, M.R.I.A.I., Lieutenant, 129th Field Company, Royal Engineers. Elder son of the late Edward Sparrow, by his wife, Annie (55, Palmerstown Road, Dublin), daughter of William Pillar and grandson of the late Jacob Sparrow, of Cairn Hill, Foxrock, Co. Dublin. Born in Dublin on 9 November 1878. Educated at Newtown School, Waterford, and the Royal College of Science, Dublin; also matriculating at the Royal University, Ireland. Was engaged as Junior Architect to the Local Government Board, Ireland for several years. Subsequently was appointed temporary Poor Law Inspector. Obtained a commission 16 December 1915. Served with the Expeditionary Force in France and Flanders, and was Killed in action, 13 August 1916, while inspecting new ground just taken from the enemy at the Battle of the Somme. Buried in the Military Cemetery, Dives Copse, near Corbie, Picardy.

His Commanding Officer wrote; "He was a great loss to us out here … He was one of the cheeriest and best officers I have met, and his men were very fond of him. There was a groan of dismay when I told them on parade about it. I had a very high opinion of him, and when he was attached to my company and belonged to another, I managed to arrange to get him transferred to me … He died doing his duty…. We have lost a good officer, and a gallant gentleman, and all of us mourn his loss with you." He was a member of the Street Stephen's Green Club; was also a keen yachtsman and golfer, winning prizes at various clubs to which he belonged."

He is commemorated on the Great War Memorial in St Canice's Cathedral, Kilkenny …'To the Glory of God and in loving memory of the following members of the Diocese of Ossory who gave their lives for their country in the Great War 1914-1918'.

Grave or memorial reference: I. C. 6. Cemetery: Dive Copse British Cemetery, Sailly-Le-Sec in France

SPILLANE, CHRISTOPHER: Rank: Lance Corporal. Regiment or service: Royal Munster Fusiliers. Unit: 2nd Battalion. Date of death: 27 August 1914. Service No.: 9892. Killed in action.

Supplementary information: Born in Athlone, Co. Westmeath. Enlisted in Limerick while living in Ennis, Co. Clare.

Grave or memorial reference: I. 8. Cemetery: Etreux British Cemetery, Aisne, France.

STACPOOLE, GEORGE ERIC GUY: Rank: Lieutenant. Regiment or service: Royal Irish Regiment. Unit: 1st Battalion. Date of death: 27 January 1915. Age at death: 23. Killed in action.

Supplementary information: Son of Mr R.G. Stacpoole, of the Constitutional Club, Northumberland Avenue, London.

From *Our Heroes*, 1916:

Lieutenant G.E.G. Stacpoole, Royal Irish Regiment, who was Killed in action on January 27th, was born in January, 1891, and was gazetted in November, 1911. He was posted to the 1st Battalion at Nasiribad, which

Lieutenant G. Stacpoole.

until recently was in Major-General K.S. Davison's Brigade of the Mhow Division. While in India he had gone in for transport work and passed the appointed course. He obtained his Lieutenancy in August last year. Lieutenant Stackpoole was the eldest son of Mr and Mrs R.G. Stackpoole, 26 Walton Place, London, S.W., and of Co. Clare.

From De Ruvigny's Roll of Honour:

Stacpoole, George Eric Guy. Lieut, 1st Battalion, Royal Irish Regiment. Eldest son of Richard George Stacpoole, of 26 Walton Street, Hans Place, London, and of Co. Clare, by his wife, Edith Maude, daughter if Sir Edward Dean Paul, 4th Bart., and great grandson of of the late Richard John de la Zouche Stacpoole, of Eden Vale, Co. Clare. Born at Sefton Park, Liverpool, 10 January 1892. Educated at Eton and the Royal Military College Sandhurst Gazetted 2nd Lieutenant., Royal Irish Regiment, 4 November 1911, and promoted Lieutenant 16 August 1914. Joined his regiment at Nasirabad, India in January 1912, and while stationed there went in for transport work, and passed the appointed course, returned to England in November 1914. Went to France in December with the 27th Division, and was killed in action at St Eoi, 27 January 1915. Buried in Dickiebusch Cemetery. His commanding officer wrote; "I very much deplore his loss, as a gallant officer, fearless, true and upright, and popular with all ranks of his Battalion."

From *Bond of Sacrifice*:

... born on the 10th February, 1892, at Albert Road, Sefton Park, Liverpool, was the eldest son of Richard George Stacpoole, of Walton Street, Hans Place, London, and of Co. Clare, Ireland, by his marriage with Edith Maude, daughter of Sir Richard John Dean paul, 4th baronet. Lieutenant Stacpoole was a great grandson of Richard John de la Zouche Stacpoole, of Eden Vale, Co. Clare, Ireland. He was educated at Eton and the R.M.C., Sandhurst, and was gazetted to the Royal Irish Regiment in November, 1911, joining his regiment in Narisabad in January, 1912. While in India he passed the Transport Course, and was promoted Lieutenant in August, 1914. His recreations were polo, football, boxing and shooting. He arrived from India, for the War, with Battalion in October, 1914, and left with it for France as part of the XXVIIth Division in December, 1914. Lieutenant Stacpoole was killed on the 27th January, 1915, in the trenches at St Eloi, and was buried in the cemetery at Dickebusch, Belgium.

Grave or memorial reference: B. 10. Cemetery: Dickiebusch Old Military Cemetery in Belgium.

STINCHCOMBE, JOHN WILLIAM NELSON: Rank: Private. Regiment or service: Royal Irish Regiment. Unit: 2nd Battalion. Date of death: 27 September 1918. Age at death: 32. Service No.: 16633. Formerly he was with the Royal Dublin Fusiliers where his number was 31457. Killed in action.

Supplementary information: Born in Miskin, Mountain Ash. Enlisted in Mountain Ash while living in Ennis, Co. Clare. Son of John Nelson Stinchcombe, and Mary Jane Stinchcombe, of Surrey; husband of Ada Mary Stinchcombe, of No. 14 Windsor Road, Miskin, Mountain Ash, Glamorganshire.

Grave or memorial reference: A. 9. Cemetery: Moeuvres British Cemetery, Nord, France.

STOKES, JOHN: Rank: Private. Regiment or service: Royal Munster Fusiliers. Unit: 1st Battalion. Date of death: 28 May 1915. Service No.: 6009. Killed in action in Gallipoli.

Supplementary information: Born in Gort, Co. Galway. Enlisted in Ennis while living in Ennis.

Grave or memorial reference: Panel 185 to 190. Memorial: Helles Memorial in Turkey.

STUDDERT, THEODORE: Rank: Lance Corporal. Regiment or service: Canadian Infantry (Manitoba Regiment) Unit: 52nd Battalion. Date of death: 2 November 1915. Age at death: 29. Service No.: 438574.

Supplementary information: Son of Jonas William and Emma Mary Studdert, of Atlantic House, Kilkee, Co. Clare, Ireland.

Grave or memorial reference: Hospital Plot. Cemetery: Thunder Bay (St Andrew's) Roman Catholic Cemetery, Ontario, Canada.

SULLIVAN, JOHN: Rank: Able Seaman. Regiment or service: Mercantile Marine. Unit: SS *Aylevarroo* (Limerick) Date of death: 7 October 1917. Age at death: 27.

Supplementary information: Son of Patrick and Mary Sullivan, of Rinevilla, Kilballyowen, Carrigaholt, Co. Clare. The 908-ton Irish cargo/transport SS *Aylevaroo* was (presumed to be) torpedoed by German submarine U-57 off Ballycotton Island. There were no survivors.

Grave or memorial reference: Tower Hill Memorial, UK.

SULLIVAN, JOHN: Rank: Lance Corporal. Regiment or service: Royal Munster Fusiliers. Unit: 8th Battalion. Date of death: 29 May 1916. Service No.: 4117. Killed in action.

Supplementary information: Born in Killaloe, Co. Clare. Enlisted in Nenagh while living in Killaloe, Co. Clare.

Grave or memorial reference: I. A. 3. Cemetery: Philosophe British Cemetery, Mazingarbe in France.

SULLIVAN, JOHN: Rank: Bombardier. Regiment or service: Royal Horse Artillery and Royal Field Artillery. Unit: D Battery, 83rd Brigade. Date of death: 17 October 1917. Service No.: 3844. Killed in action.

Supplementary information: Born in Kilrush, Ireland. Enlisted in Kilrush. Also commemorated in the 'List of Kilrush Men engaged in the War from August 1914'. This pamphlet lists the Kilrush men who were involved in the First World War until 11 November 1918.

Grave or memorial reference: VI. A. 17. Cemetery: Bard Cottage Cemetery, Ieper, Belgium

SULLIVAN, THOMAS: Rank: Private. Regiment or service: Royal Munster Fusiliers. Unit: 2nd Battalion. Date of death: 21 December 1914. Service No.: 5842. Killed in action.

Supplementary information: Born in Kilrush, Co. Clare. Enlisted in Limerick while living in Burrane, Knock, Co. Clare.

Grave or memorial reference: Panel 43 and 44. Memorial: Le Touret Memorial in France.

T

TALTY, JOHN: Rank: Private. Regiment or service: Royal Army Service Corps. Date of death: 2 November 1918. Service No.: M/416111. Died at of disease contracted while on service.

Supplementary information: Born in Kilrush, Co. Clare. Enlisted in Dublin while living in Kilrush, Co. Clare. Also commemorated in the 'List of Kilrush Men engaged in the War from August 1914'. This pamphlet lists the Kilrush men who were involved in the First World War until 11 November 1918.

Grave or memorial reference: About the middle of the east side. Cemetery: Kilrush (Shanakyle) Cemetery, Co. Clare.

TAYLOR, (GEOFFREY) GOFF: Rank: Private. Regiment or service: Royal Munster Fusiliers. Unit: 2nd Battalion. Date of death: 9 May 1915. Service No.: 5455. Killed in action.

Supplementary information: Born in Kilrush, Co. Clare. Enlisted in Kilrush while living in Kilrush, Co. Clare. Also commemorated in the 'List of Kilrush Men engaged in the War from August 1914'. This pamphlet lists the Kilrush men who were involved in the First World War until 11 November 1918.

Grave or memorial reference: Panel 43 and 44. Memorial: Le Touret Memorial in France.

THYNEE/THYNNE, JOHN: Rank: Private. Regiment or service: Royal Irish Regiment. Unit: 2nd Battalion. Date of death: 6 December 1918. Service No.: 10330. Killed in action.

Supplementary information: Born in Ennistymon, Co. Clare. Enlisted in Ennis while living in Ennistymon, Co. Clare.

Grave or memorial reference: 393. Cemetery: Chambieres French National Cemetery, Metz, Mozelle in France.

THYNNE, MICHAEL: Rank: Private. Regiment or service: Royal Munster Fusiliers. Unit: 1st Battalion. Age at death: 30. Date of death: 4 May 1915. Service No.: 6934.

Supplementary information: Born in Ennistymon, Co. Clare. Enlisted in Ennis, Co. Clare while living in Ennistymon, Co. Clare. Died of wounds in Gallipoli. In his will, dated 2 April 1915, his personal effects and property were received by Miss Mary Thynne(sister), of Church Hill, Ennistymon, Co. Clare. Son of John and Catherine Thynne, of Church Hill, Ennistymon, Co. Clare.

Grave or memorial reference: Panel 185 to 190. Memorial: Helles Memorial in Turkey.

THYNNE, PATRICK: Rank: Lance Corporal. Regiment or service: Irish Guards. Unit: 1st Battalion. Date of death: 17 May 1915. Service No.: 3179. Killed in action.

Supplementary information: Born in Ennistymon, Co. Clare. Enlisted in Ennis while living in Brighton, Sussex.

Grave or memorial reference: Panel 4. Memorial: Le Touret Memorial in France.

TIERNEY, JOHN JOSEPH: Rank: Private. Regiment or service: Royal Munster Fusiliers. Unit: 8th Battalion. Age at death: 21. Date of death: 3 November 1916. Service No.: 8/5718. Died at home.

Supplementary information: Born in Lanesborough, Co. Longford Enlisted in Lisdoonvarna, Co. Clare while living in Lisdoonvarna, Co. Clare. Son of John and Ellen Tierney, of Rooska, Lisdoonvarna, Co. Clare.

From the *Saturday Record* and *Clare Journal*, November 1916:

Lisdoonvarna War Victim
At the last meeting of the Lisdoon-varna Improvement Committee, on the motion of the Chairman (Very Rev, M.D. Conroy, P.P.), seconded by Mr McGuire, there was passed a vote of condolence ... Mr John Tierney, Sec. To the Committee, on the death of his son, John Joe, at netley Hospital, where he was invalided from the "Western Front".

Grave or memorial reference: R. C. 892. Cemetery: Netley Military Cemetery, Hampshire, UK.

TIERNEY, PATRICK: Rank: Private. Regiment or service: Royal Munster Fusiliers. Unit: 1st Battalion. Date of death: 6 July 1915. Service No.: 8479. Died of wounds in Gallipoli.

Supplementary information: Born in Drumcliffe, Co. Clare. Enlisted in Ennis while living in Ennis.

Grave or memorial reference: D. 79. Cemetery: Lancashire Landing Cemetery in Turkey.

TINCHANT, JOSE LAURENT GONZALES: Rank: Corporal. Regiment or service: Belgian Army. Unit: First Carabiners. Date of death: 6 September 1915. Age at death: 17. Killed in action.

Supplementary information: Born 4 February 1897.

From the *Clare Journal*, September 1915:

Corporal Tinchant of the Belgian Army
We learn that Mrs Bulger, of Thomond House, Lisdoonvarna, has been informed that one of her grandsons, Corporal Jose Tinchant, of the Belgian Army, has been killed in action at Dixmude. Though only 17 ½ years of age, Corporal Tinchant volunteered for service in the Belgian Army and went through all the hardships of last winter. He was fatally injured on the 6th of the present month. Corporal Tinchant was son of Madame Tinchant, a gifted lady, with whom much sympathy is felt in the loss of her gallant son; and a grandson of the late Mr Daniel Bulger, stockbroker, of Dublin.

Grave or memorial reference: Cemetery: The Churchyard at Kaaskerke/Caeskerke, in Belgium.

TOOHEY, CORNELIUS: Rank: Gunner. Regiment or service: Royal Garrison Artillery. Date of death: 26

Novemebr 1914. Service No.: 15975. Born in Bridgetown, Co. Clare. Died at home.

Supplementary information: Enlisted in Limerick while living in Castleconnell, Co. Limerick. Husband of Mrs M. Toohey, of No. 45 Evergreen Road, Cork.

Grave or memorial reference: In the east part. Cemetery: Ballinakilla Churchyard, Co. Cork.

TOOHEY, JAMES: Rank: Private.

Regiment or service: Australian Infantry, AIF. Unit: 56th Battalion attached to the Anzac Light Railways. Date of death: 11 December 1917. Service No.: 5461. Died of a shell wound to the head on admission to the 8th Field Ambulance.

Supplementary information: Born, Killuran, Broadford, Co. Clare. Occupation on enlistment, Labourer. Age on enlistment: 32 years 4 months. Next of kin: Mrs Mary Butler (sister), of No. 20 L Avenue, Newtown, N.S.W. Later changed to John Toohey (brother), Killuran, Broadford Post Office, Co. Clare. Place and date of enlistment: Liverpool, N.S.W.; Tuesday, 4 January 1916. Weight: 11st 3lbs. Height: 5ft 11in. Complexion: Florid. Eyes: Blue. Hair: Grey.

Grave or memorial reference: C. 10. Cemetery: Irish House Cemetery in Belgium.

TOOMEY/TWOMEY, PATRICK:

Rank: Private. Regiment or service: Royal Munster Fusiliers. Unit: 8th Battalion. Date of death: 10 April 1916. Service No.: 3860. Killed in action.

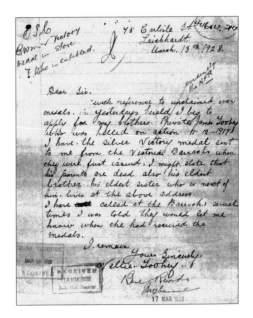

A letter from the sister of Private J. Toohey.

Supplementary information: Born in Kilkee, Co. Clare. Enlisted in Limerick while living in Kilkee, Co. Clare. I include the following article for your reference as these two men may be related.

From the *Clare Journal*, 1914:

Kilkee Man's Letter from the Front
'Stood our Ground to the Last'

From Lance Corporal Edward Twomey, a Kilkee man, to his mother:

"We have had some very hot fighting. We were in the thick of it all the time. Our regiment was posted to cover the retreat for five days, and the Germans were as thick as bees around us all the time.

When you are put on duty of that kind there's no question of giving way until your task has been completed, and we stood our ground until the last That meant in some cases that we had to be cut up, but we were selected because we could be relied on to make the best possible show and delay the enemy as long as possible.

Some of our detachments had rough luck in every way, but they carried themselves with a steadiness that won them praise from everybody, and they made the Germans realise that they weren't going to have it all their own way.

The Germans were furious over the stand our chaps made. They had never expected anything of the sort, and though they kept out of the way when we were anything approaching their strength, they were very brave about rushing us when our ammunition ran out and our weakness in numbers was obvious.

They didn't reckon on the bayonets, and when we received them that way you may guess there was a nice howl all round.

General French has thanked us for the way we behaved, and praise from him is worth a great deal more than from any other men. He is not in a hurry to say nice things about us, but when he does speak, we know he means every word of it, and maybe more. That's the way to get round the soldiers."

Grave or memorial reference: F. 15. Cemetery: Bois-Carre Military Cemetery, Haisnes in France

TRACY/TRACEY, LEROY LAWRENCE: Rank: Private. Regiment or service: Royal Army Medical Corps. Unit: 57th Field Ambulance. Date of death: 20 July 1916. Age at death: 29. Service No.: 51507. Killed in action.

Supplementary information: Born in Dublin. Enlisted in Limerick. Entered the French Theatre of War on 4 December 1915. Son of Sarah Ann Tracey, listed in the 1911 census living at No. 9 Ballydonaghan, Boherglass, Clare.

From his will:

£3, 000 Guinness pre-7 Shares and Cottage to Sarah Ann Tracey (mother). On her death to JP. Tracey (brother). On his death, house lands and fixtures to be sold and proceeds to Ralph, Ronald Tracey (cousin), RN?. Failing which to the Catholic Orphans Society Dublin, Ireland. "In the event of this will being lost return to McCaulig S. Tood, Solictors, Dame St, Dublin or to Leroy L Tracey, Engineering Inspector, Congested District Board, The Cottage, Body Ks, Clare Co, Ireland or to the Galway Office of the C. D. B. "

Grave or memorial reference: Pier and Face 4 C. Memorial: Thiepval Memorial in France.

TROY, JOHN: Rank: Private. Regiment or service: South Wales Borderers. Unit: 6th Battalion. Date of death: 21 April 1918. Service No.: 39227. Died of wounds at home.

Supplementary information: Formerly he was with the Liverpool Regiment where his number was 37869. Enlisted in Seaforth while living in Kilkee, Co. Clare.

Grave or memorial reference: D. 10. 23961. Cemetery: Hendon Cemetery and Crematorium, Middlesex, UK.

TUOHEY, EDWARD: Rank: Private. Regiment or service: Connaught Rangers Unit: 1st Battalion. Date of death: 26 April 1915. Service No.: 3984. Killed in action.

Supplementary information: Born in Clare. Enlisted in Galway while living in Gort, Co. Galway.

Grave or memorial reference: Panel 42. Memorial: Ypres (Menin Gate) Memorial in Belgium.

TUOHEY/TUOHY, PATRICK: Rank: Private. Regiment or service: Leicestershire Regiment. Unit: 6th Battalion. Date of death: 19 September 1918. Service No.: 47230. Killed in action.

Supplementary information: Born in Co. Clare, Ireland. Enlisted in Sheffield, Yorkshire.

Grave or memorial reference: V.G. 20. Cemetery: Gouzeaucourt New British Cemetery in France.

TUOHY, MICHAEL: Rank: Private. Regiment or service: Irish Guards. Unit: 1st Battalion. Date of death: 30 April 1918. Service No.: 11319. Killed in action.

Supplementary information: Born in Scariff, Co. Clare. Enlisted in Huddersfield, Yorkshire while living in Scariff, Co. Clare.

Grave or memorial reference: A. 10. Cemetery: Ayette British Cemetery in France.

TUTTLE, JOHN: Rank: Private. Regiment or service: Royal Munster Fusiliers. Unit: 2nd Battalion. Date of death: 25 September 1915. Age at death: 21. Service No.: 5868. Killed in action.

Supplementary information: Born in Drumcliffe, Co. Clare. Enlisted in Ennis, Co. Clare while living in Ennis, Co. Clare. Son of Edmund and Bridget Hehir Tuttle, of Lysaghts Lane, Ennis, Co. Clare.

From the *Clare Journal* and *Ennis Advertiser*, October 1915:

Ennis Victims of the War

In a letter from an hospital "Somewhere in France," an Ennis man, who took part in the recent heavy fighting, which was successful for the British army, describing how Lance-Corporal John Tuttle of the Munster Fusiliers, son of Mr Edward Tuttle ... says he was the first of the Munsters to fall, shot through the head, death being instantaneous. The deceased man was reputable for his quiet and amiable disposition and was very popular amongst friends before leaving Ennis.

Other Ennis men, Private. J. Savage and Private. Cahill, have, we hear, also died. The latter died of wound's.

From the *Clare Journal*, October 1916:

Roll of Honour
First Anniversary

Jack Tuttle, son of Edward Tuttle, Ennis, died at the battle of Loos, September 25th 1915, aged 21 years. Fought at the battles of La-Basee and Ypres. Writing to his sister on January 2nd 1915, as he was leaving England he said "if I go to Belgium a happier soldier never fought for that Catholic little country than I." An officer writing from the front to his father and offering him his sympathy said– "I have not known your boy particularly, but have always heard him spoken of as a good brave boy, and the kind of soldier we can ill afford to lose at present. He was very popular in his company and his comrades are very grieved at his death. The men of No. 3 Platoon, to which he belonged, had cleared our front trench and were advancing towards the German position when your son was mortally wounded, and died a few minutes afterwards. He lay back with a smile on his face and evidently in no pain. You will always have the satisfaction of knowing that your son died a gallant death like the good soldier that he was, and gave his life fighting a just cause."

Father Gleeson, the chaplain to the Munsters, in his letter to his father informing him of his death, and which he is not at liberty to publish assures him that Mass was celebrated for the Battalion, their confessions heard, and the Bread of Life distributed to every man in the Battalion, a few hours before going into battle. This will be a consolation to his relatives throughout the County and elsewhere, and a source of deep gratification to his former associates in the town, with who Jack Tuttle was very popular before he left.

Grave or memorial reference: Panel 127. Memorial: Loos Memorial in France.

TWOMEY, PATRICK: *see* **TOOMEY, PATRICK.**

TWYFORD, THOMAS: Rank: Able Seaman. Regiment or service: Mercantile Marine. Unit: SS *Castlebar* (Belfast) Date of death: 13 March 1918. Age at death: 32.

Supplementary information: Born in Kilrush, Co. Clare. Son of Mary Anne and the late Robert Twyford; husband of Teresa Twyford (*née* Hillian), of Carrignohane Villa, Carrignohane, Co. Cork. The SS *Castlebar* disappeared at sea. From 'Missing and untraced merchant vessels' in Lloyd's, 'Reported to have passed Fanad Head on 14 March and listed "missing" on 7 August 1918'.

Grave or memorial reference: Tower Hill Memorial, UK.

V

VANDELEUR, ALEXANDER MOORE: Rank: Captain. Regiment or service: 2nd Life Guards. Date of death: 30 October 1914. Age at death: 30. Killed in action.

Supplementary information: Son of Hector Stewart Vandeleur and Charlotte Vandeleur of Kilrush and Cahiracon, Co. Clare; husband of the Hon. Violet Ethel Meysey-Thompson, eldest daughter of 1st Baron Knaresborough (now the Hon. Mrs A.H.S. Howard, of Thornbury Castle, Gloucestershire).

From the *Clare Journal*, 1914:

Missing

"Missing", says the "Daily Sketch", is a most terrible word to have ever at the front of one's brain, and everyone will sympathise with beautiful Mrs Vandeleur, who is anxiously awaiting news of her husband. Captain Vandeleur, who is in the 2nd Life Guards, is the only surviving son of the late Captain Hector Vandeleur, of Co. Clare. Mrs Vandeleur is the eldest daughter of Lord Knaresborough, and was married in 1910.

Lieutenant J. B. Vandeleur.

Who was an officer in the Leicester Regiment, has been killed. He was the only son of the late Col. J. O. Vandeleur, C.B., of Ballinacourty, and was a kinsman of Captain W.M.C. Vandeleur, Moyville, Galway, whose death on September 10 has been reported; and also of that brilliant officer, the late Lieutenant Seymore C. Vandeleur, D.S.O., Kilrush, who was Killed in action in the Boer War.

The Vandeleur family has numbered many distinguished and highly placed officers in its members. There is a story told of brigadier General Thomas Pakenham Vandeleur, of the 8th Hussars, who was killed at the battle of Laswarree gained by General Lake on Nov 1 1803. The General was shot dead just when drawing his sword at the head of his regiment. He fell from his horse—a magnificent black race horse—and long after the death of his rider the horse kept his place at the head of his regiment, disdaining any other position. He was taken great care of by the regiment until it left India, and then, as the horse could not be brought home, it was shot, so that it should never fall into unworthy hands.

Grave or memorial reference: Panel 3. Memorial: Ypres (Menin Gate) Memorial in Belgium.

WALKER, CHARLES A: Rank: Assistant Steward. Regiment or service: Mercantile Marine. Unit: SS *Eupion* (London). Date of death: 3 October 1918. Age at death: 25.

Supplementary information: Son of Charles and Sarah Elizabeth Walker, of No. 20 Edward Street, Brantford, Ontario. Born at Brantford, Canada.

The 3,575 ton SS *Eupion* was built in Alloa, Clackmannanshire in 1914 for the Eupion Steamship Company. She was torpedoed and sunk west of Loop Head, Co. Clare by German submarine U-123, the same submarine that sank the *Leinster* a week later. Two other Eupion casualties are buried in this cemetery.

Grave or memorial reference: In North-East corner. Cemetery: Kilrush Church of Ireland Churchyard, Co. Clare.

WALSH, CHARLES EDWARD: Rank: Sergeant. Regiment or service: West Riding Regiment. Unit: 2nd Battalion. Date of death: 17 October 1916. Service No.: 9687. Died of wounds.

Supplementary information: Born in Leeds. Enlisted in Bradford, Yorkshire while living in Newmarket-on-Fergus, Co. Clare.

Grave or memorial reference: I. N. 7. Cemetery: Grove Town Cemetery, Meaulte, France

WALSH, JOHN: Rank: Lance Corporal. Regiment or service: Royal Munster Fusiliers. Unit: 1st Battalion. Date of death: 7 June 1917. Age at death: 32. Service No.: 3683. Killed in action.

Supplementary information: Born in Ennistymon, Co. Clare. Enlisted in Limerick while living in Ennistymon, Co. Clare. Son of Michael Walsh, of Ballygastel, Lisdoonvama, Co. Clare. His personal effects and property were sent to Mr Michael Walsh, of No. 3 River View Terrace, Ennistymon, Co. Clare, Ireland.

Grave or memorial reference: II. B. 1. Cemetery: Wytschaete Military Cemetery in Belgium.

WALSH, JOHN: Rank: Major (TP). Regiment or service: Royal Fusiliers (City of London Regiment). Unit: 22nd Battalion. Date of death: 19 February 1917. Age at death: 34. Died of wounds.

Supplementary information: Son of Mr M. and Mrs B. Walsh.

From the *Clare Journal*, February 1916:

Rapid Promotion of Young Clare Officer

The many friends of Lieutenant J. Walsh, will hear with much pleasure of his promotion to Captain. He volunteered in February, 1915, receiving a commission as Second Lieutenant in the Royal Fusiliers (City of London Regiment). When a short time in training he was made a full Lieutenant, and left for the front last November. He was home on short leave a month ago, none the worse for having spent four months in the trenches. He is eldest son of Mr and Mrs Michael Walsh, Caherogan, Miltown Malbay. Prior to his receiving a commission he was Examiner in the Exchequer and Audit department of the Civil Service, London.

To Captain Walsh we tender our heartiest congratulations, and wish him every success and a safe return to his native County.

From the *Saturday Record* and *Clare Journal*, December 1916:

Further Promotion of Young Clare Officer

It is with much pleasure we announce the promotion of Captain J Walsh, 22nd Battalion, the Royal Fusiliers (City of London Regiment) to the rank of Major. A few months ago we heartily offered this young gentleman our congratulations on his receiving his Captaincy. He is the eldest son of Mr and Mrs M. Walsh, Caherogan, Miltown-Malbay. To Major Walsh we tender our hearty congratulations and wish him every success.

From the *Clare Journal*, February 1917:

At Mass at Miltown-Malbay yesterday, the very Reverend Canon Hannon feelingly asked the prayers of the people for the repose of the soul of Major Walsh, whose death just occurred from wounds received in battle in France. Only a few weeks ago he was home on a few days leave, and he was a splendid specimen of a man. Deceased was the eldest son of Mr Michael Walsh, N.T., Caherogan, Miltown-Malbay. In their great sorrow the sympathy of everyone goes out to his parents, brothers, and sisters.

Grave or memorial reference: 23 Sp Mem. Cemetery, Ovillers Military Cemetery in France.

WALSH, MARTIN: Rank: Private. Regiment or service: Royal Dublin Fusiliers. Unit: 2nd Battalion. Date of death: 1 June 1917. Service No.: 6745. Killed in action.

Supplementary information: He won the Military Medal and is listed in the *London Gazette*. Born in Kilrush, Co. Clare. Enlisted in Limerick while living in Kilrush, Co. Clare. Son of Mrs Johanna Walsh, C/o Dunbeg, P/o, Co. Clare.

Grave or memorial reference: G. 74. Cemetery: Kemmel Chateau Military Cemetery in Belgium.

WALSH, MICHAEL: Rank: Private. Regiment or service: Northumberland Fusiliers. Unit: 9th (Northumberland Hussars) Battalion. Date of death: 22 March 1918. Age at death: 26. Service No.: 55455. Formerly he was with the C.A.V Hussars where his number was 24856. Killed in action.

Supplementary information: Born in Drumcliffe, Co. Clare. Enlisted in Ennis, Co. Clare. Son of John and Mary Walsh, of No. 30 Steeles Terrace, Ennis, Co. Clare.

Grave or memorial reference: Bay 2 and 3. Memorial: Arras Memorial in France.

WALSH, MICHAEL JOSEPH:
Rank: Gunner. Regiment or service: Royal Navy. Unit: HMS *Vivid*. Date of death: 3 October 1917.

Supplementary information: The HMS *Vivid* was a Naval Land Base. Husband of Mrs Walsh, of Cappa Pier, Kilrush.

Grave or memorial reference: Near South boundary. Cemetery: Scattery Island Graveyard, Co. Clare.

WALSH, MICHAEL: Rank: Gunner. Regiment or service: Royal Garrison Artillery. Unit: 86th Heavy Battery. Date of death: 6 May 1916. Service No.: 34518. Died in Mesopotamia.

Supplementary information: Born in Kilrush, Co. Clare. Enlisted in Kilrush. Also commemorated in the 'List of Kilrush Men engaged in the War from August 1914'. This pamphlet lists the Kilrush men who were involved in the First World War until 11 November 1918. It also says he fought in Mesopotamia and died in Turkish hands from neglect after Kut.

Grave or memorial reference: A. 3. Cemetery: Kut War Cemetery in Iraq.

WALSH, ROBERT: Rank: Private. Regiment or service: Royal Munster Fusiliers. Unit: 1st Battalion. Date of death: 12 August 1917. Age at death: 18. Service No.: 8/4364 and 4363. Died of wounds.

Supplementary information: Born in Kilrush, Co. Clare. Enlisted in Ennis, Co. Clare while living in Kilrush, Co. Clare. Son of John and Bridget Walsh, of Hector Street, Kilrush, Co. Clare. His personal effects and property were sent to John Walsh (father) Pound Street, Kilrush Co. Clare, Ireland.

Also commemorated in the 'List of Kilrush Men engaged in the War from August 1914'. This pamphlet lists the Kilrush men who were involved in the First World War until 11 November 1918. He is also commemorated in the 'List of Employees of Messrs. M. Glynn and Sons. Flour and Meal Millers and Steamship Owners. Kilrush, Co. Clare, who took part in the War, 1914 to 1918. Dated 11 November 1918'.

Grave or memorial reference: VI. F. 1. Cemetery: Brandhoek New Military Cemetery in Belgium

WALTERS, SIDNEY FREDERICK: Rank: Second Mate. Regiment or service: Mercantile Marine. Unit: SS *Eupion* (London). Date of death: 3 October 1918. Age at death: 28.

Supplementary information: Son of John and Eleanor Walters, of Myrddin House, Lloyd''s Terrace, Newcastle Emlyn, Carmarthenshire. Born at Newcastle Emlyn.

The 3,575 ton SS *Eupion* was built in Alloa, Clackmannanshire in 1914 for the Eupion Steamship Company. She was torpedoed and sunk west of Loop Head, Co. Clare by German submarine U-123, the same submarine that sank the *Leinster* a week later. Two other Eupion casualties are buried in this cemetery.

Grave or memorial reference: In North-East corner. Cemetery: Kilrush Church of Ireland Churchyard, Co. Clare.

WARD, MICHAEL: Rank: Private. Regiment or service: Royal Munster Fusiliers. Unit: 1st Battalion. Date of death: 3 October 1918. Age at death: 23. Service No.: 1107. Died of wounds.

Supplementary information: Born in Mount Shannon, Co. Clare. Enlisted in Limerick while living in Mount Shannon, Co. Clare. Son of John and Caroline M. Ward, of Scariff, Co. Clare. In his will, dated 25 June 1918, his personal effects and property were received by, Mrs J Ward (mother), Drewsboro, Scariff, Co. Clare, Ireland.

Grave or memorial reference: VIII. G. 5B. Cemetery: Mont Huon Military Cemetery, Le Treport in France.

WARD, OTHO CHARLES: Rank: Captain. Regiment or service: Indian Army. Unit: 124th Duchess of Connaught's Own Baluchistan Infantry. Date of death: 11 January 1917.

From the *Clare Journal*, January 1917:

Death of Captain Ward, Indian Army

The death occurred in action on January 11, of Captain Otho Charles Ward, Indian Army. He was the second son of major Espine C. R. Ward, R. A. M. C., who was widely connected in Clare, and was grandson of the late reverend Charles Ward, formerly Rector of Kilmaley.

Grave or memorial reference: XVIII. K. 5. Cemetery: Amara War Cemetery in Iraq.

WARD, OWEN: Rank: Sergeant. Regiment or service: Royal Irish Constabulary Date of death: 10 October 1918. Service No.: 59102.

Supplementary information: Born in Monaghan, 1879. Enlisted in the R.I.C. in 1 September 1899. Religious Denomination: Roman Catholic. Occupation on enlistment: Farmer. Served in Donegal, Derry, Belfast, Sligo, Galway and Clare. Married: 3 April 1907. Promoted Acting Sergeant 1 March 1910. Promoted Sergeant 1 February 1912. In charge of Ennis district, Co. Clare. Was travelling to Birmingham on official business when lost on the RMS *Leinster*.

Grave or memorial reference: No burial or memorial information available at this time.

WATT, EUGENE: Rank: Private. Regiment or service: Canadian Motor Machine Gun Brigade. Date of death: 24 March 1918. Age at death: 23. Service No.: 174951.

Supplementary information: Son of Robert and Georgina Watt, of No. 247 Duke Street Hamilton, Ontario; husband of Marie Watt (*née* Keane), of Lemeneigh, Newmarket-on-Fergus, Co. Clare. Next of kin listed as Georgina Watt (mother). Place of birth: Co. Clare. Date of birth: 24 January 1893. Occupation on enlistment: Manual worker. Date of enlistment: 28 October, 1915. Address on enlistment: Hamilton, Ontario. Height: 5ft 8in. Complexion: Dark. Eyes: Blue. Hair: Dark brown.

Grave or memorial reference: He has no known grave but is listed on the Vimy Memorial in France.

WHEELER, CHARLES: Rank: Gunner. Regiment or service: Royal Horse Artillery and Royal Field Artillery. Unit: 2nd Battalion. Date of death: 18 May 1918. Age at death: 25. Service No.: 69465. Died of wounds.

Supplementary information: Born in Kilrush, Co. Clare. Enlisted in Cork. Son of Charles and Mary Wheeler, of Church Square, Fermoy, Co. Cork; husband of K. Wheeler, of Carrigrohane, Co. Cork.

Grave or memorial reference: V. H. 1B. Cemetery: Mont Huon Military Cemetery, Le Treport in France.

WHEELER-O'BRYEN, MYLES:

Rank: Lieutenant. Regiment or service: Royal Warwickshire Regiment. Unit: 2nd/5th Battalion, Territorial. Date of death: 2 October 1916. Age at death: 20.

Supplementary information: This man is listed in Officers Died in the Great Was as O'Bryen, Myles Wheeler. Killed. Son of Dr Wheeler-O'Bryen and Maude Wheeler-O'Bryen, of Binghill, Sydenham, London.

From the *Clare Journal*, November 1916:

Son of Well Known Clareman
Brother an Cousin gain the Military
Cross

We take from the "Sydenham Gazette," the following concerning the death of a gallant young officer, the son of a Clareman resident in London, and nephew of Mr Robert O'Bryen, Roughan, Kilnaboy, and formerly of Kells:

We announce with deep regret the death of Lieutenat Myles Wheeler O'Bryen (Royal Warwickshire Regiment) the elder son of Dr and Mrs Wheeler-O'Bryen, of Burghill, Mayew Road, Sydenham, who has just been accidentally killed. Although only 20 years of age, he was a most promising young officer, and had been recommended for a captaincy. A fortnight ago we announced that his younger brother, Second Lieutenant Wilfred Wheeler O'Bryen, had been awarded the Military Cross.

Lieutenant Colonel R.F. Coates writes to the parents, as follows—"I am deeply grieved to inform you that an accident occurred this afternoon to your son Myles. He had just concluded practice, and had picked up a couple of bombs which had failed to explode. He then decided to withdraw the pins and throw them, in order to avoid any possibility of accident to his class. Unfortunately one exploded just after leaving his hand, and he was struck in the neck. A medical officer was at once summoned while first aid was rendered by Major Halis, who was with him at the time, but he succumbed in a very few minutes. His death has been a great shock to me. He has proved himself one of the very best of my officers, always exceptionally keen and gallant."

Major T.H.H. Carter writes— "We are all very deeply grieved at your son's death. It may be some slight comfort to you to know that he was doing his duty just as much as that he was hit when in the trenches, and that the medical officer said he could not have felt any pain. He was quite one of the most popular officers, and that he was keen and efficient is shown by the fact that he was brigade bombing officer. We all feel his loss deeply, especially those few of us who are left out of the original Battalion."

In a previous issue the "Gazette" described how the above young officer and his brother, second lieutenant W.J. Wheeler-O'Bryen, Royal Warwicks, gained distinction in France. The deceased officer was promoted Brigade Bombing Officer, and Lieutenant W.J. Wheeler-O'Bryen, who is only 18 years was given the Military Cross for the act of gallantry and devotion in the field;

Copy of recommendation for award of Military Cross for Second Lieutenant W.J. Wheeler-O'Bryen:

On the night of the 7th-8th, for very exceptional coolness, resource and courage. The extensive mine explosion which wrecked a large part of B Company's lines, caused a rush of miners, many unarmed, and also drove away our two sections of bombers, who were in a part of the line almost adjoining the wrecked area.

Lieutenant O'Bryen instantly took the situation in hand, rallied and organised and located this for the miners, posted part of platoon most skilfully at points where they could enfilade any enemy advance, and then with the remainder proceeded to get into touch with B Company and hold the now absolutely wrecked trenches. During this time he was continuously exposed to heavy shell and rifle fire, and while going up and down encouraging the men, and organising a new line of defence where the left of B Company had been blotted out. This done, he immediately set to work to rescue and dig up the wounded, still under a heavy fire, some of whom were in front of the trenches, and promptly secured what articles of identification were possible from the enemy dead.

Grave or memorial reference: III. A. 5. Cemetery: Laventie Military cemetery, La Gorgue, Nord, France.

WHELAN, MICHAEL: Rank: Private. Regiment or service: Connaught Rangers. Unit: 2nd Battalion. Age at death: 21. Date of death: 7 November 1914. Service No.: 3938. Killed in action.

Supplementary information: Born in Ballyvaughan, Co. Clare. Enlisted in Galway while living in Kilnaboy, Co. Clare. Son of Mrs Winifred Whelan, of Faherlaughroe Cottage, Carron, Kilnaboy, Co. Clare. Date of birth: 1 November 1891. Place of birth: Ballyvaughan Workhouse, Co. Clare. Height: 5ft 3 in. Enlisted in Galway in 1911. Complexion: Fair. Eyes: Blue. Hair: Brown. Occupation on enlistment: Farm Labourer.

Grave or memorial reference: Panel 42. Memorial: Ypres (Menin Gate) Memorial in Belgium.

WHITE, JAMES MATHEW: Rank: Lieutenant. Regiment or service: Army Veterinary Corps. Unit: (T CATT 126th Brigade, R.A.). Date of death: 16 March 1916. Age at death: 32.

Supplementary information: Son of Thomas and Anne White, of Tulla, Co. Clare.

From *Our heroes*, 1916:

Lieutenant J. M. White, A.V.C., was the third son of Mrs White, Tulla, Co. Clare, and nephew of James White, M.D., J.P., Kilkenny. He qualified at the Royal Veterinary College, Dublin, in 1910, and subsequently entered the service of the British South African Co., Rhodesia. On the outbreak of the war he returned at his own expense to join the colours. He contracted pneumonia while on active service in France and died on March 16th, 1916. Lieutenant White was a young man of splendid physique and a noted football and golf player.

From the *Kilkenny People*, March 1916:

Late Lieutenant J. M. White, A.V.C. —Widespread regret is felt in Clare at the death from pneumonia, contracted in France of Lieutenant James M. White, Army Veterinary Corps, third son of the late Mr Thomas White, a well known resident of Tulla, East Clare, and nephew of Dr J. White, J. P., Kilkenny, and the late Very Reverend Dean White, Nenagh.

From the *Saturday Record*, March 1916:

The Roll of Honour.
Another Gallant Young Clareman Passes Away
The latest "Roll of Honour" lists contain an announcement of the death of Lieutenant James M. White, Army Veterinary Corps, in France. He was the third son of the late Mr Thomas White, a very well known and esteemed Tulla man, and nephew of Dr James White, J.P., Kilkenny, and the late Very Rev Dean White, of Nenagh. He had received his professional education at the Royal Veterinary College, Ballsbridge, where he was one of the most popular students in his time, being secretary to the football team, and one of its most prominent players. He saw practice between Terms with Mr P. J. Howard, Ennis, and soon after receiving his diploma, in December, 1910, he received an excellent post under the British South Africa Co, in Rhodesia, which he held until some time after the outbreak of the war, when, hearing that there were not sufficient Veterinary Surgeons with our Army, he resigned, and travelled home, some 5,000 miles, at his own expense, to offer his services for the front. He received a commission and was attached as Veterinary Officer to the 126th Brigade, R.F.A., 37th Division, with which he went to France in 1915, since which time he had had no leave. This short career certainly shows a fine example of duty to his country well done. The immediate cause of death was pneumonia, contracted on duty. There is very general and sincere sympathy felt with the sorrowing members of his family, who are among the most respected and popular residents of Tulla.

Grave or memorial reference: West side. Cemetery: Henu Churchyard, Pas-De-Calais, France.

WILLIAMS, JAMES: Rank: Private. Regiment or service: Royal Munster Fusiliers. Unit: 2nd Battalion. Date of death: 27 August 1914. Service No.: 5898. Killed in action.

Supplementary information: Born in Drumcliffe, Co. Clare. Enlisted in Ennis while living in Ennis.

Grave or memorial reference: I. 4. Cemetery: Etreux British Cemetery, Aisne, France.

WILLIAMS, MICHAEL: Rank: Gunner. Regiment or service: Royal Garrison Artillery. Unit: 159th Heavy Battery. Date of death: 27 October 1917. Age at death: 42. Service No.: 3682.

Supplementary information: Born in Drumcliffe, Co. Clare. Enlisted in Limerick while living in Ennis, Co. Clare. Son of John and Susan williams, of Ennis, Co. Clare.

Grave or memorial reference: XII. C. 15. Cemetery: The Huts Cemetery in Belgium.

WILLIAMS, R.W.: Rank: Private. Regiment or service: Royal Welsh Fusiliers. Unit: 2nd Battalion. Date of death: 10 July 1921. Service No.: 4179390.

Supplementary information: Son of Mrs M. williams, of No. 3 Abbey Green, Chester. This man is only recorded in the Commonwealth First World War Graves Commisson database.

Grave or memorial reference: Spec. Memorial. Cemetery: Bunratty Old Graveyard, Co. Clare.

WOODS, JOHN: Rank: Private. Regiment or service: Royal Munster Fusiliers.

Unit: 8th Battalion. Date of death: 4 September 1916. Service No.: 5815. Killed in action.

Supplementary information: Born in Inishhehir, Co. Galway. Enlisted in Lisdoonvarna while living in Doolin, Co. Clare. In his will, dated 24 May 1916, his personal effects and property were received by James Woods (brother), Lough North, Doolin, Ennistymon, Co. Clare, Ireland.

Grave or memorial reference: Pier and Face 16C. Memorial: Thiepval Memorial in France.

WOULFE, PATRICK: Rank: Private. Regiment or service: The King's (Liverpool Regiment). Unit: 13th

Battalion. Date of death: 28 March 1918. Age at death: 29. Service No.: 307085. Killed in action.

Supplementary information: Born in Ennistymon, Co. Clare. Enlisted in Liverpool while living in Layalmeh, Co. Clare. Son of Patrick and Mary Woulfe, of Lahinch Road, Lahinch, Co. Clare. Left USA to enlist.

Grave or memorial reference: Bay 3. Memorial: Arras Memorial in France.

WYNNE, CHRISTOPHER: Rank: Private. Regiment or service: Irish Guards. Unit: 1st Battalion. Date of death: 30 March 1918. Age at death: 29. Service No.: 10850. Killed in action.

Supplementary information: Born in Drumcliffe, Co. Clare. Enlisted in Ennis, Co. Clare. Son of Mrs Mary Wynne, of Mill Street, Ennis, Co. Clare.

From the *Saturday Record* and *Clare Journal*, May 1918:

Roll of Honour
A young Ennis man, Christopher Wynne, of Mill Street, who has been out for a considerable time, has fallen in the late heavy fighting.

Grave or memorial reference: Bay 1. Memorial: Arras Memorial in France.

Bibliography

Books

Burnell, Tom *The Carlow War Dead* (The History Press Ireland, 2011)
Burnell, Tom *The Offaly War Dead* (The History Press Ireland, 2010)
Burnell, Tom *The Tipperary War Dead* (Nonsuch Ireland, 2008)
Burnell, Tom *The Wexford War Dead* (The History Press Ireland, 2010)
Burnell, Tom *The Wicklow War Dead* (Nonsuch Ireland, 2009)
Kipling, Rudyard *La Bassée to Laventie*
Lecane, Philip *Torpedoed! The R.M.S. Leinster Disaster* (Periscope Publishing Ltd, 2005)
McDonagh, Michael *The Irish at the Front* (London, 1916)
Our Heroes - Mons to the Somme, August 1914-July 1916 (Naval & Military Press Ltd, 2001)
Putkowski, Julian and Sykes, Julian *Shot at Dawn* (Pen & Sword, 1996)
Quinn, Anthony P. *Wigs and Guns: Irish Barristers and the Great War* (Four Courts Press Ltd, 2005)

Newspapers

Carlow Sentinel
Clare Champion
Clare Journal
Clare Journal and Ennis Advertiser
Enniscorthy Guardian
Flight
Irish Life
Kilkenny People
King's County Chronicle
Midland Tribune
Newhaven Courier
Saturday Record and Clare Journal

Saturday Journal
The Court Journal
The People
The Saturday Journal
The Tipperary Star

Records

Bond of Sacrifice
British Roll of Honour 1914-1916
Commonwealth War Graves Commission registers for the Irish Free State
Commonwealth War Graves Commission
De Ruvigny's Roll of Honour
Ireland's Memorial Records
Irish Battle Monuments site
List of Kilrush Men engaged in the War from August 1914
List of Employees of Messrs. M. Glynn and Sons. Flour and Meal Millers and
    Steamship Owners. Kilrush, County Clare, who took part in the War, 1914 to 1918
Nominal Rolls of the New Zealand Expeditionary Force
Public Records Office, Kew
Roll of the sons and daughters of the Anglican Church clergy throughout the world
    and of the naval and military chaplains of the same who gave their lives in the
    Great War, 1914-1918
Soldiers Died in the Great War
The Kerry War Dead (online).
The National Archives of Australia
The National Roll of honour
The New Library and Archives Canada
Wold War 1 Irish Soldiers – Their Final Testament